KU-517-334

THE SCIENTIFIC STUDY OF SOCIETY

The Scientific Study of Society

by

Max Steuer
London School of Economics,
London, United Kingdom

KLUWER ACADEMIC PUBLISHERS
BOSTON / DORDRECHT / LONDON

A C.I.P. Catalogue record for this book is available from the Library of Congress.

ISBN 1-4020-7321-6

Published by Kluwer Academic Publishers,
P.O. Box 17, 3300 AA Dordrecht, The Netherlands.

Sold and distributed in North, Central and South America
by Kluwer Academic Publishers,
101 Philip Drive, Norwell, MA 02061, U.S.A.

In all other countries, sold and distributed
by Kluwer Academic Publishers,
P.O. Box 322, 3300 AH Dordrecht, The Netherlands.

Printed on acid-free paper

Printed in the Netherlands.

DEDICATED TO

Chris Allen and Ephie Resnick

With thanks for the perfect blend of criticism and encouragement

CONTENTS

ACKNOWLEDGEMENTS

Over the years I have benefited from many conversations with social scientists, quite a number of these taking place in the Senior Dining Room of the London School of Economics. The chance to thank scholars and others who have either helped me to think about the subject, or have directly helped me with this book, or both, is most welcome. Inevitably there will be names I forget to mention, and can only curl up inside in advance at the thought of these omissions.

When the musician Buddy Rich was asked which drummers had influenced him, he replied, "All of them." This must be the correct answer. Some influences take the form of demonstrating what not to do. Others are more positive. But while everything influences one, there are particularly significant figures in one's thinking, and while perhaps not all of them would welcome being mentioned in this context, I am going to do so anyhow. Of course in the end every person is solely responsible for what he or she thinks and writes, however fortunate or unfortunate they may have been in the figures that crossed their paths. In my case, I think I have been extremely lucky.

Fred Burin, a political scientist at Columbia University, got me started by taking my ideas seriously, and by continually bringing a modest critical approach to what we and others were saying and thinking. The tendency to get carried away has to be resisted. Fancy language is one symptom. Burin always asked in a very down to earth way, what were we doing. Dick Lipsey also has this wonderful ability to go beyond convention and ask what really is needed. What really are we doing? . He has what can only be described as a powerful instinct for how the subject might grow.

William Vickrey at Columbia, and as a visitor to LSE, could actually teach originality. George Akerlof has a similar effect. Henry Phelps Brown, my supervisor at LSE, taught respect for reasoning in a very straightforward way, but looked to something higher, which was evidence. His construction of a price index running for centuries is an inspiration. Anne Bohm more than helped research students in those days, she enabled graduate students to survive when often there was little institutional support. The institution is better able to look after research students today.

Clearly there is no need for everyone to worry about philosophical matters. Some people prefer to get on with the job, which is fine, but those who look down on philosophical enquiry are mistaken. Telling examples of scholars who demonstrate the benefits of having a philosophical bent are Terrance Hutchinson, Kurt Klappholz, Joseph Agassi and Mark Blaug. They are among those who gave me an idea of what social science is about. It was always a pleasure crossing swords — it is hard to describe it in any other way — with Imre Lakatos. He was outrageous and exhausting, but at bottom cared deeply about science. Other philosophers who have been generous in talking with me as a layman are Colin Howson, Peter Urbach, John Watkins, John Worrall, Elie Zahar, Michael Redhead and Elizabeth Lloyd.

I owe a special debt to Nancy Cartwright. She certainly encouraged me with this book, and made many very helpful suggestions. Initiating the M.Sc. in Economics and Philosophy at LSE with her has been important to me, along with countless interactions in the Centre for Philosophy of Natural and Social Science, which is essentially her creation. Teaching on that M.Sc. with Richard Bradley has been truly instructive. Jim Durban is not a philosopher, but cares about these matters, and believes strongly in the proposition that there is no fundamental difference between natural and social science. On one occasion Jim helped me with a statistical problem, but beyond that, in many ways his ideas and his example are powerfully encouraging.

Among the many visitors to the London School of Economics, Roger Fisher of the Harvard Law School has an incredible fix on how developing new knowledge can help in solving real problems. My perception of the potential of research was extended and refined through working with Alex

Kwapong, Jones Afori-Atta and de Graff-Johnson in Ghana. Having Ely Devons as a mentor and colleague was another lesson in relevance.

Pete Steiner provided a strong example of being creative and open minded, and at the same time being intolerant of bad thinking. This was often demonstrated in Lionel Robbins' deservedly famous seminar. While Steiner was not the first to introduce me to strategic thinking, he made the penny drop. Ed Green was another visitor who strongly shaped my view of social science. There is no substitute for knowing a lot.

Bill Philips believed and demonstrated that ideas from one subject, engineering in his case, could successfully be applied in another area. In their different ways, Chris Archibald and Harry Johnson practised economics seriously, and so raised the endeavour to a higher level. With them the enjoyment of economics, while very real, never took precedence over the goal of improved science. In my experience, Harry Johnson was in many ways the best model of the complete social scientist.

Working with Alan Budd had the feature of being willing to break the mould a bit, and not without knowing what the mould consisted of. Bob Gould and Morris Perlman also demonstrate the importance of integrity in intellectual enquiry. I am particularly indebted to Marc Nerlove. He took me under his wing for two years and completely convinced me that ideas and technique are inexorably entwined.

Four scholars showing on a daily basis the power of theory are Ned Phelps, Douglas Gale, John Moore and Frank Hahn. Disciplined imagination is a wonderful thing. I have to keep my temper in check when people who should know better belittle the achievements of abstract enquiry, as exemplified by these and other theorists. In social psychology it has been a great help for me to know Bill and Claire McGuire. Again, there is that feature I so admire of respect for the facts and being able to get them to say something. Working with Bob Gregory encouraged and developed the vital tactic, which can be so productive, of moving back and forth between ideas and observations. The same is true of my work with Jim Ball.

In am indebted to Ken Binmore in many ways, not least for introducing me to evolutionary ideas. The Darwin group at LSE, led by Helena Cronin and including Oliver Curry, Richard Webb and Andy Wells forces me back to the drawing board time and again. In fairness to myself, it has to be said that, while often wrong, I am not always convinced by these encounters. In a similar way, taking part in Chris Caswill's intelligently led ESRC enquiry into participant research has forced me to re-think many issues. Nicholas Humphrey, psychologist, philosopher, and also a member of the Darwin group, exemplifies the usefulness of speculative enquiry, and at the same time the telling relevance of biological evidence.

Giving the Seminar in Research Strategy at LSE with many different colleagues over many years has been a weekly pleasure and a major influence on my view of social science enquiry. David Webb, Chris Pissarides, John Sutton, Nobu Kiyotaki, Leonardo Felli, François Ortalo-Mangé, Steve Redding, Andrea Prat and Michele Piccione have been co-workers in this endeavour of observing and shaping the process that goes from vague idea to significant proposition. I especially benefited in this exciting undertaking through working with Kevin Roberts. He once said that you have to keep your head down and at the same time have your eye on the horizon. Scientific advance depends on a very tight focus, but not being trapped by that.

I have been greatly helped in working on this book by comments from Richard Layard, Colin Howson, Nancy Cartwright, David Webb, and Chris Allen. Stathos Psillos read the second chapter and commented on it from a philosophy of science point of view. Peter Loizos gave initial help on the treatment of anthropology. Like the others just mentioned, the sociologist Peter Abell has read many drafts and urged needed improvement. Over the years he has had a big effect on my view of social science, and shared my concern with what we see as a growing threat of irrationality from some quarters within universities.

A very particular thanks must go to Mark Wilbor. Keeping track of the many dozens of articles involved in this study and reproducing them for me has been invaluable. Rana Rahman helped me with many administrative matters that otherwise might have overwhelmed me. Ian Moss translated from Word to Camera Ready. Bob Nobay has been enormously helpful in a variety of ways. Jane Pugh and Mina Moshkeri did the diagram of the *Xidi* house. Alex Bellamy undertook the final proof reading. Judith Moore produced the indices. Dorata Rejman and Klementina Balint-Egan frequently responded to my calls for help at the LSE Centre for Philosophy of Natural and Social Science. Cathelijne van Herwaarden at Kluwer has been helpful at every turn.

FOREWORD

Tradition recognises five social sciences: anthropology, economics, social psychology, sociology, and political science. But who knows what is going on in all five disciplines? Social scientists from one discipline often know little or nothing about the progress made by social scientists from another discipline working on essentially the same social problem. Sometimes, even the methodology of a neighbouring discipline is *terra incognita*.

The problem becomes worse when we widen the remit to natural scientists and engineers. I have found little evidence myself that they see themselves as standing on the other side of an unbridgeable gulf between two cultures. They observe the intellectual excesses of those few `new age' social scientists who see themselves fighting a `science war', but the ignorance of these innumerate critics is so apparent in their grossly naïve attacks on natural science, that they are not taken seriously. However, although natural scientists appreciate that most social science is genuine science, they seldom know much about how and why it is done as it is. This can lead to serious inefficiencies in areas in which the traditional frontiers between social and natural science are melting away. An example is the frontier between the economics of imperfect competition and evolutionary biology. Reversing the usual bias, the evolutionary biologists commonly know little mathematics, and hence find the game theory literature hard to read, with the result that they often spend their time re-inventing the wheel. At the same time, economists desperately need input from evolutionary biologists on the mechanics of equilibrium selection in the many games which have multiple equilibria.

Finally, there are politicians and other policy makers. I haven't any doubt that Max Steuer is right to argue that modern social science has an immense amount to offer planners who are willing to do their thinking long enough in advance to make serious research viable. Social scientists can seldom hope to match the advances in auction theory that have made some design problems into engineering exercises, in the sense that the theories of human behaviour on which they call have been tested in the laboratory and then applied in the field with immense success. Indeed, the billions of dollars that governments in Europe and America have made by accepting the advice of social scientists on these issues is enough to justify their total scientific research budgets on both the natural and the social sciences for many years to come. But even when social science research is less sharp or certain, it is capable of identifying bad policy long before it is inflicted on an unsuspecting public. Mrs Thatcher's disastrous experiment with a poll tax is an obvious example, but even worse was her attempt to introduce so-called `internal markets' into the British health service. No serious modelling was done. No social surveys. Even the two ludicrously inadequate role-playing exercises that were carried out suggested that the plan was unlikely to work. And it didn't. Fortunately, the last few decades have generated more enlightened governments, but there is still an enormous amount of ignorance about what the various social sciences can do for good government.

How does Max Steuer go about educating us on where social science is at, and what it can do for us? He has so little time for postmodernists and the like that he doesn't bother to refute their position. Nor has he attempted to write a book on the philosophy of social science. He has philosophical things to say about how science is done, but he doesn't say anything that even a grumpy physicist is likely to disagree with on a bad day. His approach is to show social science in action.

He began by identifying a number of major social issues, and then searched the literature to find what each of the five traditional disciplines of social science had to say on each subject. The issues are: crime, family, housing, migration, money, and religion. Nobody should expect to learn the definitive solution to the enormous problems raised by any of these issues—any more than one would expect a survey of the physics literature to reveal the solution to the problem of generating energy cheaply, or of building an anti-gravity machine. But one can hope to learn how the different disciplines of social science go about chipping away at the problems. What evidence do different disciplines have at their disposal? How do they model their problems? Who would you consult about what kind of policy problem? Where would they benefit by adopting a more inter-disciplinary approach?

No particular background in any social science is needed in order to gain an understanding from this book of what the social sciences are doing. A willingness to make the effort is the only requirement, although it isn't always easy to follow arguments in serious research papers. However, the author puts his wide knowledge of the social sciences at your disposal by translating the mathematics, diagrams and statistics employed in the research papers into everyday language.

Recent years have seen the publication of many books which claim that social science is in some kind of crisis. The authors of these silly books usually strike me as knowing little or nothing about social science—even within the discipline they call their own. In any case, Max Steuer's book provides a categorical refutation of their thesis. Nobody doubts that it is difficult to do social science well. Progress comes slowly. Worse, it is often unclear which developments constitute progress and will be seen to have advanced knowledge when we look back from some time in the future. But exactly the same was true of the natural sciences. I certainly don't feel any sense of crisis when getting on with my own research. On the contrary, I often feel a sense of exhilaration that it sometimes works out so well. Natural scientists feel exactly the same---and so do the social scientists whose work is described in this book.

Along with the crisis mentality go bold attempts to find short cuts. Every month, there seems to be a new book with a one-word explanation of human society. These books, often very popular for a time, make big claims. Characteristically, they do not build on the work of the past. The ordinary day-to-day work of social science researchers described in this book plays little part in their thinking. The implication is either that this work does not exist, or it can safely be ignored. Both implications are wrong. Quiet and steady progress is going on in each of the five traditional social sciences, and those who ignore this progress simply re-invent the wheel—often with a square circumference.

This book does us a service by providing a picture of how research is actually done in each of the social sciences. It will be useful for practising social scientists, those thinking about entering the field, policy makers, and even those who are sceptical about the nature—or even the very existence—of social science.

Ken Binmore
Center for Economic Learning and Social Evolution
University College London

PART ONE

A FRAMEWORK

Chapter One

AN OVERVIEW

PRELUDE

Political decisions, and the public policies which result in them, are often based on little more than hunch and guesswork, combined with political bias. For example, it is rare to find a pragmatic view of the market which takes account of when it can be effective, and when relying on the market will have less desirable consequences. Policies on such matters as crime, housing and immigration, with serious social consequences, are often plucked out of the air, with no apparent effort made either to draw on existing knowledge, or to investigate before acting.

It is possible to do a lot better by adopting a scientific approach to social questions. No doubt very often the scientific answer to a question where we would like to have an answer is that we just do not know. Politicians are almost all of the view that the public would rather be given a definite answer which in fact has no basis than be told that while there is a problem, it is uncertain as to whether the proposed action will be helpful. This desire for authority, sometimes called leadership, acts against a more scientific approach.

For many, the mere suggestion that human affairs can be examined scientifically is anathema. It seems to imply that political choice must be reduced, or skewed in a particular direction. But that is entirely false. Another objection is rooted in the view that human affairs are beyond scientific investigation. It is vain, so the claim goes, and diminishing of human potential, to think that such an endeavour could be anything other than sham and pretence. Again, this is a mistaken concern.

One can argue the toss back and forth about a scientific approach to society in an abstract matter. Much better is to take a hard look at what is actually going on in social science. This book tells the reader what is, and what is not, social science. It is desperately important that more people, especially the right people, become aware of this branch of knowledge. The book has a snarling face, and a smiling face. It is angry with people who intentionally, or unconsciously, confuse and mess up intellectual endeavour. The book shows how to identify these social science impostors. At the same time, it tries to appeal to people who work in social science, or who want to know about their work. Even many specialists are unaware of what goes on in neighbouring disciplines. Above all, this book is addressed to those who should be aware of this branch of science. These are the people who take decisions that affect the lives of other people.

NORMAL SCIENCE

This is an unusual book about science. Most books on science cover the great ideas of key figures in science. They tend to concentrate on critical moments when big breakthroughs occurred. Science becomes drama and adventure. We suddenly discover a new and intriguing concept, such as chaos theory. Small changes in initial conditions can have huge consequences, raising deep issues about predictability. Science writers report on things like the race to crack the genetic code, or a new theory about dinosaurs and why they disappeared. This is entirely understandable.

There is a little problem in concentrating on great thinkers and big changes. Science is not like that. Scientific work goes on day by day, and it is done by reasonably intelligent and well-trained people who do useful work within a structure of ideas and information. Amazingly, that structure gets better as time goes by. It enables us to understand and do things today that we could not have understood or done in the past.

In this book I take a recent period, most of the decade of the 1990s, and examine the workings of a branch of science over that period. Due to the progressing nature of science, I would have preferred to deal with the decade ending on the date of publication of this book. Unfortunately, that was not possible. It takes time to analyse material and produce a book. The period on which I report is the most recent I could manage. It is an ordinary period in the story of science, much like any other ordinary period, as well as being the most recent I could manage. What we see is how science is actually working today, or just a few days ago.

SOCIAL SCIENCE

The branch of science I am writing about is a large branch that goes under the name of social science. The term covers a number of distinct disciplines, such as economics and political science. Social science is about human beings and what goes on in their institutions and interactions. Society is fundamental to human existence and therefore can be transparent. One might not be aware of it. In the same way, fish probably do not have a concept of water. They live in it and that is the way things are. What occupies their attention is food, mating, and getting away from predators.

Humans also think about fulfilling their needs, wishes, aspirations and desires, and may or may not be aware that all this takes place in a social medium. Humans interact with each other in face-to-face interactions, and in very remote and round about ways. The social unit, so to speak, may be a few friends, a workplace, a town, and all the way up to a giant nation, and beyond. Social science studies all levels from the family to the global society, and how the various levels affect each other.

Turning to animals instead of humans for a moment, we might note that some animals are loners, only getting together in pairs to reproduce. Others are very social. What it means to be 'very social' is that they are continually relating to each other. Social animals typically develop a hierarchy, and take their places in it. A single individual, or a few of them, may impose actions on the rest. Alternatively, the social system may be self-organising without any key figures. Males and females may behave differently. There may be division of labour, in the sense that some members of an animal group may specialise in defence against enemies, or in raising the young, or in providing food. The social behaviour of animals is an interesting and increasingly studied area.

The study of social interaction among humans can provide insights into understanding animal interactions, and the social behaviour of animals may be helpful in understanding some aspects of human society. In spite of the scope for cross fertilisation of ideas, essentially the subjects are separate. Social science, as the term is generally used, is about human society. That is how it is used in this book.

Most people start out in some kind of family. They pick up one or more languages. They are socialised into patterns of behaviour. They take part in institutions such as schools, prisons, armies, clubs, churches, professions, and productive units like stores, farms, factories and offices. People have multiple and interacting affiliations. Simultaneously they are part of a family, a friendship circle, an ethnic grouping, a community, a working association, a fan club, a religion, and so on. They are subject to social forces, which come from close by, along with forces whose origins are quite remote. By remote forces I mean effects associated with markets, as well as those coming from political pressure and the laws and conventions of a society.

Some individuals may have important positions in one or more markets, or in the law making activities of government. They may be active in shaping laws and taking market decisions. While some individuals appear to have power, and probably can exercise power, when it comes to these more remote social forces, most people have little say and are simply swept along with the flow. Social science studies all of this, the face-to-face and the more distant social interactions.

Social science directs particular attention to those aspects of society when and where things go wrong. Big areas of enquiry are unemployment, or rioting and war, or crime and social disaffection. But social science is also interested in the ordinary and normal such as skateboarding and other fashions, how people team up in marriage and in other ways, and decisions such as moving from one place to another. Social scientists study both social problems and social non-problems. Both are studied out of inherent interest, and with the object of finding solutions. The study of non-problematic social interactions, institutions and events, as well as being inherently interesting, can be important to the understanding of social problems.

Few people have any difficulty with the notion that someone might want to investigate the public transport system of a city. The investigator might want to find out how the system works in the sense of who controls it and how it is financed. They might be interested in the relation between those managerial and finance features and the performance of the transport system in moving people about. Probably the study of the system will have the goal of trying to improve the performance of it. All this is easy to grasp.

Another investigator might be interested in whether people are marrying younger, getting divorced more frequently, and the consequences of these trends for child development. Again, this is understandable, and the motive for that investigation might be its potential for recommending helpful changes in the divorce laws, and in the laws on child custody. Ultimately this kind of research hopes to be part of a process leading to an improvement in existing laws and practices. The difficulty in understanding the concept of social science comes in convincing people that the transport system and the marriage system both have aspects that fall within the domain of social science.

Any social arrangement is part of the subject matter of social science, from a bowling club to a parliament. How to win bowling matches is not part of social science, though conceivably the social organisation of clubs could have some bearing on competitive success. It is the common element of people interacting through large scale or small scale means, through large institutions like the World Bank and the global financial markets, and through smaller groupings like street gangs, which is studied by social science. That these matters, these interactions, can be studied scientifically, is not obvious and the concept of scientific investigation does not sit naturally with the uninitiated.

THE 'SCIENCE' IN SOCIAL SCIENCE

The next chapter of this book is about science. One cannot understand social science without some understanding of science as an activity different from other activities. People tend to confuse engineering with science. Both are important endeavours, but they are not the same. It is easier to visualise engineering than science. Engineering produces hardware and science produces understanding. The trappings of science, like white coats, microscopes and Bunsen burners can mistakenly come to epitomise the essence of science.

A popular phrase nowadays is 'rocket science'. But there is no such thing as rocket science. Physics and chemistry are sciences that contribute to the engineering of rockets, along with other natural sciences. Given the popular misconceptions about science, it is not surprising that using the term social science does not seem natural. The phrase social science does not appear to refer to something that is the same as natural science, according to popular criteria. Where is the equipment, the impressive display? Where is the success that we attach to science? What does social science have in common with the atom bomb or the double helix?

It all depends on what you think of as being essential to science. Is it experiments? Is it the discovery of laws? These are big questions, and in the next chapter they are addressed. My answer is that neither equipment nor success goes to the essence of science. The objective is what is crucial, and that objective is understanding. A science is a connected body of concepts, facts and explanations. As we shall see, this feature of connected ideas is crucial to scientific understanding, in contrast to other types of understanding. This is true of social science and of natural science.

Of course there are differences between sciences. There are differences between anthropology and physics, between biology and political science, between chemistry and sociology. As a group the social sciences differ in emphasis from the natural sciences. For example some sciences, both natural and social, rely more on controlled experiment than others do. On the whole, social science uses less controlled experiment than natural science. The natural sciences, too, differ from one another in the way they approach problems. But the overwhelming and critical feature of seeking explanations, and putting explanations to the test, is common to all scientific endeavour, be it natural or social science. This position is developed and defended in chapter two.

FRIENDS, FRAUDS AND PRETENDERS

Everyone has his or her blind spots. Among mine are opera, poetry, and motor racing. I have nothing against these activities, and maybe one day I will get into one or more of them. Some people have a blind spot with science. Why, I do not know. They may be afraid of its discoveries. A former friend once remarked, please do not mention the universe to my wife. It upsets her. There may be a problem with religion. Science and religion are rather at odds, however ingenious the efforts to either keep them apart, or to reconcile them. It is not so much that one is saying the earth is a few thousand years old and the other is saying it is older. More to the point is whether one prefers unchanging truth, certainty and faith, as against a willingness to accept not knowing, but having curiosity, and being willing to question authority, work with tentative conjectures, and live with answers that develop over time.

Some people seem to resent what they take to be the authority and arrogance of science. One day they say you should not eat butter, and the next day they say eat all you want. What about folk wisdom, the stored up knowledge of the ages? Acupuncture works, so the argument goes, and so much the worse for science if science cannot explain it. Why does science reject the concept of ley lines on the body, when acupuncture works? Why should we respect science if some scientists say that eating beef is safe and others say it is not?

There are bound to be disagreements at the frontier of scientific inquiry. And there are many instances where changes are made in what is accepted knowledge. Usually the changes are small, but sometimes they have wider consequences. Defining the state of knowledge at any particular time is not a simple matter. None of these undoubted facts about science can legitimately be used to denigrate the activity.

Other objections to science come from its successes rather than its short lived, or long lived, failures. For these objectors the problem is that on balance science does work. Engineers make atom bombs and political and military forces deploy them. Science made it possible. People are more than entitled to wonder whether future understanding will be applied in desirable ways. Some are prepared to judge the risks as being so high that on balance a policy of halting scientific enquiry is best. If one feels, as I do, that on balance mankind has overwhelmingly benefited from science in the past, the policy of halting science amounts to arguing that the future will not be like the past. Granted that up till now, on balance, the applications of knowledge have been broadly beneficial, it is logically conceivable that this may not be true in the future. But such a conclusion is unnecessarily pessimistic, in my view.

Attacking science does not leave the rest of the horizon unaffected. A policy stance which is hostile to science is likely to result in irrationality. It encourages all kinds of barbarism, with proven records of horrible outcomes. The case for encouraging science rests partly on a realistic appraisal of the alternatives.

We live in a period when all forms of science are under attack from many quarters. Maybe that has always been the case. No matter. Social science is particularly vulnerable to attack compared to natural science, and the attacks today take many forms. The third chapter of this book concentrates on attacks that take the form of doing something that pretends to be social science, while in fact being something else. These are attacks from the inside, and they are particularly insidious.

No one is obliged to be in a university in any capacity. Being sceptical about the value of academic knowledge is fair enough. Understanding and explaining is the job of universities. Spreading confusion under the guise of knowledge is a growing trend in many universities. I regard these activities as being deeply hostile to social science. If you do not like science, that is all right. Do not do science. In the third chapter I discuss some invalid alternatives to social science. They are invalid in the sense of being fraudulent. I also discuss some valid alternatives. They are valid alternatives in the sense that they do something related to social science, but are not social science. Literature and history are two prominent examples of valid alternatives.

WHAT ARE THE SOCIAL SCIENCES?

On my reading there are five distinct disciplines, or subjects, which together make up the social sciences. If you ask laymen what are the natural sciences, they will come up with answers like physics, chemistry, biology, astronomy, geology, and so on. How many natural sciences there are depends mainly on how far down the divisions one wants to go. Is molecular biology a separate science? It also depends on judgmental factors in that the divisions between disciplines are often complex, blurred, and overlapping. If you ask the layman to name the social sciences, almost anything can come up as an answer.

An interesting thing is if you ask professionals in a place like the London School of Economics and Political Science to name the five social sciences they will take the question to be a bit of a puzzle. The answer is a bit unsure. Very often lecturers do not have much trouble in identifying three social sciences. These are not always the same three. Few people can list all five. I take some encouragement from the fact that when I supply the missing subject, or subjects, people usually agree with my list.

Why social scientists find it hard to identify the social sciences is a little mysterious. My guess is that is has to do with specialisation. It is healthy, indeed it is essential, to specialise. It also is healthy to be aware of what other researchers are doing. This book has an angry side and a benign side. It is angry with those who confuse themselves, their students, the public and the people who take decisions about social matters. Some of these experts in obfuscation say social science does not exist. Some say they are doing science when they are not. And some believe that there is something called social theory, for example, which claims to do the same job as science without being science. This book sets out to show that these people are badly mistaken. The method of the book is to make the case more by example than by argument. If someone says there are no green frogs, you can try to argue with them. The best thing to do with such people is to walk into the room holding a green frog.

This leads me to the happy and smiling side of this book. It aims to show in a convenient and organised way to actual social scientists, potential social scientists, and any interested parties, what goes on in social science, across all five major disciplines. I am not offering an abstract discussion. Most of the book simply lays out what social scientists do. I am more interested in what they actually do than in what they might do, or should do, or could do. Understanding knowledge, employing it in real applications, and adding to it all depend on some understanding of the current state of knowledge. And that is what I want to present.

SELECTING TOPICS

Each of the social sciences directs attention to certain social phenomena that are hardly considered at all by the other social sciences. Economists work on the velocity of circulation of money, but this is not of much interest to anthropologists and political scientists. On the other hand, there are lots of topics where all of the social sciences take an interest. In general they address these topics in very different ways. I felt it would provide a deeper insight into social science by seeing how these disciplines operate on common topics in their characteristically different ways, than to see them at work on very different topics.

Chapters five through ten are the heart of this book and set out the research that has been published in professional journals on each of six topics. These central chapters are organised in different ways. Let me explain. One of the topics is crime. For this chapter the material is grouped according to discipline. This is the simplest form of organisation. What do economists have to say about crime, what do sociologists have to say, and so on.

Another method of organisation is according to aspects of the topic. For example, on the topic of migration we have a number of sub-topics. Why do people migrate? What happens to them when they arrive in the new destination? The different disciplines then slot in according to the sub-topic, or sub-topics, on which they do research.

One chapter is organised according to the kind of knowledge the research is aiming to provide. Are the researchers trying to find some facts? Or are they offering explanations in a purely theoretical exercise? Among other possibilities, the researchers might be putting their theory, or someone else's theory, to the test to see how well it fits the facts. This is organising a chapter according to the kind of scientific information that is being provided. Social sciences tend to specialise in the kind of knowledge they are seeking. It is interesting to see which disciplines place more emphasis on uncovering facts, and which devote more energy to constructing explanations.

A further organising principle, which is used in the chapter on housing, is according to policy relevance. I find all the research on housing to be of interest, whether or not I can see how it might be used to improve some public policy. But policy relevance is an issue and this provides the organising principle for this chapter. Some of the investigations are quite remote from what I can see as a possible policy application. Other work seems to have immediate relevance to pressing problems of the day. It is informative to see how research carried out in the different social sciences compares in terms of policy relevance.

SUPPORT DISCIPLINES

Chapter four contains brief introductions to each of the five social sciences. These characterisations are intended to provide some kind of simple introduction. Of course, my thumb nail sketches are of little or no importance compared to what goes on in the six chapters that follow. The best definition of social psychology, or anthropology, or sociology, or any discipline, is what the scientists working in that discipline actually do.

Nevertheless, going in cold might be tougher than is necessary. Hence these brief introductions.

Science is rarely easy and rarely exciting. We might as well face that. Covering this book will, I believe, provide the stalwart reader with accurate and pretty recent snapshots of the work of the social sciences. These pictures of social science research as currently undertaken can be found in chapters five through ten. There is no substitute for reading the central chapters, other than going to the journals themselves. I hope I have made it a little easier to form a mental map of this territory of knowledge by briefly describing the disciplines in chapter four. The main aid to understanding provided by this book is the digestion of material that has been done in chapters five through ten, and not in the brief summaries.

Chapter four also takes up the fascinating question of what makes some disciplines like history and linguistics, as wonderful and important as they are, not the same as the five social sciences. That difference typically comes about either because these subjects work in a different way, or because they are too narrow in focus. History is an example of the first, and demography is an example of the second.

Other subjects I do not include with the five social sciences are the subject matter oriented disciplines, like international relations and trade union studies. These are perfectly reasonable areas of enquiry, but these enquiries proceed by drawing on the five social sciences, and much else, like history. In chapter four I flesh out the argument that a relatively narrow subject matter, narrow compared to economics or sociology, as the sole defining characteristic of a field, makes that field different from the five social science disciplines.

I feel justified in leaving out subjects like demography and geography because at their core they address a single aspect of human society, and as they move from their cores, they employ the other social science disciplines. The proof of my claim that I am right to settle on the five disciplines I have chosen can be found by asking which disciplines have substantial things to say on each of the six broad social topics I have selected. My claim is that the only subjects that do so are the fields that I am identifying as the five social sciences.

Not everyone will agree with my arguments for organising the fields in the way that I do. And certainly we are dealing with blurred borders when we define subjects. Nothing critical, other than pride, hangs on whether or not I have left out a subject that should be here. But I do not think I have, and I think that my concept of the five social sciences is reasonable.

I was about to say, 'which I am calling the five social sciences'. This would be a more than a little ridiculous, as everyone else also calls them the social sciences. I am reminded of a passage in Ronnie Corbett's autobiography. He refers to a friend who frequently used the curious phrase, 'what I call', as in, 'what I call a good looking woman', or 'what I call the game of polo'. I suspect that there are a number of points where I appear to be presenting something as an idea of mine that is well known in the subject. This is always a danger when an economist, as in my case, or any other specialist, strays out of his or her speciality. I have tried to avoid this kind of unintended appearance of arrogance, but no doubt not entirely successfully.

PULLING THE THREADS TOGETHER

After our extended view of how each of the five social sciences —
Anthropology
Economics
Political Science
Social Psychology
Sociology
addresses each of the six topics —
Crime
Migration
Housing
Money
The Family
Religion
an attempt is made to summarise what the five social sciences are like, and how they relate to each other, on the basis of the evidence presented in the six substantive chapters. What kinds of questions do these subjects ask? How do they go about finding answers?

Clearly there is an important element of judgement in making these generalisations. There is no purely objective way of identifying typical approaches or typical questions. People may certainly differ as to how important they feel statistical enquiry is to political science, for example. Philosophers who study social science, particularly economics, have quite different views as to what it is that economists are actually doing. We have to be aware of this, but not put off by it.

I could take the line that I have presented what these subjects are doing. There is no need to go beyond that. Let the reader draw what conclusions he or she wants to draw. Fine. I support that. But I feel some obligation to give my view as well. What is anthropology? What is sociology? I believe we can make a number of reasonably valid statements about the subjects, and this is done in chapter eleven. This chapter also contains a defence of the existing structure of social science. There is, I believe, a logic to the way the field is organised. I suggest reasons as to why we have five disciplines, and not four or six.

Chapter eleven also takes up the vexing question of interdisciplinary enquiry. This means using more than one social science to tackle a scientific question. I find this area vexing because some scholars, and more frequently funding authorities and administrators, seem to advocate interdisciplinary work for its own sake, whether or not there is a need for it. This may be due to nothing more than empire building. Alternatively, it may reveal a rather fundamental misunderstanding of scientific enquiry. Scientific enquiry is not comprehensive. Different researchers tackle bits of a problem. Inevitably that does some damage, but it also makes possible manageable and solid progress.

I cannot resist suggesting that there is a tendency for academics and researchers who are a bit light on discipline, or put another way, who have a shaky grasp on their alleged field, to be drawn to interdisciplinary enquiry. One purpose of this book is to provide a possible basis from which to address interdisciplinary issues. Chapter eleven tries to draw on the experience of the previous six chapters to take up questions like does employing a single discipline in a research exercise tend to lead to incorrect conclusions, and when and for what do we need interdisciplinary research?

This penultimate chapter also raises the challenging question of how we rate social science. This is deep water indeed. However, we have had a look at all the research, on six major topics, published in English language professional journals, for the best part of a recent decade. Surely there is some basis here for saying, 'it looks a bit thin', or, 'wow, this is an impressive body of knowledge'. I try to give my view. I think it is fair enough to do so. The important consideration is that through reading chapters five through ten, the reader is in an equally good position to make an evaluation. I urge all readers to do so.

RESEARCH, PURE AND APPLIED

One could say, there is no need to make some kind of general judgement about the state of social science. It is enough to give the facts. This is the work. This is what it consists of. I feel I cannot agree with that stance which is based on purity and detachment. The reason is simple. All around us there are horrible social malfunctions. There are natural disasters as well. But even some of the natural disasters may be related to social considerations such as how we use energy, and how we farm. Other social problems have little to do with natural disasters. They relate to more purely social matters like income inequality, political instability, repression and a host of other social matters. If a case is to be made for more use of social science, it must depend in part on how well the social sciences are doing.

Issues like homelessness are not just a matter of too few homes, or even primarily a matter of physical supply, so I maintain. Prior to coming to power, a prominent New Labour politician said that when they got to power they would solve the problem of people living rough on the streets by building more dwellings, and, incidentally, reduce unemployment in the process. Once in power, we heard nothing more about this. Who is right? Am I right, or the New Labour politician? Is the best answer to homelessness to be found from intuition and political conviction, or from social science? There is no need to oversell the achievements of social science, but underselling is dangerous as well.

Very often the scientific answer to a question is, 'we just do not know'. That can be a terribly important piece of information. It is nicer to have an answer, if we have one. But if we do not have an answer, it is usually better to know that.

When making policy decisions we have the option of turning to social science. How important it is that we take that option depends on how much is at stake. It also depends on how much better the answer coming from social science is likely to be compared to the guesses of politicians and the armies of gurus who stand by ready to offer opinions. This provides one of the motives for attempting some general appraisal of the achievements of social science.

Just as an aside, it is worth emphasising that I am interested in what follows from social science, and not in the off-the-cuff opinions of social scientists. There is a big difference between the two. Social scientists have every right to express their opinions, just like anyone else. A number of social scientists seem to feel that their status as perhaps being former researchers entitles them to preferred opinions on matters which they have not studied, and maybe no one has studied. This is unworthy behaviour.

The relationship between democratic decision-making and scientific decision- making is no simple matter, and the last chapter attempts to clarify some of the important issues. This concluding chapter also discusses the greater success of economics as applied social science compared to the other social sciences. It argues the case for greater use of the other four, and questions the wisdom of treating lawyers as all-purpose intellectuals.

IN A NUT-SHELL

This is a book about the findings of the five social sciences as can be seen in fairly recent research undertaken on what I hope is a representative sample of topics. The book could have been called, Social Science: What It Is, How It Works, and How to Spot the Impostor.

I have made every effort to stay very 'hands-on'. We are not dealing here with the guiding principles of social science. This is not a book about what social science could or should be like. It attempts to be a fairly objective report on recent research.

The facts, including the facts about the content of a science, any science, are vital, but they do not speak for themselves, to use a popular phrase. They have to be organised in order to squeeze the meaning out of them. I have tried to construct a framework for simplifying the task of thinking about what are complex and illusive matters.

This book is organised in three sections. The first part sets out a framework for thinking about social science. The second part is the heart of the book. It illustrates social science in action. The third part draws some conclusions and implications for social policy that appear to follow from the fact that we are fortunate in having made a start in understanding the social aspects of mankind.

Chapter Two

WHAT IS SOCIAL SCIENCE?

FRIENDS AND ENEMIES OF NATURAL AND SOCIAL SCIENCE

One of my motives for writing this book is the growing presence of people in universities who are antagonistic to science in any form, yet call themselves social scientists. Some are anti-science without realising this. Others champion their hostility to a scientific approach to society. Another motive for writing this book is to break down some of the insularity between social science disciplines. I hope that my view of science is broadly acceptable to this group of supporters of social science, and that seeing what goes on in surrounding disciplines proves of interest.

As to those modern thinkers who either have a very different view from mine of what constitutes social science, or think the whole enterprise is both impossible to do and wicked to attempt, I hope to make inroads into their closed world. I will do my best to argue with these sceptical writers who tend to be prolific, energetic, muddle headed and popular with students. But I will argue by example. I do not intend to identify these scoundrels by name, and will resist the temptation to engage in abstract debate. They know who they are, and they do not need me to advertise for them. I know it is difficult to get the ear of this misguided *avant guard*. They have made big investments in the unfortunate intellectual positions they have adopted, and they tend to confine their reading to books and articles written by each other. But perhaps even they will agree that the proof of the pudding is in the eating.

My main goal and fervent hope is to interest some people who have never given even a moment's thought to addressing the boundless range of social issues in a scientific fashion. Lots of people have opinions about such diverse things as famines, the effects of television on children, a common currency for Europe, and life on housing estates, without realising that these topics, and a myriad other social mysteries and social problems, can be studied scientifically. Discussions in pubs which are not about sex or football are almost all about society in one way or another. People do find party politics, the pay of City traders, house building in the south East, war wherever it is going on, and so on, to be of real interest.

Even sex and football can be looked at from a social point of view. And anything which exists, including things of a social or societal nature, can be studied scientifically. My main aim is to describe and analyse how this is done. I am fully aware that a scientific approach to society is not the only approach. I do think that it is an interesting, attractive and potentially very useful thing to do. In passing, I hope to make a case for social science, along with describing and explaining what it is.

The whole of this book is an answer to the question, "What is social science?". Most of the answer provided is very practical and 'hands on'. It deals with what social scientists actually do, not with what they might do, may do, or could do in principle. This chapter is different. It operates at a very general level. In order to understand social science, it is necessary to have a framework for thinking about science as a whole. Social science is a part of the picture. So let us begin with the big picture, a picture of that amazing construct which is science.

SCIENCE AS CULTURE

There is nothing more peaceful than a herd of cows lying down in a field. As they ruminate together, is it possible that they are thinking? Probably, yes, they are. But are they wondering about how they came to be there, and what awaits them at the end? I doubt it. But suppose they did. They would not get very far with these questions because they are not very good at thinking. Even human beings, who are supposed to be good at thinking, a characteristic that allegedly distinguishes them from other animals, find these difficult questions. But perhaps among the millions of cows and the many millions of hours they spend thinking, a few unusually able and lucky ones from time to time manage to construct an important question, and maybe even to find some plausible answers.

The big problem for cows is that these discoveries are not transmitted to their fellows. Cows a thousand years ago, and a thousand years in the future, will probably have much the same thoughts as cows today. They lack the capacity to transmit ideas across generations. In other words, they do not have much in the way of what could be called a culture, or an accumulation of knowledge. There is some growing evidence that cultural transmission among animals may be more important than hitherto expected. But whatever might be found, it will still be very minor compared to the central and over-riding role of the capacity to absorb and build on the ideas of the past which is the truly distinguishing feature of humans compared to other animals.

Of course humans today may choose to think about the great mysteries, and mundane puzzles, much as people did a thousand years ago. They can do that, but they do not have to. With suitable training, we can draw on the thinking of others. There are many, many traditions of thought. When people set about to build a house, a car, a football team, make a work of art, design a constitution for a government, or a treatment for a patient, they can draw on the handed down experience of the past, and in most cases, they have to draw on the past. They could not even make a start without doing so.

The truly distinguishing feature of humans beings is that we can absorb constructions from the past, language being the outstanding example, and pass these hard won achievements on to others. Most people contribute nothing memorable to the language they speak, but many of the contributions of those who do add something new are added to the total and retained. That is the great feature of cultural transmission and development. Along with art and technology, science shines as one of the great and growing traditions of human culture.

Art changes, evolves, and responds to events and conditions of the past and the present. It does not in any obvious sense show continual improvement. Nor need it do that. It has other aspects of grandeur. Science is also a truly amazing human activity, and this is partly because of its cumulative and progressing nature. Scientists today may be no better than scientists in the past, but science is unrecognisably better. This intellectual structure which is science is such a marvel in itself that it would be a glory of mankind even if it had no practical consequences whatsoever.

While some people care about science for its own sake, the achievements of science interest relatively few people. What effects most people, whether they know it or not, is the practical consequences of science. The growth of scientific knowledge has changed life on this planet for everyone. The great advances which we see in health and life expectancy, in communication, and above all in productivity have all been made possible by the development of new knowledge. Science is not the only source of new knowledge, but it is the most organised, the most continuous and the most fundamental source of knowledge. Of course knowledge has to be applied in order for it to have these great beneficial effects. Some of the finest achievements of engineers and others can be seen in developing an application of a discovery of science. But without the scientific knowledge in the first place, there can be no application of it. Undoubtedly practical experience adds to better practices. Science is not the only source of technical improvement. But many truly heroic leaps have come from science, and could not come from any other source.

No doubt there are serious problems that come with new knowledge, and adverse applications are always possible. There are different schools of thought as to how to respond to the possible destructive uses and the unintended consequences of science. Some people feel that scientists themselves have a special responsibility to work on certain problems, and not to work on other questions. Others feel that whether experiments should be done on human embryos, for example, is a matter for governments to decide, and scientists have no special role to play in these essentially ethical and political decisions. Tragic consequences of new knowledge are by no means confined to examples like Hiroshima. In the process of looking for new answers, mistakes are made, and these can have terrible effects. However, allowing fully for any and all of the unfortunate consequences of scientific knowledge, there is still an overwhelming case that so far mankind has reaped enormous net benefit from the progress of science.

Untold millions live longer and healthier lives. Many millions are incomparably better educated and have greater choices. Many have standards of living which even as little as a hundred years ago were inconceivable. Even in what are the rich countries today, nine out of ten people had hard lives working on farms in the year 1900. Today there is a richer life for most people in advanced countries. Only a tiny part of these gains which many experience came at some cost to others. The vast bulk of the gains for the millions who are gainers come from the advances of science. This is the single most fundamental source of what I see as human progress.

UNDERSTANDING

One of the proofs of the achievements of human understanding was the lift-off from the surface of the moon of the lunar module, bringing the two astronauts up to the circling spacecraft. There could be no full-scale rehearsal for this event. The functioning of the machine sitting on the moon's surface depended on many factors including the moon's gravitational pull, the near vacuum conditions, and the temperature at the time. None of these could be measured directly. They were deduced from scientific theory. They could not be duplicated on earth. Engineers had to build a machine capable of taking account of these conditions. No doubt the engineering achievement in building this machine, which had to work the first time without testing under the actual conditions, is immense. It is comparable to constructing the temples of Luxor. But even the greatest engineers of the past could not have built the lunar module. They could not draw on the vast array of scientific knowledge necessary for that endeavour.

Some years before the Russians launched Sputnik, an uncle of mine tried to persuade me that it was impossible for humans to launch an artificial satellite. His understanding of why the moon stayed in orbit was shaky. As a child it was not easy for me to argue with him. How do we know the gravitational pull of the moon, he would ask? Even as an adult it is not easy to explain to a sceptic that through complex chains of reasoning, combined with observations that can be made here on earth, we can be pretty sure about how some things work thousands, and millions, and even light years away. Can we be certain? Certainty is not possible. Nor is it necessary. Only a fool insists on certainty.

When the Sputnik went up, my uncle had a number of options. He could have maintained that the scientific community was mistaken. Those beep-beep-beeps coming over the radio had some other source. In fact, the line that he took is not unusual in those circumstances. Much to my frustration he maintained that the reasoning which led him to argue those years ago that an artificial satellite could not be launched from the earth was essentially correct. He just missed out on one small, trivial consideration. I found the argument unfair. Why could he not simply say that he was wrong? Perhaps he felt that an adult must always be right in arguing with a child, and in addition, as a lawyer, he probably was pretty innocent of scientific reasoning.

But what is "scientific reasoning"? Not only is science amazing, it is also mysterious. Philosophers of science struggle with dozens of issues including how scientific knowledge is acquired? What distinguishes science from other activities? What are "facts"? What are scientific "laws"? Is there such a thing as the "scientific method"? Can we identify valid and invalid methods of investigation? In these opening chapters I want to provide a working picture of what it means to be scientific. It would be foolhardy in the extreme to expect to make a contribution to the high level debates that engage the philosophers. Those are important and intricate debates. Some of the greatest scholars of the past and the present have worked, and are still actively working, on these questions, and many other related questions. I can eavesdrop on these fascinating discussions, but that is as far as it goes.

Most of my views come from being a self-conscious practitioner. Many good, and even super good, scientists have nothing but scorn for an interest in methodology. "Get on with the job" is the cry. Fair enough. If a scientist does not feel the need for methodological enquiry, and can do good work without thinking about the methods he or she is using, so be it. But I want to think a bit about these issues, as a necessary step in describing a particular part of science, which is social science.

Natural science studies the physical world in all its forms, both living and not living. Social science studies the social world in all its forms. The borderline between different kinds of science is not sharp. It is a blurred border. Much of psychology, for example, stands at the border between the physical and the social. Nor is science, in any form, the only way of gaining understanding. There is art, history and philosophy, to name but three alternatives to science. Again, the border between science and these other forms of understanding is also fuzzy at points. This state of affairs is perfectly natural and understandable. There is no need to make much of it, though some critics, who, for one reason or another, want put down science, seize on this fact.

There seems to be a growing tendency in some circles to maintain that if there is no sharp distinction between things, then the categories themselves are flawed, and probably are meaningless. Unless there is an unambiguous test which will classify every case as 'science' or 'not science', or 'art' or 'not art', then the category itself is suspect. This is utter nonsense. There are several reasons why. For many purposes it is useful to distinguish between states which vary continuously. Water, for example, can be warmer or cooler. People can be older or younger, richer or poorer, and so on. Where is the dividing line between hot and cold, young and old, rich and poor? Of course there is none. Any conventional border will be arbitrary. For some purposes we may not need a border. For other purposes it will be useful to define one. To say that the border is arbitrary does not mean that there is no meaningful variation. Hot is not the same as cold, and rich is not the same as poor. Apart from continual variation, there are complex categories and it may be difficult to classify certain particular cases as being in the category or not in it. *Night Fishing at Antibes* by Picasso is a work of art. An unmade bed may be a debatable case. That some cases are hard to classify does not mean that all, or even many, cases are problematic.

There are armies of people who do not like science. Most of these people do not like any form of tight, careful reasoning, such as what goes on in a game of chess. They may feel deep down that they are right about various things, but know from experience that people employing logical reasoning appear to be able to successfully question some of their views. Sometimes people who are opposed to science tend to draw the invalid conclusion from their debates with others that reasoning itself is at fault. While there is pleasure to be gained from casual and informal thinking, there also can be great excitement in tight reasoning. I doubt if I would take the trouble to write at length about science if I did not like it. I do. I also like lots of other things including the music of Jerry Lee Lewis. I do not see these things, like philosophy and art, as being in competition with science, and there is not any need, and probably very little meaning, in attempting to rank these things in some way. But for the most part, my affection for social science is beside the point in the argument of this book. I want to do something a little more objective. I want to describe social science — show what it is. And somewhat more ambitious, I want to show how it works.

HOW DOES SCIENCE, NATURAL OR SOCIAL, WORK?

Any discussion of social science is likely to begin with science in general, including natural science. While social and natural science have much in common, there are differences and we will come to these. The common elements are by far the more important. All science has to do with understanding, and the potential for controlling things in order to achieve some end. What it means to understand something is itself a tricky matter, partly because there are levels of understanding. I may know that stinging nettles irritate my skin without having any idea how they do that. Knowing that they have the capacity to irritate, and that word may understate the amount of discomfort they can cause, is a kind of understanding. To be told that the active agent is a kind of acid with a certain name adds to understanding. What the acid does to human skin and why this generates painful sensations takes understanding much further. Knowing whether the nettles evolved this capacity as a defence against being eaten, or whether it is a by-product of some other need of the plant, also adds to understanding. Among other things, the process of understanding is a process of linking up ideas.

Understanding often takes the form of recognising that a particular case, or even a large class of cases, such as lightening, is an instance of a more general principle. If there is a range of things which I think I understand, bringing something hitherto not understood into that range is part of the process of understanding. This way of looking at things implies that one may be mistaken in thinking one understands. There still is a case for striving to understand. Going deeper into relationships may be fruitful in developing better theories.

Successful control may involve very little linking up of ideas and specifying of mechanisms. I may know nothing more than that wearing gloves will stop me from getting stung when I am weeding in the garden. Many sophisticated thinkers maintain that understanding is largely illusory. All that we have is complex, and simple, rules that work and enable us to predict when an eclipse will occur, for example. We really do not know how anything works. I find this extreme instrumentalist view hard to swallow, but I am prepared to concede that if I knew much more than I currently do, I might see the wisdom of it.

Meanwhile, I take a rather common sense view of understanding, and see it as the goal of scientific enquiry. Scientific understanding is not the only kind of understanding. It does have special characteristics, and among these I emphasise the connected nature of scientific explanation. Of course understanding is never certain or complete. Things are always understood in terms of other things. The pattern of dependence is not like a circle that turns back on itself. Rather it starts from a core and spreads out becoming weaker as it goes further from the core. The end is always the limit of what is currently understood. We can understand a very limited range of things, and can see where the bounds of understanding tail off into mystery.

There is a tendency to see the scientific endeavour as hugely, if not uniformly, successful. Important thinkers like Newton and Galileo have made the physical universe much more understandable. And great successes in probing the nature of physical entities from the largest to the smallest continue on an almost daily basis. After resisting understanding for most of human history, biological science is at last yielding priceless insights, building on work as diverse as that of Darwin and Crick and Watson. But we must not be mesmerised by success. We can predict when an eclipse of the sun will occur, but we do not know enough about the weather to predict whether the eclipse can be seen from a particular place on the earth.

The standard reply today to this last problem is that some physical phenomena are extremely sensitive to initial conditions, and small unobservable, or difficult to observe, differences can have large consequences. That may be the case. And it is a kind of progress to know more about why we do not know how to predict certain things. Yet, the argument about initial conditions may turn out to be wrong in the case of weather prediction. Fundamental changes in the way we look at weather may come along. Radically new theories of the weather may dramatically improve forecasting and show that the 'initial conditions' argument largely missed the point. We do not know. What we do know is that weather forecasting is an area where science has had very limited success. Fairer might be to say that is has been unsuccessful.

There are many areas where the track record of science is poor or worse. Where did AIDS come from and how can it be cured? Nowadays there may be more of a consensus in the scientific community about the 'where' question than about the 'what to do' question, but consensus does not mean that the scientists are right. There is some suggestion that very recent years have seen a slight decline in the amount of CO_2 in the atmosphere. One has to be a bit careful, not to say sceptical, about these measurements, and very cautious about the explanations for this apparent decline in CO_2 that are offered. Political pressure can force scientists into expressing an opinion. We might want to draw a distinction between what science has to say and what scientists have to say. Particularly when a committee of sixteen scientists say that British beef is safe and will not cause CJD, one senses a yielding to pressure. From what we know, it looks as if the chances of being infected are slight, and if the beef can be lethal due to prions, probably few people will be effected. How do we know this? Lots of people eat beef, and few people have come down with CJD. Possibly in the future many more will succumb. The real scientific answer in this question and many other questions is 'do not know'. Similar remarks could be made about the impact on people and on the environment of genetically modified foods.

THE COMMON ELEMENT IN SCIENCE

It is not success which is the key characteristic of science, in spite of its many and great successes. The crucial thing is the goal of the endeavour. The goal is in some sense to add to knowledge. The aim is to have more and better understanding. Perhaps equally characteristic is the collective nature of the scientific endeavour. If I try to see whether planting my potatoes earlier will add to the size of the crop, I may be trying to add to my understanding. I might even be successful. But that is not science. I have neither drawn on nor added to that great body of knowledge out there that is science. Just as success in business might be making money, success in science is improving the structure of knowledge. How much is understood? Do we now have a better understanding? As a practical matter, it may be very difficult to know whether a new idea — cold fusion, for example — is a step forward or backward. Hopefully, in time we shall know. To say that the goal is better understanding does not mean that it is easy to determine immediately whether this goal is being met by a particular research programme. But it does say what the goal is.

Thousands of people over hundreds of years have worked on that enormous structure which is the whole of science, natural and social. Only a tiny handful of the science workers work on more than a very small part of the structure. There are a few great scientists who have occasionally had an impact over a sizeable range, but this is rare. Compared to the whole, even quite significant scientific work is only on a small part of the structure.

What that structure consists of is never simple to specify at any point in time. Deciding what is in and what is out of the accepted body of knowledge is not easy.

Only a fraction of all the written records that are publicly available would be held by scientists working today to embody current knowledge. No one person even has an opinion over the full range about where the subjects stand at this point in time. In most cases there is a fair amount of agreement among specialists about particular small parts of science, but it is not perfect agreement. Nor is there any guarantee that current opinion will always be superior to earlier opinion. It is likely, but occasionally there are exceptions.

Science is a human endeavour undertaken by people in universities, government establishments, private firms, and a few unaffiliated individuals. On the whole it is self-policing. Dozens and dozens of establishments, scientific clubs if you like, recognise the affiliation of their members and the authority of other clubs. They recruit new members, regulate the promotion of individuals to positions of prominence, and decide on the publication and dissemination of findings. Scientists are not like lawyers or doctors. You do not need a license to practice science. No one can stop you from doing it. On the other hand, if you want access to some of the complex and expensive equipment used in scientific research, or more basically, if you want to be paid a living wage while doing science, then the establishment has the power to decide 'yes' or 'no'. Membership in the club usually requires a Ph.D. degree, which tends to mean in itself that one has aspired to membership in the establishment and accepted the authority of the establishment.

SCIENTIFIC ESTABLISHMENTS

Most of the development of science takes place within establishments. The existence of these self-conscious and mutually supportive clubs is on the whole a good thing. It would be difficult to see how science could work without them. If there were no science establishments, new potential practitioners would have to find their own ways to educate themselves. There would be no agreement as to what was known and not known. People would get some help from the past, but using past findings effectively would call for great luck and astounding judgement. Essentially, aspiring scientists would have to figure everything out for themselves. The task would be too daunting.

There have been instances where someone outside the establishment has been successful in championing an idea that initially ran counter to accepted knowledge. Usually what keeps such people outside the club is not their lack of knowledge. Typically it has to do with career path, and the radical nature of their ideas. Madam Curie is an example in natural science. Karl Marx is an example in social science. Rejected for a time, and maybe for a long time, these successful invaders from outside the clubs have ultimately been brought into the fold. When this happens, the scientists and their ideas become a part of the establishment. This is rare, but it can happen.

The fact that science has a kind of worldly, official presence is also helpful in the application of scientific knowledge, and in other dealings between science and the wider community. The funding of science is a prime example of this last advantage. With competing claims for support, the layman would be helpless, or nearly so, in deciding who should get money and who should not. These decisions would have to be made by scientists, if they were to be made at all sensibly. But here is the problem. Apart from a very few rare individuals, tolerable mastery can only be achieved over a very small bit of science.

Scientists themselves relate to the vast body of science that lies outside their specialism in almost the same way as do laymen. Scientists have some cultural affinity, and sometimes a bit of common skill. They may share some amount of mathematical technique. Perhaps more than anything, they share a feel for scientific activity. In addition, there is a culture of learning, and the experience of being at a university. But this is not enough for decision-making about people and ideas. Intelligent decisions depend on knowledge of the various sciences. In order to tap into this, we have to rely on the establishments, and that is the best that we can do.

Occasionally one of these clubs can go off the rails. A very small establishment can fall prey to a little clique of perverse, and yet politically astute, individuals. These situations are unlikely to last. Neighbouring specialisms glance over their shoulders. They begin to smell a rat. Most of the tiny specialisms have some territorial ambitions. If they see weak and misguided work nearby, that is an invitation to move in. At the same time it is important that the scientific community, in its parts and in the whole, be open to challenge from the outside. A perfect monopoly would not be desirable. Nor is there any easy way to achieve this. Yet some privileged status, which is part of having an establishment, appears to be essential to the scientific endeavour.

A small digression on the World Wide Web is in order. People refer to it as increasing the amount of information, and above all easing the dissemination of information. It is common to favour using the word 'information' rather than speaking of 'knowledge'. Perhaps the implication is that the specialist has knowledge, and anyone can acquire information. It is doubtful if this distinction will stand up under closer examination. If I want to find out about the genes for eye colour, I can get any number of articles off the web, and any number of individual assertions. Indeed, if I am so inclined, I can put a piece on the web about genes, though I know nothing about the subject. Is that knowledge or information? Neither. Sound information about how things work is knowledge. A reliable figure for the rate of inflation in Thailand is information about that country. Those who know this figure have a bit of knowledge about Thailand.

I cannot see much in the knowledge/information distinction. But what is clear is that the web downplays establishments due precisely to the open access features which Bill Gates and others feel are so important. They may be right. The web may serve some purposes other than convenience. It may be desirable to have a place where anyone can get some kind of hearing. My prediction is that the web will have no qualitative effect on science. The establishments will continue to function. Anyone may propound a physics idea on the web, but members of the physics establishment are far more likely to be listened to, and with good reason. Books and journals will go on being the repository of discoveries, though they may be available on the web. Books and journals do not have open access. They have editors. That is an important part of an establishment. No one has the time to read everything put out by the establishment, even in a small field. To devote much energy to reading unedited contributions on the web is unlikely to prove a good investment of time and energy.

SCIENCE AS STRUCTURE

I think of a science, any science, as a large, complex structure. I use the word structure to emphasise the interconnected nature of the pieces that make up a body of science. The pieces do not stand alone. This is central to natural and social science, indeed, to all science. We may ask, what are these pieces, and how do they fit together? Both are difficult questions and both need answers. It may be easier to begin with the 'fit'. Parts of the structure fit together very neatly, and parts relate to each other in a higgledy-piggledy fashion. By a neat fit I mean either that the pieces can be derived logically, one from another, or relate to each other in a unique and unambiguous relation.

It is nice to have clearly specified relationships between parts of science, but science can make progress when they do not exist. Some of the connections are suspected rather than established. It is not unusual for two partly inconsistent, or even wholly, inconsistent, substructures to coexist in a part of the overall structure of a branch of science. Any one piece may connect to some other pieces for sure, and still other pieces tentatively. There may be alternative connecting routes between pieces. And the routes themselves are pieces, often being 'terminals' in one context and 'routes' in another context. It would not be possible to build a physical model of such a structure, and it certainly would be dangerous to move about in such a structure if it could be built.

There are different kinds of pieces in the structure of a science, but the main pieces are explanations. 'Running electricity through a steel bar raises its temperature because...' is a typical piece of the structure. Enclosed within a general verbal statement of this kind we can often find more precise strands. These are typically stated in mathematical formulations, which predict how the temperature in a specified bar will vary as the strength of the current is varied, including the responses over time. Every explanation rests in principle on other explanations, about which we may have a firm or less firm idea, or maybe no idea at all.

Imre Lakatos, the philosopher of science, used to say that scientific laws are infinite in length if properly specified. Perhaps the fact that explanations rest on other explanations is what he meant by infinitely long statements of scientific laws. He also felt that the pieces that make up the scientific structure could best be classified hierarchically, that is, in order of importance. That was a mistake. There is no such thing as a universal ordering according to importance. Importance always involves a purpose. Important to what particular scientific objective? The pieces relate to each other in dozens of different ways. Simply ordering according to a possible importance is not particularly revealing. We can suggest a few of the ways propositions in science relate to each other.

Some of the pieces may in themselves have little or no characteristic which could be called explanation. The 'piece' might simply be a formula that relates heat to electricity, with no attempt at saying why the relation holds up. Alternatively, a piece might do nothing more than indicate membership in a class of objects. Statements of the kind, '...all objects we call "A", are members of a group we call "B"', can be useful statements without in themselves offering any explanation. Naturally, it all depends on what we mean by an explanation. If it is the case that it always rains when I am on holiday — assertion "B" —, it is a kind of explanation of why it is raining now to point out that I am on holiday — assertion "A". In other words, '...all holiday days are rainy days (B), and this is a holiday day (A), hence it is raining". There is no mechanism here. But nor is there any mechanism in the original formulation of the law of gravity.

The absurd example above involves the idea of 'all' holiday days. And the law of gravity involves the idea of 'all' objects pulling on each other. 'This turtle has four legs' is a *fact*. It is not just a true statement; it is a particular kind of true statement. There is no 'all' about it. It refers to a single, observable case. Statements of fact may be wrong, just as theories, or explanations may be wrong. Maybe this turtle lost a leg in a fight, or has an unusual genetic make-up such that it only grew three legs. In which case the statement that this turtle has four legs is a factual type of statement that happens to be wrong.

FACTS, THEORIES AND ASSUMPTIONS

A lot of people use the term 'facts' to refer to true statements, and theories to refer to guesses. This is a misleading usage. Facts tend to be specific, and to be amenable to sensory observation. It gets trickier if the statement is "... turtles usually have four legs." For most purposes, that is a factual statement. But what about, "...all turtles who have not been injured or had a genetic defect have four legs."? My view is that whether something is correctly classified as a fact or not depends on its place in the structure of the argument. Statements based on particular sense observations are almost always facts in most explorations. It is a fact that the blades of the particular radiometer in front of me rotated when I exposed it to the sunlight. It is a higher level fact that the blades of all properly built radiometers rotate when they are exposed to sunlight. The larger statement is a fact primarily because it can in principle be observed, and the statement does not go beyond saying what will be observed. In short, it does not say why they rotate.

A useful trichotomy is between *facts, assumptions* and *theories*. Theories are statements about why things happen. They are explanations. What constitutes a fact, for example, depends on the structure of the scientific investigation. For some purposes it may be a fact that unemployment is falling. Part of what makes it a fact for that investigation is that the parties concerned believe it is the case, accept it as a fact, and are trying to explain it. On another occasion, other parties, or even the same parties, may regard the statement 'unemployment is falling' as the explanation of why people are spending more, for example. They may endeavour to test whether or not that is the correct explanation by making certain relevant observations — in other words, by finding out whether that explanation is consistent or inconsistent with other facts.

Assumptions are structurally very much like facts. For the purpose of a particular agreed investigation, we take them for granted. However, there are a few differences. The facts tend to be either the starting point, the puzzle, which initiates the investigation, and also the litmus test for resolving the investigation. We try not to make up the facts. One way or another, they should come from observation. Inventing facts is going against the grain of the investigation. Assumptions are made up. They are selected, if you like. Very often there are conventions about what assumptions are made in a particular kind of investigation. This has the advantage of helping to isolate particular causal relations at work in the area. Other kinds of assumptions may simply be a way of ruling out what is held not to matter for a particular investigation. Alternatively, they may help to specify where an explanation is expected to apply. It is also common to make assumptions according to the need to make a problem tractable.

I would like to dwell a bit on the word 'theory' because theories are at the heart of science, and elaborate on my assertion that this word is so often misused in ordinary speech. In the context of science, theory means 'explanation'. Any explanation, like any assertion that something or other is a fact, may be wrong. Sometimes people use the word theory to mean what they think might be the case, or is being suggested could be the case, and the word fact to mean what is the case. One can hardly say that the way people use words is wrong, but I do think this usage which emphasises reliability is confusing.

For the purposes of this book, and I claim for the understanding of science generally, it is best to use the term theory to mean explanation, whether that explanation is believed to be correct and has been shown to be consistent with the available evidence, or is possibly correct, or is wrong. An explanation is an explanation, whether it is the correct or not the correct explanation.

Another popular use of the term theory has to do with ideal circumstances. "Theory is one thing, reality is another." It is that kind of silly statement to which I object. A recent book has the title *Human Rights in Theory and in Practice.* What the title means is; what rights should be, and what in fact they are. The same idea is contained in the sentence, "In theory the police treat all suspects in the same way, but in fact they are harder on ethnic minorities." This use of the word 'theory' here is in terms of normative arguments. Like it or not, we all have values, and think some states of affairs are better than others. Disputes over values involve arguments about what is best and what should be the case in a better world. Issues of this kind are called normative questions. The debate is over what should be the 'norm', or standard in a particular situation. It is confusing to call statements about norms 'theories'.

Science, as science, has nothing to say about normative matters. However well we explain what is going on, we cannot go logically from an explanation to an inference about what should be done. Having said that, it has to be pointed out that very often when people appear to disagree about matters of value, or normative matters, what they really disagree about is how the world works. One person may favour the death penalty and another oppose it because they hold different views about the ability of the penalty to deter murder. That is a disagreement about the facts of the case. It is also possible to disagree about the death penalty on grounds that are independent of any facts.

The term theory, as one of the key pieces in that structure that is science, is synonymous with the term 'explanation' and has no normative content. For such a usage, to say something is all right in theory, but not in practice, makes no sense. If an idea is not a good explanation of what is going on, it is not all right. Even the grammatical transformation, 'all right in explanation', shows that the use of the term 'theory' to mean 'ideally' is a nonsense usage in the context of science.

Normally there are a variety of terms used in science to mean explanation, such as theory, hypothesis, conjecture and law. Typically we find the term 'law' used for relatively old ideas and ideas that are held to be unusually likely to be reliable in the sense of yielding correct predictions. The term law also tends to be attached to connecting links in the structure of science which are used frequently in scientific investigation. Is it a good idea to call some explanations 'laws' and others 'theories', for example? It probably does not do much harm, as long as it is recognised that the terms refer to precisely the same type of thing. They both mean 'explanations', nothing more and nothing less. The same goes for the terms 'conjecture' and 'hypothesis'. Which term is used to describe or refer to an explanation tends to depend on how long the explanation has been around, how reliable it is felt to be, and how frequently it is employed in scientific reasoning. Of course these are important distinctions. And in investigating problems they are relevant considerations. But using the term law rather than theory does not tell us anything specific. A law may turn out to be wrong, just like any other explanation. A law may be a well travelled connection between pieces of the scientific structure today, but may be little used in the future. All in all, it is probably better to stick to the term theory in all cases where one means 'explanation', and discuss the issue of reliability explicitly when needed, rather than assigning the term hypothesis, or law, to particular explanations.

ORDINARY SCIENTIFIC WORK

These are the pieces, or elements, of the scientific structure, and we have said a bit about how they relate to each other. The next question is, what is scientific work? What do scientists do? The answer is obvious at a fairly general level. Though obvious, surprisingly often it is ignored. What scientists do is work on that structure which is scientific knowledge. They do not tackle problems from scratch. Exactly how they work on the body of science varies from case to case, and is not easy to specify. Again speaking generally, scientists improve and add to the pieces which make up the structure, and they rearrange the way that they are put together. Occasionally an investigator discovers a redundant piece, or group of pieces. Two different names may in fact refer to the same thing, if looked at properly, and this means that an unnecessary piece can be removed. One of the jobs of a scientist is identifying and chucking out unnecessary material.

Far more common than the removal of redundant pieces is the effort to achieve some kind of coherence or consistency. Progress in science is not orderly. It is not uncommon for discoveries to be made which appear to be valid, as valid as existing ideas, but in certain respects they are inconsistent with other avenues of understanding. The discovery of inconsistencies between different parts of a scientific structure is a common stimulus to further enquiry. Maybe one or more of the ideas are seriously flawed. Perhaps a new setting in which the troublesome facts or explanations can all be placed can be found which will remove, or partly remove, the apparent inconsistency. It is far from easy to do this. Rationalising a section of the structure of science is among the most challenging tasks for a scientist.

The body of science is continually growing. The growth process is not held back very much by existing inconsistencies and outright mysteries. Scientists do not wait for order and consistency in the existing structure to be achieved before moving on. For example, explanations are continually advanced for facts that have not been touched on before. Usually the first attempt to explain new facts is done by drawing on closely related, if not identical, explanations which have worked reasonably well in other contexts. But sometimes new facts which have been discovered, or familiar facts which have not been studied very much, call for quite new explanations. And then again, even though we seem to have a plausible explanation of something, a new and different explanation may be proposed. The two, or more, rival explanations may coexist for some time and in this way add both to the size and the inconsistency of the science structure.

The discovery of new, usually complex, facts is an important part of scientific work. Finding these and adding them to the stock of accepted information is another task of working scientists. A related aspect, which is a kind of growth, is greater precision. Better measurements may add to precision, as may more precise formulations of explanations. Sometimes greater precision removes what was thought to be an inconsistency. It is equally able to uncover a problem where none was seen to be there before.

Science is not common sense. It is not something we all possess, or could possess if we were only trained to use it. Science is that great structure out there. No one person made it or can even begin to master it. Individual workers attempt to improve tiny parts of it. These parts may be important for some human need, but they are nevertheless tiny when seen against the backdrop of science as a whole. Most of the findings of science are outside of and contrary to common sense experience. The earth is moving, not the sun, even if it does not look or feel that way.

The collective endeavour of science is extraordinary. There is no other example of a combined effort of even remotely this scale stretching over time and place and having a single purpose. In this case that is the purpose of adding to understanding. This in itself implies a remarkable feature of science, namely, it is always provisional and subject to change. It is only human to defend ideas in the face of attack. There are reactionaries in the science establishment. And it is quite right not to abandon ideas at the first hint of a better alternative. But in the end, change is the name of the game. Why, how and at what point a general change in perception occurs is interesting, but the facts of change, and more remarkably, of improvement, cannot be denied.

Scientists work on the structure, and also use the structure to address problems. Somewhere in that structure are pieces related to each other which can be used to calculate the gravitational force that a lunar module will experience on the surface of the moon. It often is no trivial matter to be able to use scientific knowledge in a particular application. Yet, if repeated over and over again in well-specified circumstances, it may become quite trivial to apply a bit of science. The struggle to apply, when it proves difficult, can be a major source of improvement in the scientific structure. The distinction between doing science, in the sense of working on that structure, and applying science to achieve some specified end is clear in many cases and blurred in many other cases.

IS SOCIAL SCIENCE THE SAME?

This description of science has treated natural science and social science in exactly the same way. At the level of generality we are working at here, they are much the same. The goal of understanding is the same. The image of pieces and how they are put together is equally applicable. So is the discussion of theories, assumptions and facts. There are differences between social and natural science, and for the most part they are differences of degree. That is why the same general descriptive statements apply to both. So why do we find at the extreme the assertion that social science is not possible, and short of the extreme, the view that it is a completely different activity from natural science?

I can only guess as to why these views, which are generally hostile to a scientific study of society, are so common. A lot of it must be nothing more than sheer ignorance. If you think that the essence of natural science is something which is fixed, certain and successful, then social science looks so different as to be legitimately seen as being something else. That view rests on a false understanding of natural science. We have to concede that natural science is more successful than social science, but that is not the point. We would like to be more successful in social science, and usually have to content ourselves with very modest gains. The point is that success is not the critical test of the endeavour. In some cases sheer guesswork may be successful. There is also the fact that social decisions have to be made whether the science is there to inform them or not. But none of this means that we cannot do social science. It does mean that we should not oversell our achievements. It is also worthwhile to point out that hunch, guesswork, prejudice, instinct, habit and all the rest of the non-scientific armoury are just that. In the next chapter we will take a closer look at hostility to social science. Now is the time to highlight differences between social and natural science.

Most of us have some idea of what it is like to be a child, a consumer, a worker, and so on, and these categories are part of the subject matter of social science. Individuals are the elements of society. Typically the study of various aspects of society involves theories about the behaviour of these and other elements. In other words, in social science, we study ourselves. An individual is not a society, but is a part of a society, and as such is an object of study. Most of us have some experience of being in a family, and theories about families are in some obvious sense closer to home than theories about charged particles or reproduction in frogs.

It is inevitable that people have opinions about almost all social phenomena and these phenomena are the subject matter of social science. Everything from the causes of crime to the consequences for unemployment of an increase in the money supply — all these things which people experience directly to some degree — will inevitably result in many people holding opinions on many topics. The layman will have more of an idea about car theft than about financial fraud, and more views about not having to change money when going abroad than about integrated monetary policy. But it still is the case that much of social science is about things we try to understand in a non-scientific way. It is about things that impinge on daily life. Most people are happy to concede that there are specialists who know a lot about viruses. They are more inclined to ignore, or doubt the existence of, specialists who know a lot about the social factors effecting why marriages last or break up, or the social effects of television violence on children.

THREE DIFFERENCES OF DEGREE

I think people have a different view of social science compared to natural science because of the subject matter of the latter, rather than because of any real difference in how they two bodies of science work. At the same time, there are actual differences, more of degree than of kind. The single greatest difference is that society in all its aspects is, or may be, changing. What was true yesterday may not be true today. To mention three very obvious examples, credit cards, television and computers may change the way societies function in important respects and in certain areas, or may have no discernible effect at all. There is always the possibility that what was fairly well understood in the past may turn out to be not true at a later date, due to the changes I mentioned, or due to some other changes. Many people have much higher incomes than forty years ago. How does this affect saving for old age, dating behaviour in children, and attitudes towards foxhunting?

The way the physical universe functions may be changing as the universe ages, if it ages, but the pace of this change is slow for all practical purposes. There is little reason to think that a hydrogen atom is different today from what it was like in the past. The biological universe is clearly changing much faster than the physical universe. Creatures exist today which were not around ten million years ago, and *vice versa*. That in itself does not mean that the underlying principles of life have changed, but it does rather suggest that it may be harder to find those principles than in the case of the physical universe. Much more than the physical and biological realms, the social universe is a place of deep seated and of superficial change.

This does raise the question of what are the principles, and what are the superficial aspects. Both can be important. I may be more interested in whether locusts will attack my crop than I am in the general principles of swarming insects. Whether or not there will be an attack tomorrow, or this spring, is in one sense a contingent, or a superficial matter. In the physical universe, a great deal of what is interesting and usable has to do with what is not changing, like the various forces that physicists describe. It may be that when it comes to social investigation, it is precisely the superficial and contingent which is interesting. In some sense, in the physical universe the underlying principles are a large part of the story. In the social universe they may be there, but they may be a comparatively small part of the story.

There are two sides to this issue of change. The changing component may be the more interesting component when it comes to social matters. At the same time, there may be very little which is not at least in principle subject to change when it comes to the objects of study of the social sciences. Many people would agree that it is unlikely that France, Germany and the United Kingdom will go to war again against each other over the coming two hundred years, if ever, even though they frequently did so in the past, including in my lifetime. Assuming this prediction is right, what has changed that has caused this rather desirable difference in behaviour between these countries? Could it be that after a certain amount of warring, people become pessimistic about it being able to achieve anything? Or are people less inclined to go to war when they have higher incomes, or know more about each other? Perhaps the military might of the United States puts big countries and former allies off war. Or is it all four factors which combined produce the result, and no two factors could do that? We just do not know. We may be in the same world today as in the past when it comes to the causes of war, or we may be in a fundamentally different world.

EXPERIMENTS

The second great difference between social and natural science has to do with experimentation. I once worked with a group trying to find an insecticide to kill a particular bug. What the researchers did was lay out rows and rows of little containers with five bugs and a little of what they ate in each, and then they put a different bit of chemical in each container, and had a look to see how the bugs were doing. I was amazed at the number of containers and the variety of chemicals used. I would have thought the scientists knew some general things about this bug, and what would be likely to have an adverse effect on it. They told me they did, but there are surprises, and once they had a collection of chemicals that killed the bugs, they would be much better able to work out why certain chemicals were killing them. It was also suggested that if one of the effective chemicals was much cheaper than the others, they might not bother to work out what was killing the bugs, and just use that chemical. But that is another story. What struck me was how easy it is to line up containers, and by sheer dint of coverage, find the chemicals that killed this bug. The great thing was that every container was the same, for all relevant purposes, apart from the chemical. The scientists could experiment. This is much less of a possibility for social scientists.

Natural science often employs clever pseudo-experiments in situations where it is not possible to do genuine experiments. Examples of this are bombarding a metal sphere with charged particles in an effort to simulate the northern lights, and passing electrical charges through a gaseous medium to simulate the conditions when the building blocks of life were forming on earth. Another example is attempts to construct a physical model of the Gulf Stream, and then vary temperature to see what happens. In some cases drastic changes of scale may not matter, and in others they may invalidate any results of the mock experiment. Lots of areas in natural science are not amenable to experiment, and even pseudo-experiment is hard to imagine in some areas. But many questions can be resolved through experiment, and this is in contrast to social science. Some experiments in social science do seem quite effective, such as leaving wallets around and observing whether they are reported or not. And in other cases people are asked to play games as if they were making high-level business decisions. This is a kind of experimentation with considerable uncertainty as to whether behaviour in the world closely follows behaviour in the experiment. Some attempt has been made to test social theories using animals. Here the hope that behaviour out in the wild will be similar to that in the cage has a good chance of being at least partly right. What can be deduced about co-operation and rivalry in humans, for example, is less certain.

The plain fact is that social science can make some use of experiment, but this will always be to a significantly lesser degree than in natural science. Frank Paish, an LSE economist, once said if anatomy and dissection were not allowed, but it was possible to make drawings of corpses after big battles, anatomy would be like social science. However, the problem is worse than that. With luck, eventually the ravages of war might duplicate every cut the anatomist might wish to make. However, the social changes induced by history come all of a piece. We may observe the effects of reducing or expanding the money supply. Every level of interest rate may be available in the record, but that is not like every possible cross-section slice of a limb. The reason is that the limb itself is relatively constant compared to the variations of society. The same change in the money supply may have very different effects depending on other conditions of society. Of course there are ways to try to come to grips with the inability to experiment in the investigation of most social phenomena. This is not the place to seriously explore the limits and achievements of statistical inference. Impressive techniques can be employed. The need for these methods comes in large part from the inability to experiment. This is a difference in degree between social and natural science.

OPEN TO BIAS?

A lot of play is made of the assertion that natural science is objective, but social science cannot escape from values and subjective biases. A more extreme version of the 'science only pretends to be value-free' school holds that even natural science, and, believe it or not, even pure mathematics, are products of human effort and therefore tainted by human prejudice. If it can be argued by some that physics is designed to serve the interests of well-off white males, then what is the hope that social psychology, for example, might be held to be, if not entirely free of any value bias, at least not destroyed by it? I do not think that these kinds of issues of potential lack of objectivity in social science are as important as the problems that come from the rapid changing of societies and the limited scope for experiment. However, the facts of social change and the limited scope for experiments do relate to the accusation of bias in social science. They result in it being harder in the social world to find empirical tests of theories. However, from the fact that it is harder it does not follow that social science is hopelessly contorted through lack of objectivity.

The fact that social science has less scope for crisp empirical tests of its propositions than natural science helps to open the door for attacks on social science on the grounds of not being value-free, and therefore of not being scientific. The firmer the basis of knowledge, the less scope for criticism on the grounds of possible bias through practitioners holding particular values. But regardless of the actual objectivity of the enquiry, these kinds of attacks will always be possible. If Newton's laws can be called nothing more than aggressive male posturing, how much worse the problem for less secure endeavours. We can assume that such attacks will always go on, however demonstrable knowledge becomes. Social science will always be particularly vulnerable to them. The bottom line for social science is to strive to be more objective, not to claim to be totally value-free.

The choice of topic to investigate is not something that can be scientifically determined. It is, however, influenced by scientific progress itself. I had the good fortune to be able to ask the Nobel Laureate Kenneth Arrow what he thought today about the general equilibrium programme which had occupied him to a great extent and to which he contributed so significantly. His answer was that doing the work was more or less irresistible as each new answer threw up new and difficult, but solvable, problems. This inherent logic of discovery is an important element in what scientists choose to work on. There are other forces influencing the choice of problem.

If a funding body wants to pay for space research, the scientists will not come up with a submarine. Funding is bound to influence the development of science. This is likely to be more important at the more applied end of science, and more important in the short run than the long run. But it cannot be denied that social and political factors influence the development of science. All sorts of things influence the choice of research programmes, and the perceived interests of parts of society, particularly powerful parts, is one of these.

Will these kinds of considerations also influence how problems are tackled, and worse still, will they bias the results? I think a fair-minded observer must answer 'yes' to both questions. Scientific research, natural and social, and maybe more in the case of social than natural science, will respond to and be influenced by the powerful special interests of society. However, it would be totally naïve to think that if the research was not undertaken, the view of society held and promulgated by the special interests would be closer to the truth than the findings of admittedly influenced scientific investigation. Science exists in a social context, and it is natural to assume that it is likely to respond to, and be broadly supportive of, that context.

Why are a number of social scientists interested in homelessness? For one thing, it is perceived to be a serious problem. It is also probably the case that social scientists, like people generally, feel that people without places to live offends their values as well as raising political concerns. Research on homelessness might have the goal of finding the most effective way of reducing the number of people sleeping rough in our cities. Alternatively, it might have the goal of improving the lot of those who do not have places to sleep and live. There is bound to be some overlap between the two research programmes. The goal of 'improving the lot' is easy to say, but cannot be given objective meaning. Nevertheless, the focus of the two research programmes would be different in ways that we can loosely anticipate.

There is plenty of ambiguity in the stated objective of the first programme unless we specify what is meant by "effective". A policy for reducing the number of people sleeping on city pavements would be unlikely to be effective if it did not have fairly wide support, and that would include some concern for the homeless themselves. However, the motivation behind a research effort with more emphasis on reducing numbers compared to one with more emphasis on helping the homeless would be different. Yet both would very likely be concerned with finding out who are the homeless, and the factors that lead people to becoming homeless. And both would want to determine what types of alternative accommodation would more readily induce people to leave the streets. Undoubtedly the preferences and values of the more powerful elements in society will influence the development of social science. This is an exciting fact to the anti-science camp, but we should not make too much of it.

Clearly there are very sensitive areas of social enquiry. Research on when and where a *coup d'état* is likely to be more successful is one of these. Even more sensitive is research on the best ways to organise and fund coups. While conceivably this work could be carried out using the highest standards of objectivity, the knowledge itself might prove to pose a threat to democracy. As anyone can see the possible consequences of the investigation, the research may gain little support, or attract little interest, from scholars who like democracy. On the other hand, this might be exactly the most valuable information to a state which wants to take action to lower the possibility of *coup d'état*. There is a minefield of dangers when it comes to the choice of problem, and guessing which way the bias will go.

There have been many cases where research has been stopped, or hindered, because it appeared to be against the interests of a certain group. The study of potentially adverse effects of putting babies and young children in day-care has been fiercely attacked as being against the emancipation of women. This is at best short-sighted, given that roughly half the individuals in day-care will grow up to be women. Sometimes it is claimed that undertaking the research itself will influence social behaviour. For example, it is claimed that social enquiry into teenage sexual behaviour in itself promotes promiscuity. This so called 'reflexivity' view sees social institutions and social behaviour as being very sensitive to the activity of acquiring knowledge, and to the knowledge itself once produced. These views are themselves theories that should be investigated. They are not valid arguments against social science.

One would expect much of scientific research to have the potential of furthering the generally accepted ends of the society in which it takes place. This will influence what is studied, and how it is studied. It may bias the results. There is no need to claim otherwise. While being aware of the ever present, and often hard to detect, influences away from objective results, social scientists should and do aim to reduce the amount of bias in their work. It is a service to social science, and indeed part of its activity, to look for bias and correct it when it is detected. The potential for error in scientific work is not an argument for not undertaking scientific investigation.

The problem of bias is greater in social science than in natural science. It differs in degree rather than in kind. There is less content and less stability in the social science structure than in physical or natural science. The subject matter changes more, but not so much so that past work has no explanatory power in the present. Studying things may effect what has been studied. Of course these factors require special care. One it tempted to say that because of these considerations, including the fact that the role for experiments is much more restricted, that social science is more difficult than natural science. But that is not the case. It is a bit like saying that some musical instruments are easier to play than others. This is false. All musical instruments have potentials that even the most gifted player cannot reach. The possibility with any instrument is limitless, so how can we say that one is harder to play than another? Similarly, all the sciences contain challenges beyond what anyone can achieve. The fact that there is more danger of bias in the study of almost any aspect of human society than there is in the study of the physical or biological sphere does not mean that social investigation is in any meaningful sense harder to do. It does call for particular care. That is all. How important the particular problems of social science are varies from one social science to the next.

These differences between natural and social science, and the possible pitfalls, not to say bogeymen, of the latter are easily exaggerated. The Nobel Prize winner Amartya Sen once suggested that economics, one of the social sciences, had not had the benefit of being worked on by a first rate mind. When I reported this comment to a fellow economist, Leonardo Felli, he said that this is because first rate minds like to work on difficult, but solvable problems. In social science we have difficult unsolvable problems. What we do in social science in response, he suggested, is make up difficult problems of an essentially mathematical nature and pretend that they are social science. That may be a modern disease. To a great extent, mathematics has replaced scholarship as a beside-the-point test of relevance. But this concession should not be taken to imply that mathematical methods are of no use in social science. They are immensely important. The issues of how to advance our subjects are difficult and real enough. We do not need 'pretend' problems, like is it legitimate to use mathematics in social investigation, on top of the real problems in our way.

THE SOCIAL SCIENCES

It is convenient, and fairly conventional, to think in terms of five different social science disciplines. In alphabetical order, they are anthropology, economics, political science, social psychology and sociology. Because social structures are highly interconnected in the most elaborate and complex ways, there are numerous points of contact and overlap between the five disciplines. Yet the disciplines remain recognisably distinct. They can be characterised in terms of both their subject matters and their methods. But they clearly do not fit neatly into airtight compartments.

There are some scholars who see the divisions between these five disciplines as having no more justification than historical accident, which is no justification at all. The five subjects and the establishments they generate, and which in turn work to perpetuate the subjects, are a fact of university life. In principle it could be that rather different ways of carving up the field would make more sense. It could be that more, or fewer, subjects could address the different aspects of society in a way that leads to greater understanding of social reality. The thrust of this book is to maintain that the five relatively distinct disciplines which make up social science are not simply, or largely, arbitrary ways of organising training and research. There is a good deal of logic in how the subjects divide up the field. We will see in later chapters the distinct ways in which they address different topics.

I know of no convincing case for carving up the territory in a different way than is done at present, or for combining, or sub-dividing, existing subjects.

This is not to say that as society changes and our knowledge of it improves, it will never be the case that basic changes in the structure of social science disciplines will be desirable. It may be that as knowledge advances a very different structure of subjects would be more helpful than the present divisions between the subjects. If a different structure would be better, it might be adopted. Even if better, it is not clear that such changes will occur. They may happen. They will not happen tomorrow. Meanwhile, the five disciplines make up the basic organising principle of social science. I will argue that this arrangement is advantageous. It works reasonably well, in spite of society itself being integrated in complex ways. The existing structure of social science subjects is helpful partly because the different subjects make investigations manageable. But that is just part of the benefit of the present structure. More important than that, the subjects in a very important sense are able to complement each other.

One way of answering the question, what is social science, is to examine the territory around it. What is not social science? In the next chapter we will step across some of the fuzzy borders surrounding social science. We will concentrate on the non-scientific borders. Some of these crossings lead us into territory that is indifferent to social science. Other forays lead into friendly territory, and some surrounding territories turn out to be pretty hostile.

Chapter Three

VALID AND INVALID ALTERNATIVES TO SOCIAL SCIENCE

Some people have a talent for discerning that certain things which appear to be dissimilar are in fact similar or even the same. Other people emphasise the opposite side of the coin and take pride in showing that certain things which are often taken to be the same are in fact different. Both can be valuable discoveries. Usually the most appropriate and realistic stance is to note that certain methods, or disciplines, or subjects, which is what we are discussing now, are similar in some respects and different in others. The fact that things have much in common does not make them the same. The differences may be very important for some purposes.

ART

We can all agree that scientific understanding of society is not the only kind of understanding. A concrete example is useful in comparing the understanding that can come from literature with that of social science. Economics, sociology and political science all study the Great Depression. Each subject comes at the topic from a different perspective, and each has the goal of explaining different aspects of this social event. These social sciences are not directly concerned with creating for the reader the subjective experience of being an unemployed urban worker, or a hopelessly indebted farmer, or showing the reader what it was like to be any other participant in the depression.

The novel *The Grapes of Wrath*, in sharp contrast to social science, does have the goal of providing a picture of what it was like to be there. That is very different from the economics monograph *The Great Crash*, which attempts to explain how this depression came about. I have no problem with calling "what it was like to be there" a kind of knowledge, and "why it came about" another kind of knowledge. I do have a problem with the claim, if it were to be made, that they are the same. Art is a wonderful vehicle for creating in the person who absorbs the art the emotions and feelings of various experiences. It is not particularly suited to explaining the causes of the events described. Social science does not have the goal of reproducing experiences. It has the goal of explaining things. Art is not social science. It is a perfectly valid alternative mode of understanding.

Of course, the subjective experiences people have often play a crucial role in understanding social events. Whether people perceive something as hard luck or unfair, permanent or possible to change, frightening or terrifying, and so on, may for many problems be important data for social scientists. The skills of the artist may be very similar to those of the scientific investigator. Anthropologists specialise in understanding what the world looks like from the inside of various communities. So do some film makers and novelists.

Taxi Driver and *Glamorama* put you in the shoes of certain characters who one feels one can recognise and know that in some sense they are not pure invention. The artists have given us insight into significant ways of living and feeling that are present in the world. There is some generality here. It is not just these particular characters who engage our attention. They are socially significant. That is as far as the artist need go. What it means to be "socially significant" does not have to be directly explored in a work of art. It does have to be in a work of social science — significant to whom, and in what way, and with what consequences.

The important differences between art and science as ways of approaching society have to do with generality and accuracy, with the audiences both engage, and with relations between works of art compared to the relations between works of science. *Crime and Punishment* and *The Stranger* are novels with something in common and they are helpful in illustrating all three differences. In both novels the reader gains insight into the experience of being particular people caught up in a particular murder. Novels are not usually about murders, or businessmen, or workers, in general, but are about particular people and particular events.

When prisoners on Death Row are taken to the electric chair in the novel *The Green Mile*, we are there with both the condemned men and the prison guards who have to carry out this awful task. Different prisoners and different guards would result in a different novel. This is especially true of the narrator in the novel. For many novels the character and humanity of the explicit or implicit storyteller is the basic content of the novel. We would get a different answer to the implied question, what is the death sentence like, for example, with a different author, or the same author writing about different characters.

When we say that "art provides the experience of being there", it is worth asking exactly what do we mean? Are we referring to what it is like to be those particular characters, or the reader somehow in those characters, or the experience in general? I would suggest that all three are involved, with varying degrees of emphasis in particular plays, novels, films or whatever. The novel *American Psycho* is an interesting example. Taken as a simulation for the reader of the experience of being a trader in financial markets in New York City, it tells the tale through an extreme character who is hardly characterised at all. This tends to heighten what the author takes to be the significant and hidden, or repressed, features of a certain slice of contemporary life.

It can be argued that authors, and other artists, make general statements through the particular. For the most part, these are implicit statements. The act of showing what it is like to get married, commit a crime, work in a certain trade, go to war, or suffer some humiliation, is bound to involve some kind of implicit theory. Part of the task of literary criticism is to attempt to make explicit the implicit theories of works of art. Science is explicit. We may disagree about the significance and accuracy of a scientific theory. What the theory is saying is usually not a matter for dispute. It can also be argued that works of art not only have lots of meanings, the richness of a work of art may lie precisely in its breadth of meaning. *The Stranger* may mean something rather different to you than to me. Which is the 'true' meaning is not a helpful question. Scientific theories do not mean different things to different people. Scientific work addresses itself to that structure which is science. In that sense it has a single audience, personified by science specialists. Art is addressed to all mankind. The ability it has to mean different things to different people is a strength. In science the lack of a clear and unambiguous meaning is a weakness.

We learn from art, or perhaps better, enrich our lives through art, in much the same way as we learn from experience. The virtual experience which art provides is not real, but it may go to more significant layers of a subjective event than much of ordinary life. It is less real, in the ordinary sense, but often it is more focused. One can relate to experiences in a work of art which are totally remote from one's own life. Few of us have been outside a space vehicle in orbit to undertake repair work on it. Yet we can know something of it through imagination and having gone through fear, loneliness and demanding work in other contexts. It is reality passed to us through the mind and emotions of another person. That other person, the artist, may bring more to our experience than we often do ourselves, or at least something very different and valuable. Even familiar experiences portrayed in a work of art may be more telling than much of what life itself often provides for us. Art works both with the familiar and the unfamiliar. Apart from its capacity for generating an experience which we may be unlikely to have in real life, we get an appreciation of the events told and expressed in the novel which we are incapable of having without the benefit of the guide, who is the artist.

THE BASIC DISTINCTION BETWEEN ART AND SCIENCE

But now we come to a crucial distinction between art and science. A new theory in science has to deal fully and explicitly with existing theory. The significance of the scientific idea lies in its relation to the current body of science. A work of art has a very different relation with other art. There is no sense in which *The Stranger* has the goal of improving on *Crime and Punishment*. New works of art generally do not replace or refine existing works. There is no question of the two novels offering rival views, only one of which may be right. Artists differ greatly in the extent to which they inform themselves of the history of their art. They may be aware of other work and be responding to it, but that response may or may not be apparent to the people who read the novel or come to the play. Each artist is working on her own project. In sharp contrast to the arts, scientists work on the same project.

It has been pointed out many times that if a particular scientist had not produced a certain piece of work, another scientist eventually would have done so. It is inconceivable that the nature of the genetic code would have remained unknown without Crick and Watson, or that biologists would not have a theory of natural selection if Darwin had not provided it. Indeed, in both cases, historians of science report on a race to reach certain discoveries and theories. Sometimes scientists are well aware that others are trying to solve the problem they are trying to solve, and they know who these competitors are. The reason for this that scientists all work on parts of the same structure of ideas. A gap or incongruity can be seen by all scientists. While artists certainly influence each other, the influence is not so direct because they are not working on the same thing in quite the same way that scientists address the same problem. Beckett does not replace Shakespeare. We cannot maintain that Faulkner was right and Vidal was wrong. We certainly can have different preferences. We may rank their achievements differently. But they and their works are in no sense obliged to deal with each other in the way that scientists and their work deal with one another.

Rival, or contradictory, scientific theories may co-exist for a time, or even a long time, because scientists have not figured out a way of resolving the conflict. It may be difficult to find implications of the two ideas which are different and which can be subjected to empirical investigation. But if this can be accomplished, this is a classic route for resolving conflict. Sometimes deeper logical investigation accomplishes the same task. Works of art are not rivals in the same sense. We need not compare them at all. We certainly do not have to say if one is true and another false. If I report that I went to see a new play last night, it would be odd for you to ask me whether it was true or false. You might want to know how much I enjoyed it. If you are a particularly serious chap, or lady, you might be interested in whether it moved me, and in what way. Did it give me a new insight into love or boredom? It may be very informative. Maybe I never thought about psychoanalysis, or AIDS, that way before. But works of art do not link up in the same way that scientific work links up. Works of art compete for our attention and appreciation. Scientists try to extend and improve explanations.

HISTORY

Though there are those who contest the view that art is different from social science, many other people feel that the point hardly needs to be made, and pointing out the differences between the two activities is pretty easy stuff; shooting fish in a barrel, as they say in America. When it comes to social science and history, the border between them is much fuzzier, and it is no easy matter to delineate it. The first point to dispose of is the idea that history is about the past of mankind, and social science is about the present. Of course much of the work of social scientists is applied work on current problems, or more basic work which is suggested by current problems, or simply takes off from current events. There are practical reasons why it is easier, as well as potentially more useful, to work on present day material, or fairly recent material, and these include data availability and the possibility of making all kinds of observations, including undertaking surveys. We may be able to ask some pertinent questions of those people who participated in removing the Berlin Wall, but we cannot question participants in the French Revolution. However, these practical considerations do not rule out doing social scientific investigation on any period that contained a society. Certain commonly employed methods will be impossible to use, but others will still be available.

It is also possible to write a history of any period, including right up to the present. My ignorance precludes me from giving specific examples, but

I would be willing to bet that one or more histories of the end of the Berlin Wall have been written. Of course most of actual history is about periods before the twenty-first century. But it is not the case that history is in principle about the past, let alone the ancient past, and social science is about the present, or recent past. That most of it works out that way does not mean that there is anything in principle to separate the two activities in terms of the periods they investigate.

History is narrative. Historians chronicle events. It is intended that the story told have a literal truth. This is achieved by sticking to the evidence. Where crucial evidence is currently not available, historians continue the tale by arguing the plausibility of certain events. Of course many histories may be written about the same place and period. We may tell the history of farmers and their farms, or kings and their courts, or possibly the interaction between the two. And all of these can be done in an endless variety of ways. We cannot tell the history of everything. Selection of what history to write is a kind of abstraction. It always involves leaving things out. This is something it shares with theory.

Naturally, even when writing about the same events, historians may give very different interpretations to the subject matter. There is often a great deal of explanation in historical writing. A migration, it is asserted, was caused by religious persecution, or a famine, or maybe both. How does this differ from social science? The difference may be very slight. It may not exist at all. We really are in a grey area, when it comes to difficult cases. Happily, not all cases are difficult.

An over-simplification, which nevertheless points us in the right direction, is to say that historians deal with unique events, and social scientists deal with general explanations. But it is complicated. Take the example of voyages of discovery. The explorer may have certain motives, and so may the government which pays for the exploration. The decision-takers in the government may be motivated by possible commercial advantage, by the desire to be seen to be powerful, by curiosity, and any number of other considerations. The historian may wish to tell the story of Columbus, or NASA, and a big part of the story might be what is motivating the participants. These are unique events. There is no obligation on the part of the historian to come up with a general theory of voyages of discovery. This immediately suggests two questions. How does the historian know whether his explanation is right or not? And if it is right, might it not be applicable, suitably modified, to other cases?

Some historians are well trained in one or more social science, but in most cases the appeal is to common sense rather than science. The phrase 'common sense' refers to what are generally accepted arguments or explanations by a particular body of people in a specified context. One man's platitude is the next man's revelation, as R.D. Laing once pointed out. Common-sense arguments are far from universally agreed. Common sense says that children will love their parents, if reasonably treated by them. It also says that they may not, and more, they may love them if unreasonably treated. While the broad body of common-sense views may contain contradictory elements, they do tend to be consistent in individuals and to come in clusters. Social psychologists study these groupings and can provide documented examples. Off the cuff, one might hazard the guess that people who feel that it is common-sense to be very worried about genetically modified food plants are inclined to hold that privately owned train companies pay less attention to customer comfort. The basic point about common sense is that the views are not linked up as in science. Even though they tend to come in clusters, they are stand-alone propositions which are not derived from combinations of ideas.

The work of historians can be quite brilliant in its formulation of a coherent tale, in its search for evidence, and in its appeal to common sense. Of course it is an exceedingly important activity, and Margaret Thatcher was wrong in thinking that it did not matter. How did we come to our present position is an absolutely central question, not only for practical applications, but for understanding ourselves. Often the historian provides the best answer we can have to this question. At the same time, the reach of historical explanation is either too great for science, or its aim is too specific. This distinguishes the activity from social science. Granted that where possible, many schools of historians are inclined to draw on social science when they can. In these cases history becomes a kind of applied social science, at least in part. And not infrequently social scientists proceed by constructing case studies. These exercises have much in common with history. They appear to be little histories, but they are not developed with the same goal which motivates historians. They are preludes to understanding rather than finished products.

Toynbee, Marx, Hicks, Spengler and others have endeavoured to construct general theories of history. I join with those who judge these efforts to be unsuccessful in accounting for significant amounts of past events. However, were an effort of this kind to be successful, that would take it beyond the sphere of narrative construction. It would be providing a science of society. Such a construct would certainly be quite broad and general in its level of explanation. Whether it would have much predictive power is doubtful. But why speculate about the nature of something we do not have. It is an interesting philosophical question as to why we can never have a theory of history, if indeed that is the case. I do not propose to go into it, but take it as a cue to turn to another legitimate alternative to social science, which is philosophy.

PHILOSOPHY

Most of knowledge has its roots in philosophy. The natural sciences have largely moved away from their philosophical origins. At least working scientists take that to be the case. While many practitioners in natural science may care little about philosophical matters, philosophers of science are very interested in many of their endeavours, including research in quantum mechanics, theories of the origin and nature of the universe, and evolutionary theory. Many of the great puzzles, such as what is and what brings about consciousness, are as much on the philosophy agenda as that of neurologists and psychologists. However, one suspects that as better theories and more telling evidence come to bear, this and other questions will tend to move away from the philosophical realm and become largely aspects of science.

All intellectual effort has philosophical underpinnings. These metaphysical stances can exert subtle and not so subtle influences on how enquiry is undertaken. It can sway what is studied and how it is studied. Fundamental issues such as the nature of causality and what it means to understand something are always present, whether acknowledged or not acknowledged. There certainly is no requirement for active researchers to have explicit views on these deep matters. Opinions differ as to whether it helps scientists to think at this philosophical level about what they are doing, or whether it just gets in the way. Weinberg says drawing the attention of scientists to philosophical concerns is like telling a tiger on the chase that all flesh is grass. However, it is not unusual for scientists, particularly senior figures, to occasionally chance their arms and write philosophical pieces. Sometimes this works well, though certainly that is not always the case.

The process of gradual distancing of philosophy from natural science is much less the case with social science. Indeed, the situation in social science is quite the opposite. At times it seems as if half the supposed social scientists are shirking the job and doing amateur philosophy instead. I will talk about this more when we come to illegitimate alternatives to social science. Academics can be seen to engage in what observers of the behaviour of animals call displacement activities, because it is just so difficult to do social science. One of these displacement activities is philosophy. Two other popular ones are scholarship and mathematics. But apart from all that, there are perfectly reasonable and legitimate reasons for social science to have more and closer links to philosophy than natural science.

Political science in particular is often indistinguishable from political philosophy. Philosophical figures like Adam Smith retain an interest for economics researchers to this day. Three factors contribute to the prominence of philosophy in the analysis of society. One is its relatively short history. It takes time for the structure of a science to become sufficiently large and elaborate to have enough mass so that contacts with philosophy become relatively unimportant. A second factor is caused by the difference of emphasis in social science methods. I will elaborate on these. The third factor is the greater importance of values and ethics at the heart of social investigation. Having said all that, philosophy is not the same as social science. It is a legitimate and important activity, and it can bear on understanding of society. Like art and history, it is a valid alternative approach to understanding social reality.

If more controversies in social science could be resolved through an appeal to evidence, the historical links to philosophy would be less pertinent and less compelling. The restricted scope for experiment compared to natural science means that metaphysical predisposition tends to play a larger role in forming a concept of what society is and how it functions. This is true both of large-scale issues and much more narrow and specific questions. There are important questions concerning the very nature of social reality compared to physical reality. The nature of what we are studying is problematic and the fact that social change is always occurring compounds the problems that result from the limited scope for experiments. For many studies there is always a reasonable possibility that the social world has changed in a way that alters the relationships under investigation. This means that appeals to evidence through observing over time, without being able to experiment, tend to be more suggestive than definitive.

Yet even if it were possible to have sharper empirical results in social science, the importance of value-judgements in social affairs would result in closer ties between social science and philosophy than we observe in natural science. Though the goal of all science is understanding and prediction, the objective of improved social arrangements impinges on social science investigation much more directly than with natural science. Notions of justice and fairness are important factors in many social interactions. What people take to be just is a factual matter, but it slides so easily into questions of the nature of justice as investigated by philosophers. Social questions involve groups of people ranging from the whole of mankind down to small communities and families. What counts as an improvement in social arrangements? If everyone in the relevant group has more, but inequality between the better-off and the rest has increased, is this progress? The usual assertion is that this is not a scientific question. And of course that is correct. But many social enquiries sidle up to such questions, often with a fuzzy border between science and values.

The other inescapable link to philosophy is the social scientist's continual struggles with the methods of enquiry. It is quite possible to get on with the job and let the philosophers worry about the validity of the methods investigators employ. Two things argue against this. In scientific debate we do not just argue over conclusions. We tend to defend what we are doing as being a particular case of a more general way of doing science. So willy-nilly, investigators are drawn into methodological debate. The other reason for not leaving it to the philosophers is that philosophers of science are often perceived as having a flawed view of the subjects they study. Common complaints are that they fail to recognise that a subject has changed, and that what we teach students is different, and should be different, from the applied practise of a subject. It may be useful for students to learn how to solve optimising problems, for example, even though we know that out in the world people often are not very good at optimising. Whether the social scientist sees the philosopher as a valuable commentator or a misguided busy-body, at least some practitioners should keep up with the debates.

The great philosophers of the past, and many working today, offer a world- view of human life on this planet. What are the responsibilities of an individual to society, and visa versa? What do the present occupants owe to the future? What is a just war? These and many other issues in philosophy are worth exploring. Definite answers may not be forthcoming, but so be it. The death of Diana prompted some philosophers to take a poor view of the widespread grief in the United Kingdom and elsewhere. Not surprisingly, others did not agree. Parts of philosophy tend to deal with large and lasting questions, questions that perhaps are impossible to resolve. Along with art and history, philosophy has a place in the investigation of society. These three areas are examples of valid alternatives to a scientific study of society.

PRETENDING TO BE SOCIAL SCIENCE

The invasion of social science by frauds and impostors echoes some earlier events in natural science. Scientific rogues, like Pilatre de Rozier in the eighteenth century, had charm and also ability. A modern social science example of an outrageous impostor is Carlos Castaneda who persuaded the Anthropology Department at UCLA that his novels were genuine pieces of research. They awarded a Masters degree to his first book, and a Doctorate to another completely fictitious work. Scholars all around the world were taken in. A distinguished British anthropologist reviewed his work in the most glowing terms. Very basic questions like what language his informant spoke were never asked. The informant could never be found, nor did his alleged culture tie in with any known investigations. The scholars involved in this case were quite remiss in their duties.

It is hard not to take some enjoyment from seeing highly placed academics taken in by a talented faker. Could natural science be so easily fooled? Some observers of the cold fusion episode would say yes. But when it comes to matters of degree, it is clear that the social sciences are much more vulnerable to wilful efforts to defraud. However, the conscious prankster, like the people who pretend to have medical degrees, and sometimes perform complicated operations under difficult circumstances, is not the real threat. The real threat comes from tenured invaders of academic departments. More and more important posts in academic institutions are going to people who argue variously that social science is not possible, or if it is possible, it is not desirable, or that the definition of social science should include activity which bears no resemblance to science in any form.

A number of people have tried to account for these sad developments. Some observers find the explanation in various successful campaigns coming from such diverse sources as literary criticism, feminism, and political correctness. These and other factors are held by some observers to be responsible for the current powerful move away from social science. They may be right. It is an interesting and important sociological question as to how this vogue for masquerading as social science came about. I have no new explanation of this unfortunate state of affairs, but I would like to offer help in identifying the different kinds of illegitimate alternatives to social science.

SOCIAL REVELATION

Recent years have seen a rash of books with titles like *The Network Society, The Risk Society, The Audit Society, The Entertainment Society, The Consumer Society, The Complaining Society,* and so on. These books have a lot in common. Perhaps their most important feature is that they are very easy to read and understand. We all agree that intelligibility is a virtue. And making things difficult for no reason is a pretty bad thing to do. Nor do I want to defend any kind of puritan virtue along the lines that something which is not difficult to understand is not worth knowing. But making knowledge appear to be easy by drastic falsification is a much greater disservice to knowledge than making something unnecessarily difficulty.

It is inevitable that science, at the very least, will be a little difficult. This is not to say that we lack communicators, science popularisers. On the contrary. We do have very able science popularisers writing today. Making science, be it social or natural, available to a non-professional audience is a most important activity. This is very different from achieving ease of understanding by ignoring science while pretending, probably unconsciously, to do science. Making difficult things accessible is fine. Misleading people is wicked.

The fact that simple books are likely to be phoney follows from my earlier argument about the structure of science. Science in any form is a body of knowledge worked on by many participants over the years. It is a complex interconnected body of potential explanation. It is always changing. It is never neat and coherent. To actually use a part of this structure in an effective way calls for quite a lot of knowledge of where to look in the structure, the ability to combine parts of it, and facility in handling the pieces. This is unlikely to be easy. The simplest way of spotting pretend social science of the one word — risk, globalisation, network — variety mentioned above is to note that this kind of work does not relate to the body of scientific knowledge.

Writers in this vein strike out as if they had a gift of enormous insight and originality. This is understanding through revelation. These writers do not need that body of knowledge which is science. Somehow the truth has been revealed to them. Their work does not draw on existing knowledge and does not add to it. They write as if these matters had never been investigated before. Starting out as if nothing had been done before makes for easy reading. This is not the same as informing about society. For that task these books are almost totally useless. At least that is my judgement. But whether useless or not, what is unforgivable is suggesting that this is social science. It is something else. It is social revelation.

Writers who feel they are lucky enough to have had important knowledge about the world revealed to them, and are prepared to pass on their revelations to others, are most likely spinning a tale — what my wife calls 'making it up as they go along'. There is no need to relate such work to the work of others. It could be argued that even if the particular writers seemed to be building little structures of ideas, even if rather off on their own, other investigators might slot those little structures into the large structure which is the body of science. This has never happened, and there are good reasons why it is unlikely to happen in the future. The most obvious is that revelations tend to have little in common with intelligible explanation.

There are other reasons why it is very unlikely that these essentially self-contained and isolated exercises could form a part of the structure of science, even if their originators did not work in that way. The structure of science, even a new social science, is likely to have thousands, if not tens of thousands of strands and connections, and been worked on by many practitioners over a period of time. That someone innocent of all this effort and refinement could come up with an idea, or set of ideas, that could be attached to the structure of knowledge is so unlikely as to be virtually impossible. It would be like making a complex mechanical structure, with no idea of what its use might be, and finding it was a perfect carburettor for a particular car engine, or chain-saw.

The producers of social revelation tend to mix unsupported assertion of unlikely propositions with blatant platitudes. 'Capitalism is nearing its end and there are more computers around today than twenty years ago.' A natural response is to ask what makes you believe the former, and what is the relevance of the latter? Social revelationists try to make out that the wild assertions are as firmly based as the platitudes. That is part of the function of referring to the platitudes. What the two have in common is that they appear in the same book. They are cited by the same author. The assertions are not related in terms of an intellectual structure. For their fans and followers, that this work has no scientific significance is quietly ignored.

SOCIAL CRITICISM

A slightly different invalid activity than peddling revelation is best described as social criticism. These writers are rather like literary critics, music critics, or any other type of critic. Instead of addressing their attention to works of art, they criticise social phenomena, large and small. A really knowledgeable critic is a wonderful person. Shaw's music criticism is interesting to read long after the performances which none of us now around could have attended. Criticism can open doors. The art critic Norbert Lynton does not like Giacometti. When you read his review of Giacometti's show at the Tate, there is no hint of this. What we have is a beautiful summary of the work and help in how to appreciate it. Much poor criticism is not like that. It is essentially about appraisal. 'I liked, or did not like, his latest film'. Liking is one thing and intelligent reaction is another thing.

Of course anyone can be a critic. Film criticism is a particularly interesting example. In order to read, we more or less have to know how to write. But to be a film critic, or a music critic, it is not necessary to understand filmmaking, or be able to play music. The critic need not be a creator of work. The critic responds to the work. Presumably honesty is some kind of requirement. 'This is what I actually felt about this movie.' Presumably almost anyone can give an honest report, so what makes one critic better than another? Having a similar take on films, books, or concerts as oneself could be useful. Writing well cannot hurt. But what about qualifications? A good critic should know a lot about the subject, have seen a lot of films, read a lot of criticism. Maybe being very worldly and steeped in lots of culture could help as well.

The social critic is much like the film-critic, or any other kind of critic. There is the 'liking' and 'not liking' element. This may refer to a particular institution, a political party, a style of leadership, or even a whole country. But going beyond preferences, well-developed sensitivities may endear a social critic to others with similar acuteness. A film like *American Beauty* may appeal at the time of viewing, but on reflection, and aided by a good critic, one may conclude that maybe one was 'taken in' a bit by the film. Exactly this process can be seen in social criticism. Like political satire, the social critic alerts the reader to what he might have found out on his own, if he gave a bit more thought to the matter. For example, the critic of a foreign-aid programme may reveal that less was given than was implied, that the motives were suspect, and that the aid was not very effective in achieving particular goals. Social critics are particularly alert to hypocrisy and misrepresentation.

The social critic may argue that democracy is more circumscribed in a particular country than is generally believed. Perhaps the chief executive may in effect go to war without explicitly declaring war or going through the allegedly required parliamentary processes. These are not insignificant insights. A knowledge of social science could help the social critic. Yet the critic is not doing social science. It becomes an invalid alternative when it pretends to be social science. Quite obviously the goal of criticism is not to refine or add to the body of knowledge. It is not beholden on the critic to refer to the current state of scientific knowledge. Criticism may involve very little in the way of chains of reasoning. And where it does, guesswork and intuition may bridge many of the gaps. In the end, the honest critic says, 'this is how it seems to me'. Who knows, or cares, whether he or she draws on social science to a great or a little extent in making these judgements? The critic certainly is not taking up the goal of changing the body of science. But is the activity a form of applied social science? It need not be, and generally will not be, because in the end the critic is reporting a subjective take on social events. If it is applied social science, it ceases to be pure social criticism.

SOCIAL POETRY

A speed-reading enthusiast once explained to me that rapid reading could save an enormous amount of time, given the quality and content of much of what one reads. Serious material with a lot of content is a different matter. He went on to describe what it is like to 'speed-read' Blake. For him it was like travelling in outer space, with rockets, flares, and potent images racing at him in bewildering confusion. Some writing has the objective of creating this kind of sensation, however slowly, not to say ponderously, it may be read. The objective is not so much coherent thought as it is the telling image. Certain words and phrases light up the mind and produce a feeling of deep understanding. The insight may border on the transcendental. If the reader, or the listener in a lecture hall, desires a short-cut to supposed understanding, the social poet is there to provide it. Indeed, what I am calling social revelation, criticism and poetry all have this element of bypassing the intricate connected paths of science.

The social poet has a special kind of offering which is different from the others. It has something to do with creating the experience of being there. Like the picture of a starving child, the full horror of flood, draught, war and pestilence as social events can be captured emotionally. Associations in the mind are activated and combined to literally cast a spell. Social poetry can be high art, when done well. Even when done quite badly, it often works pretty effectively on an audience. The social poet typically offers a cameo of where we are in the world today. We recognise that description as revealing what we almost knew, but needed to be told. We are provided with an answer to the question, what is the social world like which we are living in today? Of course, you and I may be living in quite different social worlds. There clearly is no such thing as, 'what life is like' just now. For the social poet, that is a quibble. He is not referring literally to particular people in a particular place. He is referring to the spirit of the age, a kind of metaphysical essence.

The social poet may be asking us to accept that beyond the superficiality of contingent events lies a deeper reality. This is a rather high level endeavour. It is a search for the true essence of social reality today. A more modest goal might be to suggest that there is a description which fits fairly well, as a sort of average, to a class of individuals, and hopefully this covers the audience at hand, or the likely readers of a book. Satisfied consumers of social poetry experience a kind of recognition which is sometimes called the 'a-ha', or penny-dropping, experience. Images can be fired off of money moving around the world, lots of computers, insecurity of jobs, loss of traditional authority, and so on. Alternatively, the social poet may conjure up the modern experience of air travel, or working in a particular trade. We who have never worked in that trade, and even more some that have, may sense a kind of poetic truth in the description. Very much like art, social poetry attempts to provide the experience of being there. Good social poetry can be very successful in doing this.

In this chapter I have written about 'valid' and 'invalid' alternatives to social science. Art, history and philosophy are described as valid. Social revelation, criticism and poetry are condemned as being invalid. Is this fair? There clearly is a taste for these activities which I castigate. While I personally have little use for them, others take them seriously. The distinction should not, and does not, turn on whether I like them or not, but on whether they pretend to be social science. This is the key point. Calling something science, something which departs fundamentally from that endeavour, is not just harmless labelling. It distorts and degrades intellectual endeavour. If someone prefers these ways of addressing the social, it is hard to argue with that. No one is obliged to do science. But to pretend that this is science will mislead many people, and may in the end keep them away from the real thing.

If the easy is the same as the hard, by all means let us do the easy. But is it the same? Claiming that revelation, criticism and poetry are science is a con. It fools students, and it fools those responsible for the allocation of university funds.

Most people get most of their information about the social world from journalism, either television, radio, newspaper or magazine journalism. I have not included journalism in the discussion because it does not pretend to be an academic subject in the sense of having a single specific subject matter. It is a great profession, and when done well is a joy. We need more and better schools of journalism. It is not characteristic of journalists to claim to be scientists of any kind. They report what is going on. Their work is often maligned. Sometimes this is justified. They may invade privacy, fail to stick with a story, be superficial or inaccurate. One has to be careful about taking these complaints too seriously. Often there is a lot of special pleading in these complaints. As with any large activity, there is good work and less good work.

What journalists are not expected to do is to come up with new theories. Day after day, and usually under the tightest of schedules, they report on the widest range of events in the world. Many journalists are specialists in the sense of concentrating on a range of activities. They are not specialists in the sense of creating new knowledge. The activities I have called invalid alternatives are not like journalism. These alternatives to social science are tainted with pretence. They pretend to be social science. This is not harmless fun. It carries a heavy cost.

SEEING VALUE IN INCOHERENCE

I would like to conclude this chapter by mentioning a particular strand of the social poetry school which makes a virtue of incoherence. The claim is that rational thought has failed mankind. It failed to deliver what it promised, namely, the solution to all our problems. That nobody ever made such a ridiculous promise is quietly ignored. Careful thought is the best way we have of addressing problems. It carries no guarantee of success. Even where it succeeds, it may take a long time. There can be false starts. Many people may have to work on the problem. The advocates of irrationality defend their approach through the claim that rationality does not always work. Of course it does not. It never claimed to solve all problems. It does claim to be preferable to intentional irrationality.

The practice of using words in bizarre ways and creating sentences that have no specific meaning is a terrible disservice to knowledge. There are people, usually badly educated people, who find this kind of writing attractive. It stimulates their minds much as does severe physical privation and certain drugs can do. I see little virtue in using the appearance of thought to achieve incoherence. I prefer to use martinis. But be that as it may, let us agree not to call incoherent thinking and writing 'social science'.

The valid alternatives to social science as means of thinking about society require some discipline in order to help understanding. They draw on prior knowledge. The invalid alternatives have a great levelling effect. No one knows more than anyone else. We are all equal. A popular attempt at justifying this position, and to my knowledge the only attempt, is to argue that in some dramatic way there was a great change in the way the social world behaves, and this change renders all previous knowledge inapplicable. Both the nature of this change, and when it took place, are discussed in vague and unconvincing terms. Even if there could be convincing discussion of 'when' and 'what', usually called the move from modern times to post-modern times, there is a fundamental error here.

There is no need to link what is studied to the method employed. If I want to study mental illness, I should not proceed in a mad or irrational manner to do so. I do not have to be asleep to study sleep. Even if there was a sudden change, and I see no evidence for that, valid and familiar methods of study may still apply. New phenomena may call for new methods. Most likely they will not. That is one thing. The fact, if it was a fact, that the world has become chaotic does not mean that our thinking about the world has to be chaotic.

Part of the appeal of incoherence is that whether you write it or read it, you can never go wrong. No one can say, here is a contradiction, here is a non-sequitor, or the evidence says otherwise. Incoherence involves no sustained argument; hence there is no error in the argument. Of course, if a method insures that you will not say anything wrong, it also insures that you will never say anything right. Practitioners of one kind or another of what we can call the 'pretend social science' persuasion know next to nothing about natural science. That does not stop them for one moment from making derogatory remarks about science. And for every attack on natural science, there are ten attacks on social science. These self-appointed philosophers resent the claim that there is such a thing as knowledge. For them, one opinion about society is as good as another.

Yet even the firmest advocate of the view that knowledge is an illusion wants to have a highly qualified pilot flying the plane. Knowledgeable pilots cannot always stop planes from crashing. But when it comes to immediate life and death matters, even fools and charlatans reason conventionally and more carefully, and will favour approaches which improve the chances of success. Of course there are no guarantees that the search for better knowledge will be successful in all cases. In some cases knowing more will not help. And we are never going to be one hundred percent sure that we have a reasonably good understanding of a social matter. None of these considerations make a case for pretend social science. It is time to turn to the real thing.

Chapter Four

THE FIVE SOCIAL SCIENCES AND THEIR SISTER SUBJECTS

DIVISIONS BETWEEN DISCIPLINES

It is interesting to ask if the way academic subjects are set out today is an almost inevitable outcome of their development, or whether the picture might just as easily have developed in quite a different way. The history of academic disciplines can be thought of as the subjects evolving alcng the natural contours that their subject matters suggest. Alternatively, they may be seen as having a highly arbitrary element, and being mainly shaped by individual personalities and other accidental factors.

At the very broadest level, it is hard to imagine a different breakdown in natural science than that between physical and biological science. When we come to more detail and the finer divisions within and between subjects, perhaps there would be other ways of dividing up the fields that would produce more coherence and more efficient specialisation. What works best at one point in time in the history of a group of subjects may not be optimal as knowledge grows and new problems are uncovered. Even so, it is not usually helpful to change the structure of academic subjects.

Nowadays there is quite a fashion for arguing that the old divisions between subjects are no longer relevant. 'Interdisciplinary' is 'good'. Discipline based work, by implication, is not. The case for changing the structure of disciplines is very rarely made by well-informed scholars. And those who do argue for new structures, or no structure at all, ignore the fact that there are costs associated with changing the structure of academic establishments too frequently. These costs arise mainly from changes in the training of specialists. They also can come from unproductive disputes between establishments as to who is the central authority and the normal beneficiary of funding in a particular area.

Along with these concerns go potential disputes over titles and degrees, and who has the right to determine student admission, curricula and the editing of publications. I have discussed elsewhere the importance of having scientific establishments. In order to function well they require some stability. So here is the balancing problem — enough stability to avoid costly disputes and enough flexibility to accommodate changed circumstances. Two broad features determine a discipline; the subject matter and the methods normally employed in investigating that subject matter. Economics uses a more mathematical approach than political science. The subject matter of economics tends to centre on production, wages, inflation, domestic and international trade, unemployment and many related topics, such as the nature of firms. Political science concentrates on the actions of governments, voting, legal structures, authority and its breakdown and the use of force. Ultimately, it is the subject matter that determines the scope of a subject, yet it is the methods of investigation which are the prominent characteristics.

It is reasonable to ask if the more mathematical approach used in economics compared to political science is essential, or particularly helpful to that subject. Might some of the other social sciences be more mathematical with advantage, and economics less mathematical, if they had followed different historical paths? A popular answer to that question is 'no', on the grounds that economics deals with more measurable aspects of society. This is not a very convincing answer. The number of crimes is as measurable as agricultural output. The answer lies more in the taste for modelling and more precise specification of theories in economics, which we will examine later.

Maddox, the former editor of *Nature*, discusses how attempts to apply mathematical approaches to biology in the early years of the last century were largely unfruitful. The great breakthroughs in that field turned out to have little to do with mathematics. However, Maddox speculates, it may well be that progress over the coming years in understanding what cells are and how they work will depend on good modelling and a more mathematical approach to the subject. The false start with mathematics made in the past may prejudice practitioners today against that approach, just when it may very much be needed. This episode suggests that there are periods where mathematics is critical to progress in a subject, and periods where it is much less important.

The relatively short histories of most social sciences may not have given enough time for this kind of change to be observed. A central proposition in economics, which has proved very fruitful, is the idea that people have objectives and they pursue them in reasonably straightforward ways. The other social sciences tend to place more emphasis on cultural influences on behaviour, along with imitation and adopting roles. Again, some writers have attempted to defend this difference in approach between economics and the rest on the grounds that, for example, people are fairly rational when it comes to spending money, but much less so when deciding who to marry. In fact, there is very little reason to believe that people are more rational in economic behaviour than in other aspects of social interaction. This realisation has led to a kind of economics take-over, where the optimising theories of that subject are applied in areas which are not normally thought of as falling within the economic sphere. It has also led to the application of insights from the other social sciences to the analysis of markets and other traditional economics concerns.

The sociologist Peter Abell has suggested that maybe there should be two social sciences instead of the five we have. One could deal with goal directed optimising behaviour, wherever it occurred, and the other could emphasise institutions and culture. This is an intriguing suggestion, but my investigation has led me to conclude that there is a lot of sense in the continued existence of the five disciplines that we find in social science. We will examine this issue in much greater detail in the coming chapters, and especially in chapter eleven.

As an introduction to the six substantive chapters coming up, I will briefly characterise the five social science subjects, going in alphabetical order. This could be a very controversial activity, if taken too seriously. Specialists may feel that the characterisations are unduly confining, and that they give insufficient attention to some core activities. I do not want to argue too much about these matters. In the coming chapters we examine in a very factual way what actually goes on in the subjects as they address particular topics. That is what really matters. How we choose to describe the subjects in abstract terms is much less important. But especially for those less familiar with social science, even a sketchy overview can be helpful.

These brief characterisations will also serve to differentiate these disciplines from two kinds of 'sister' subjects I will be discussing. One kind consists of the subjects which work exclusively on a specific input to social behaviour. The other kind is made up of those subjects which draw on one or more of the social sciences in the course of addressing particular topics. First, an overview of the five social sciences.

THE FIVE SOCIAL SCIENCES

Anthropology

An important consideration motivating many anthropologists, particularly in the early days of the subject, was the feeling that all human societies are important, and with the spread of industrialisation and higher standards of living around the world, many traditional societies would disappear. So one clear goal was simply to record what was there while it was still possible to do so. In this tradition, the subject matter of anthropology was what used to be called primitive societies, or the remote corners of less developed countries. These societies were thought of as not changing in fundamental ways for many years and certainly were not caught up in modernisation. Physical and social remoteness from Europe, America, and other higher income areas defined the subject matter. The objective of preserving information about these communities was primary. All aspects of these societies were of potential importance. Where the other four social sciences tend to concentrate on particular aspects of society, anthropology tends to take in the whole of the community under study. And at least in the past, description has tended to dominate over explanation.

Describing a society is by no means a simple and obvious undertaking. There are potentially an infinite number of facts to be reported, so some selection is inevitable. Immediately we run into the issue of bias. The goal is not to describe a society from the perspective of another society, but in some sense to be objective. Acquiring wealth may be central in our society, but doing the right thing with respect to ancestors may be more important in another society. A possible approach is to record what is happening on film. This medium is used more in anthropology than the other social sciences. But as the great filmmaker Eisenstein pointed out, film is the ideal medium for lying. When is the camera to be on, when off, and what is it pointed at, not to mention the subtle and yet powerful ways of influencing the interpretation of a scene. As a means of reducing the power of the filmmaker, it has been suggested that still cameras might be located around a village, for example, and set to go off at predetermined intervals. This, it is argued, would give an objective record of what went on. However, for the pictures to be informative, they have to be interpreted. So we are still are left with the problem of potential bias in the analysis.

Anthropologists tend to be the least judgmental of the social scientists. In an effort to avoid criticising institutions or practices, or even simply describing them from a point of view different from that of the community being studied, they are inclined to approve of all that they find, at least implicitly. A belief widely held in a traditional society may strike most people in a high-income society as fanciful, magical, or just plain false. An anthropologist is unlikely to be concerned with that kind of appraisal of the belief. Rather he or she would have the goal of trying to empathise with the belief and to understand the perceptions and feelings of people who hold that belief. This leads to a central and much discussed dilemma of anthropology.

The kind of understanding to which anthropology aspires has much to do with seeing a society from the inside. That does not quite mean becoming a member of that society, because the knowledge gained has to be reported back. It has to be made intelligible to the members of the anthropology discipline, and to the wider academic community. One great skill of the anthropologist is the ability to comprehend a community as that community looks at itself, and yet retain a scientific objectivity in that understanding.

Because anthropologists aim at a more comprehensive view of other societies, they tend to study smaller communities where their objective of covering the major elements in the society has a better chance of being fulfilled. It is also the case that traditional societies tend to be made up of smaller and relatively more self-contained groupings than we observe in high-income societies. Of course, smaller groupings can be identified in the high-income countries. A significant amount of modern anthropology is devoted to the study of communities nested in modern society. For example, physicists specialising in experimental 'atom smashing' are a relatively small group who almost all know each other and have a kind of common culture. They have been the subjects of anthropological investigation. This work is not particularly concerned with the theories the physicists are exploring. It sees the small particle community as a kind of 'tribe' and explores their customs, their evaluations of colleagues and others, and their general mode of behaviour. Reading this work we learn something about what it is like to be one of them. We do that without knowing any physics or experimental techniques at all.

This subject has the feature of getting under the skin of a society. It often will explore not just the religion, or family practices, or ways of organising work, but to some extent the several interrelated aspects of a community. The dominant mode is for working on smaller communities. Description, or 'reporting back', is more to the fore in anthropology than explanation. Field trips to remote parts of the world, remote when viewed from the starting point of universities, are still the norm. But increasingly the perspective of anthropology is brought to bear on communities and groupings located within the societies which were not studied by anthropologists in the early years of the subject. Crudely put, these are the societies that embrace more advanced technologies. In a phrase, anthropologists are more interested in the culture of communities than other social scientists.

Economics

Economics, traditionally and narrowly defined, has to do with markets, money, making a living, production, prices, wealth, employment, and related concepts. Explanation dominates over description, and little attempt is made to capture the flavour of what is being studied. A typical question for investigation might be what will happen to the price of airline tickets if duty-free sales are no longer allowed, or the overall consequences for employment of banning duty-free. A non-economist may see no reason to link duty-free to the cost of air travel. Economists are trained to analyse the major connections between elements in an economy, and how the various aspects of the system will respond to changes brought about by government policy, technical change, natural disaster, or any other initiating factor. In this sense the subject typically takes a more comprehensive view than the layman does in thinking about economic matters. At the same time, it sees various questions as amenable to analysis without considering society as a whole.

There are many exceptions to any generalisation that might be put forward about economics. Given the difficulty of making progress in understanding, it is not surprising that almost everything under the sun is tried from time to time. But it is fair to say that typical of the subject are certain characteristic assumptions and practices. These include a very simple model of what motivates people. This does not mean that economists are naïve and unable to appreciate the complexity of human emotion and other factors influencing behaviour. Rather they guess that very simple ideas of how people function, or behave, or work, will contain enough of the truth to be useful, and will allow an explicit analysis of an issue. A related simplification is to assume that the past can safely be left out of the picture. Economists are pretty confident that a higher tax on cigarettes will, among other effects, cause more effort to be devoted to getting around the tax. They will make this prediction without knowing the history of taxes in an area.

The normal unit of economic analysis is the entire economy, which is often taken to be synonymous with the nation-state. If we are considering an 'open' economy, then we may have to take account of consequences going beyond the borders and involving international trade, for example. This means thinking about parts of the world economy. Because of dealing with very large and complex units with innumerable interacting parts, economists often proceed by postulating how a single company, or worker, or consumer might behave, and then add up, or aggregate, the responses of thousands or millions of actors, all assumed to be behaving in simple and comprehensible ways. If too much variety and richness of responses is postulated, it may not be possible to derive any overall result for the economy.

The path that an economy might follow over time in responding to some shock, such as a big rise in the price of oil, is of interest to economists and these kinds of dynamic paths are often examined. But much of the work of economists is about what happens when the adjustments have worked themselves out. In other words, there is a preference, again on the grounds of needed simplicity, for asking what the 'equilibrium', or final working out might look like. A tax on building houses on Greenfield sites might not effect builders and developers tomorrow, but over time we might well observe a different distribution of houses as a result of the tax. For many purposes, it may be helpful to have some idea about that equilibrium adjustment even if the path leading to it cannot be specified.

The usual working method of economists is to analyse one change, or one situation, at a time. This will entail assuming that other relevant considerations do not change significantly. This is called the ceteris paribus assumption, and like the simple assumptions about behaviour of economic agents, ignoring the past, and concentrating on equilibrium, it tends to arouse criticism, or worse, from non-economists. They see these practices as too unrealistic and too restrictive. Admittedly, they may be essential for explicit analysis of issues. A more intuitive approach, employing what might be held to be plausible speculation, is seen as having advantages. And so it might.

But the economist is likely to argue that if a phenomenon is too complex to be analysed explicitly, it is unlikely to yield to intuition. This argument tends to play down the successes of intuition in complex situations. More to the point is the argument that science depends on explicit propositions. A Chancellor may have to take a leap in the dark about a proposed tax change. A person in that position cannot wait for better knowledge. An economist is quite prepared to say that we do not know the answer. A clear model is the objective, however long it may take to develop it. The advantages of this approach are that when results are achieved they link into the existing structure of ideas, and they can be explained to other potential users who can make use of the ideas. Intuition is not similarly transferable. It is hard to teach people to be successfully intuitive.

Economics is particularly geared to analysing large-scale systems with complex interactions. It is a highly developed method of studying competitive processes. Indeed, economics could be described as the study of competitive interactions involving purposeful behaviour. The insights of economics can be applied to any area of competitive interaction ranging from the living creatures in a coral reef to political parties in a democracy. The normal approach in analysing competition is to assume that the various participants in the arena have goals, such as making money, and they adopt strategies which give them as good a chance as possible to go as far as they can in achieving their goals, given the circumstances. Economics has been called the science of decision-making because it studies optimising behaviour. The methods economists employ often prove useful in analysing behaviour far outside what we think of as the economic sphere, including areas normally discussed in the other social sciences and in biology. We could do an economic analysis of optimal foraging strategies on the part of starlings, for example.

Two additional related features of economics are the quest for efficiency and appraisal of the well-being of collections of individuals. As the focus is on whole economies, which are large systems, efficiency is as much about how the pieces — firms, workers, governments, consumers — fit together as it is about the workings of single entities. The concepts of both efficiency and well-being involve value-judgements, and to that extent are outside of social science. However, once judgements are specified, explanations of the interactions can be scientific. The various features of economics, particularly explicit modelling and dealing with large complex systems, make the subject amenable to mathematical formulation. The optimising methods of calculus and game theory are commonly used. Economic data is used both to test theories and to estimate the magnitude of various effects. For example, a higher price for a product may reduce the number of sales. The question is often one of by how much will sales be reduced. Statistical techniques for inferring information from historical data, rather than from experiments, are widely used in the subject.

Political Science

The central concern of political science is government. Governments tend to be complicated entities, and how they work is a challenge to understanding. Often there is a formal structure, and an equally, or even more important, informal structure. The laws of a society have to be interpreted and are not enforced uniformly. Simply to describe the nature of a government, or a part of it, is a first step to understanding. Political scientists attempt to explain why a particular society has the government that it has. Who is really in control? What interests are being served by the governmental arrangements we observe? Finding the answers to these questions leads to a broader definition of political science. It can be thought of as the study of power.

Wealth can yield power, and power can produce wealth. The interaction between the political and the economic structure of a society has been more the concern of political science than much of economics. Political economy, as a branch of economics, is an exception to that generalisation. That there can be power without wealth is a basis for the distinct subject of political science. In many circumstances, people achieve, or are granted power, and are expected to exercise that power to bring about certain social ends. Using the power to acquire personal wealth is almost always in violation of the formal rules of the society, and usually against the informal customs. It is nevertheless difficult to prevent, and one of the important subjects of political science is corruption. Equally important is the study of the many other possible abuses of power.

Many people, ranging from Mafia bosses to leaders of street gangs, may have power. Governmental power is not the same. It allegedly has legitimacy. How legitimacy arises, and what is its nature, is an important concern of political science. Much play has been made of the concept of consent, either actual or implied. Difficult cases arise when one country, or group, conquers another people or territory. Questions of precedent, and how far back is it sensible to go in saying who is the legitimate authority, are important to political analysis.

Force is common in changing governments. Invasions, coups, revolutions and civil wars are familiar parts of the political process. Sometimes they fail and sometimes they succeed. But even determining what is success is often not straightforward. A government may be the heir to a revolution, but the promoters of that revolution, whether alive or not alive, might well not recognise or agree with the government they in fact created. Governments also change through peaceful but non-democratic means. There may be well defined rules of decent, or a more or less free choice on the part of the departing monarch or dictator, or those serving him or her.

Just as the bulk of economics is about the market, the bulk of political science is about democracy. The most technical and mathematical aspect of political science has to do with voting. Even in a democracy, not everything is subject to a vote. There are practical reasons for this as well as matters of principle. The courts, and other institutions, have authority in many areas. Where voting is deemed to be appropriate, there are many possible voting systems. Determining the consequences of different systems, and designing voting systems that will satisfy what are believed to be desirable characteristics, are among the problems addressed by the theory of voting. Different parts of a democratic system of government, national and local among them, may best be served by different voting systems. The goals of a voting system cannot be set by science. The consequences of different systems can be studied scientifically.

Political science studies political parties and other influential groupings. It looks at the process of law-making and law-enforcement. While historical methods are important in this subject, for many problems statistical techniques can be used to measure the importance of competing explanations for observed political institutions and behaviour. Comparative studies within and between countries are common. Some involve quantifiable elements and call for fairly sophisticated statistical analysis. In other cases more qualitative approaches are used. The great classics of political science on authority, constitutions, voting, alliances and power are more alive in this subject than the classical literature of other social sciences.

Social Psychology

The whole of psychology has a central social dimension. Human beings interact with other human beings, and a large part of human intelligence is devoted to these interactions. However, the conventions of social psychology as a discipline mark off certain interests and approaches. As close as the subject is to psychology proper, and as much as it draws on theories and evidence from the larger discipline, social psychology has a reasonably well circumscribed area of interest. How the healthy mind works, and the illnesses and problems the mind is subject to, are not central to social psychology. It does not have a medical orientation. It is interested in how people come to hold the views they do hold, without coming down to the mechanics of learning, memory, and subjective mental phenomena. Gender issues can be important in the subject. For example, men may hold different views about money, on average, compared to women. Do they? And if so, what are these differences? These are potentially socially significant questions falling outside the scope of individual psychology.

The effect of drugs on the mental state of individuals is an interesting area of investigation. How the drugs bring about these effects is also interesting. Social psychologists are more concerned with the group dynamics of drug taking, and the opinions various parts of society hold about drugs. Exactly the same observations could be made about homelessness. A psychologist might want to explain why a particular person became homeless. The social psychologist is interested in the general phenomenon of homelessness. This interest includes questions such as what are the attitudes of the various strata of society towards sleeping rough? What would be the consequences of various policies designed to reduce homelessness?

Social psychology studies the views that people hold and the behaviour induced by those views. Hostile attitudes towards members of other races is an interesting example. Which types of people in which circumstances are particularly prone to prejudice against others? What are the consequences and how do people deal with being victims of prejudice? The mechanisms of peer pressure and the factors influencing conforming to popular views are important areas of study.

Equally important are those factors leading to independence of mind and the ability and willingness to stand apart from popular views. People's opinions have their origins in many sources. They are influenced by first-hand experience, the views of people around them, and from the media. This applies equally to action in the political sphere, or the lack of it, and to buying a razor. Advertisers make use of the insights of social psychologists, as do policy makers. An example of the latter might be the effect of television and computer games on the development of young people. There might be a sound case for encouraging limited viewing, or influencing the content, away from violence for example.

There are two senses in which the social psychologist explores the social. One has to do with general tendencies and the average attitudes or responses of larger sections in society, rather than individuals. The second has to do with the way being in society shapes views and behaviour. Social psychology is the most experimental of the social sciences. For example, juries form judgements. The group dynamics of this kind of decision-making can be studied by observing different mock juries exposed to somewhat different versions of a case as a way to study how these variations work through to different decisions. There are also applications where large data sets, for example, cohorts of children exposed to lots of television and those not exposed to very much, are used in a non-experimental way in an effort to discover consequences.

The tendency in social psychology is to look for associations and to be very much guided by data of one kind or another. Less attention is given to theory construction than in economics, for instance, and much more attention to learning from evidence. What does the man in the street believe, and who is he? Do the French have a different attitude towards nuclear power and high speed trains than the British, or is the difference in policy due more to physical differences between the countries or simply the decisions of political leaders?

Surveys are the main investigative tool of the social psychologist. Designing and interpreting survey information is a proportionately large undertaking for social psychology compared to other social sciences. Over the years a huge stock of questionnaires have been developed and these are used over and over again. Where possible, and it usually is possible, social psychologists will normally use an off-the-shelf survey rather than make one up. There are two big advantages in this apart from the saving of effort. One is it tends to bring some objectivity to the undertaking. If an investigator invents a survey to measure fear of crime, for example, rather than using a standard survey, there may be unintended biases in the framing of questions. The other advantageous factor means that surveys are used many times over and in many contexts, and a great deal of information about the surveys themselves is acquired as time goes by. Obviously, nothing would be known about a made-up survey as to the kind of results generated by it in other uses than the one in which its author happened to apply it. Knowing one's way around the enormous stock of surveys, and having the necessary statistical tools for interpreting the results of surveys are important skills of the social psychologist.

Sociology

Kenneth Boulding once wrote that economics is about exchange, by which he meant voluntary exchange. I am prepared to do this for you, or give you this product, if you will pay me a certain amount. Take it or leave it. Political science, so Boulding suggested, is about threats. If you deal in drugs, I will put you in jail. If you try to secede and form an independent country, we will invade. It is not easy to fit voting into Boulding's threat description. And finally, sociology for Boulding was about what he called love. There were exchange relations, threat relations, and love relations. Sociology studies cases where we do things together, not exchanges and not threats. Not many sociologists would recognise that description. For example, deviant behaviour, such as crime and suicide, is a favourite topic. There is nothing particularly co-operative about either. But there is some truth in the idea that sociology has a kind of residual status in the social sciences. If the topic does not fit under any of the other four disciplines, it will very likely find a place under sociology.

In the early days of the subject, it was felt that a grand theory of society would be constructed, much like an economic theory of the market linking together capitalists, workers and consumers. But this sociological theory would contain economic life as part of it, and integrate it with a broader theory of society generally. It was envisaged that economics would take its place as a sub-division of sociology. Few sociologists pursue this kind of endeavour today. The subject is much more modest in its objectives, while remaining almost without bounds on what might be investigated.

We have to be careful to distinguish what is called 'pretend social science' in the previous chapter from sociology. It is true that the pretend writers and teachers tend to fit more easily under the sociology banner than that of economics or any other social science. This is partly because of the more open agenda of sociology, and partly because of the early history of grand social theorising in that subject. But sociology as social science has nothing to do with the 'pretend school' and investigates a wide range of matters in a perfectly sound way.

What are the dynamics of neighbourhoods going up and down? Who migrates from one country to another, and why? How much social mobility is there in a society? Are crowded restaurants offering better food at lower prices, or is there a herd element in choosing where to eat? What is the status of dealers in their communities? Do people living in trailer parks help each other? What sort of people play pivotal roles in neighbourhood networks? It is difficult to describe the subject without listing topics. The question is, what do they have in common?

An important feature of sociological investigation is the characterisation of customary behaviour, culture, and adopting roles. Where economics emphasises rational calculation with clearly specified objectives and the range of actions open to agents to work towards achieving their objectives, sociologists are more inclined to examine where the objectives are coming from. People have a place in a community. The community is a reality. We do not invent a language, though we speak it in our own way. We do not invent the institutions or structures of society.

Economists and sociologists can both study workers in a particular industry. They will tend to ask different questions. The same goes for decisions like how many children to have, and what education to undertake. The sociologist sees a bigger role for conventions and institutions. The economist, particularly nowadays, is also happy to attempt to explain institutions and customs. But the type of explanation typically offered by economists is likely to give an exclusive role to efficiency and to competing agents. The sociologist may have a richer range of theories in accounting for why policemen and firemen wear uniforms.

Apart from a tendency to choose different subject matter, and a tendency to explore different kinds of explanations of the same subject matter, sociological investigation is like that of the other social sciences. Theories are put forward: some optimising theories are taken straight from economics at one extreme; some cultural conformity and role playing theories are advanced at the other extreme; and the full middle range explanations are used as well. Theories not from the extreme have the advantage of being more plausible, but usually are much harder to formulate precisely and to apply to particular problems. Whatever type of theory is being used, evidence is brought to bear when possible to test the theories. Sometimes these facts come from published data, and sometimes from purpose built surveys and other direct observations. Evidence is also used to measure the importance of particular effects. Older people may be less likely to migrate than younger people, but measurements must be taken if we are to know how much less likely. Experiment is occasionally possible in sociological investigation, but usually to a very limited extent. The reason for this is that the sociological domain is the community, or the society, or some part of it, and these cannot be readily manipulated for the purposes of science.

THE INPUT SISTER SUBJECTS

Demography

Having briefly sketched out the nature of the five social sciences, it is time to answer the question, why five? For example, is demography a social science? My answer is that it is scientific, and it is about society, but it is not a social science in the sense of the subjects discussed above. It has a very specific objective. It describes, predicts, and theorises about populations. Of course for many social questions it is vitally important to know how many people there are and what is the age profile of the population. The explanations for the demographic facts that we observe can involve all the social sciences in varying degrees. And certainly the size and nature of populations can have implications for many social investigations. It is the rather more specific focus of demography that sets it apart from the other five social sciences.

As a scientific undertaking, the better-defined objectives of demography are a real advantage. Some very creative and very careful work goes into the study of populations. Classifying demography as distinct from social science is not a judgement about either quality or importance of any type of work. Demographers may justifiably feel superior to some of the woolly headed activity in social science. That is not the point either. The distinction purely has to do with the range of interest. It would be quite understandable to argue that range is not a relevant consideration. Other features mark off the socially scientific from what is not social or is not scientific. But I still maintain that demography is qualitatively different from the five social sciences.

The proof of the pudding is in what demography has to say about a range of topics that are central to the concerns of social science. I have chosen six topics for this study of what social science actually has to say. The topics were chosen through informed guesswork. There is no doubt in my mind that six other topics could have been chosen with equally good results. The first test of a good result is that each of the five social sciences must have a fair amount to say on each of the six topics. As we shall see in subsequent chapters, the topics chosen do meet this test. Demography does not have much to say on these topics. On topics like money and crime it would be stretching things to hold that there is any significant demographic literature. On topics like migration and religion, demography is more concerned with quantification, accounting if you will, than with explanation. This important distinction between demography and the five social sciences would be equally well illustrated by any other choice of topics.

All knowledge has some connection with other branches of knowledge. This implies that the whole structure of knowledge is a connected structure. There is nothing that exists completely off on its own. Nevertheless, there are centres of gravity. There are more and less densely connected parts in that structure which is science. It is these groupings which roughly, not perfectly or precisely, define a discipline. We can see demography feeding into all the social sciences. And we can see influences from all of them on demography. Yet it is not located in the same way as the five social sciences. If one refuses to accept this argument, then my study is incomplete. It purports to examine how all the social sciences address six different topics. The claim is that it covers all the social sciences. It could be that I have dealt with some, but not all, of the social sciences. So be it. The argument is about conventions and convenient groupings. Whether one takes my position or not is of little consequence. We can still be friends.

Geography

Another subject that feeds into all of social science, but on my reckoning is not in itself one of the five, is geography. All individuals, and institutions, and groups of individuals have to be somewhere. Location is significant for many issues. It is safely set to one side for other issues. The obvious importance of location, like the obvious importance of numbers in the case of demography, does not mean that geography is one of the social sciences. Applying the same test as above, the geography literature has little to say on the topics of money and crime, for example. Detailed maps may pinpoint crime hotspots. This information may be very important for many issues on the social science agenda. It is essentially an input, rather than a discipline like political science or social psychology.

Map-making appears to play a much smaller role today in academic geography than in earlier times. The importance of knowing where things are and how to map this knowledge, along with the navigational skills vital to being able to get to specified places, is no less important today for commerce, military activity, and government. Yet as an academic discipline, the techniques of making the maps take second place, or no place at all, behind the application of location to a wide range of issues.

Far from being mapmakers, geographers are more likely to be environmentalists and urbanists. As such they may draw on knowledge from fields as diverse as biology and engineering. The issue of location may turn up in investigations of anything from AIDS to bus transportation.

Geography can be an umbrella for interdisciplinary study; the only limitation being that the studies have some locational aspect. We will be turning to the topic of interdisciplinary social science, and discussion of this aspect of geographical study can be held over until then.

As a discipline in its own right, geographers work on the discovery and reporting of location in innumerable contexts. This information can be of crucial importance to studies in social science, and in other sciences. To go beyond reporting the facts and to explain why things are located where they are located involves theories outside of the discipline of geography proper. The same can be said about theories of the consequences of location. Economic geography, for example, attempts to explain concentrations of activity and their implications. Political geography has analogous undertakings. Like knowing numbers of types of people, knowing where they are located is in itself an input to social science. It is not one of the five social sciences.

Lingusitics

Linguistics is my last example of a scientific investigation of a phenomenon with social implications which is not a social science. Some prominent linguists like to bad-mouth social science and will not object at all to being excluded from social science. Demographers and geographers like to claim a social science position, which is fair enough. But for reasons set out above, they are not usefully grouped with the five social sciences. When linguists disparage social science, they never mention economics. The target tends to be what I have called 'pretend social science' in the previous chapter. Let us hope that these attacks on social science come from ignorance, and not from a desire to be superior.

The study of language has a psychological and a physiological side. How are sounds made? And what is the nature of the human capacity for language which is so different from that of other animals? These are not directly social matters. But so many of the aspects of language, such as differences in speech associated with social classes, have a social science link up. There is useful exchange of knowledge between linguists and social scientists, but this does not mean that linguistics is a social science in the sense of the five subjects outlined above. The distinction does not rest on the important areas of linguistic investigation which are not social. It has to do with the focus of social linguistics.

Criminal groups, for example, may have special linguistic features. So may people working in financial markets. What these differences are is one thing, and what causes them to exist is something else. There is no need to repeat the arguments made above about special skills in generating facts and combining these facts with concepts from other disciplines. The bottom line is that the linguistic literature does not address the topics that are common to the five social sciences.

THE INTERDISCIPLINARY SISTER SUBJECTS

Among the university subjects commonly grouped within social science faculties are subjects like industrial relations, media studies, management and international relations. Are not these subjects as much social science as the five subjects listed above? The 'no' part of the inevitable 'yes and no' answer has to do with the distinction between discipline based subjects and subject matter based subjects. It goes without saying that this distinction has nothing to do with importance. I say it anyhow, just to be on the safe side. I want to suggest that the five social sciences, as I identify them, are qualitatively different from the interdisciplinary subjects. That does not make them better or worse, more or less difficult, or more or less useful. I simply argue that they are different in particular ways.

Subject matter based subjects

What I am calling the five social sciences have broadly defined subject matters. In addition, they have specific techniques, literatures and histories that have to be understood by those who wish to master one of those disciplines. The very specifically subject matter based subjects do not have a similar discipline base. Take the case of my wife's niece who is doing a degree in 'sport'. This is a new undergraduate university subject. It is clearly subject matter based. No one would deny that sport is an important topic. Some, like myself, find it a little too important in its professional and performance aspect, but that is irrelevant.

There clearly are many economic aspects to sport; the funding from television, advertising, and other sources, as well as the consequences of different funding arrangements. There are medical issues about training, diet, drugs and related questions. The politics and sociology of sport are complex and interesting. All of these disciplines feed into this interdisciplinary subject. However, if we wish to design a new method of allocating World Cup tickets so as to avoid past chaos, should we go to an economist, or to a sports specialist? What about testing for the use of proscribed drugs? Do we want a sports specialist or a medical specialist? Who is best at a particular investigation is one consideration. The nature of the distinction between discipline based and subject matter based subjects is another.

International Relations

Let us take international relations as an example of a subject matter based rather than discipline based activity. Nations relate to each other in a host of ways. Warring relations and peaceful relations are among them. International government, along with other associations such as regional groupings and worldwide systems like international mail and telephone systems, link nations. Attempts to grapple with environmental and economic issues at the international level result in temporary and more lasting institutions. This is a sample of the subject matter of international relations.

Experts in these areas draw on history, economics, politics, social psychology as well as sociology and anthropology. It is entirely right that they do so. Indeed, it is essential. Economic considerations are important in understanding the behaviour of national negotiators in forums such as the IMF, the World Bank and the World Trade Organization. But economic considerations are not the only considerations, even in what seem to be predominantly commercial settings. So international relations experts draw on all the social sciences in varying degrees. The relation is not symmetric. Anthropologists and social psychologists, along with economists and political scientists, do not of necessity draw on international relations.

Industrial Relations

Industrial relations is another subject matter based social science. Specialists may turn out to be helpful in resolving industrial disputes and in achieving greater fairness in the terms of employment. Economics is vital to understanding in this area, and so is political science and sociology. The five social sciences can all be applied here. Everything that was said about international relations applies to industrial relations as well. For example, the industrial relations literature does not address most of the topics that we are turning to shortly, and yet they are examined by all the core social sciences. That is the crucial test.

Media Studies

The fastest growing subject matter oriented social science is media studies. Again, all the five social science disciplines are of potential relevance. If we take a question like how should the BBC be funded, economics holds much of the answer. It does not hold it all. There are issues of decision-making in Parliament and the public perception of non-commercial media which involve political science and social psychology.

Whether media specialists can master enough economics and psychology to be useful in policy making is problematical. One media specialist writes that 'common-sense' is the base of media studies, not social science. That stance absolves that writer from having to draw on the five social science disciplines. Those with some familiarity with one or more of the core disciplines may find starting from common-sense results in an unnecessarily long road to useful conclusions.

Anything could be a university subject. We could have a degree in roads; the economics of roads, the politics, the aesthetics, their effects on communities, the engineering of roads, and so on. I have made clear my preference for discipline based rather than subject matter based enquiry. The five social science disciplines feed into any number of applied areas from management to poverty. These are the subject matter based sister subjects.

CHOICES AND METHODS

In the following six chapters we see how the five social sciences have addressed six different topics in the last decade of the last century. The goal is to provide a reasonably up-to-date picture of current research. Maybe twenty years rather than tens years would have provided almost as up-to-date a picture, and given greater coverage. The reason for taking ten years is expediency. Ten years seemed doable. There a few cases where reference is made to slightly earlier work which was published in the nineteen eighties. If what seemed to be a particularly useful reference lay outside the 90's, it was included. However, absolutely no attempt was made to cover the subjects in their entirety and examine classic contributions. That simply is another exercise. The last years of the last century were largely excluded also for reasons of expediency.

The six topics chosen were crime, migration, housing, money, the family and religion. Why these six? For one thing, I think they are all interesting and important. The most binding consideration was that all five social sciences should have a fair amount to say about any topic chosen. If the topic of inflation was selected, for example, it could be that the anthropology literature might not have much to say on the topic. If the topic was civil wars, maybe economics might be thin on the ground. In order to facilitate the comparison of the methods and achievements of the social sciences there had to be a good chance that all the subjects would have a fair amount to say about each of the topics. In the event, these six turned out beautifully.

There is a reasonable amount of research available on each of the six topics from each of the five social sciences during the 90's. I attribute this outcome to good luck in making my educated guess. There undoubtedly is another set of topics which would work equally well for this experiment in the study of knowledge. I believe, and this in only a belief, that any other set of topics would yield broadly the same picture of what the social sciences are like. Certainly there has been no attempt to load the dice in favour or against any subject, or to affect its characterisation.

In addition to the rather arbitrary time period chosen, there were two other important decisions. This study is confined to the English language literature. I am pretty sure that as far as economics is concerned, that has little impact. Most of economics is available in English, and what is not is not materially different from the English language literature. In the other social sciences, there may be characteristically different and important research that has been published in languages other than English. The assumption I have made is that the English language material is representative of the whole. Information in support, or to the contrary, of this assumption would be welcome.

The second decision was to confine the study to the journal literature. This ignores books and web sites. Again, as far as economics is concerned, this does not bias the results to a significant degree. Very few researchers produce material that is wordy enough to require book length reporting. There are exceptions. Most of the economics book length material are summaries, or textbook presentations, of research that first appeared in the economics journals. This is probably less the case with the other four social science subjects. For present purposes this would not bias my report unless the book literature was significantly different from the journal literature. It is hard to see why that would be the case, but it may be.

Much of the material from the Web is not edited. The journal literature goes through professional screening. This makes it more the establishment statement of the subject than other sources. And that is what I am after. I want to see the subjects as undertakings of what could be called the official clubs of the subjects. It is not my job, and I am not qualified to say what should or should not be taken as establishment knowledge. That is what the journals do for me.

When it comes to which journals, I have been very much in the hands of the British Library of Political and Economic Science at the London School of Economics and Political Science. I assume that this collection is as comprehensive as it claims. Colleagues at LSE were consulted. Internal evidence suggests that certainly the main journals organised by the long established professional associations in each subject have been consulted. Many of the newer journals have also been consulted. The appendix has a comprehensive list. These are the journals that appear to dominate in each of the five social sciences.

There are journals which concentrate on the topics I take up, rather than on a particular social science discipline. Examples are journals on crime, or on housing. Contributors to these journals may be from any social science, or from outside the academic sphere. On the whole, I have not used these journals. Apart from the need to save effort, the goal is specifically to see what refereed articles in each of the social sciences have to say on these six topics, not what 'housing' or 'family' or 'religion' journals have to say.

A bit of judgement and the need for choice does come in when a decision has to be made as to whether a particular article reports research on the family, for example, or on children, to take an example. If in doubt, I opt for inclusion. But it all depends on my doubt, or lack of doubt. More serious is what is social science. Not everything in a social science journal claims to be social science. There are philosophical pieces on methodology, or the ethics of certain kinds of research. A piece may purport to be about 'money', for example, but in my judgement is a prelude to research or a speculation as to what might be undertaken.

Some political science journals contain some pieces which are more like high-class current affairs than anything scientific. Again, if in doubt, I include the problematic article. I rather take the risk of including something which perhaps should not be there, than exclude something which it could be argued should be there. I am aiming for totally comprehensive coverage of the English language journal literature in the 90's by the five social sciences, on the six topics. If I include something which arguably should not be there, the reader can make a judgement. If I leave out something, the reader may not know about that research and cannot make a judgement.

There is one exception to this goal of including everything. When it comes to economics, I am selective. As an economist I know something of the literature, and know that it is vast on most of the topics compared to the other social sciences. If I find half a dozen scientific articles in a subject on a topic, I feel pretty pleased. In economics there may be ten, or a hundred papers for every one in sociology. It just is a much bigger enterprise with many, many more researchers. Fortunately, I feel as an economist I can be selective without misrepresenting the subject. In the other subjects less familiar to me, with a few exceptions I simply report everything in specialist journals written on the topics in the decade under review.

This completes the framework and introduction to the scientific study of society. I have outlined a view of scientific enquiry which places emphasis on science as a structure of connected ideas. One way or another, scientists work on that structure. Activity which goes under the name of social science, but is not scientific, has a number of features. It is characteristic of activity of the pretend social science kind that it does not address the scientific structure. In social science this structure is essentially like that of natural science, but differs in degree in certain respects. The term social science refers to five distinct disciplines. We turn now to the work undertaken by researchers in those disciplines.

PART TWO

SOCIAL SCIENCE RESEARCH

Chapter Five

CRIME

A WORD IN ADVANCE

This is the first of the six substantive chapters which contain the central point of this book. A few words of explanation and advice are in order and could prove to be helpful before starting on this material. On the surface this is a chapter about crime. There are illustrations that range from petty crimes, like short-changing customers from foreign countries, all the way to murder, rape, organised crime, and crime committed by the government itself. Evidence is examined to determine whether crime is typically a rational act, given the circumstances of the criminal, or due to dysfunctional states of mind. We explore problems that arise in attempts to prevent crime. These cover such matters as the behaviour of the police, decision-making by juries, and the content of the law.

Policies designed to deter crime may or may not achieve the intended objective. They may have little effect, or drive it elsewhere. Public opinion may influence responses to crime, and be influenced itself by media coverage of crime. Of course, the public is not a single entity. It can be divided by race, income, gender, class and cultural orientation. All of these can influence who commits crime and what is done about it. Some crimes, like assault and theft, cause clear harm to the victim. Other crimes, like consuming drugs or pornography, are deemed to be dangerous for the individual consumer, and by some accounts for society as a whole. Judgements on these matters vary across communities. Part of our goal is to understand the causes of these variations and their consequences.

While the surface objective of this chapter is an understanding of crime, the core objective is an understanding of social science. Crime is just an example. We will see others. All of these examples, or illustrations, are used to explain in a realistic manner what has in fact been going on in the attempts by social scientists to understand social phenomena, including the phenomenon of crime. Crime is the vehicle of the moment. The subject matter is social science. This has consequences for the chapter at hand.

A systematic treatment of any one of the individual topics that come under the general heading of crime would require at least a large book, and more likely many books. The examples presented here cover most of what social scientists have produced in the decade of the nineties. Nothing is said about the history of the various subjects. We are eavesdropping on conversations and debates that have been going on very recently. We have no idea what went on before and what led to the current investigations. Yet these enquiries all have long histories. In some cases they have roots going back for centuries. This chapter is not intended to boil down a coherent story of any one aspect of the giant subject of crime. It is intended to cover more-or-less everything written in English in the leading journals over a brief current period.

The reader is invited to discover the current state of social science from actual examples. There is little or no attempt to be selective. If it is in the journals, it is, or should be, in the chapter. The organisation of this chapter, unlike some subsequent chapters, is by social science discipline, rather than by type of crime, or aspect of crime. We see how economists study a range of crimes, how sociologists do that, and so on. The organisation by social science discipline is intended to highlight the distinct nature of each subject, rather than what each contributes to the understanding of the different crimes, and aspects of crime, that fall under the general heading of crime.

Whether an economist directs attention to gun legislation or to tax evasion, it is economics that is being done. A sociologist may study delinquent behaviour of youths living on the street, or changes in the numbers of people sent to prison. The discipline being brought to bear on the topics is still sociology. The ultimate subject matter of this, and the other chapters, is the nature of these scientific disciplines. The five subjects have common elements and clear differences. Typically the different subjects employ different techniques. Some work very close in with in-depth interviews, and others examine national and international data. They differ in their theoretical orientation, and so tend to ask different kinds of questions. In the end there is one society out there, but science proceeds by slicing off a little piece of the problem.

All such slices do harm in the sense of distorting reality. We make slices because they are necessary. We cannot work on the problem all at once.

Some alternatives to science do try to do it all at once. I have discussed this elsewhere. Here we are looking at social science. Part of the skill of the scientist lies in making a slice in such a way that the understanding gained from the enquiry more than compensates for the inevitable distortion involved.

There are two great problems that must be mentioned before getting into the material. One is the issue of statistical inference. Many of the studies of crime we will cover employ quite advanced statistical techniques. Some of these methods appear to be simple, and in a way they are. And some are extremely complex. None have been invented for the particular studies at hand. They come from standard off-the-shelf statistical practice. This does not make them uncontroversial. Far from it. All of them involve methodological decisions that can be debated.

It would be nice to have an alternative to standard statistical inference and be able to get the conclusion from the facts without it. Unfortunately, this is not to be. For the most part, the data do not speak for themselves. They must be put in a framework in order to help to answer our questions. These techniques are explained in textbooks, and are themselves the subject of continuing investigation by specialists. I have tried to indicate how the statistical reasoning leads to the conclusions the researchers reach. And I have tried to convey whether these are best seen as hints, suggestions, reasonable possibilities, or highly reliable results. This is done in a most superficial manner, and without apology. A serious analysis of the statistical inference used in the studies which employ these techniques would over-burden the book to an intolerable degree.

Even more serious for the writer, but not for the reader, is the problem of theoretical context. Science is a body of connected ideas. Most of the studies of crime we are about to examine rehearse the state of the theory of their problem before going on to add their element to the great body of knowledge. A full understanding of the significance of each piece would require examining that intellectual context. Only passing attention can be given to that in what follows. The reader need not worry about this, nor be particularly disadvantaged by it. Rather, it is just something to bear in mind. Very rarely does a scientist break completely new ground. With a well travelled topic like crime, it is safe to say that every contribution either adds a bit to an existing structure, or challenges that structure at some point. It would be completely overwhelming to try to rehearse the context for each article. Please just bear in mind that a structure of ideas exists for every investigation.

As a child I liked those little flip books where you could fan the pages with your thumb and watch a mouse appear to run about. The rapid passing of the pages created an image of movement which was not present in any one page. That image was the point of the experience. I see this chapter on crime in much the same way. A series of pictures, rapidly reviewed, will hopefully provide a dynamic and pretty up-to-date picture of each of the five social sciences as they address the common topic of crime.

INTRODUCTION

Crime is a part of all societies. As long as there are rules, and an incentive to break rules, there will be crime. The concept varies from place to place, and time to time. The law may be secular, religious or less formal. Great variations exist as to which behaviour is deemed to be criminal, rather than merely being a breach of preferred customs. In some sense, most crime serves the interests of the criminal. Some criminal behaviour, or deviant, behaviour, will have its roots in personal disorder, and may not be motivated by self-interest, as normally understood.

Whatever the motive for crime, we can expect societies to attempt to control the amount of crime and to reduce the adverse consequences of it. If no attempt is made to enforce some rules in a society regarding theft and physical harm, for example, or if the attempts have little success, that social structure is vulnerable and is likely to be replaced with another. Of course, what constitutes a crime varies enormously across societies, as do the means taken to address crime. Even in a society fully set against all activity it regards as criminal, the resources available to deal with crime will be limited, and this means that there must be priorities. Some illegal activities will receive much more attention than others.

Most individuals seem to adhere to, and to support, most of the laws and less formal customs of their various societies. Indeed, this broad social consensus is almost the definition of a society. It is not clear why, on the whole, people behave in a law-abiding fashion, or at least try to keep up the appearance of doing that. Imitation, social imprinting and religion appear to be important explanations, as does rational calculation on the part of individuals who understand the consequences of failing to conform.

There does seem to be quite a universal tendency for most people to accept authority. In a person's early years, this is most commonly the authority of the family. In later years people become aware of the wider community and tend to accept the authority of it. Often children argue in terms a concept of fairness and are aggrieved when it is violated. Later in life a reputation for being honest and trustworthy can be an asset in itself. But internalising ethical views and conforming to accepted practices are not exclusively features of behaviour that respects the law. There are criminal and deviant strands of culture which also induce imitation and loyalty.

What are the rules of a society? How did they come about and how are they evolving? What determines the extent to which the rules are supported? Who deviates and why? These are fundamental questions for social science. They are closely related to more down-to-earth questions regarding law enforcement. The ideal codification of the law within a society is never fully agreed, let alone achieved, and much wider differences of opinion as to what the law should be are obvious when comparing countries. What are proper and improper types of competitive behaviour in commercial activities are disputed, as are rules about sexual behaviour, alcohol and drugs, the personal exercise of force, among many other matters. What should be the law, and more especially how to enforce it more effectively, are questions high on the agendas of many political leaders and their followers.

Social science is concerned with every aspect of the law and law-breaking activity. Most people have views as to why crime in general, or particular types of crimes, are becoming more common, if indeed that is the case. Popular opinion is one thing. Determining the facts and their explanations are two rather different things. Understanding how the amounts and kinds of criminal activity respond to different policies of enforcement, and other measures intended to reduce the adverse effects of crime, is a difficult and demanding scientific undertaking. Some aspects of the subject have been investigated, but certainly not all aspects. The studies that have been undertaken display varying degrees of success. By no means all that we would like to know has been found out with any significant degree of reliability. In this chapter we will see what research has been undertaken by the five social sciences in the 1990's. This is very far from being a comprehensive report on what has been researched about crime. It only covers a few recent years. Earlier work, some of it of great importance, is not discussed. Our objective is to create a picture of how social science is conducted today, as well as learning something about crime.

It is interesting that the different social sciences have their favourite aspects of crime and types of crime. Social psychologists, for example, place a great deal of emphasis on the crime of rape. Economists do not look at it at all. They are far more inclined to study corruption on the part of government officials. Political scientists are especially interested in enforcement issues, and so it goes. In what follows we will see both differences of subject matter and methods of investigation.

Before turning to what researchers have been learning about crime, a further word about statistical inference is in order. Statistical inference is something quite apart from reporting the figures. How many murders were committed in a country over a certain period? The answer to that question is a reasonably accurate, or less accurate, figure. It has nothing to do with explaining the causes of murder. Partly because of the very limited opportunities for experimentation, social scientists have taken from statisticians a great variety of techniques for inferring causal relations from the data at hand, and also developed some new techniques themselves. This type of investigation is much less common in anthropology, but it is occasionally used there, and everywhere if it comes to that, in the social sciences.

Some readers of this book will have the necessary background in statistical inference to understand the arguments in the studies that use those techniques. Those readers will be disappointed by the lack of detail given below. While I want to go quite deeply into to what social scientists do when they investigate a problem, to actually explore the logic of statistical investigation would triple the length of this book and make it unreadable for the majority of potentially interested people. I therefore have adopted the strategy of referring to statistical evidence where appropriate, but not examining the nature of the reasoning involved. One has to learn the techniques in order to appraise them critically. Alternatively, one can simply be aware of the results as I report them, but not be able to appraise them.

ANTHROPOLOGY

It was quite a surprise to me that only half-a-dozen, or so, studies relating specifically to crime were undertaken by anthropologists during the period covered by this study. Casual impressions of both minor street crimes, such as begging and cleaning car windows at road intersections in London, and more serious crimes, such as those portrayed in Mafia movies, strongly suggest the family and community basis of much crime. The ethnic and sub-culture aspects of crime are examined by some social scientists, but not very much by anthropologists. This lack of studies is surprising because it would seem to be a natural focus for anthropological research. I can only very tentatively offer a couple of guesses as to why these practitioners have chosen not to study crime very much.

One reason might be due to the working methods of anthropologists and the need to achieve immersion in the community under study. It could be that anthropological research on crime would almost necessitate becoming a criminal, at least temporarily. It might not be all that easy to gain access, and quite risky if one was successful in doing so. The second reason has to do with the descriptive and non-judgemental aspect of the subject. Anthropology is the least normative of the social sciences. It has a primary goal of reporting what is there. To classify something as a criminal act is already to pass judgement, or very nearly so. As it happens, neither of these explanations is very convincing. In every society people judge certain activities to be criminal, and have attitudes towards, and make responses to, crime. The crime in a society could be studied from a perspective within the society but outside of the criminal practice. As we shall see, while there are not many studies, there are a few telling examples of this kind of enquiry.

Food sharing among the Meriam

The most traditionally anthropological study of crime is that of Rebecca Bird and Douglas Bird who wrote about what they call "tolerated theft" among an aboriginal group called the Mer. (Bird and Bird, '97) These are island dwellers in the Torres Strait of Australia. The main activities of these Melanesian people are gardening and fishing. The study is about how they dispose of the meat of the large sea turtles of the *chelonia mydas* species that are caught and slaughtered by the Meriam. Bird and Bird studied this turtle hunting over the eleven months from May 1994 to March 1995. During this period 132 turtles were caught, and they produced on average over 65 kilograms of edible meat each.

The whole business is pretty unpleasant to many Western sensibilities, and the turtles are protected under Australia's Endangered Species Act. The Meriam are allowed to do this hunting provided it is done with traditional methods, for their own consumption, and not for export. The Meriam are aware of the threat that hunting poses to the survival of the species, and raise baby turtles for eventual release into the sea. The turtles have a better chance of survival when they are older, and need to be cared for up to that time.

There are two forms of hunting. One is capture of female turtles when they come on land to lay eggs. It is quite easy to catch these creatures in this way, as they are relatively helpless on land. Women, and even children, take part in this hunting. Far more difficult is capturing these large animals when they are feeding and mating in the ocean off the islands. This is arduous and hazardous, and is only done by fit and skilled men. The slaughter of the turtles is a messy and also an arduous business, in which the pain of the turtles is not a consideration. This is done by men who specialise in the activity.

When a turtle is caught, there is far more meat than can be used by the family who made the lucky capture and the specialist butchers. While these islanders apparently do have access to refrigeration, they do not freeze turtle meat to any significant extent. The meat that is not consumed by the family is given away, and this is really what Bird and Bird are interested in studying. Food sharing is common in traditional societies, and much studied by anthropologists. The reason why turtle hunting, eating, and meat sharing falls under the topic of crime is that Bird and Bird come to the conclusion that the central reason for giving away turtle meat is that it is easier to give it away than to prevent it being stolen.

Some of the surplus turtle meat is distributed at public feasts and some is given to particular chosen families. In the nesting season observed by Bird and Bird, when it is easier to catch turtles, forty-five turtles were disposed of at public feasts, which were attended by about thirty households. In the other season, only nine turtles were allocated to public feasts. The families of successful hunters consumed about six percent of the turtle meat in the nesting season, and half that amount in the other season, when around fifty households attended the feasts. Some parts of the turtles are regarded as much better to eat from the point of view of both taste and nutrition. According to Bird and Bird, the mix of better and less good meat that is retained by the family able to catch a turtle is exactly the same as the mix of meat that is given away. This runs counter to an intuition that the captors would retain the best meat.

We might find it odd that people in a relatively small community, and presumably friendly to a normal degree, have to give away something of value to avoid having it stolen. As we shall see, other anthropologists also question Bird and Bird's conclusion. In spite of some doubts anyone might have, this is a fascinating study. What is striking about the method Bird and Bird employed is the way they followed up every successful capture of a turtle and measured with precision how much meat was obtained, of what quality, and what was done with it. The detailed facts of turtle meat sharing are the main focus of their empirical investigation. Little attention is given to other possibly relevant facts.

The authors entertain three possible explanations of the meat sharing which they observe. The first is that it might not be giving at all. It might be trade. A test of this proposition would probably require observation over more than one year, and certainly would require observing the flow of other things, fish and vegetables for example, to those who give away turtle meat. This was not done. If I wanted to know why meat was being given away, I would be inclined to ask the givers. Their answers need not be taken at face value, but they could be suggestive. Bird and Bird do not report any such questions or answers.

A second idea the authors put forward is that the giving is a form of insurance. Who will capture a turtle, and when, is very uncertain. By giving away meat when I have some, I create an obligation to give me meat when I am unlucky at hunting. The third idea, which is the one Bird and Bird favour, is that meat not eaten would be taken away by stealth or by force, so it might as well be given away. They defend this conjecture largely by what I have called "the residual method". (Steuer '98) This method, popular with UFO enthusiasts and others, looks for evidence in support of some conventional explanations, and if none is found, take the absence of evidence for certain specified theories to be an argument in favour of the remaining theory. As the evidence in this study is not consistent with either of the first two ideas, Bird and Bird assume that the data supports the "tolerated theft" idea.

It is invalid to infer that if disposal of turtle meat is not a form of trade, or of insurance, it must be a response to the possibility of theft. There are any number of other possible explanations, or combinations of explanations. The one I favour is status seeking. Academics tend to be status maximisers, so I may be biased. There are many reasons why young men would want to improve their status in the community. It could have to do with securing a desirable marriage partner, or partners outside of marriage. The authors pay passing attention to this idea, but dismiss it because the meat is not particularly distributed to families with marriageable daughters. This ignores the fact that a man can get a good reputation as a successful hunter and a generous provider by giving to the community broadly. His good reputation could further his chances with families with sought after daughters, even though the gifts were not especially directed to such families. Indeed, it might seem crude to single out such families, and run counter to other traditions of the society.

Bird and Bird argue against both trade and insurance by noting that: (1) there is no tendency to give more meat to households with one or more successful turtle hunters; (2) significant amounts of meat are given to non-hunters; and (3) there is no tendency for those who hunt in the difficult feeding and mating season when the turtles are in the sea to give meat to others who hunt in that season. Some support for the "tolerated theft" hypothesis is found in the observations that: (1) the more families live near a lucky hunter, the more meat is given away; (2) large families, who could be a bigger threat, are given more; (3) and very little is given to geographically distant families. The authors also find support for their conjecture in the fact that less is given away when it is easier to catch turtles. My goal is to report interesting work rather than attempting to improve it. However, it must be noted that these facts uncovered by Bird and Bird are consistent with many explanations other than the tolerated theft explanation.

It is customary for articles written in the journal *Current Anthropology* to be commented on by other scholars following the article. Elizabeth Cashdan, Richard Davis and Robert Attenborough, among other anthropologists, make the point that Bird and Bird give little attention to reputation as a possible motive for generosity. A number of other commentators feel that Bird and Bird work with an unduly restricted range of possible explanations of what they observe. This is probably the case. However, the power of the study does not lie in its formal tests of a number of theories. It lies in the picture of a community which is memorable and persuasive. And it lies in the incomparable data on turtles caught and what happens to their meat. Other investigators can build on this information.

Crime and Delinquency in the United States

Increasingly we can see anthropological insights applied not in remote traditional societies, but in contemporary United States. Linda Kaljee and her co-authors used a technique called ethnographic observation — non-invasive and, as much as possible, objective observation — of focus groups to learn how adolescents and their parents perceive and react to violence in and against their communities. (Kaljee and colleagues, '95) The setting is a mainly African-American area of Baltimore. The authors begin by discussing the horrific crime figures among poor Americans generally. White households with incomes of less than $7,500 experience 53 violent crimes per thousand. The figure is 56 for African-Americans. No significance figures are given, but the difference is probably not significant. So it appears that what matters is income, not race. 'Violent crime' means murder, assault or rape. For households with incomes above $50,000, the figures are about half, being 27 and 26.

As part of establishing the background to their study, Kaljee and her fellow authors refer to an extraordinary survey which found that seventeen percent of the children living in inner city Chicago had witnessed a homicide. (Roper, '91) If we want to do something about this, part of the relevant information for effective decision-making is the perception of violent crime among those most at risk from it.

The method the authors employed was to get together groups of people from the neighbourhood, get them talking, and then report in their article what they take to be the telling remarks. They do not try to have a statistical breakdown of the kind that says such-and-such a percent of the people feel this, and so many feel that. Typical of anthropology, they want to identify core situations, and then let you, the reader, experience what they experienced. Kaljee and her colleagues are quite open in saying that they had a certain set of prior expectations. These included the importance of street gangs, and the view that poor people are exploited, and this results in what is called "institutionalised violence". At the same time, they do not want to lead their respondents. They describe the kind of statements used to get people talking as follows.

> "What kinds of things do people in your neighbourhood worry about; what contributes to these problems/worries? What is being done by the government to address these problems? How has your neighbourhood

> changed in recent years? What kinds of things do kids do when they are not in class? Are there groups of kids that hang together? What kinds of groups are these? How do you become a member/Is it important to be a member?" (p.375)

The results of this experiment in structured listening run counter to the authors' expectations in many ways. The respondents were not particularly inclined to take up the topic of street gangs. They just did not figure prominently in their discussions. Nor did the idea of institutionalised violence and exploitation gain support. What did come out far more than anticipated was the importance of drugs, though not exactly as one might expect. The respondents did see drug dealing as major cause of violence. However, the dealers were held in some kind of macho respect, especially by actual and potential female partners. A young woman is reported as saying, ""Some of [the youths who sell drugs], makes them feel big. They glad they got that reputation. I never met a drug dealer who didn't like his reputation. Never." (p. 377) The grammar is a little hard to follow, but the sentiment is clear.

There is an odd kind of apparent contradiction in this reported attitude towards drugs and drug dealing. It is seen as a major source of difficulty. At the same time, dealers have employment, of a kind, in a community with massive unemployment. There are reports of opinions to the effect that police are not doing much by moving drug-dealers from place to place. A certain sympathy for the dealers is expressed, and some are believed to be "moderate" in the sense of not being violent. Only one actual dealer is reported as being present and speaking out in one of the focus groups. He is taken to be of the 'good' kind, and certainly sees himself in that way. "Me, I mean, well I consider myself a type of drug-dealer that's nice to everybody." (p. 377)

Given the crime statistics which are all too familiar for an area like the African- American area in Baltimore, it is natural that fear of violent crime is a part of the culture. However, the extent of the fear reported in this study goes well beyond what the authors anticipated. The actual words of children and their parents take us to the heart of the study.

> "...you have to be on guard at all times...you never know when somebody is going to be shooting...I've got to get home before dark...all the older people are scared to sit on their own step...you never know with the drugs going on...It's drugs around our neighbourhood and a lot of people getting robbed...you be dead and everybody you love be dead..." (p. 376)

Kaljee and her co-authors are more inclined to see drugs as a symptom than a cause of the prevailing atmosphere. They conclude that the people they observed saw the threats as coming from 'out there', so to speak. They distance themselves from the violence. "These parents do not feel 'ownership' of the violence in their communities." (p. 376) The overall conclusion of the study contains a kind of contradiction. Certainly people feel both threatened and vulnerable and see this danger as something relatively new. The source of the trouble is held to be external. At the same time, the focus group participants express a need for change in the community. What these changes might be, and how to bring them about, is not explored in the study.

Delinquency and membership in street gangs go hand-in-hand for many young people. James Virgil has studied initiation into gang membership in over twenty Chicano, or Mexican-American, *barrios*, or neighbourhoods, in Los Angeles for more than twenty years. (Virgil, '96) Sixty life histories and three hundred structured interviews were conducted. This was supplemented by "many pages" of ethnographic observation. Virgil concludes that initiation, usually taking the form of several gang members beating up a prospective recruit, is a rite of passage for the recruit and a rite of solidarity for the gang. He sees parallels with initiation rites in pre-industrial tribal societies.

The distinct *barrios* are territories to be defended. The initiation, apart from its symbolic value, is a useful screening device to find suitable members. It takes some courage and some fighting skill to hold out for a time when seriously outnumbered. Girls rarely meet the test, and many boys fail as well. The typical age for initiation is twelve to thirteen. The article does not attempt statistical or other formal analysis. It reports the authors well founded take on the initiation into street gangs and provides a number of telling quotations that give a graphic picture of a pretty brutal slice of life in Los Angeles.

> "If you wanted to get in, one, two, three guys, you go against them...If you just stood there and let them hit you and they whip your ass and you don't do nothing, your going to get an ass whipping for nothing. I guess I took an ass whipping to be able to back up the *barrio*." (p. 150)
> An outsider straying into a *barrio* may be at serious risk.
> "They stabbed him and threw him into the bushes. The dudes that got him in were loaded and were *muy locos* (real crazy)...They kept getting him in and getting him out and finally they just stabbed him." (p.151)

Not all gang members have to go through the initiation hurdle Virgil describes, depending on reputation and local variations in the custom, but it is the norm. The young age of initiates, being in junior high rather than grammar school is striking. So is the strength and robustness of the street gang culture. It is difficult to argue with the author's conclusion. "Until such time that major social institutions, such as the family and schools, are able to win over control from the street gangs, the latter will continue to socialize and enculturate large numbers of *barrio* youth and subject them to street baptism." (p. 153)

The next and last study of delinquency in America straddles the boundary between anthropology and sociology. The subject matter is characteristic of anthropology, but the method of study is more sociological. Linda Weber is a sociologist and Andrew Miracle is an anthropologist. The third author is Tom Skehan, a Research Associate with the Centre for Youth Development in Texas. This is a study of what is called 'bonding', or the extent to which young members of a community come to accept the positive values of that community. (Weber and colleagues, '95) The primary goal of the study is to compare three racial or ethnic groups — White, African-American and Hispanic — in terms of the importance of different factors leading children to take up the values of their families. Following the work of Travis Hirschi, the authors hypothesise that weak bonds lead to delinquent behaviour. (Hirschi, '69).

Weber and her colleagues have undertaken a complex and ambitious investigation. I cannot do justice to it in a brief report. Broadly, the authors find considerable support for the view that bonding mechanisms differ comparing one ethnic group with another. Over two thousand forms were distributed to schools in the Southwest, Midwest and Southeast of the United States. 864 forms were returned, and 755 of these carried permission of the parents to use the results in the study. Attention is given to the likely representativeness and probable sources of bias in the results.

Delinquency is measured by using a modified version of a set of questions employed by Delbert Elliott and his co-workers in the National Youth Survey. (Elliott and colleagues, '83). These questions covered behaviour like: theft of small, medium, and higher valued items; aggravated assault; selling marijuana and joy-riding.

The survey included twenty-eight questions designed to compare the role of fathers and mothers in communicating with their children; in knowing what the children are doing; in being with them and involved in family activities. Examples of the questions are:

> "How often does your father/mother know where you are when you are away from them?
> How often do you share your thoughts and feelings with your father/mother?

Do you want people to know who your family is?
During the school week, how many afternoons do you usually spend with your family?
When your family makes rules, how often do you follow them?" (pp. 366 – 367)

Sophisticated statistical analysis was employed to determine the importance of fathers and mothers in 'bonding' in the three ethnic groups, and the effects of bonding on delinquency in the three ethnic groups. In spite of the quite large sample and the statistical care, the authors are generally cautious about comparing different communities. They do feel that a *prima facia* case is made for cultural differences. For example, family pride was found to reduce delinquency for Whites and Hispanics, but not for African-Americans. Female communication appeared to reduce delinquency in Hispanic children, but not for Whites and African-Americans. Males were more delinquent than females for all three ethnic groups. While older White and African-American children were more delinquent than younger children, this was not true for Hispanic children. Other results were found tending to support differences across ethnic groups in a picture that is far from simple. For example, a large role for mothers may be associated with neglect on the part of fathers, or just be an additional civilising influence.

Anthropologist as Expert Witness

In any multicultural society there is an interesting potential role for anthropologists in the courts as experts on cultural differences across members of different communities. Michael Winkelman\f"n" takes up this question in the context of American law. (Winkelman, '96') The fundamental premise is that the law applies to everyone, and no one is allowed to break the law because of his or her cultural orientation. Marijuana smoking by Rastafarians who claim a religious role for the practice is an interesting case. For all crimes, guilt is held to be independent of cultural orientation. But mitigation, or excuses, related to culture can be relevant to sentencing.

Winkelman identifies three related but separate applications of the concept of mitigation because of the culture of the convicted criminal. The first has to do with the extent to which the perpetrator acted in a voluntary way in committing the illegal act. What is wholly voluntary in one culture may be required, or hardly voluntary, in another culture. The second issue has to do with intent. This can have implications for both determining guilt and for appraising the severity of a crime. Intent has to do with the state of mind, or as it is called, the *mens rea,* of the individual. Knowledge of cultural considerations can help the court in attempting to determine a person's likely state of mind. The third consideration is that of non-responsibility. A strong cultural orientation may be relevant in establishing the degree to which the defendant was in fact responsible for his or her actions.

The author provides one example, among others, of a Mexican who undoubtedly killed his wife's lover. In some societies this is not murder. Crimes of passion are viewed very differently in different cultures. An interesting angle in this kind of case is whether the culture of the victim could be relevant. A person engaging in an infidelity who believes that this could be legitimately punished by death might have less legal comeback, so to speak. Winkelman does not discuss this.

In the 1990 annual meeting of the American Anthropological Association, some objections were raised against allowing cultural considerations to enter into the deliberations of the courts, and the possible role of anthropologists in this activity. It was argued that many cultures do not share the official, not to say politically correct, attitude towards women that exists in America. What would be an abuse in America might not be in the country of origin, or the sub-culture, of the accused. Some members of the Association felt that allowing scope in the courts for consideration of cultural differences in the relations between the sexes was inappropriate because it would damage the position of women. It goes without saying that social science, including anthropology of course, cannot resolve the ethical issue on its own. However, in so far as the debate turns on the facts of diverse cultures, as well as matters of principle, professional anthropological knowledge could be helpful.

An Anthropological Dispute on Rural Vigilantism

The great strength of anthropology is its ability to draw on trained intuition and capture subtle but important considerations. The great weakness inherent in this approach is the lack of more objective tests of whether a particular interpretation is right or not. Perhaps unfortunately, it is not very common for anthropologists to repeat the work of other colleagues as a further test of their conclusions. There are cases, indeed classic cases read by all those learning the subject, where later interpretations concluded that the work of distinguished earlier investigators was fundamentally flawed. For example, a culture that was found to have little or no aggression by the first visitor, was found to be intensely aggressive by a later investigator with a better knowledge of the local language.

A fascinating recent example of completely opposed anthropological findings occurred in work on community self-help groups in the Philippines, which go under the names *barangay tanod* and *Bantay ng Bayan*. These groupings are made up of villagers who get together to help each other with certain aspects of farming, for example, or to protect themselves from criminal exploitation. Timothy Austin says that these rather informal self-help groupings are firmly embedded in the culture. (Austin, '95) This much is not in dispute. What is hotly contested is that an organisation called the Civilian Army Force Geographic Unit, or CAFGU, is an organisation comparable to the traditional clubbing together which is such a prominent part of the Filipino personality. It is suggested that when people get little protection from the police or from the courts, it is only natural that they band together for their mutual protection, and the CAFGU can be thought of in that light. Austin provides an abstract, or summary, of his article, and I would like to quote it in full.

> "Building upon field research, two predictably allied features of Philippine society are explored: the time-honored patterns of neighborhood or village cooperation (self-help) long associated with Filipino culture and character, and the continuing emergence of citizen volunteer security organizations. A variety of informal features of self-help are described along with variously formalized and official networks of social control. How these security and peacemaking activities fluctuate but persist in a turbulent socio-political setting is discussed." (p. 10)

The critical part is the reference to, "...variously formalised and official networks of social control.". It is difficult to see how the more traditional groupings could be described in terms of 'social control'. Austin grants that there are differences, but is clear in saying that the CAFGU is, "...composed of civilian volunteers...The new CAFGU is more of a civilian-orientated military auxiliary. Citizen volunteers are now screened and trained by the Philippine Army and receive a small allowance." (p. 16) This description is hotly disputed by Kathy Nadeau and Vel Sumingutt (Nadeau and Sumingutt, '96) They take the greatest possible exception to this characterisation and give a very different picture. The only point of agreement between the two reports is the importance of the CAFGU in fighting communism.

Nadeau and Sumingutt see the CAFGU as having nothing to do with traditional self-help activity. Far from helping local people, they see it as a perpetrator of, "...gross human rights violations...". (p.245) They make reference to the Justice of the Peace Commission of the Association of Major Religious Superiors of May 1989 which found, among other things, that the CAFGU were responsible for thirteen murders in Mindanao between July of 1987 and November of 1989. There was also a significant amount of robbery, assault and other crimes. One of the murder victims was a Protestant pastor. The authors also refer to the Philippine Alliance of Human Rights report of 1993 which discusses 553 atrocities committed by the CAFGU, including a case in August of 1989 when three CAFGU members killed ten people and wounded fifty-seven by throwing grenades into the crowd at a beauty pageant.

Austin makes no mention of any of this violence. His emphasis is on volunteer groups, mainly for the purpose of self-help, and forming spontaneously out of the community. They have the goal of protecting people and preserving the peace. Nadeau and Sumingutt assert that CAFGU members are not volunteers. "...military commanders would simply send orders to barrio captains to send able-bodied men...Barios whose leaders failed to send representatives are labelled "communist" territory...usually targets of military operations, including aerial bombings and shellings that led to...mass evacuations...". (p. 245) Far from the picture given by Austin, Nadeau and Sumingutt see the long arm of United States intervention. "In fact the use of civilian militia is an extension of the U.S. psychological warfare doctrine currently known as Low Intensity Conflict...Many of the lessons learned there (in Vietnam) were subsequently transferred to the Philippines starting in 1987...The Philippine Military Headquarters in Manila and military commanders in the provinces also designed new strategies, some dating back to the Huk campaign, to recruit members into the CAFGU and vigilante groups." (p. 247, my bracket added)

Austin does agree that the CAFGU is much involved in fighting communism, and that the village members are often employed in more dangerous activities than the regular Army soldiers. They might appear to be doing more dangerous things, but he attributes this in part to their greater knowledge of the local terrain. In addition, Austin argues that the villagers saw themselves as less vulnerable. "Another explanation given by locals was that the CAFGU volunteers were believers in, and wearers of amulets (*anting-antings*), which some believed would even repel bullets." (p.16)

While it is possible that both articles may be giving false pictures of an aspect of life in Mindanao, it certainly is the case that both cannot be broadly correct. The integrity and the accuracy of anthropological investigation seem to call for some resolution of this extraordinary difference of presentation.

It is not unusual for different people to come back from holiday in the same place and report completely different experiences. Maybe they like different things. But even if they have the same preferences, one may have got sick, or robbed, or sunburned, and this coloured the experience. The dispute between these articles about the CAFGU cannot be seen in that light. It may be simplistic to maintain that either the CAFGU is an indigenous volunteer organisation, acting in the interests of its members, or it is a largely foreign dominated organisation prepared to sacrifice its members and often wreck havoc in the rest of the community. The truth may be more complicated. However, here we have a case where one author asserts that the CAFGU is fundamentally a self-help body fighting crime. The other authors say it is organised from outside and is a perpetrator of crimes. As I say, while they both may be wrong, they cannot both be right. One would hope that the editors of anthropology journals like *Human Organiszation,* which published both papers, would be keen to see further investigation. The structure of knowledge which is anthropology cannot live indefinitely with both views.

SOCIOLOGY

Where anthropologists have been a bit reticent to study crime, sociologists have a rich tradition that deals with virtually all aspects of crime. The number one question is who commits crime? The second and third questions are why, and what can be done to discourage criminal activity. We know that some kinds of criminal behaviour are associated with relative poverty, family background, ethnic minorities, particular schools, and certain contributing experiences. These things tend to go together. The great scientific problem is separating out the causes of crime. For example, how important is the influence of an unfortunate family, and how strong is the effect of poverty? What I am calling an "unfortunate family" for the moment is also likely to be one which is relatively badly off economically. Here is where advanced statistical technique comes into play. We cannot run the clock back and change one circumstance at a time; such as the school an individual attended, and see how that affected behaviour. The best we can do is to apply advanced statistical techniques to the data we can collect on many individuals in an effort to separate out causal factors. The dominant sociological approach to the study of crime is large-scale collection and analysis of data. Liberal use is made of these methods in the studies reported below. Other approaches are also illustrated in this section.

Most of the sociological research on crime done in the 1990's has to do with violent behaviour, including murder, and with theft. I am not aware of any generally used term for these kinds of crimes. One might call them 'base individual crimes'. These are to be distinguished from both organised crime and white-collar crime. Some attention is given to these other two categories of crime in this section. More coverage of the more commercial kinds of crime, be they organised crime or white-collar crime, will come up in later sections.

Of course the most common method of dealing with serious crime is prison. Sentencing is not a purely mechanical procedure, with everyone convicted of a certain crime going to prison for the same amount of time. Sociologists look at the factors which lead to a prison sentence, and the length of sentence. Social attitudes are important. These are very rarely based on something we could call objective knowledge. It is interesting to see how popular opinions are formed. The climate of opinion has a good deal to do with policies on crime, and the responses individuals make, including moving to a different neighbourhood. By moving, people hope that there will be less danger of attacks on the street and less likelihood of robbery at home.

Sentencing

Dawn Robinson and her colleagues have studied the effects of contrition on the part of the accused person on the sentences given out. (Robinson and colleagues, '94) They want to answer the question: if the offender appears to sincerely regret what happened, and is able to convey this to the court in the course of the trial, what will be the consequences as regards the imposition and length of a prison sentence? Of course we cannot experiment to find the answer. We cannot run real trials, and keeping everything the same, have the accused adopt a very contrite manner for one trial, and then run the trial again, but suppressing the contrition. To get around this problem, the authors employ methods very similar to those used in social psychology, as we shall see in a later section.

Robinson and his fellow researchers asked eighty undergraduates to read a version of a hypothetical trail. Half of the participants were given a version full of remorse, and the other half read one virtually devoid of emotion. The crime described in the written material was committed by a drunken driver who killed a pedestrian. In both written versions there is no uncertainty about the immediate facts in the case. The accused clearly committed the crime and is guilty as charged.

After reading their respective versions of the trial, both groups were asked to fill in the same questionnaire which was designed to elicit their views on four basic questions: (1) how emotionally distressed was the driver; (2) how often did he drive while drunk; (3) how likely was he to do this in the future; and (4), what would be the appropriate sentence? The first point to emerge from this mock experiment, and from other casual evidence reported by the authors, is that expressing the right emotions does indeed have some effect on sentencing. The deeper purpose of the study is to determine the mechanisms that bring this about. Why does contrition tend to reduce sentences? There are obviously a number of possible explanations, such as that guilt has made the person suffer. Another view might be that a display of contrition shows that this is a 'nice' person at heart, and a lighter sentence would be suitable.

Robinson and her colleagues draw on what is called 'affect control theory' to explain the effects of contrition in criminal trials. The theory was originally advanced by Osgood, Suci and Tannenbaum. (Osgood and colleagues, '57) This theory is intended to explain how observing the emotions displayed by people influences the views observers hold about these people, and what they predict to be the likely future behaviour of the people they observe.

Emotions of the observers, in turn, are conditioned by the settings, the kind of person they believe they are seeing, and the nature of that person's behaviour. According to how the act is evaluated, the potency, or power, of the act and its consequences, an emotion is elicited in the observers. In the present experiment, the undergraduates characterised the driver as being a sad, sorry and more remorseful person if they read the contritė version. In other words, the two versions had their intended effects. But how this view of a more contrite person effected sentencing was interesting.

The critical dependence is on how the display of contrition effects the perception of the individual being tried. Analysis of the questionnaires indicated that if the display of contrition was believed, but the view of the kind of person the driver was did not change, the remorse of the accused did not lead to a lighter sentence. On the other hand, if the respondents saw the remorse as part of the evidence that this was not characteristic behaviour on the part of the accused, then the remorse led to a lighter sentence. (p. 185) So while contrition works in some cases in terms of reducing time in prison, this is because these are cases where it changes the perception of the accused as being a person less likely to offend again.

While contrition may have an effect on the sentencing of particular individuals, it is unlikely to have a measurable effect on the overall size of the prison population and changes in it over time. The number of people admitted to prison each year, and the rise in this number, is disturbing. During the period 1948 to 1965 there was a low of 43 people sent to prison per 100,000 of the population in the United States, and a high of 51. The figure fell to 36 in 1968. This is not much variation. But by 1981, the figure for annual admissions per 100,000 of the population doubled to 70. And over the next eight years it rose to 128. One might have thought that the number of prison admissions must be closely related to the amount of crime. This does not appear to be the case.

Reported crime grew rapidly over the period of relatively stable prison admissions in the United States, and it increased only twelve percent from 1975 to 1991, which is precisely when we can see a great surge in prison admissions, seven times the growth in reported crime. The United States is not alone in having a rapid increase in incarceration rates. Many of the higher income countries had the same experience. David Jacobs and Ronald Helms set out to explain the changes in admission to prison in the United States over these years. (Jacobs and Helms, '96)

Previous research provides fairly strong evidence suggesting that the proportion of young males in the population, unemployment, and out-of-wedlock births are the main factors explaining incarceration rates. Jacobs and Helms start from this position, but go on to modify it in important ways. They draw on ideas due to Marx and Weber in an informal way which suggest that the legal system is not entirely neutral. This view holds that the way the law works tends to support the interests of the better-off classes in society, and so economic inequality leads to more repressive measures, and more prison admissions. A related consideration is racial tension. This is also treated by the authors in terms of economic inequality. One of the variables they use to capture racial divides in their statistical analysis is the ratio of median non-white income to median white income. The conjecture is that the greater the income differences on average between the two racial groups, the more people admitted to prison.

Building on other work which shows that initiatives of political officials have a major impact on popular concern about crime, Jacobs and Helms include two political variables in their analysis. One is the degree of Republican influence, including whether the President is Republican, combined in an index measuring the proportion of Republican Congressmen and mayors. In support of this variable, they draw on studies showing that Republican administrations at all levels of government tend to devote more resources to fighting crime. The other political variable is whether the year is one with a presidential election. The conjecture is that an election, and the promises that accompany it, tends to promote an atmosphere in which crime moves up the scale of popular concern. The idea being that, responding to this election time atmosphere, the courts send more people to prison.

The last important variable used by Jacobs and Helms is out-of-wedlock births. This is seen as an indicator of family breakdown. They then refer to work showing that family breakdown leads to crime. There are at least two ways to think about this. One is to argue that periods of greater breakdown cause both more out-of-wedlock births and more crime. The other way is to argue that when the children born out-of-wedlock grow up, they are more likely to commit crimes. The researchers adopt this second line of reasoning, and use out-of-wedlock births nineteen years ago to explain prison admissions today. I have a slight problem with this. If family breakdown ultimately results in more people going to prison because it results in more crime, we already have this effect in the crime figures. The volume of crime is one of the factors the authors include in their analysis. So I am inclined to see this wedlock variable, which works well in the statistical analysis, as being some kind of indicator of policy swings rather than a producer of criminal activity. But having said this, I am a little mystified by why the wedlock variable works best with a nineteen-year lag.

The authors also use the past year's crimes as an explanatory variable. But this is not just the figure as it comes. That figure proved to have an insignificant effect. Instead of employing the figure for the number of crimes last year, they square that figure, and then subtract each year from the previous year. This has the effect of exaggerating variations. They call this the threshold effect, and suggest that when crime reaches high levels, people get more sensitive to further increases. However, the variable does not actually track a particular threshold.

There are a number of general observations to be made about this important study. First, using the techniques of 'multiple regression', the researchers are attempting to see how all the effects on prison admission work together. This is to be preferred to some previous studies that examine just one effect in isolation. Second, they are trying to avoid the effects of trends. Lots of things are going up together, or down together, with little or no actual causal interaction. The price level in many countries is rising, and so is the number of heart attacks. It is unlikely that the one is the main cause of the other. To address the problem of trends, Jacobs and Helms use year to year changes in all their statistics, rather than the levels of the figures. Two, or more, things may in general be going up, but are they changing together year by year? That is a much more stringent test.

A word should be said about the data used in this study. The same comment applies to most statistical studies in the social sciences. The vast bulk of the statistics researchers have to use were not collected for the purpose of research. Typically governments collect statistics for other purposes, and these have to be adopted, or treated creatively, to help with scientific study. In the present case, the authors bring formidable care and ingenuity to the task of marshalling the data they need. For detailed discussion one must refer to the published paper. It can always be argued by other researchers that the results which were found are suspect because the data that were used, and how they were manipulated, were inappropriate. Of course a general charge of this kind has no value. It has to be shown specifically, and in fact it has yet to be shown, how the figures and their manipulation has led to invalid inferences in this case.

There are a number of new and interesting results Jacobs and Helms found about the causes of changing prison admission rates in the United States. An important negative result, in contrast to earlier studies, is that national levels of unemployment do not effect the rate of incarceration. It is always open to other investigators to challenge this conclusion. But for the moment, bringing more potential explanations to bear on the problem simultaneously does suggest that the previous findings regarding the effect of unemployment were mistaken.

A highly significant finding was the importance of the ascendancy of the Republican Party in increased incarceration. The other political variable, an election year, was also found to be significant. National inequality of income proved to be the most significant factor, while the income difference between blacks and whites, as a separate consideration, did not play a role. These findings about the importance of income inequality are worrisome, given the current run-away growth in income differentials, particularly fuelled by rises in executive salaries, in the United States.

One possible factor, which is noticeable by its absence in this study, is the role of drugs in explaining the growth of annual prison admissions. Casual observation suggests that the big rise since the middle sixties in people going to prison each year coincides with an increase in the drug problem. With prison admission rising significantly in many advanced industrial countries, and drug using rising as well, it is reasonable to suspect a connection. Of course, this has to be investigated. Jacobs and Helms devote only a footnote to drugs. (pp. 348 – 349) They are mainly interested in making a case for the importance of their two political factors. This brings the investigation very close to what we will find later when we look at political science. It also leaves inviting room for subsequent researchers, who will be well advised to adopt and modify the 'simultaneous' approach to unravelling what-is-causing-what used by Jacobs and Helms.

For a comprehensive review of the sociological work on sentencing, and a fascinating study in its own right, one could not do better than refer to Jo Dixon's work on the Minnesota State Court during the first half of 1983. (Dixon, '95) Her data set begins with 1,532 convicted felons and follows their sentencing fate during the period. She separates out the question of whether or not those found guilty went to jail from the question of how long was the sentence of those going to jail.

Broadly speaking, there are four major contending theories of sentencing. One is the notion of political oppression mentioned by Jacobs and Helms. In contrast, the formal legal perspective sees the rules of sentencing being applied equally and dispassionately across the different classes and races in society. A third position holds that the courts themselves adopt traditions, or conventions of sentencing apart from the formal legal requirements. A hybrid theory combines the political and the court convention approaches. Among other objectives, this theory tries to account for why blacks are more likely to go to jail than whites, and to go to jail for longer periods. The argument turns mainly on the greater and more effective use of pleas by whites, which is alleged to be built into the system.

Dixon is sceptical about many of the findings of previous studies of sentencing. She favours a more integrated approach which in principle allows at the same time for the effects of the political, social and organisational context in which the courts are operating. In particular, she is interested in the effectiveness of sentencing guidelines, and on the effects of 'judicial bureaucratisation' and 'prosecutorial bureaucratisation'. In addition to being something of a mouth-full, these last two terms call for some explanation. The former has to do with whether the court is highly specialised, or judges tend to do a bit of everything. The latter term similarly refers to specialisation. 'Low judicial bureaucratisation' in effect means that any case may come before any judge. 'High prosecutorial bureaucratisation' means very specialised prosecutors.

The 'yes' or 'no' question of whether the convicted felons went to jail or not is analysed by Dixon using what is called the 'logit' technique. The length of prison sentences is analysed using what is called 'least square regression'. In both cases the results support the view that less specialised courts produce results supporting the formal legal theory of sentencing. The more specialised, or 'highly bureaucratised' courts produce outcomes supporting the 'court tradition' theory of sentencing, where pleas play a major role. An important finding of this study is that which theory of sentencing is most applicable depends upon the kind of court it is.

Along with the kind of court it is, the race of the felon and four legal considerations are analysed in attempting to explain the sentences given out. The legal factors are: the severity of the crime; the individual's criminal history; one or multiple charges; and was a weapon used or not. In contrast to a number of other studies of sentencing (see, for example, Myers and Talarico, '86), Dixon finds no effect of race on the sentences of the Minnesota Courts. This is quite a dramatic finding. She attributes it to the power of legal sentencing guidelines.

Minnesota was the first state to implement statutory guidelines. "The intent of the guidelines was to establish a set of consistent standards for sentencing that would increase uniformity..." (p. 1170) She goes on to say that in states that do not have such guidelines, there may well be an effect of race on the sentence given for a crime. She takes this result, if it were to be found, as further evidence that the setting of the court determines which theory of sentencing is most applicable.

One cannot leave this topic without emphasising the enormous data problems that had to be faced in doing this study. The upshot of this heroic effort is that if you know the kind of court, and the criminal history and actions of the convicted person, you can predict the sentence. Being told the race of the offender does not improve the prediction. Does this mean that racial prejudice is not responsible for the disproportionate numbers of African-Americans in United States jails? Certainly not. Prejudice may be the root cause of much crime. What it does say that the courts in Minnesota appear to ignore the race of felons when doing sentencing. The one problem I might have with this conclusion has to do with pleas. We see from the statistical results that they are significantly related to sentences. And it could be that they also correlate closely with race. If so, they may be masking the effect of race on sentencing. So much for sentencing. Next we turn to studies of the factors influencing criminal behaviour.

The Causes of Crime

In this sub-section we will look at four investigations of the causes of crime. The first study takes up what is called the 'sub-culture thesis' of violent behaviour. "He fell into bad company." How often have we heard this explanation of a life gone wrong. Marvin Wolfgang and Franco Ferracuti were among the first to subject this very plausible idea to a more precise formulation and to empirical test. (Wolfgang and Ferracuti, '67) Since that time there have been many studies of the 'sub-culture' explanation of the differences between groups in the incidence of violence. The idea is that some groups hold to values which support, or fail to condemn, violence. These values cause others in the group to adopt a violent mode of behaviour, who would not have done so in the absence of the group ethic.

Richard Felson and his colleagues are critical of some of the large-scale, or macro-level, work on the 'sub-culture' theory on the grounds that these studies assume that a race, or region, or class can be treated as a group. (Felson and colleagues, '94) They suspect that these are inappropriately large aggregates for this theory. For them the sub-culture effect is more potent when there is the potential for face-to-face interaction. They also argue that a proper test of the theory involves measuring the group culture directly, rather than simply assuming that those groups that are found to be particularly violent have a culture which supports that behaviour.

In order to meet some of these problems, Felson and his colleagues used data collected from a large sample of male students attending 87 randomly selected public high-schools in America. Following a questionnaire and interview procedure devised by Jerald Bachman, over 2,000 sophomores, and the headmasters of their schools, provided an enormous amount of detailed information. A total of twenty-two questions were asked which were intended to measure violence and delinquency. Examples are: "Did you hurt someone badly enough to need bandages or a doctor", [have you] "taken something from a store without paying for it", and "do you cheat on tests". (pp. 156 –157) Many other questions were addressed to the respondents personal values, such as agreeing or not agreeing with, "turning the other cheek...". (p. 159) After the initial interviews and questionnaires, a second wave of questions was administered in the students' senior year to determine how being at the various schools effected them. Indices intended to summarise the culture of each of the high-schools were constructed from the averages of the individual responses. A variety of statistical techniques were employed to attempt to determine which were the factors leading to interpersonal violence, theft and vandalism, and school delinquency.

A helpful factor for this study is that students have little choice over which school to attend, so that self-selection is unlikely to effect the results. While these results are based on statements, or written answers, and not on actual acts of violence or theft, they are highly suggestive. The study provides good evidence for the importance of the sub-culture effect. This was anticipated, but that should not detract from the result. It is one thing to think something is highly likely to be the case. It is another to have real evidence.

There was one quite surprising result that came out of the investigation. This was a strong tendency to find more violence in the high-schools which placed more emphasis on academic attainment. The authors cautiously offer an explanation for this finding in terms of frustration on the part of less able students. They refer to 'strain theory', due to Merton, which suggests that criminal and deviant activity is an option which is sometimes taken up by young men who find it difficult to succeed in more socially accepted ways. (Merton, '57).

People living in America are rightly concerned about the high rates of homicide that can be found in their country, as well as other types of violent crime, and crimes against property. These high rates do not exist everywhere, and a truly impressive body of literature has grown up which attempts to explain variations in the rates of crime across the United States. Are the differences which can be observed as we move from place to place due to the presence of cities, ethnic minorities, poverty, or social disintegration? Is there a kind of tradition of criminal activity that is stronger in some places than in others? Augustine Kposowa and her colleagues have reviewed some twenty fairly recent studies that attempt to account for variations in crime rates. (Kposowa and colleagues, '95) It is a complex story and there is no easy substitute for reading their survey. All the studies they review use multiple regression techniques which attempt to find a statistical relation between the amount of crime and various potential causes. Tests are employed to see if apparent associations could be the result of chance and have no causal significance. By combining the explanatory factors in different combinations, attempts are made to see if, for example, certain ethnic groups living in cities contribute substantially to the amount of crime, but do not do so in rural settings.

Depending on the kind of data used, and the various combinations of explanatory factors employed, quite different results emerge from the various studies. It is not at all unusual for the results of one study to contradict the results of another study. Sociological investigators are up against a very complex set of interacting causes. One can detect progress, but we are far from having a satisfactory understanding of these kinds of crimes. Kposowa and her team reviewed important past work, and also undertook a massive study of their own. The unique feature of their work was to take the county as their unit of analysis. The data are for the year 1980, and over 3,000 counties of the United States, or 98 percent of all counties, were included in the study. Seventeen factors were examined for their possible ability to explain the number of homicides, other violent crimes, and crimes against property.

Though there are a lot of them, it is worth looking at these seventeen potential explanations of criminal activity in some detail. For one thing, they are used quite widely in many studies apart from the Kposowa investigation. It also is interesting to see what is not included in the list of possible explanatory factors.

I. We begin with the South of the United States. The South is known to have a high rate of homicides. Is this because of other factors, like poverty, which may be more important in the South, or is the South an independent factor in the rate of crime? This is the 'sub-culture' variable in this study.

II. Three 'ethnic' variables are included. These are the proportions of African Americans, Hispanics, and Native Americans in each county.

III. Poverty enters both as an absolute figure — the proportion of people below the poverty line — and the degree of inequality in the county as measured by the 'Gini coefficient', a popular measure of inequality.

IV. Social cohesion is measured through church attendance, divorce rates, the proportion of migrants, and the population turnover of the county.

V. The economic variables included as possible explanations of crime rates are the level of unemployment and the proportion of professional workers.

VI. Demographic variables used are education, the median age, and the proportion of residents aged five to seventeen.

VII. Finally, the proportion of people living in large cities, and the density of population in the country complete the seventeen variables.

One interesting omission to note for future reference is that there are no variables included intended to measure the efforts made to deter crime. Candidates for this might be the numbers of police compared to the population of the county and the severity of punishment if caught. Some

States, and hence the counties in them, have the death penalty. Others do not. As we shall see, these considerations, not included in sociological analysis in the 90's, are taken up by other social sciences.

It is not practical to report in detail on all the results found by this study by Kposowa and her associates. Their argument for the county as a unit of analysis is quite persuasive, and the large volume of data this generates allows the authors to include these seventeen possible explanations in a simultaneous study as well as breaking the data down in a variety of ways. Letting all the variables work together reduces the chances that something which appears to be a cause of crime, but in fact is not, may simply be correlated with something else which is a true cause of crime.

Many of their results are consistent with those of earlier work. Much of this work was on crime in urban areas. The part of the Kposowa work which focuses on urban counties confirms earlier work showing a strong association between crime rates and income inequality, divorce, proportion of the population which is Black, and population turnover. The significance of the proportion of the population which is Hispanic is a new feature of this study. Equally important with the positive findings is the failure to find any explanatory power in whether the county was in the South of the United States or not. Nor was there any effect on crime from divorce, the proportion of the population who were Native American, or from church membership.

The picture changes when we take rural counties on their own, rather than all counties together. For rural counties, being in the South does contribute to homicide rates, as does poverty and the proportion of the population that are Native American. The difference in results between rural and urban areas is a crucial feature of this study, and this bears on the kind of crime as well. Violence is associated with church membership, divorce, population change and Native American proportions in rural counties only. With crime against property, population turnover and the Hispanic proportion are significant factors in rural areas but not in urban areas.

Many more questions can be addressed with this large data set, and the authors discuss a large sample of them quite fully. We will have to conclude our report with the question of unemployment. While agreeing with other studies that found unemployment to be a significant factor in explaining property crime, it did not help much with violent crime, and not at all with homicide. Restricting attention to rural counties brought out more strongly the significance of unemployment for property crime and its lack of impact on the rates of violence and homicide.

It is well known that young men between the ages of fifteen and twenty-nine do a large proportion of murders. The psychologists Daly and Wilson attempt to relate this finding to the effects of evolution through natural selection. (Daly and Wilson, '88) They emphasise the evolved nature of human beings. The sociologists Fred Pampel and Rosemary Gartner take a very different line in their study of homicide. (Pampel and Gartner, '95) For these authors, it would appear that there is nothing in human nature, so to speak, to relate to murder. It is a more a matter of circumstance. Pampel and Gartner start from the observation that if murders are committed largely by young men, the proportion of young men in a society will be the main factor explaining the amount of murder. In addition to a natural propensity of youth towards crime, the authors suggest that a large cohort of younger people makes it more difficult for members of that cohort to secure jobs. In addition, they argue that a large cohort tends to result in lower wages for the cohort, and reduced prospects for promotion. These frustrations could also contribute to the murder rate. (pp. 243 – 244)

The empirical puzzle which Pampel and Gartner want to unravel is the fairly well established proposition that there tends to be a reasonably stable relationship between murder rates and the proportion of young men in a society as we move through time. However, when we compare one country with another at a moment in time, there is no stable relationship to be found between homicide and youth proportions. Quite reasonably the authors suggest that certain factors present in some societies and not in others may weaken, or wipe out, any such relationship. They do not simply want to call this mitigating factor the 'culture' of the society and leave it at that. Instead they propose that, crudely put, societies with a strong collective element, in contrast to more market oriented and individualistic societies, are likely to work against any relation between youth and murder.

Quite a lot of ingenuity, and a willingness to speculate, is needed to construct quantitative measures of the extent to which a country has a collectivist, or left leaning, environment. A mix of expert opinion and more objective facts, like the amount of social security and the extent of membership in unions, are employed. A 'collectivism' scale is constructed for eighteen countries. After reasonably sophisticated statistical analysis, Pampel and Gartner conclude that the data is consistent with the idea that societies which promote the idea that 'we are all in it together' — what the authors call "collectivist class identities" and "solidaristic policies" — are able to weaken the relation between the proportion of young men and the murder rate. They see their work as a first step. They acknowledge that the availability of guns may be at work along with, or even instead of, a collectivist environment. One would have thought that a measure of weapon availability would be possible. It would be interesting to see how this relates to homicide, along with the other factors like urbanisation, income inequality and unemployment.

The last study in this sub-section brings a new and interesting wrinkle to the relationship between variations in the amount of crime and the proportions of white and non-white people in American communities. (Liska and Bellair, '95) The basic idea is quite simple. It may well be that a higher proportion of non-white people in a community contributes to the amount of crime. But it is also likely to be the case that the amount of crime has a longer-term impact on the racial composition of a community. If whites are wealthier, and therefore more able to move out of high crime areas, we could observe effects running in both directions: the racial composition effects the crime rate, and the crime rate effects the racial composition.

The idea of this two-way causality is pretty straight forward, but the task of investigating it statistically is not easy. Allen Liska and Paul Bellair work with a sample of over one hundred United States cities with populations over fifty thousand. The study covers four decades from 1950 to 1990. Many different relations are examined, partly to see how their data on violent crime relates to findings in other studies. They also subject their central concern to a variety of statistical tests. In their core model, there are four relationships going on. Past robbery rates are allowed to influence current robbery rates, and past proportions non-white to influence current proportions. In addition, the robbery rate a decade ago affects the non-white proportion today, and the non-white proportion today affects the robbery rate in the next decade. All four relations are examined to determine if they can be found to play a significant role. The results are encouraging for the central idea, with a number of interesting features.

As we move from decade to decade, the strength of the relationship between the percent non-white and the robbery rate has been growing. The proportion of the variation which appears to be explained doubles over the forty-year period. With other changes going on, including a general rise in the robbery rate, it at first appears that the affect of robbery on racial composition is declining over time. An extra robbery per thousand of the population initially raises the non-white proportion in the 1950's by three percent. For the next decade the rise goes down to less than two percent, winding up in the 1980's to less than a fifth of one percent, or so the data suggests.

However, the hazards of correctly accounting for simultaneous effects are well illustrated by examining the effect of robbery on the change in the non-white proportion in the next decade relative to other effects. This turns out to suggest that the effect of robbery in the previous decade has a small, but constant effect on increases in the non-white proportion throughout the period under study. (pp. 595 - 596) The picture is confusing, and the last word has yet to be said. But the broad point that Liska and Bellair want to make is getting off the ground. If we see more crime in places with a smaller non-white proportion of the population, this may be due in part to a past exodus of the better-off white population from the area.

Street Life

Like the anthropologists, the sociologists are particularly interested in street life, and especially homelessness, as an influence on crime. Where the former tend to employ a close-in, subjective method of observation, the latter tend towards broader statistical investigation. John Hagen and Bill McCarthy note that sociological theories often attribute delinquency to unfavourable family influences. Very little attention is given to young people living on the streets, especially in empirical work. (Hagen and McCarthy, '92[ii]) One obvious reason for this is that there are great difficulties in getting a good sample of street populations. It is much easier to work with students. However, working for over a year through shelters and drop-in centres, and exploring parks and streets in Toronto, the authors were able to get information on 386 teenagers living on the streets. They compare these homeless young people in downtown Toronto to 563 students.

Hagen and McCarthy study serious theft. They construct an index from six inputs: (1) stealing from cars; (2) taking items worth more than $50 from stores; or (3) from individuals; (4) illegal use of a credit or bank cards; (5) breaking into a building and taking something; and (6) stealing a car. The index takes account of whether or not the crime was committed, and how often. There is no doubt that the street youths, with an average score five times higher than teenagers at school, are more prone to crime. The subtle question the authors wish to answer is how much of the difference can be attributed to being on the street, as against being a particular kind of teenager. It is quite obvious that the street adolescents are not the same as the students. For one thing, two-thirds are male.

The street teenagers are three times more likely to be involved in ten or more serious thefts than the students, and where over one quarter of the 'streets' have done thirty or more thefts, less than one percent of the students reach that level. While it is nice to have a clearer quantitative picture, the comparison is hardly surprising. Hagen and McCarthy use three indicators of being inclined towards delinquency: family class; the 'health' of the family; and being employed or unemployed. These factors are assumed to place young people at more or less risk of being involved in theft. Some teenagers in adverse circumstances nevertheless live at home, and others wind up on the streets. The basic result of this study is that being on the street in itself contributes greatly to the probability of being involved in theft. How much street life contributes compared to adverse family situations remains a bit problematical. The authors address this issue, but they cannot be sure that those people on the streets are in some meaningful sense the same as a group of comparable youths who are not on the streets.

Broadly, and not unexpectedly, older male youths from families where the breadwinner is unemployed are more likely to be on the street. The family not being intact contributes, as does conflict with teachers. The comparison the authors want to make is with young males with all these features who are not on the streets. But do they differ only in not being on the streets?

In another study the authors consider the motives of hunger and the need for shelter as potential causes of criminal activity on the part of street youths. (Hagen and McCarthy, '92 [I]) They are working with essentially the same sample as in the other study. The extra dimension is to ask exactly what about being on the street leads to more crime. The answer the authors find is that basic need explains the greater propensity of street youths to turn to crime.

The need for shelter is also included. And along with the earlier emphasis on theft, the crime of prostitution is added to the questions asked. The data suggest that hunger can lead directly to the stealing of food, and along with the need for shelter, can lead to serious theft and prostitution. As we might expect, men are more inclined to steal and women to engage in prostitution. Being on the street makes it all the more difficult to get legitimate employment, and the link between lack of work and basic need passes through to crime.

The policing of streets is a fascinating and controversial area. Many concerned observers argue for community policing. The police should be seen walking the streets, rather than riding in cars, or worse still, not seen at all. The police should be friendly figures with good relations with the people on their beat. Others claim that too obvious a police presence is provocative and in itself leads to anti-social behaviour. It is also felt that police attitudes on race are important to the well-being of the community. Sometimes this takes the form of advocating that the police have a similar racial composition to the people they are policing. A further consideration is that the police should have exemplary attitudes on racial, and other matters, and not reflect any of the inappropriate attitudes that may be present in the community.

Clive Norris and four colleagues undertook careful observation of the police with respect to their habits regarding stopping people in the street. Their observations covered fifteen months in 1986 and 1987. (Norris and colleagues, '92) They managed to persuade the police to allow them to accompany them on their street patrols in one division in Surrey and two divisions in London. A single observer went along in each case. A total of over 800 hours of observation were recorded.

Of course, sometimes the police are approached by members of the public. These incidents are excluded from the study. Only actions initiated by the police are recorded. Allegedly, the person or persons are stopped on suspicion of some wrongdoing, though perhaps of a minor nature. At each incident, the observers filled out forms which stated who was stopped and what was the demeanour of both the police and the people stopped. Intoxication was also noted, as was the outcome in terms of no action, a warning or more formal action.

The authors do not discuss the question of whether their presence affected either the police or the people stopped by the police. It might be interesting, though not easy, to surreptitiously make the same observations of the police on patrol. One also might wonder if the particular divisions which agreed to the study are representative of the police generally.

Stopping people is not very common. The researchers observed one stop on average approximately every four hours. This resulted in information on more than two hundred stops involving over three hundred people. The statistical test known as Chi square was employed to see if there was a racial element in who was stopped. The result was overwhelming evidence of a greater propensity to stop Black people compared to the United Kingdom proportions of Black and White people. A different comparison might be with the proportions of the two races on the streets, rather than the national compositions. Ideally, but hard to do, would be a comparison that took account of suspicious behaviour. The researchers do find a larger proportion of Whites than Blacks stopped for obvious misbehaviour, and a larger proportion of Blacks than Whites stopped on suspicion. But whether there were more grounds for suspicion in one case than the other is not examined.

Apart from the greater tendency to stop Blacks, the police come off rather well in this study. There is some evidence that among those stopped, Whites are more likely to be intoxicated than Blacks. But once people are stopped, the police in this study do not reveal any racial prejudice. The observers noted the calm and civil behaviour of both the police and the people they stopped. They describe the police attitude towards the Black people who are stopped as "neutral", and observed a somewhat negative attitude on the part of the police towards the White individuals who are stopped. (p. 222) The authors conclude that the police do not exhibit prejudice once people are stopped, but do stop Black people, particularly men under thirty-five, unduly often.

Suppose it was the case that a particular recognisable group, by skin, eye, hair colour, body type, or whatever, was more likely to be up to no good than the general population. We could ask whether the police would be right to observe such people more carefully. Whether the answer on the question of observing is 'yes' or 'no', we could go on to ask whether the police would be right to take action with respect to such people on weaker evidence than for the general population. Sociology on its own cannot tell us what the police should do as they patrol the streets. But it can uncover important information which could influence what we might conclude. For example, it might shed light on how different policing strategies effect both behaviour and perceptions of the police. Clive Norris and the team relate their findings to the extensive literature on policing and race in the United Kingdom.

Crime and the Media

Clearly the newspapers, and other media, want to attract large audiences. Crime stories, particularly reports of sensational crimes, are one way of doing this. At times it may be in the interests of the press or television to exaggerate the extent of crime and to provide biased reports on the nature crimes being committed. Philip Schlesinger and his co-researchers quote the example of a 'crime wave' which was manufactured by a newspaper in Cleveland in 1919. (Schlesinger and colleagues, '91) This type of activity can well have an effect on the public perception of crime and on policies designed to deal with crime. Severely distorted information could have an adverse effect on policy.

The media are dependent on various government agencies, and others, for their information about crime. These sources of information are often in competition with each other and have their own goals. So even if the press, for example, was as objective in its reporting as is humanly possible, the information given to the press is at least somewhat shaped by political and institutional interests. Schlesinger and his colleagues trace out how groups in the United Kingdom such as the Home Office, the Metropolitan Police, the Prison Services and Customs all have their own needs which can be helped or hindered by how crime is treated in the media.

Following a brief discussion of important earlier studies of the content of newspaper and television reporting of crime, the authors present their own findings. For a two-week period in the late 80's they compiled figures on the major television channels and national newspapers. They worked with ten categories of offences ranging from public order offences, drugs, sexual offences, violence against the person and so on. The newspapers were divided into 'quality', 'mid-market' and 'tabloid'. A rather clear pattern emerges of more of an emphasis on sex and violence in the tabloids, and more emphasis on property offences in the quality press, with the mid-market papers falling between the two. The pattern of coverage in television mirrors the 'mid-market' of the press.

The researchers also recorded whom the national newspapers referred to or quoted in their crime reporting. This list included members of Government, the Opposition, the police, judges, and all the way down to the members of the general public. Here we can see a very sharp difference between types of paper. The qualities tend to refer much more to figures in government, and to experts. The tabloids pay much more attention to victims of crime, and to criminals and suspected criminals. Finally, analysis of front-page newspaper coverage confirms the earlier finding that the tabloids go for sex and violence, and the qualities go for crimes against property. There is one possible exception in that mid-range papers now tend to go more with the qualities, and even exceed them in some categories, rather than falling in the middle in terms of front-page coverage.

The Special Projects Group of the research Department of the BBC allowed Schlesinger and his colleagues to insert some questions relating to fear of crime in the Omnibus Surveys they conduct. This exercise revealed a "consistent" relationship between being a tabloid reader, a heavy TV viewer, especially of the less up-market commercial channel, and worrying about becoming a victim of a crime. This fear was concentrated on mugging and physical attack in general. The authors make a *prima face* case for a complex set of interactions between the competitive jostling of various groups who supply information, the way crime is covered in the media, and the public perception of crime.

White Collar Crime

We conclude this section with a brief discussion of two sociological studies of white-collar crime. They are slightly out of the mainstream of the subject where there is a tendency to concentrate on robbery and violent crime, especially homicide. These two studies are no less interesting for being a bit unusual. Bruce Wiegand centres his investigation on the popular view that if one wants to sell black-market dollars in Belize City, and hence get a better rate than the official rate, the people to approach are East Indian merchants. (Wiegand, '94) His first task is to establish that this is more than hearsay. He does this to his satisfaction through surveys of households in Belize and surveys of merchants. These results tend to confirm the suspicions, but not as strongly as I would have anticipated.

Only one third of households thought that East Indians are involved in this black-market more than other ethnic groups. Among merchants, just under half see East Indians as being particularly associated with the foreign exchange black-market. The other type of evidence comes from senior officials, such as Presidents of the Chamber of Commerce, an Economic Officer of the United States Embassy and a Director of Research at the

Central Bank. These informed figures definitely agreed that East Indians were very much involved in black-market money, and much more so than other ethnic groups.

Wiegand agrees that the economics literature gives a good explanation of why a black-market exists, namely, that the official rate is over valued keeping an excess unsatisfied demand for dollars. He turns to sociology to explain why a particular ethnic group is especially involved in meeting this demand. Some of the theory is close to, or the same as, explanations coming from economics. Central to the argument is the need for trust when dealings are afoot that cannot be enforced in the courts. East Indians are more involved in international trade than other groups with a weaker, or non-existent, international network. Under-invoicing in order to claim to custom officials that goods cost less than they actually did, and thereby reduce the tariff burden on imports, is common.

A culture of trust is established, along with a need for foreign exchange to pay for the imports. Wiegard concludes that there is nothing special in the culture of East Indian importers to account for their prominent position in the foreign exchange black-market. It is the circumstance that generates the specialism. I would be inclined to add an informational point. If it is believed that East Indians specialise in that market, more opportunities for that trade will come to them with lower search costs, and that will encourage them to enter that market.

ECONOMICS

We might expect that economists would be interested in the economic costs of crime. As it turns out, this is not characteristic of much of their work. One study done in the '90's is related to this question, and we shall have a look at it. The consequences of huge profits from the trade in illegal drugs is another matter that might be explored, but in fact there are no articles on this in the major economics journals in the nineties. What we do find in large part are two types of studies. One is on how people respond to efforts to deter crime. This question is much the same as that addressed by sociologists, but the answers given by economists can differ. The other popular topic is cheating the government by not paying taxes, and cheating by the government.

Most of the studies of crime done by economists employ the same fundamental assumption about human behaviour. Work in this discipline starts from the position that people have more-or-less well defined objectives. Given the situations they are in, they make decisions which they believe will enable them to achieve their objectives to the fullest extent that they can. Modern economics tends to relax some of the more traditional and extreme assumptions such as that people have all the relevant information at hand when making decisions, and can calculate consequences effortlessly and perfectly.

Nowadays, agents are assumed to be 'boundedly rational', meaning that information may be hard to get, incomplete, and inaccurate. And even with the information in hand, the problem of finding the best course of action may not be solved perfectly, and certainly will not be solved without effort. In many circumstances it might not be worth it to agents to put in all that much effort. Taking boundedly rational considerations into account, economists nevertheless see people as trying to do the best they can, according to their own lights and according to their circumstances.

Among the implications of this broad approach to the analysis of crime is the conjecture that illegal activity is best seen as a rational choice in certain circumstances. The emphasis is on the notion of choice, and on some explicit or implicit cognitive process leading to choices. The sociologists, and in their own way, the anthropologists, are not completely adverse to the idea that people pursue goals in a somewhat sensible and rational matter. But much of their work has to do with the way the circumstances in which people find themselves shapes the goals they pursue, as well as their ways of going about meeting their objectives.

The method of economics differs from other social sciences, as we will see, in placing more emphasis on more fully specified explicit theories of behaviour. This does not mean that evidence is not important to economic analysis. Far from it. We will see telling examples of bringing the facts to bear on theories. However, the taste for formal analysis does mean that some attention is given in the economics literature to pure theory in the sense of deriving the consequences of a set of assumptions combined with conjectures about how people behave. This approach of working with fully specified explicit theories necessitates using simple assumptions. When a fair number of simple assumptions are used together the analysis may be complex, but the underlying simplicity leaves the analysis tractable.

Ultimately we would like to confront these theoretical efforts with evidence that may prove them to be quite accurate, or to be very poor theories. As a practical matter, that may be difficult to do. Meanwhile, especially when working with fairly plausible assumptions and theories, the results of purely theoretical analysis can be interesting. Our intuition can easily lead us astray. An exercise in pure theory may show us that what we thought were the implications of a set of conditions is not the case, and that the actual implications are very different from what we thought they were. Even when the results of theory are pretty obvious and confirm what we thought, explicit and careful specification places the argument on a much firmer scientific basis. Another potential benefit of explicit theory is generating some unexpected implications, along with the more obvious ones.

Cheating on Taxes

Timothy Besley and John McLaren take the position that it is relatively easy to collect taxes in traditional, less developed, societies, and in reasonably advanced economies. The former have the advantage of face-to-face relations and readily observed benefits from the use of taxes. The latter have the modern machinery of good record keeping. It is the middle level of societies, that are in transition to being 'developed', that have the greatest difficulty in collecting taxes. (Besley and McLaren, ' 93) One need not agree with this comparative point to see that tax collection can be a major issue in developing countries. A particularly knotty problem has to do with the wages of government employees, especially tax collectors. Outside influences, such as the IMF, along with some internal pressures, can lead to the need to balance the budget. In a nutshell, the dilemma is that lower wages will reduce government expenditure, but if they effect tax collection adversely, lower wages will reduce revenues as well.

Besley and McLaren put forward a theoretical analysis, or 'model', in which it is assumed there are two types of tax collectors. Some are always honest, and regardless of circumstances they collect what is due and hand it over to the government. Others are opportunistic. They will behave honestly when it pays to do so, and dishonestly when that is personally more rewarding financially. The proportion of the two types clearly influences the outcome with different wage policies. This proportion is taken to be determined outside the system. The consequences of different proportions are examined.

The authors assume that all tax payers prefer to pay bribes lower than their tax bill in return for not paying taxes. One of the central features of their model is the 'bargaining' variable which specifies how the gains from cheating on taxes are divided between the potential taxpayers and the tax collectors. There are a number of other such considerations which we will explain. The heart of the model brings together all the possible levels of the different factors assumed to affect behaviour and traces out how they work together. Tax collectors caught at cheating simply lose their jobs, and taxpayers simply pay up the full tax due. The more forward-looking is a tax collector with a good salary, the less likely he is to risk loosing a good job.

It is assumed that there is always some chance of getting caught by an inspector. The proportion of tax collectors that are inspected each period is not solved for optimally in the model. In principle, it would seem reasonable to determine jointly the wage of tax collectors and the number of inspectors.

However, this does lead to considerable complexity, even in this stylised formal model. So the authors opt for letting the frequency of inspection vary along with the other key variables in determining outcomes. The number of tax collectors is fixed in the model, and is determined by the size of the population, which also is assumed fixed. In every period, a certain proportion of the population has an income above the tax threshold, and owes tax at a fixed rate. Tax collectors are randomly paired with citizens who may or may not owe any tax.

The authors examine the implications of three different wage policies in the setting which they have specified. One policy is to pay a high enough wage so that no one has an incentive to cheat. The dishonest collectors still act honestly because they take account of the chance of being audited and the value of their job. The second strategy is to pay a wage which brings in the proportion of honest potential collectors in the labour pool, but gives an incentive to the dishonest collectors to cheat. The third strategy is to pay what they call the 'capitulation' wage that only brings in dishonest collectors, as honest collectors command a higher wage in the outside economy. In each period a certain proportion of the tax-collectors leave the government through natural wastage, and through being caught cheating.

This is a complicated area, even when we employ the Besley and McLaren model. With their limited number of factors, each specified as simply as possible, the results can be very different depending on exactly how the various considerations act together. We cannot do justice here to the precision and subtlety of the analysis. However, certain broad trends can be noted. First, it rarely makes sense to pay tax collectors enough so that even the dishonest among them have no incentive to take bribes rather than collect taxes for the government. In order for this high-wage policy to actually add to the government's net position — extra revenue collected minus extra wages paid — several conditions must all hold. Most citizens must be liable for tax, and there must be a pretty high proportion of corrupt tax collectors. In addition, there has to be a lot of monitoring of collectors, in itself a costly undertaking. For quite a range of variation of the levels of the factors involved here, the middle option of paying a wage which attracts both honest and dishonest collectors, but gives an incentive to the dishonest to cheat, gets squeezed out. Unfortunately, in the model at least, the best option may be to pay the lowest possible wage and only collect taxes through the monitoring of tax-collectors. However, here we might well ask, why have tax collectors at all? Why not simply rely on inspectors?

Presumably the answer depends partly on an assumption, not stated in the article, that the inspectors themselves act honestly when dealing with a tax-collector, but might not if dealing with a taxpayer. The other part of the answer would involve the impracticality in a less developed country of some reasonably effective self-assessment on the part of taxpayers. Otherwise, only a random sample of taxpayers would be approached, as by assumption we have many fewer inspectors than tax collectors. This may be less acceptable than everyone being approached by a dishonest collector, and some ultimately paying the full tax to the government when an inspector shows up.

This is an interesting, if somewhat discouraging model. One is left with an uneasy feeling that the assumption of inspectors who always act honestly is likely to effect the results in ways that would differ significantly from what happens in the world. There is also the assumption that honest tax collectors can be identified by the private sector where they earn a wage premium. Why cannot they also be identified by the government and paid a premium as tax collectors? One may anticipate further theoretical work along these and related lines.

Jens Andvig and Karl Moene suggest a more general model of corruption. (Andvig and Moene, '90) It could be applied to the issue of collecting tax, but is intended for any circumstance where a government official will give an illegal advantage to someone in return for a bribe. Unlike the Besley and McLaren theory above, Andvig and Moene assume that the willingness of members of the public to offer bribes depends on circumstances. They have a kind of supply and demand model, with the public demanding corruption, and some officials being willing to supply it. The supply also depends on circumstances. The variable which brings about an equilibrium in their model is not price, but the amount of corruption itself.

The main objective of the authors is to account for the wide divergence in the amount of corruption in different countries. The essence of the analysis is that on reasonable assumptions about the behaviour of government officials and of the public, we are very likely to see a great deal of corruption, or very little. The middle ground of a fair amount of corruption is an unstable equilibrium position. If small random movements cause the system to veer away from the middle towards either increasing corruption, or a bit less corruption, the dynamics of the system are inclined to reinforce this movement.

Both the public and the officials benefit more from engaging in illegal behaviour when there is a lot of it about. By the same token, corruption is less rewarding when there is less of it about. The returns to adopting a corrupt strategy go up when there is more corruption, and down when there is less. The reasons for this have to do with the costs associated with finding a corrupt partner, and the costs when getting caught. Members of the public will have lower search costs in finding a corrupt official when the proportion of them is high. And officials who are caught by another corrupt official will face smaller penalties then if caught by an honest official. So for them as well, the willingness to be corrupt rises when there is more of it around.

Turning away from taxes for a moment, it is often claimed that competition will in itself tend to eliminate corruption on the part of government officials, or forms of preying on firms such as protection rackets. Christopher Bliss and Rafael Tella raise a number of interesting examples, such as health inspectors collecting bribes rather than closing unsanitary restaurants. (Bliss and Tella, '97) These corrupt inspectors may also collect bribes from clean restaurants that may fear being closed on trumped up technicalities. The authors' basic argument is complex, and leads to a disturbing conclusion that competition will not necessarily get rid of corruption. They operate with three notions of what it means to have more competition. The first says that firms face each other more directly through, for example, lower transport costs. A second concept depends on firms being more similar to each other in terms of their costs. The third has to do with the extent to which costs of production have a large fixed, or overhead, component. The analysis rests on fairly advanced economics, and concludes that increases in these three possible aspects of competition will not necessarily reduce corruption.

The main reason why it is sometimes felt that competition will reduce corruption is that lack of competition creates above normal profits. This surplus provides a motive for anyone who can exert power over firms to do so, and cream off some, or all, of the surplus for themselves. A simple little tale that motivates this theoretical investigation is that of desperate poverty leading to some people selling matches on the street corners. With anyone able to enter this activity, there will be some eventual number of street sellers where it is just worth it for him or her to stay in this activity. This is competition. Now along come fierce men making threats and extracting some money from the unfortunate match-sellers. The arrival of these men makes the activity less attractive, and some match-sellers give it up. The remaining sellers do better in the sense of selling more matches, but wind up with only as much money as before, if the 'protection' men are skilful in setting the right level of rake-off. The rather hopeful presumption that competition will eliminate corruption is weakened by this analysis.

Is Risking Arrest Rational?

Jeffrey Grogger begins his insightful study of criminal activity by noting that one third of all young men in Philadelphia in the recent past were arrested before the age of eighteen. A similar proportion of men between the ages of eighteen and thirty in California were arrested for crimes carrying a jail sentence. (Grogger, '95) Apart from the fact that these are disturbing figures in themselves, the amount of crime and subsequent arrest poses a problem for economic analysis. Grogger goes on to quote figures showing that men arrested before 1980 earned less in subsequent years than those who were not arrested. The loss in income due to arrest on average amounted to about fifteen percent. It comes about as a combination of arrest making it harder to get a job, and leading to lower paid work when succeeding in getting a job. This is a substantial penalty for risking being arrested. It calls into question the assumption that people generally act in a forward-looking rational way, and will try to maximise their income.

There is one way of rescuing both the notions that people are optimising agents, and it pays to risk being arrested. It could be that the people who are arrested are different from those who are not arrested. Even if they were not arrested, they would not earn the same income on average as those who were not arrested. This possibility seems plausible enough, but Grogger brings exceptional ingenuity to bear in teasing the answer out of the available data.

United States law requires that all employers covered by unemployment insurance law, which is likely to represent well over 90 percent of all jobs, must report quarterly earnings of each of their employees to the relevant state unemployment insurance agency. In California this is the Employment Development Department (EDD), which normally retains data for five quarters. As it happened, the agency was subject to a court case, and this caused it to retain data from the first quarter of 1980 to the last quarter of 1986. Grogger used earnings figures from 1980 to 1984, and has a sample of people arrested in 1985 or later taken from the figures of the California Justice Department's Adult Criminal Justice Statistical System (ACJSS). These figures cover convictions and jails sentences, as well as arrests, and are broken down for the more serious felony offences, and the less serious misdemeanours.

Matching up individuals in the two sets of data, ACJSS and EDD, was no easy matter. It was done through a combination of Social Security numbers and last names. The match rate overall was something over 60 percent. The essence of the approach used by Grogger to finding out the effect of arrest on earnings was to ask what were the earnings of an individual before being arrested, and after the arrest. Instead of comparing the earnings of arrested men to those who never were arrested, we compare earnings before and after arrest for a group of men who we know from the data will be arrested. The statistical method used attempts to control for age and race, two factors that significantly influence earnings in any case.

Grogger looks at effects over time, and finds that the immediate effect of arrest is to reduce earnings by approximately four percent, instead of the fifteen percent differential found in less sophisticated studies. For six months to a year and a half, the effect is on the order of two to three percent.

After that the data suggest that there is no discernible effect of having been arrested. Rather than a lasting fifteen percent fall in earnings, the effect of an arrest seems to be more like a fifth of that at first, falling to zero in a year-and-a-half. The simple fact is that those arrested did not have the earning potential of those men who were not arrested.

Grogger finds that jail sentences similarly have small and only transient effects on earnings. Even though the chances of arrest are pretty great if one commits a crime — about one arrest for every six crimes, and about one in three felony arrests results in a jail sentence — the loss in earnings is not that great. This is powerful evidence that for those who do risk arrest, it is not a wildly irrational decision in terms of loss of earnings. Grogger speculates that lack of education may lower earnings potential and make crime an economically attractive option. This results in an apparent relation between committing crimes and low income, but the true causal factor for low incomes in this group of men might be lack of education and nothing to do with criminal behaviour. (p. 66)

An interesting extra thought on the role of education in the control of crime is provided by Marcellus Andrews. (Andrews, '93) His mathematical model of an entire economy can only be followed in detail by a trained economist. In spite of Its highly simplified assumptions regarding almost everything from what is produced and how, to the nature of the population in this 'thought experiment', one cannot avoid considerable complexity. No one likes difficulty for its own sake. The problem calls for considerable mathematical skill in order to keep track of what is going on. The essence of the model is that in order to be productive, workers must be educated. Everyone in this society is either working, in school, unemployed or in prison The uneducated form an 'under-class' who receive welfare but have little reason not to engage in crime. The society engages in the costly activity of apprehending criminals and putting them in jail.

The hypothetical world which Andrews is analysing is inherently dynamic. Decisions taken by society at one point in time have consequences in subsequent years. All the important magnitudes are subject to change. Investment in education today effects the size of the employable workforce in the future, and given the rate of population growth, it effects the size of the under-class. Controlling the threat of crime from the under-class requires investing in prisons as well as the police force and legal system needed to get the right people into prison. It turns out that for a plausible range of assumptions about the various relevant magnitudes, keeping the under-class from destroying the society sooner or later is impossible. Not enough law enforcement can be provided. It just gets too expensive.

The alternative is to invest more in education. This policy will not get rid of the under-class. Not everyone succeeds in getting adequately qualified.

But now the need for prisons is greatly reduced. The need to contain the wayward members of the now much smaller under-class is a burden the society can support, and this support can continue on a sustainable basis.

Deterring Homicide

Harold Brumm and Dale Cloninger emphasise the distinction in their work between the actual risk of serious punishment, and what people perceive to be the risk. (Brumm and Cloninger, '96) Economists often work with what is called the 'rational expectations' hypothesis. This notion comes in several forms, but centres on the theme that people have a correct theory of what is going on. Only the strongest defenders of the starkest version of rational expectations could reject the distinction between perceptions and reality out of hand when it comes to risking punishment for murder. The key problem for the researchers is determining what are the perceptions.

The authors work with a complex structure where the murder rate depends on perceptions of being punished and other things, and perceptions depend on the murder rate and other things. Of course, we cannot observe perceptions, but they are assumed in the study to depend on the execution rate, population density and population growth, and the number of police per violent offence, along with the murder rate. The murder rate is held to depend on the proportion of the population that is non-white, the proportion between the ages of 25 and 44, and the unemployment rate, along with the perceived risk of punishment. The key point is that perceptions are assumed to influence the murder rate, and the murder rate is assumed to have an influence on perceptions. With this theoretical formulation, it is possible to estimate perceptions.

The data used to estimate these simultaneous effects was collected from fifty-nine cities spread over thirty-two American states. The figures are for the year 1985, except for the execution rate which is a weighted average of execution rates for 1980 to 1984. Later years are weighted more heavily. This implies that more recent experience counts more heavily in influencing perceptions. The execution rates are for states. All data are city specific, except these rates which are assigned to each city according to its state.

Brumm and Cloninger are essentially interested in two theories: the deterrence hypothesis; and the effect of numbers of police, which is called the resource saturation hypothesis. Both receive support from the data. The greater the perception of punishment, as specified in the formulation, the fewer the number of homicides. In turn, the perceived risk of punishment is found to go down the higher the murder rate, and to go up the larger number of police per number of violent crimes in the city. A great deal of statistical conjecture goes into these tentative findings that execution rates and police numbers per violent crime do deter murders through their effects on perceptions. The authors repeatedly warn that these results should be treated with caution. That certainly is the case, but this is probably among the best evidence on the matter that we currently have. It would be wise to treat other arguments and evidence, and especially guesses and gut feelings, with at least equal caution.

Hiring Illegal Labour — An Experimental Investigation

The issue of illegal immigrants has been particularly high on the political agenda in the United States since 1980. While there are no accurate figures, it is clear that the number of such immigrants, particularly from Mexico, has been large and rapidly growing. This led to the passing of the Immigration Reform and Control Act in 1986. One aim of the legislation has been to reduce the incentive to come to the United States by making it harder to obtain work. This is done by making it a criminal offence to knowingly hire an illegal immigrant. It is recognised that it is easy to obtain false documentation, and an employer might be found guilty if an illegal immigrant was hired who possessed counterfeit papers. So far so good, but the situation gets much trickier. In the 1990 Immigration Act it is made an offence to discriminate in hiring. Refusing to hire a worker possessing an apparently genuine identification card may be taken to be evidence of discrimination.

Jose Pagan has studied the delicate situation in which employers might find themselves given the two pieces of legislation. (Pagan, '98) The worker knows whether he or she is legal or not, but the employer can often be uncertain. Pagan is in favour of a counterfeit-proof national identity card. As part of his investigation, he designed and administered an experiment intended to shed light on how employers might behave in the outside world.

In the natural sciences there are experiments where the sample of material under investigation is highly likely to be perfectly representative of what that material is like wherever it exists, provided it is not in a black hole or in some other grossly disturbing circumstance. The experimental procedure has the effects of excluding irrelevant complication and allowing more precise observation. There are other types of experiments in natural science which work on the principle of analogy, which may or may not be revealing of how the world works outside of the experimental situation. One such experiment consisted of passing electric charges through a gaseous compound thought to be like the atmosphere of the earth before life existed. The goal was to see if the resulting molecules bore some resemblance to the building blocks of life. Another example consisted of passing charged particles over a sphere to see if their behaviour produced results similar to the aurora borealis. Yet other examples of this latter kind of experiment can be found in using an artificial body of water to test some theories about the behaviour of oceans.

Social science experiments are clearly of the latter kind. The test material is rarely representative of the wider world. More than that, the circumstances are only vaguely analogous. There is nothing much to say generally about this kind of activity. One can neither embrace it unconditionally nor dismiss it out-of-hand. It all depends on the particular examples. As more experiments are performed, a culture of preferred test-procedures is evolving. The present paper provides us with an example.

Pagan worked with thirty undergraduate economics majors drawn from two universities. The students were divided into six groups of five each. They were paid five dollars to participate, and the winner in each group received twenty dollars. Two distinct experiments were run, each with twenty-five trials. A trial consisted of the experimenter writing a number from 50 to 100 on a board. For Pagan, this number represented potential employees, and the students were taking the role of firms who are hiring these employees. This was not explained to the students, who simply competed in a game of acquiring the maximum number of points.

Once a figure was announced by being put on the board, the students could choose to acquire up to this total in the form of red tokens or blue tokens, or a mixture. Red tokens counted as three points, and blue tokens as one point. The red tokens were seen by the experimenter to represent illegal workers who are more profitable to the firm, if undetected, because they received a lower wage. The chances of being caught holding red tokens varied in different rounds. This was explained to the participants in the experiment. In one third of the rounds there was a ten-percent chance of being checked for possessing red tokens; in one-third there was a fifty-percent chance; and in one-third a ninety-percent chance of being checked for holding red tokens. If detected, the student player lost all the red tokens in that round, and was charged an additional one point for each red token held.

There were two types of session run. The one described above was called 'blue-token-certainty'. The second type involved blue-token-uncertainty. In these sessions, in addition to the red token penalties, a student selected for a check faced an additional round of potential penalty in the form of a fifty- percent chance of loosing half of his or her blue tokens. The blue token loss, when imposed, was not subject to an additional fine on blue token holdings, as was the case with red token holdings.

The results showed that the greater the risk of being inspected, the less likely the students were to hold red tokens. This result was common to both kinds of trials, but significantly stronger when there was blue token certainty. By analogy, Pagan argues that we have here some evidence that firms will be less inclined to hire illegal immigrants when it is clear to them who is legal and who is illegal. (p. 96) He uses this to support his advocacy of a national identification card. He may have a point. But I would be inclined to agree with those who would expect that an ID card would reduce the amount of hiring of illegal immigrants, without running the experiment. I would not have any idea by how much illegal hiring would fall, and the experiment would not help me with that. Nor would I know how to balance this gain against the administrative cost, and possible loss of civil liberties, due to a mandatory ID.

Gun Control

The American Economic Association published a series of papers dealing with the politically charged issue of gun ownership and the consequences of different regulations in the market for guns. Edward Glaeser and Spencer Glendon start from the position that people are more likely to own guns when it is in their interests to do so. (Glaeser and Glendon, '98) Their data comes from the General Social Survey over the years 1973 to 1994. In each year approximately 1,500 people were asked a number questions related to pistols and rifles. This resulted in over 20,000 observations. The authors used straightforward statistical techniques to produce a broad picture of handgun and other gun ownership. While they are not really able to answer the question as to whether gun ownership, or non-ownership, is on the whole rational in some sense, they do produce an interesting statistical picture.

Not surprisingly, the authors find that hunters own guns, but not pistols, and that people living in large cities are less likely to own guns. Blacks are less likely to own guns but slightly more likely to own pistols. Marriage increases gun ownership, though young babies reduce it. Older children are associated with more gun ownership. Women are less likely to own guns, and people over forty, and those living in the South of the United States are more inclined towards gun ownership.

Glaeser and Spencer find that higher income leads to more gun-ownership. They offer three possible explanations. One is that guns are expensive, and people with higher incomes have more to protect. Rather ominously, they suggest that higher incomes enable the users of guns to avoid "adverse consequences" of gun use. Neither fear of crime nor having been arrested seems to be associated with gun ownership. But lack of trust in publicly provided justice and fewer police in the area do seem to be factors in gun ownership. Another strong positive factor seems to be the social impact of living in a community that favours guns. The authors suggest that this may be due to fewer adverse consequences when owning guns is the norm. Finally, they argue that gun ownership is more common when there is a culture of retribution. They deduce this from finding a positive association between owning guns and answering 'yes' to the question, "Would you approve of hitting someone who hit your child?" (p. 461)

In contrast to the empirical study of Glaeser and Spencer, John Donohue III and Steven Levitt constructed a model in the tradition of 'game theory' in an attempt to explain the doubling of the juvenile homicide rate over the period 1985 to 1995. (Donohue III and Levitt, '98) This was a period when there was a slight decline in the homicide rate for adults. In the framework of their model they have a very interesting point to make. They note that over the decade street gangs were much more involved in distributing drugs, a profitable activity. There was also much more carrying of guns by juveniles. The authors are sceptical of the view that fighting is always going on, but with guns there are more lethal encounters. On the contrary, if there is a high cost to fighting, we might expect less of it.

Game theory is a mathematical tool for the analysis of strategic interaction between participants. It can be used for the analysis of games, but is used by social scientists to analyse both co-operative and competitive interaction. The key elements in any game are: who are the players; what strategic actions can they take; and what are the consequences, called 'pay-offs', of what they do. The current example is fairly typical, with two players in a competitive situation. Each has to decide whether or not to fight, without knowing the decision their opponent will take.

The authors construct a model with perfect rationality, and explain that it probably does not say much about such tragedies as domestic shootings and suicides. In their analysis willingness to fight is necessary for gaining a reward, and loosing entails a cost. Not being willing to fight has zero consequences. A key factor in the model is the ability of the participants to predict the outcome of a fight. When there are no guns, physical appearance may give a pretty accurate prediction of the outcome of a fight. Guns make the outcome very unpredictable.

It is precisely this unpredictability which leads to more cases where both parties opt for a fight. In the model each 'player' has a component of his level of ability which is known to himself and to the other player. He also has a component that is not known to either player. The cost of violence is low if the means of fighting are either hardly lethal at all, or extremely lethal. But when the outcome is least predictable, and the means of fighting are quite lethal, the cost of violence is high. With predictability, the cost of violence is low, however lethal. The model makes a convincing case for predictability as a potentially important factor in the debate about guns.

In America a number of states have adopted laws which allow citizens to carry concealed handguns. These so-called 'shall issue' laws have been the subject of much controversy. Those who place more emphasis on the 'facilitating' effect of these laws anticipate an increase in the amount of crime because it is easier for criminals to obtain weapons. Supporters of the laws expect a greater relative impact from the 'deterrence' effect. They believe that potential criminals will be less likely to engage in crime knowing that the victims may be armed. A famous article by John Lott and David Mustard (Lott and Mustard, '97) found that there was a significant drop in both violent crimes and crimes against property as a result of shall-issue laws.

These results have been held to be misleading by two economists, Hashem Dezhbakhsh and Paul Rubin. (Dezhbakhsh and Rubin, '98) They object to both the statistical method of Lott and Mustard and to the breakdown of data used by them. The difference of conclusion is entirely dependent on the approaches taken, as both pairs of researchers used the Lott and Mustard data which covers murder, rape, aggravated assault and robbery, as well as auto-theft, burglary and larceny, for over three thousand counties for the decade 1982 to 1992.

The fundamental difference between L & M and D & R is that the former assumes that the same statistical relation between crime and its causes can describe all counties. D & R use a method which allows for different statistical relations between crime and its causes in the counties with shall issue laws compared to those counties which did not pass these laws. This apparently rather innocent difference in approach throws up a very different conclusion. In contrast to L & M, D & R find much smaller effects, and in various directions. While there may be a very small reduction in the number of murders, there seems to be a general tendency for the number of robberies to go up by large amount. Other crimes respond differently according to the state in which the county is located.

An additional benefit of the research done by D & R is some explanation of the difference in outcomes. Counties which spend more on policing tend to be those where shall issue laws reduce crime. The authors reason that the deterrent effect is not influenced but the facilitating effect is reduced by having more policing. A worrying finding is that counties with more arrests, and therefore perhaps more criminals, are counties where the shall issue laws tend to increase the amount of crime. They also find that young white women, and the elderly, are less frequent victims of crime when shall issue laws are passed, and that there is little evidence that these laws facilitate gun owning by young males. These latter findings go more in the L & M direction, but to a more modest degree.

One wonders if efforts to reduce crime can have the unintended effect of moving it elsewhere rather than actually bringing it more under control. If economists are right that there is a large element of rational calculation in the commission of crime, we might expect crime to move to places where it is more beneficial to the criminal. It would seem that these possible spillover effects have not been studied very much, if at all. Stephen Bronars and John Lott took this on, again in the context of the shall issue laws. (Bronars and Lott, '98) The data is the same as in the other studies. The main difference of method is to allow the laws in an adjacent county, defined as one with a geographic centre within fifty miles of the geographic centre of the home county, to have an effect on crime in their home-county.

The results of this study are striking. With the exception of assault, allowing people in a neighbouring county to carry a concealed handgun raises the volume of some crimes in the adjacent counties by significant amounts. Bronars and Lott report a seven-and-a-half percent increase in rape, over four percent in robbery, and four-and-a-half percent increase in murder. It would appear from the data that the shall issue laws move crime away more than does increasing the number of arrests. Including spillover effects tends to show larger effects of allowing concealed handguns than have been found in previous studies.

Not unreasonably, the authors conclude that if all states were to adopt these laws, there would be a large drop in crime. However, one might wonder a bit when the biggest spillover effect seems to be on rape. There may be other perceptions and attitudes which cause one state to pass a shall issue law and another not to do so, and these could be changing and having a big effect. I just find it hard to picture going to another county to commit a rape because that county does not allow concealed handguns. But the statistical evidence is more important. Clearly these empirical results are very sensitive to specification, as we saw from the study by Dezhbakhsh and Rubin. Gut feelings are no more than that. There is pressing need for further statistical investigation.

SOCIAL PSYCHOLOGY

The social reality which we observe comes about because of the actions taken by the individuals who make up society. These actions, in turn, depend on the perceptions and opinions held by individuals. Where the other social sciences tend to concentrate on the consequences of individual actions, social psychology directs attention to the thought processes that result in actions. The subject has three main concerns. First we want to know what is going on in people's minds. Second, we want to explain how people come to hold the views they hold. And finally, we want to study the links between mind-sets and actions. These concerns bear very powerfully on the study of crime. Along with sociology, social psychologists devote proportionately much more of their research to this topic than do the other social sciences.

As we shall see below, within the topic of crime there are interesting concentrations of effort in social psychology. More attention is devoted to rape than to any other crime, with seven major articles in the journals in the nineties. The other social sciences have a passing interest in rape in so far as it falls under the general category of violent crime. These other subjects tend to pick out murder for special consideration rather than rape. But for social psychology, rape holds particular fascination. The other favourite topic is the behaviour of juries, with six major pieces in the literature over our period. These two topics share the characteristic of being difficult to observe. Information about what went on in an alleged rape, or in a jury room, has to be inferred from indirect evidence, as both activities are normally only observed by the participants. Some of the studies discussed below could be assigned to either the 'jury' topic or the 'rape' topic, or to both. I have divided them between topics on judgements as to whether the main interest in the research was jury behaviour as such, or generally held views about rape.

Rape and juries are not the only activities we usually cannot observe. The content of people's minds, and the processes that lead to opinion formation, cannot be observed directly. This is one of the factors which makes social psychology more reliant on experiment than the other social sciences. Fortunately it is also the case that the questions that social psychologists want to answer can often be studied quite naturally in an experimental way. Two similar groups are exposed to different stimuli and then can be tested for differences in opinion. To perform these tests, researchers typically draw on the great stock of off-the-shelf questionnaires at their command, rather than by making up new questions. This practice has the great advantage that a good deal is known about how the tests function in many different settings. A made-up questionnaire may be more specifically tuned to the problem at hand, but has the disadvantage of not having been tested over and over in a variety of circumstances. The other feature of social psychology, shared by economics and sociology, is fairly sophisticated statistical analysis in a number of studies. Inferring causes of differences in outcome between two or more groups requires advanced statistical techniques.

How Do Juries Decide?

Juries in criminal trials, as we all know, are instructed to return a not-guilty verdict if there is a reasonable doubt that the defendant did not commit the crime. This is very different from of deciding on balance whether the defendant it is more likely to be innocent or to be guilty. It is a bit of a mystery as to what it actually means to say that there is no reasonable doubt. Estimates made by judges tend to find that jurors typically take it to mean that there is around a 90% likelihood that the accused is guilty. (McCauliff, '82) Saul Kassin and David Garfield have studied the effect on standards of proof of showing jurors a graphic video of the victim of a horrific crime. (Kassin and Garfield, '91) Among their numerous and important findings, they report that seeing the video resulted in an average of 77% likelihood as the required standard of proof. Subjects in their experiment who saw the same disturbing video, but not relevant to their particular crime, or were shown no video at all, settled on standards of proof of 93%, which were in line with many other studies showing around 90% as the average standard. But for the group who were told they were seeing the actual pictures of the victim in the crime they were hearing, seeing the video significantly changed the meaning of 'reasonable doubt'.

Any judge's decision about allowing the controversial practice of showing "blood and guts" videos to jurors involves balancing the effect in terms of evidence of guilt against the arousal of prejudice or other inappropriate emotions. In an effort to gain an insight into the effects of graphic material on jurors, Kassin and Garfield held mock trials, complete with transcripts and a mock courtroom. Three groups of sixteen subjects, with eight men and eight women in each, were presented with the same trial information running to 49 pages. Two groups were shown an actual colour video taken at a crime scene in New York City of a murder victim with stab wounds. One group was told it was the victim in the crime in which they were participating. One group was told it was from an unrelated murder, and the third group was not shown a video. In addition, all participants were tested using the Juror Bias Scale. (Kassin and Wrightsman, '83) This seventeen-question test aims to measure a person's leanings, or bias prior to any knowledge of a case, in terms of deciding how likely it is that the defendant committed the crime, and what standard of proof should be applied.

A typical item in the test aimed at probability-of-commission is an agree/disagree scaling on "any suspect who runs from the police probably committed the crime". And a typical item aimed at views on reasonable doubt is "too often jurors hesitate to convict someone who is guilty out of pure sympathy". (p. 1461) Depending on how their scores compared to the mean, all of the subjects were classified as either prosecution-biased or defence-biased.

Generally speaking, seeing a horrible video, but one that was not relevant to the trial, had no effect in this experiment. The results were much like not seeing a video at all. But seeing a video of what was thought to be of the victim had interesting effects. Prosecution-biased subjects thought it was more likely that the accused did the crime, and defence-biased subjects thought it was less likely that the accused did the crime. These two effects of the video more-or-less cancelled out, with no net effect of seeing the video. This was not the case when it came to standards of proof. Here there was no effect on defence-biased subjects, but a marked lowering of the standard of proof for the prosecution-biased subjects. This does suggest that seeing a video could tip the balance in favour of conviction in some cases.

Kassin and Garfield report a closely related study of level of damages awarded which found that colour photographs influenced jurors, but not black-and-white photographs. (Whalen and Blanchard, '82) The graphic nature of the depiction does seem to matter and is a result consistent with the current finding. One result of the current paper, somewhat at odds with the literature, is that seeing the video tended to lower the subjects' estimate of the amount of murder going on, but to raise their estimate of the likely increase in future amounts of murder. This is comparing the thirty-two subjects who saw the video with the sixteen who did not. Seeing what a murder actually looked like made the participants feel this must be a very rare event, but at the same time frightened them into thinking there might be more of these crimes committed in the future. These are suggestive results. It should be remembered that they were derived from a fairly small sample.

David Shaffer and Jeffrey Kerwin conducted a study of how 'dogmatism', in contrast to pro-defence or pro-prosecution bias, affects decisions of juries. (Shaffer and Kerwin, '92) Their results support the conjecture that more dogmatic individuals are more likely to follow the instructions of judges. 240 introductory psychology students were divided into 40 six-person 'juries'. The reward for taking part was a course credit, which would seem to be much more of an inducement than the $3.00 payment in the previous study. An average dogmatism rating was given to each jury. Each participant was told they were answering a "Social Values" questionnaire, but in fact were given the dogmatism test designed by Troldahl and Powell and published in 1965. Every jury was classified as dogmatic or non-dogmatic according to its composition of high and low scoring individuals, such as to have an equal number of each type of jury.

The juries were told about a drug arrest in which the police set up a 'sting'. The accused was definitely guilty of providing a small amount of heroin, but two different scenarios were given to different groups. In one there were strong extenuating circumstances, due to the conduct of the police, which favoured the plea of entrapment, and in the other scenario there was less in the way of extenuating circumstances. This experimental set-up resulted in ten juries in each of four cells. The cells were dogmatic/extenuating, non-dogmatic/extenuating, and so on. The law of entrapment was explained to all the participants, as would be done by a judge, with the conclusion that if the police acted improperly, they would have to find the defendant not guilty.

Each juror had to give a verdict on a nine point scale from 1 = definitely acquit, with 5, = uncertain, and 9 = definitely convict. There is an interesting kind of tension here because dogmatic individuals are more likely to find the accused guilty, but are also more likely to follow the instructions of the judge. The researchers hypothesised that the more dogmatic juries would be more inclined to follow the instructions of the judge and therefore take more account of the entrapment argument. The data bares this out, with a mean score of 4.88 on the nine point scale for the dogmatic juries when there was less extenuating circumstances, compared to 6.36, which is a much greater tendency to convict, on the part of the non-dogmatic juries. When extenuating circumstances were stronger, average conviction scores fell a little to 4.22 for the dogmatic juries, and quite a bit to 5.00 for the non-dogmatic juries. These results suggest that more dogmatic individuals may be more likely to support the rules, as laid down by the judge, than to go by their generally believed tendency to act on moral imperatives.

A large literature, with many interconnected theories and statistical tests, can be found in social psychology on the extent to which jurors obey the instructions and rules laid down by courts. Richard Wiener and his colleagues report on much of this material, and conduct a complex statistical test of their own. (Wiener and colleagues, '91) They take as their hypothetical example a rape case in which the students and other subjects standing in for jurors were given repeated instructions and tested for their decisions and the reasons as the case went on. The results do suggest that participants who were drawn from the local community of the university, but were not students, were inclined to depart from the rules of the court in many cases. Their own sentiments influenced them far more than they did for the student subjects. The authors attribute this to the academic environment where students are accustomed to following instructions. There may be something in this.

However, the average age of the students was little over nineteen, and the average age of the residents was nearly twice that of the students. Also, only half of the residents had been to university. That there is tension between the rules of the courts, and what jurors see as justice, particularly in a rape case, is well established. The extent to which jurors will bend the rules, and why, are less well known.

A number of studies over the years have addressed questions such as how the ethnic and gender composition of both juries and the accused effects the way juries come to decisions. Some of this work is summarised in a paper by Harmon Hosch and his colleagues. (Hosch and colleagues, '91) The outcome sometimes hinges significantly on nature of the crime. Hosh and his fellow researchers were particularly interested in detecting differences between a more 'collectivist' culture as represented by Mexican-American university students compared to the more 'individualistic' culture of the Anglo- American students.

A large number of students took part in a two part study, the essence of which in the first part was that a mother knew her son was subject to physical abuse from the father and did not take the required steps to protect him. In the second part students read a similar case about a daughter who was sexually abused by her father, and again the mother failed to take steps to protect her. In both cases the father was convicted and in prison, but a statutory responsibility of the mother was the subject of a trial.

To the credit of the researchers, they are straightforward in reporting that, in both parts of the experiment, they failed to find any effect of the two cultures, as represented by the two ethnic groups, on the matter of guilt. They did find a gender difference, similar to those of other studies, in that women were more inclined to find the defendant guilty. This is tentatively explained by women having more regard for the welfare of children. The cultural difference did emerge when it came to sentencing, with the Mexican-Americans imposing harsher penalties when they found the accused to be guilty. The authors suggest this is due to stronger family, community and traditional values in the students from a Mexican background than an Anglo background. However, this may not be the exactly the same as the individual/collective divide. They also reported twice as long recommended sentences for sexual abuse than for physical abuse. The authors appear to be unsure as to whether this is because the one abuse is more important than the other, or whether the abuse of females is a more serious crime. They conclude by suggesting that this could be the subject of further investigation.

The penultimate article to report in this section straddles the line between the study of attitudes towards rape and study of the behaviour of juries even more than one or two articles discussed above. Chris Kleinke and his colleagues attempted to determine how expressions of intent to commit rape, or the opposite, and expressions of remorse, or lack of such expressions, effect potential jurors and others. (Kleinke and colleagues, '92) They were concerned with a wide range of judgements such as the seriousness of the crime, potential for rehabilitation, and recommended prison sentences. Subtle distinctions are drawn in the paper between blame and responsibility. In one experiment the subjects viewed one of four videos performed by two actors playing the 'rapist' and the 'interviewer'. The rapist either said he intended the act from an early stage, or alternatively got carried away. And he either felt sorry for the victim, or simply, "...did what I had to do." (p.530) The two alternatives were combined to make the four possible combinations. The second experiment involved reading about the rapist's replies rather than seeing a video, and different questions were addressed.

The psychology and sociology students taking part in this study were asked to evaluate the rapist using the Personal Attribute Inventory. (Parish and colleagues, '67) This device has one hundred adjectives, fifty positive in nature and fifty negative. Respondents are asked to select thirty adjectives which best describe the subject, and the score is made up of the number of negative adjectives chosen. As in the sociology study discussed in the previous section, remorse definitely has an influence, as does intent. The former leads to recommending shorter sentences, and the latter to longer ones. Interestingly, there were no gender effects when the video was used, but there were, with the usual finding of men being more lenient, with the written form of reporting. The authors suggest that seeing the video had two effects. It left less room for doubt through hearing the rapist describe his crime, so the men had less room to excuse him. At the same time, the video made the rapist more of a real person, softening the views of the women.

The last study in this section is truly fascinating. While it says a great deal regarding the practice of allowing hypnotically elicited evidence in court, it has much wider implications regarding general gullibility. It is relatively easy to test the reliability of hypnotic recall by observing subjects at a point in time, and sometime later sending them back to that time under hypnosis and seeing what they report. This has been done on many occasions, and the results show clearly that reports given under hypnosis are unreliable, often highly fanciful, and readily influenced by the hypnotist. The present study is not of that kind. Rather, Graham Wagstaff and his colleagues asked ninety British undergraduates to express their views on the reliability of a witness. (Wagstaff and colleagues, '92)

All the students heard the same seven-minute recording of an elderly female witness who woke up in the night and by chance saw a man leaving a building across the street and getting into a car. She is able to provide telling detail and to identify the burglar in the courtroom. The students were divided into three groups of thirty each. The first group was told that the woman was initially unable to provide any information, but having been sent back to the night in question under hypnosis, her memory came to life and that is what she is reporting on the tape. The second group was also told that initially the woman could not remember anything, but a psychologist employed a 'guided memory' technique, and was eventually able to help her to provide this testimony. The third group was told nothing.

Each group was asked to give a judgement on the basis of what the witness said as to whether the man she picked out in the court was guilty or not guilty. The results are worrying. For the group who thought this was evidence brought to life through hypnosis, 19 found the defendant guilty and 11 not guilty. Those who were told this was guided memory evidence voted 13 guilty and 17 not guilty. And finally, those told nothing voted 10 guilty and 20 not guilty. Due to the relatively small number of students in the experiment, the Chi-square test, which is standard statistical procedure in these circumstances, concluded that there was a significant difference between the hypnosis group result and the no-memory aid result. The difference between the guided-memory result and either of the other results could quite easily have come about by chance. However, the main result of danger in the courtroom from the false belief in hypnotism is very persuasive. The authors note that studies in the United States and Australia attest to the widespread belief in the accuracy of hypnotism, though this has not been studied in those countries, as it has in this experiment, in the context of evaluating evidence supplied by a witness.

Rape

The social psychological literature on rape is mainly concerned to find out what factors influence decisions as to whether or not a rape has taken place, and judgements about the seriousness of the offence. Depending on the situation in which the allegation was made, there may be more or less grounds for the alleged rapist to assume that the sex was consensual. Such factors as the amount of force involved, or threat of force, and the relationship between the two parties, including knowing each other, if that is the case, and class and racial differences, seem to influence popular perceptions of this crime. Some studies also examine the so-called 'rape myth', or the theory that the threat of rape is endemic in society and a part of the means of subjugating women.

A typical example of the first kind of study involved adjusting a tale of possible rape so that roughly half of the subjects taking part in the final version found the accused guilty of rape. Seventy-one students from a "Midwestern American university" took part in the experiment. (Hymes and colleagues, '93) They came from an initial group of ninety-six students, some of which were used to adjust the tale, and some were dropped for technical reasons. Robert Hymes and his colleagues asked the students to read some 'testimony' which the authors describe as follows.

> "The victim met the defendant in a college bar and went out to his car with him to smoke a marijuana cigarette. The victim testified that after she and the defendant had smoked the cigarette, the defendant raped her. The testimony of a police officer and a

doctor indicated that there was evidence of sexual activity and that there were bruises on the victim's arms and legs. the defendant claimed that after he and the alleged victim had smoked the cigarette, they engaged in passionate kissing and caressing. The defendant claimed that the alleged victim seemed to enjoy his attention and made no attempt to stop him from removing her clothing. The defendant stated that he was under the assumption the alleged victim had consented to engage in sexual activity." (p. 630)

The students were divided into four groups, one of which was told that both parties were White and another was told they both were Black. The other two groups were told they were of mixed races, with the victim being White in one version and Black in another. They were asked whether they thought a rape had taken place, and how sure they were on a scale of one to ten, with ten being complete confidence. Subjects who found the accused guilty were asked to recommend a prison sentence from zero to one hundred years.

The results are of considerable interest. Before reading on, it might be wise to take a guess, and then compare your guess for male and female students to the data. As it happens, the students were more likely to find the defendant guilty in the mixed races cases, and it did not matter which way around. And there was no significant difference between male and female students. For male students taking part there was no difference in sentencing according to the racial pattern, but the female students recommended longer sentences for the same-race cases than the mixed race cases.

This study by Hymes and his colleagues suggests that racial bias can be influenced by the nature of the crime, and who is the victim. In this case there was no general tendency to find the Black defendants more likely to be guilty, but mixed race defendants definitely were more likely to be found guilty. The authors tentatively explain the longer recommended sentences from women when the story was one of same race by suggesting that crimes against one's own group are regarded as more serious. It is interesting that the group is here thought of purely along racial lines, rather than as a student group, or a marijuana-smoking group.

Christiane Brems and Patricia Wagner worked with 220 college students in a study designed to distinguish between attitudes toward violent rape and violent theft. (Brems and Wagner, '94) All of their subjects were tested using two scales. The Attitudes Toward Women Scale (Spence and colleagues, '73) was used to determine whether students held 'traditional' or 'profeminist' views. They were also tested as to whether they saw the world as essentially fair or unfair using the Just-World Scale. (Rubin and Peplau, '75)

In two different experiments, the subjects were asked to read particularly graphic and horrifying descriptions of violent attacks in a lift in the one case, and on the street late at night in the other. Both stories were varied to describe vaginal and oral rape in the one case, and no rape but theft of jewellery and all other valuables in the other. The main goal of the research was to explain differences in the views people hold as to degrees of responsibility for what happened, and how blame should be attributed. The authors felt that type of crime would matter, along with attitudes towards women and views of the world as essentially just or unjust. In the event, none of this was borne out by the first experiment. The problem in the view of the authors was that this first story had no ambiguity. The woman was perfectly entitled to be in the lift, and there was nothing in her behaviour to prompt either a rape or theft.

In the judgement of the researchers, and apparently of the student subjects as well, a woman walking home alone at night in a "sexy, strapless black evening dress" (p. 368) is more ambiguous. Unlike some other studies, neither just-world beliefs nor the gender of the respondents seemed to matter here. But attitudes toward women, and whether the crime was rape or theft, did seem to matter. First, we look at the two crimes, ignoring the kind of respondent. In the case of theft, the woman was judged to carry more of the responsibility and the attacker less of the blame, compared to the rape story. But attitudes towards women, on the other hand, had an effect regardless of whether the crime was theft or rape. The profeminist respondents, compared to those with more traditional attitudes towards women, were inclined to attribute less responsibility for rape or for theft to the victim, and place more blame in both cases on the attacker.

Nyla Branscombe and her colleagues conducted an experiment in which a hundred student subjects were asked to read about an alleged rape and make judgements. (Branscombe and colleagues, '96) As part of the experiment the students were invited to construct new stories in which either the man or the woman acted differently, and in which either sexual intercourse still took place, or did not take place. Here is the researchers' initial story.

> "The incident began with Jeff walking Mary home. Because of the late hour and the long distance that Jeff would have to travel, Mary invited him to stay overnight on her sofa. They enjoyed mutual kissing and touching, but when intimacy progressed more rapidly than she would like, she became uncomfortable. Eventually, Mary stated that she was only willing to continue if he had and would use

> a condom. They continued kissing with Jeff stating that 'I don't have one but we won't go that far.' After a few minutes, Jeff ignored her request to stop and forced intercourse occurred, with Mary yelling and hitting him. (p. 1046)

The subjects invented other tales such as Mary not inviting Jeff, or Jeff refusing the invitation. Obviously these changes meant there was no rape. Other changes might or might not result in a rape occurring in spite of the change. Having produced these counterfactual stories, the subjects were asked to assign blame to Mary and to Jeff on a scale from 0% to 100% on the original story. The results showed that Mary received more of the blame when the counterfactual construction resulted in a different outcome as a result of action that she took. And she got less of the blame when different actions on the part of Jeff changed the outcome. But where Mary changed her action and still a rape occurred the amount of blame assigned to her was at its lowest. The authors use these results to argue that lawyers can influence juries by focusing on possible different behaviour on the part of either the assailant or the victim, and by postulating different outcomes.

Branscombe and her fellow researchers were rightly worried that the counterfactual the students chose to imagine might well be related to their judgements about relative blame. They conducted a second experiment involving a larger number of students. This time the tale involved initially mutually agreed kissing and undressing in a car in a parking lot, rather like the tale used by Hymes and his colleagues above. At some point the passion ceased to be mutually acceptable, and a possible rape occurred. This time the student subjects were shown one of four versions of a video performed by an actor, but which they were told was of the argument of a lawyer.

The actor either emphasised different possible actions on the part of the man, or on the part of the woman, and either imaged a case in which rape still occurred, or did not occur. Interestingly, this resulted in much the same outcome as the first experiment. More blame was attributed when the hypothetical action resulted in no rape. If the lawyer directed attention to the victim, and what she might have done, this appeared to have the effect of making her more to blame. In contrast to the first experiment, there was more blame in general for the assailant in the parking lot compared to Mary's flat.

A third experiment was conducted in which the tale was about two women driving poorly, resulting in a serious accident. Again, the device was used of showing one of four versions of an actor believed to be a lawyer argui9ng in court to separate groups of students. And as in the rape cases, directing attention to possible alternative driving on the part of one driver or the other, and telling a counterfactual in which the accident was avoided, or not avoided, had the expected influence on assigning blame. Here neither party desired the outcome, and the two parties to the accident were so similar that the subjects could not possibly have had general biases about who was to blame. Coming back to rape, the authors conclude by referring to much earlier work which recognised that showing that the victim could have taken action which could have changed the outcome makes it much harder to convict the defendant. They maintain that their study adds to this by showing the significance of the tactic of focusing attention on one party or the other, and on possible outcomes, in the effective use of counterfactuals.

As these studies show, special problems arise in determining what happened when the attacker and the victim in a rape know each other. The issue of consent comes more to the fore, and there is more ambiguity surrounding responsibility and appropriate amount of blame. I might just lay my own cards on the table and say that in my view, which I take to be the generally accepted civilised view, either party has the right to call a halt to sexual activity at any time, including during the course of what started out as consensual intercourse. Few people would hold that violating this principle during intercourse with an acquaintance, or closer companion, is the same thing as brutally attacking a stranger in a park. Suresh Kanekar and her colleagues at the University of Bombay undertook a number of studies of the perceptions people hold regarding alleged rape of an acquaintance. (Kanekar and colleagues, '91 and '93)

All the experiments done by Kanekar and her researchers involved having sizeable numbers of university students read short descriptions of an alleged rape. For different groups the tale is varied in several different ways. One change has to do with the victim, who might be divorced or married, or a schoolteacher or a call girl, for example. Other dimensions of change include evidence of physical resistance or not, and lodging a complaint with the police, or not. Along with these variations, the researchers test for differences of response according to whether the man was a stranger, acquaintance, friend, fiancé or husband. Typical information that the student subjects were asked to read is as follows.

> "A young woman who works as a stenotypist in an office in south Bombay was raped by a man a few days ago. The rapist is the manager of the office in which the victim works and the two, naturally, were acquainted before the incident. The victim has lodged a complaint with the police." (p. 1530, '91)

Different groups of students received versions where 'manager' was replaced with 'watchman', for example, along with 'the two were not acquainted'. In other versions the last phrase is replaced with 'has not lodged a complaint'.

In these two studies which focus on the issue of acquaintance rape, the respondents were asked to make a number of judgements. These included assigning fault to the victim on a scale of –10 = not at all her fault, up to + 10 = totally her fault. The same scale is used for assessing the likelihood that a rape took place, with – 10 = not at all likely. In addition they were asked to recommend years in prison over the range 0 to 45 years.

We can see that a very large number of combinations of circumstances can be generated by considering different victims, different assailants, complaint or no complaint, and so on. The main statistical objective, employing a technique known as an analysis of variance, is to determine how combinations of factors interact with each other, to influence judgements as to whom should be believed and how serious the crime was. Kanekar and her colleagues attribute part of the motivation for these studies to an incident in 1984 when two policemen raped a woman in a police station. Their sentences were later reduced by the Supreme Court partly on the grounds that the woman "was of questionable character and easy virtue". This judgement produced a strong reaction, particularly among feminists in India. The issue of rape has been central to the relations between men and women in all countries, and has been the subject of scientific investigation in many. The authors review this extensive literature with thorough discussion of the theories researchers have advanced.

Kanaker and her fellow investigators used large groups of student subjects — often in the hundreds — to discover the prevailing attitudes. In most cases their findings are consistent with earlier work, and because of the quality of the work, increase the reliability of the results rather than breaking entirely new ground. We find that women are inclined to see less fault for the victim than men and to recommend longer prison sentences. They are more confident that in fact a rape took place. All subjects tend to agree that there is less fault for the victim in rape by a stranger, and when a complaint is lodged. Naturally, physical injury adds to the recommended prison sentence. Female subjects opted for longer prison sentences in the not acquainted case, but did not differ from men otherwise. All subjects were more inclined to attribute greater fault to a call girl than to a schoolteacher. In this respect the Supreme Court of India could be seen as reflecting general opinion rather than progressive opinion.

Perhaps not central to this work, but nevertheless an interesting result has to do with comparing husband, fiancé, friend, acquaintance and stranger. The statistically significant results tend to be found in contrasting husband with stranger. However, it is at least suggestive to see that there is the smallest amount of fault attributed to the victim in the case of stranger rape, but more fault for fiancé than husband, and more fault for acquaintance than friend. When it came to estimating likelihood that a rape took place, this was judged least likely for a husband and most likely for a stranger. What is odd is that 'fiancé' is not all that far from 'stranger', and more likely to have been rape than friend or acquaintance. It has to be emphasised that these differences are not statistically significant.

The last sub-topic under this heading concerns the theory that the implicit threat of rape plays an important role in the relations between men and women in a very general way. Gerd Bohner and his colleagues conducted experiments in the United States and in Germany to see how reading a report of a rape effected self-esteem in men and women. (Bohner and colleagues, '93) Central to this theory is the concept of 'rape myth', or the view that much of the blame for rape can be put on the victim. Women who accept rape myth are believed to conduct themselves in ways that perpetuate male dominance. Important feminist literature holds that women are intimidated by rape and that this is an aspect of the interaction between all men and all women. Bohner and his co-authors report on an extensive literature designed to determine the validity of the view that rape is important in male dominance, and that the 'rape myth', which is accepted by some people and rejected by others, plays an important role.

Following on, and extending earlier work, Bohner and the team tested their subjects for self-esteem, social confidence, and trust and attitudes towards women using standard off-the-shelf tests. They were also tested for the degree to which they accepted or rejected the rape myth using 15 questions from a measurement devised by M. Burt and published in 1980. Eighty-five German students took part in the first experiment that involved reading fictional reports of a violent rape and of a violent assault in which the victim was a man. The main thrust of the experiment was to see the immediate effect of reading these reports on general self-esteem as measured by the Hormuth and Lalli test of 1980.

Among women who rejected the rape myth, reading about the rape had the immediate effect of lowering their self-esteem. There was no such effect on women who tended to accept the rape myth. This latter group has lower self-esteem generally, as is confirmed in a number of studies. The most worrying part of the Bohner study was the rise in self-esteem on the part of men who accepted the rape myth. This fits in loosely with the feminist theory that rape is a part of social control of women by men, though not the theory that all men and all women are involved. The links could be developed with more precision, but the data so far is troubling.

There was little effect of the reports on men who rejected the rape myth. The control of providing a reading on assault for comparison convinced the researchers that it was rape in particular, and not violence in general, which was having the effect. However, one might wonder about the effect of having a male victim in the control reading. The experiment was repeated with 120 university students in New York City with strikingly similar results.

Grant Muir and his colleagues examined the possibility that the larger number of rapes in America, 42 per 100,000 compared to Scotland with 30 per 100,000, might be due to more acceptance of the rape myth in America. (Muir and colleagues, '96) Over three hundred students from a Scottish university and nearly eight hundred students from an American university were tested using the Illinois Rape Myth Acceptance Scale. (Payne, '93) As in other studies, men in the two countries scored higher than women. The result which the authors take to be evidence in favour of the view that rape myth is important in explaining the incidence of rape was that American students scored higher than Scottish students. Had the average gone the other way around, we would have strong evidence against the theory. But as only two countries are involved, and there are so many other possibilities, one has to be very cautious. It would be interesting to see if the results could be extended over a large number of countries.

Costin and Kaptanoglu report on a survey in Turkey, and compare their results with results they obtained in England, Israel, the United States and West Germany. (Costin and Kaptanoglu, '93) Their focus is a bit different from that of Muir and his researchers. They related rape myth acceptance to other beliefs about women's rights and their proper roles in society. They find high correlations across groups of students, teachers, nurses and clerical workers in rape myth acceptance and "restrictive beliefs" about women. This is not without interest, and does seem to hold in a number of countries. What it shows is that certain views tend to go together. It does not show either the causes or consequences of these views.

Judging from Appearances

Many people feel they can tell if a person is lying, or is guilty of a crime, by observing what they look like and how they behave. Aldert Vrij conducted an interesting experiment in which ninety-one police officers were asked to tell from watching a video who was lying. (Vrij, '93) They were also asked to indicate how confident they were in their own judgements on a scale of one to seven, with one being not at all confident. I find the average confidence level of 4.8 to be pretty high, without really specifying either a comparison or prior expectations.

It turned out that confidence in their abilities to detect lying was not justified. There was no relationship between the level of confidence and proportion of subjects who were accurately assessed. The videos used in the experiment showed a group of subjects being interviewed by an actor playing the part of a policeman. The subjects were all asked the same five questions regarding whether or not they had stolen headphones in their pocket. Each subject was interviewed twice, once when in fact he had the headphones, and once when he did not. The police were able to guess correctly just under half the time.

Vrij wanted to find out how good the police were in detecting lying, and he also wanted to discover, if possible, what were the factors leading to the judgements the police made. The subjects filled out standard questionnaires designed to measure such characteristics as social anxiety and self-consciousness. In addition they were rated on things like hand movements, dress, eye contact and hesitation in answering questions. From this Vrij was able to identify five factors which led the police to believe the person was lying. These were hand and arm movements, untidy dress, self-consciousness, anxiety and failure to smile. As it happened, only one factor correlated with lying, and that was fewer hand movements. If I were a policeman who wanted to defend my ability to detect lying in spite of these results, I would argue that there was no real pressure on the subjects as they were taking part in a game. People who lie in circumstances where it matters to them are under pressure, and this is what can be detected.

It seems to be quite well established that people have views as to what criminals look like, and how appearances vary with the type of crime involved. Neil Macrae and John Shepherd took this one step further by controlling for attractiveness. (Macrae and Shepherd, '89) Their method is ingenious. They used a large sample of subjects to rank photographs according to honesty, aggression and attractiveness. Interestingly, honesty was correlated with attractiveness, but aggression was not associated significantly. The five pictures rated most and least honest, and most and least aggressive were identified. A second group then chose two pictures — the man most and the man least likely is be dishonest, and the two most and least likely to be aggressive. These four photos were then used in the final stage. The authors explain that the final four were equally attractive, which is important to the experiment, but do not explain exactly how this was achieved.

Fifty male and fifty female students at the University of Aberdeen were then randomly assigned to one of four groups. They were shown a video of one of the four pictures, and told through voice over that the person was alleged to be involved in a theft or an assault, according to whether the photo came from the honesty or aggression category. If appearances played no role, we would expect little agreement between the Aberdeen students and the previous selectors. But in fact there is a high degree of agreement. For the assault photo judged previously to be unlikely to be guilty, five of the twenty-five students thought him guilty, and twenty thought him to be innocent. Much the same occurred with the theft photos. There was less agreement regarding the photos previously judged to be of guilty men, but all went in the same direction as the previous selectors. For assault, 14 found him guilty and 11 innocent. And for theft, 17 found him guilty and 8 innocent. (p. 190) It would be interesting to see a larger sample of respondents, and to reverse the photos, while giving the same information about the kind of crime alleged. But the case for the prevalence of stereotyping is convincing.

It is an important luxury of scientific investigation that when we do not know the answer, we can live with that. Indeed, we must live with that. If we do not know, that is the state of affairs and we are not forced to make a guess. However, I would not be surprised to learn that in day-to-day life lots of judgements are made when there is no real evidence, and worse, no need to make a judgement. Edmund Howe has done work on how past crimes influence judgements about present accusations. (Howe, '91) The legal position is that past crime can be introduced to help assess the credibility of a witness, but not to influence judgements about the present accusation. One might doubt if jurors can keep the two considerations separate.

Howe worked with a relatively small sample of 44 students. He postulated ten crimes ranging in seriousness from murder to disturbing the peace. The bottom line of a complex study was that when accused of a crime similar to the previous conviction, there is much more presumption of guilt. Reliable figures on what are the facts about repetition seem to be "extremely sparse". A study done by the National Institute of Justice (Beck and Shipley, '87) found that if the first crime was murder, robbery, assault, burglary, fraud or larceny, the second arrest was more likely to be for the same crime than for one of the other five. On the other hand, the same study reports that if the first crime was against property, the offenders were equally likely to commit a violent crime while on parole as those parolees whose first conviction was for a violent crime.

Social psychologists have done a good deal of work on confessions in criminal investigations. This includes attempting to predict who will confess, and designing strategies to encourage confessions. A popular view is that vulnerable people are more likely to confess. J. Pearse and his colleagues were able to test 160 suspects and observe them during police interviews. (Pearse and colleagues, '98) From the original group of 197, only 24 refused to take part, and another 13 had to be dropped for a variety of practical reasons. A standardised interview was used to appraise the mental state of the suspects over the past week, and they were given four tests. These were for suggestibility (GSS 2, Gudjonsson, '97); anxiety, (STAI,

Spielberger and colleagues, '70); vocabulary and comprehension (Wechsler, '81); and reading (Schonell and Goodacre, '74).

The researchers applied a logistic statistical procedure to the data. Instead of accounting for a continuous range of outcomes, this method identifies factors that help to predict one of two possible outcomes — in this case, of course, whether the suspect chose to confess or not to confess. The data firmly rejected the hypothesis that the more vulnerable suspects were more likely to confess. Two factors which made suspects less likely to confess were having a legal adviser present, and having been to prison. Two factors which increased the likelihood of a confession were admitting consuming an illegal drug in the past twenty-four hours, and being young. One might try to make a case that both of these latter two factors can contribute to vulnerability. Maybe our expectation that the vulnerable suspects are more likely to confess is correct, but youth and drugs are better predictors of vulnerability than the interviews and tests that were employed.

Thomas Petee also used a logistic statistical analysis to determine which factors led suspects being granted pre-trial release. (Petee, '94) He worked with a sample of 498 felony cases in Lucas County, Ohio, over the period 1981 to 1989. According to the legal guidelines, six factors are supposed to be taken into account in making this decision. They include the seriousness of the crime, failure to appear for a hearing in the past, and employment status. Only the last of these failed to contribute some predictive power. However, demeanour and race also exerted significant influence. While demeanour has a large subjective element, it is reported in the comments of the pre-trial agency, and Petee classified the reports as either 'good' or 'bad'. Race combined with seriousness also exerted an influence. So legal and extra-legal factors were found to influence judgements about pre-trial release.

There is no denying that race plays an important role in judgements about crime and fear of crime. Keith Parker and his colleagues distributed a questionnaire to Hispanics and Blacks on subway trains and waiting at stations in New York City. (Parker and colleagues, '93) As in a number of other studies, fear of crime and estimates of the likelihood of victimisation are significant in all categories tested. This study confirmed that women are more fearful than men. What is new in the study is the ethnic comparison. Hispanics came out higher on both fear and victimisation. The authors hazard the guesses that Blacks may take more precautionary measures such as travelling in groups and at certain times, and were more socially integrated. (p. 730) One cannot place a lot of confidence in these guesses, nor are we asked to do so. The information about how people feel and the judgements they make is important. Relating this to the real risks would also be helpful in learning about judgements. Hispanics in New York City are more fearful of crime than Blacks, but are they also more likely to suffer from crime?

Police under Pressure

In the more liberal democracies we expect the police to act honestly, and even more important, to employ force cautiously and with circumspection. People will readily protest and vigorously complain if it is believed that the police acted in an irresponsible way, particularly if the public at large is put at risk. At the same time, it has to be recognised that the police are human, and many factors effect their performance. There are circumstances when the police will perform in a better fashion, and times when less satisfactory conduct can be observed. Two studies have attempted to investigate police action when arriving at a potentially lethal encounter, and another to investigate police use of high-speed chase.

Aldert Vrij and Liesbeth Dingemans tested the effect of physical effort on response at a crime scene. (Vrij and Dingemans, '96) For example, it might be necessary to run some distance to get to the place where the incident is unfolding, or one might arrive by car with little exertion. In particular, Vrij and Dingemans were interested in the effect of exertion on how the police perceive the degree in aggression in a criminal, and how aggressive they themselves feel. The third question was whether they chose to shoot or not to shoot in the circumstances.

The experiment involved eighty volunteer Dutch police officers. Half exercised vigorously for one minute and half did not, and all were then exposed to a simulator which it is claimed mimics a real experience very effectively. The arrival of the police subject interrupts an attempted robbery. The male or female subject in the experiment has a 'virtual' partner who appears on the screen and is kicked by the robber. The robber then aims to shoot at the subject of the experiment.

80% of the exercisers shot at the robber, and all of the non-exercisers did so. This difference was statistically significant. In addition, the police were asked questions about the level of aggression they perceived in the robber, and again the exercisers judged this to be significantly less than the non-exercisers. In a second similar experiment the police were told why they were asked to exercise. In this next virtual crime scene a known troublemaker was interrupted while threatening a woman with a knife. For this experiment there was no significant difference in the proportion of 'shooters', but the questions about own and perceived levels of aggression came out the same as in the previous experiment, namely, exercisers reported less aggression.

The authors refer to earlier work that found the opposite to their results. Exercise led to more aggression and more aggressive behaviour. They attribute this difference to the fact that in the earlier experiment there was a substantial delay between exercise and the confrontation. It is difficult to have an opinion about this. Vrij and Dingemans offer two explanations for their results. One is that, knowing that they have exercised, the police are more inclined compared to the non-exercisers to attribute the aggression they feel to their internal state than to the stimulus from the simulator. The second theory is that being tired reduces physical activity, including the activity of shooting. One may wonder if a minute on an exercise bicycle can produce the same effect as running through a city to get to a robbery. Most people would guess that being physically stressed would increase the chances of shooting. At the very least, this study introduces doubt about that. On the other hand, one could conjecture that physical strain reduces the chances of making the right decision, and include experiments where it was 'right' not to shoot.

When the police decide to engage in high-speed pursuit by car there is an obvious risk to the public. Of course, there are times when not giving chase can put the public at greater risk. These are not easy matters to regulate. Policies across American states vary greatly from giving considerable discretion to almost forbidding high-speed chase, unless there is a clear and immediate danger if the pursuit did not take place. Robert Homant and his colleagues have studied the role of personality in the decision by police to engage in high-speed pursuit. (Homant and colleagues, '94) They worked with 69 patrol officers in a co-operating department in a major American city. This included all the officers with over two years' experience. They were tested for their taste for sensation seeking using the Sensation Seeking Scale (Zuckerman, '79) They were under considerable pressure from a sergeant to complete the questionnaire, and all did so. The authors constructed their own risk preference scale using scores from '1' for disagreement to '7' for agreement on three questions about risk. One question had to do with enjoying challenge. Another emphasised the inescapable role of risk in law enforcement. And a third held that taking a chance occasionally was needed in order to be a good officer.

Interestingly, there was no correlation found between sensation seeking and risk. These two factors were used to account for the extent to which officers had engaged in high-speed pursuit. Pursuit was measured in three ways. One was to read two scenarios and indicate on two seven point scales both how likely they were to pursue, and how intensely they would do that. The researchers also had access to records of the number of pursuits that resulted in damage to police vehicles. Finally, the policemen were asked how many high-speed pursuits they initiated over the past year. These three sources of information were combined into a single index of pursuit activity.

The results showed some explanatory power, though not a great deal, from sensation seeking and attitudes towards risk. Each has an effect, but even together they leave a lot of the variation between officers unexplained. The police station was in the process of reviewing its policy on high-speed chase, and the number of pursuits had been coming down for some time. It could be that there was not enough opportunity for pursuits to discriminate more effectively between officers. And there may be other factors in accounting for individual decisions. The authors quite rightly put these forward as very preliminary and mainly suggestive results. Ideally, we would like to know how personality effects 'type one' and 'type two' errors, as the statisticians call them. Officers might pursue when they should not, and fail to pursue when they should. One would need a very large run of data to have confidence that on average officers faced the same decisions regarding chase, and the observed differences in response were due to their personalities, and not to their circumstances.

Minor Crimes

We conclude this section by looking at social psychological studies of two relatively minor crimes. One is running red lights, and the other is short- changing. These certainly are minor compared to murder and rape, but at the same time, most of us, happily, are more likely to be annoyed by them than to be victims of serious crime. Yoel Yinon and Emanual Levian observed nine hundred and sixty traffic light changes in two Israeli cities. (Yinon and Levian, '95) They were interested in social effects on driving, which have received much less attention than such considerations as drivers' personalities, and physical skills. For this study, the presence or absence of other cars at the intersection is the social consideration.

The presence of other cars was categorised in fours ways: The car was on its own; at least two cars behind it; one or two cars on the driver's side; and at least two cars behind, and on either side, or one side, of the driver. So we have a progression from being completely alone up to greater presence of other drivers. 120 cases were observed for each of the four possibilities when the drivers were men, and the same when the drivers were women. The authors note that in general women are more law-abiding, but were curious as to whether they would be more or less law-abiding in the presence of other cars.

In general they were less inclined to jump the lights than men were, except when no other cars were around. Eleven percent of men on their own committed this offence, and twelve percent of women. At the other extreme, with lots of cars around, forty percent of men crossed before green was up, and thirty-two percent of women. By London or New York standards these figure look high, but may depend on the exact nature of the roads and the light change timings, including amber conventions. The authors are torn between explaining their results through the distraction of other drivers being around, or because of a desire to compete with them. It is also a little unclear from the report how multiple violations at a single observation were handled. It could be simply that one person jumping the light is a strong incentive for others to do so as well. In principle this might be tested by planting drivers who could try to lead others astray, but there would be ethical implications.

Fredric Rabinowitz and his large team of researchers conducted a classic study of dishonesty by having pairs of Americans enter shops in Salzburg and either underpay or overpay a shilling for a purchase of cards costing four shillings. (Rabinowitz and colleagues, '93) The two conspirators randomly changed roles, one doing the paying and one noting such things as whether the change was counted or not, eye contact, and the number of people in the store at the time. They settled on 32 shops in the Old Town tourist section and observed 96 cashiers. Underpaying and overpaying was evenly distributed across shops so as to minimise costs or benefits to the shops as a result of the experiment. The experimenters worked with three categories. If the cashier counted the money and kept the difference on an over payment it was classed as 'dishonesty'. Not counting was called 'carelessness'. And counting but not asking for another shilling when there was an underpayment was classed as 'indifference'.

On any reckoning, there was a lot of dishonesty. Only 15 of the 50 cashiers who were overpaid returned the shilling, though there is some inconsistency with this figure when we come to look at male and female confederates making overpayments. 22 who kept the extra shilling did not count the money, but 13 did. Of those who were underpaid, only a few less, 22 compared to 24, asked for the extra shilling. While there was more accuracy on the underpay than the overpay, the difference was not statistically significant.

What is quite interesting is the cashiers' behaviour according to whether the purchaser was male or female. Unfortunately, the figures the authors report for the sex breakdown are not consistent with the aggregate figures — possible carelessness on the part of the researchers and the editors of the *Journal of Social Psychology*. Ignoring that for now, they write that 25 female confederates overpaid, and 6 got change returned. 23 females underpaid, and change was requested on 14 occasions. So far so good. This is in contrast to the 25 men who overpaid, where the difference was returned on 14 occasions. More money was requested from 11 of the men who underpaid. The authors note that on the underpay side, the difference between men and women shoppers is not significant, but on the overpay side it is.

This study must have been fun to carry out, and it certainly is fun to read about. But what are we to make of it? First, it highlights the role of carelessness, which occurred in 44% of the overpay cases. Only 26% of these were put down as examples of dishonest behaviour. We do have a question here about the ability of cashiers to feel or otherwise observe the amount of money without overtly counting it. There was less carelessness in the underpay case at 30%. This could be due to self-interest, or it being more obvious when three shillings are tendered instead of four, compared to five instead of four in the overpay case. More dishonesty occurred in this study than one in Canada, but there the overpay was 70 cents rather than 9 cents in the present study. Less dishonesty was found in the present study than one done on foreign travellers, again, in Athens, Paris and Boston. That study did not allow for a carelessness category. The apparent tendency of female cashiers to take advantage more frequently of their female customers than their male customers is not without interest. The authors make a case for more investigation along these lines, possibly supplementing the fieldwork with interviews with the cashiers. That might prove to be harder to achieve.

POLITICAL SCIENCE

Whatever political system a country may have, it is impossible for the government to keep tabs on more than a fraction of what people are doing. Most of the day-to-day interactions between people take place without any direct acknowledgement or intervention on the part of local government, or of a higher tier of government. People tend to go about their normal business without explicitly referring to the state. Nor do they attract the attention of the state. However, there is always the possibility that the political system will impinge on individuals, depending in part on their actions. This potential action of government exerts a continuing influence on individual behaviour, especially in the area of criminal activity.

The political process is the main determinant of what is seen as crime, and what is to be done about it. Ultimately, crime is to be met with force of one kind or another. Most governments aspire to being the only institution in society that can sanction the use of force. All governments jealously guard their monopoly on the legitimate use of force, and indeed, on any use of force at all. As well as being an attack on individuals, the use of force by criminals is a challenge to the power of the state. Political science is about power, particularly the right to use force. But this simple word 'power' refers to an endless array of somewhat related and somewhat different interactions.

It is not easy to define and delineate the political nature of society. The political process is not separate from the economic and social setting which it regulates, and which in turn is shaped by the beliefs and actions of people in society. There is a continuing struggle over power. Interest groups, or coalitions, form and dissolve, and are interwoven and juxtaposed on each other. One outcome of this evolving process is a body of formal agreement which takes the form of laws on what is to be seen as crime, and what is to be done about criminal activity. Much of the order in society is political in nature. This aspect of order tends to have its most obvious presence in the laws of a country, and in the enforcement practices, which can in turn exert their own independent influences.

The content of the law defining criminal activity, and the enforcement practices of the authorities, are clearly parts of the consequences of political processes. Political scientists attempt to explain both the content of laws in a country, and how they are implemented. They direct attention to crimes done by individuals, organised crime, crimes done by firms, and by governments themselves. The problem of crime in society is often an important item on the political agenda, with some crimes rising in the attention they receive, and others moving away from centre stage. How politicians respond to, and manipulate, the issue of crime is another important topic.

Traditionally the methods of political science rely less on statistical investigation than is common in sociology and social psychology. There is also less use of formal models, both as self-contained means of analysis, and as the structure of an empirical investigation, such as we see in economics. There is some formal modelling and a good deal of statistical enquiry, but less than in most other social sciences, apart from anthropology. Like anthropology, the emphasis is on particular events. However, the scale of the enquiry is much broader, typically being national in scope. The focus is on law, where the rule of law dominates, and at all times on power, and the actual or potential exercise of force.

State Laws on Drugs, and in Use of the Death Penalty

It is disturbing how much of social science investigation concentrates on the United States and we will return to that issue. However, for many enquiries in political science, the structure of that country provides the best laboratory that we have. In that country there is some variation in state law, a common national economic and legal system, unrestricted movement, and some common culture. Completing the picture is the large number of states, and the different responses they generate. In this setting, Kenneth Meier has investigated variations in the laws and law enforcement relating to illegal drugs. (Meier, '92) He points out that while the federal government sent twenty-two thousand drug cases for prosecution in 1989, state governments made over one and a third million arrests for drug offences in that year. (p. 41)

Meier notes that while taxes, for example, need to be addressed at almost every legislative session, the illegal drug question may or may not come up, depending on the political environment. A factor that might influence this environment is the extent and nature of "visible" drug use. Marijuana use might cause less perceived need to act.

It undoubtedly is the case that race is heavily involved in the drug issue in the United States. The author of this study refers to literature on how Chinese immigration led to laws prohibiting opium-smoking, though not other means of taking the drug. Other writers have documented how harsh national and state laws on marijuana aimed at Blacks and Mexicans tended to be relaxed in the sixties and seventies, when this drug became more popular with young middle-class Whites. Quoting surveys undertaken by the National Institute on Drug Abuse ('88), Meier reports that the proportion of Blacks who have ever used an illegal drug, at 37%, is much the same as the proportion of Whites, which is 36%. The proportions using a drug in a chosen month are also much the same with 7% of Whites and 8% of Blacks. But whereas 12% of the population of America is Black, 40% of those arrested for drug related crimes in that country are Black. (p.43) There is something here that calls for explanation, with a likely candidate being discrimination.

In the political arena there is universal condemnation of drug use in the United States. But there does tend to be some difference of approach in the two parties, with the Republicans being relatively more keen on enforcement and stern punishments, and the Democrats placing a bit more emphasis on education and treatment. Other interest groups with particular concerns about drugs are those who are involved in enforcement or in treatment, and those firms who are in the alcohol sector.

Meier uses careful application of a wide range of data to determine the effects of race, the political environment, the amount of drug use, the importance of the alcohol industry, and the power of other interested bureaucracies, on the variations which can be seen across states in their laws on drugs. Starting with marijuana, separate regressions were run on whether the state has decriminalised the drug (a logit exercise), the size of fines imposed, length of jail sentences, and light penalties. Not much of the variation can be accounted for using the factors mentioned. This might be because the drug law policy of a state is better seen as a package involving interaction between fines, jail, and so on. Taking them one at a time may be misleading. But this is a most impressive investigation nevertheless.

A similar statistical exercise is done on variations in the state laws on heroin and cocaine. And further work is reported on both arrests, and the effectiveness of the drug laws, in controlling drug use.

While conceding that his work is "hardly the last word", Meier's results point to a number of tentative conclusions. (p.66) There is strong evidence that the so-called drug war is directed more at minorities, while there is no evidence to show that they are more involved in drugs. Another conclusion relates the amount of drug arrests in a state to the amount of drug use in the state. The author finds only a very modest impact of the proportion of liberal voters on state drug laws. Interestingly, the extent to which a state is host to the alcohol industry did relate both to the toughness of its drug laws and to how vigorously they were implemented. Finally, the interested parties mentioned above did have some impact on both drug laws and their implementation. Meier mentions in particular that states with larger treatment bureaucracies tended to have weaker laws, but enforced those laws more effectively.

This subject presents the researcher with a data nightmare. Getting any figures for many factors is a real challenge, and ensuring that the figures are roughly comparable across states can be difficult. We have to be grateful for this first step in attempting to explain why different political constituencies adopt the policies they do, and implement them in the way that they do. Meier suggests that harsh laws may have a symbolic role, which is often toned down when it comes to implementation. Politicians may feel the need to be seen to be doing something, and passing laws is one way of achieving this. Whether the policies are implemented, or have good effects if implemented, may be a secondary consideration.

David Nice has undertaken a study of the variations across American states in the use of the death penalty. (Nice, '92) His work has a formal similarity to that of Meier in explaining differences in drug laws. Nice constructed a scale going from 0 to 4 to measure the involvement of the states in the death penalty. '0' means there is no death penalty law. The highest rating of 4 meant that three conditions were met: the law permits use of the penalty when the offender is under 18 years of age; at least one person was on death row; and the state had executed someone over the period 1977 to 1987. As well as using this scale as a dependent variable, or 'what is to be explained', the author used proportionate numbers on death row, and the execution rate, as two additional aspects to be explained.

The explanatory factors employed in this study included state ideology. One indicator Nice used was the proportion of voters who voted for McGovern, the liberal candidate, in the 1972 presidential election. Another measure was a survey done over the period 1974 to 1982 by Wright and colleagues ('85), where voters were asked to classify themselves as liberal, moderate or conservative. Three demographic factors used in the study to explain differences in state use of the death penalty were the proportion of Blacks in the state, the median income, and the proportion of residents living in metropolitan areas. While the data does not allow perfect consistency, the goal is to focus on the year 1976. The final explanatory factors were the 1975 murder and nonnegligent manslaughter rate, and the growth in this rate over the years 1970 to 1975.

Two factors show up strongly when it comes to the extent of use of the death penalty — voting for McGovern was associated with less use of this punishment, and the murder and nonnegligent manslaughter rate encouraged use of it. The proportions on death row were statistically related to the same two factors, with urbanisation also being positively associated. When it came to executions, the murder and nonnegligent manslaughter rate dropped out of the explanatory frame, and the proportion of Blacks was significantly associated.

The one factor that runs consistently through Nice's study is the political climate. Conservatives are more inclined towards use of the death penalty, and liberals less so. Whether the death penalty is effective in deterring murder is another matter. As in the case of drugs discussed above, the pressure on politicians is to be seen to be doing something. The effectiveness of the measures employed is another matter.

Crime and Race in America

Studies of state variations in both drug laws and use of the death penalty in America show the importance of race. Jon Hurwitz and Mark Peffley directly address this issue. (Hurwitz and Peffley, '97) They conducted a large survey of Whites in Lexington Kentucky. Five hundred adult Whites were interviewed for up to twenty minutes to determine their attitudes towards Blacks as potential criminals. Central to the study was the description of two different crimes. One involved beating a man and stealing his car. The other involved embezzling thousands of dollars from a telephone company. In discussing both crimes, some respondents were told that the suspect was White and some were told that he was Black. Two questions were highlighted: how likely is it that the suspect is guilty; and how likely is he to commit a similar crime in the future.

The survey by Hurwitz and Peffley also elicited opinions on the 'furlough experiment', where prisoners were allowed weekends at home prior to completing their sentences. Those interviewed were asked whether they approved in the case of Black and of White prisoners, and how likely they thought it was that the prisoner would commit a crime while on furlough. Similar questions were asked about such matters as the likelihood of rehabilitation of prisoners, and the wisdom of spending public money to help people to get jobs. All the questions were directed to the Black/White issue, either by referring to prisoners, where appropriate, or to neighbourhoods.

The authors are convinced of the importance of media presentations in shaping public perceptions, and the effects of these perceptions on policy debates. Much of this discussion is entirely plausible. However, their data provides a picture of what White people in Lexington believe, not why they hold the opinions they do. It is clear that stereotypes play a significant role. Whites have a very negative view of Blacks when it comes to violent crime. This does not hold for other types of crime. While the issue of race is likely to influence White opinions about punishment of crime, it does not carry over to views about preventative measures. Support for job creation initiatives, for example, does not seem to be effected by whether the target is a Black neighbourhood or a White neighbourhood.

Mafia Culture, and Mafia-Like Organisations in Russia

The power of the Mafia in Sicily has a long and controversial history. Different factions have given support to it, and others interests have opposed the activity. Attitudes range from toleration, resignation, fear, envy and outrage. From something known, but not to be discussed openly, the Mafia problem is not only a favourite cinema topic worldwide, but also popular reading material in Sicily itself. Jane Schneider and Peter Schneider bring an anthropological perspective to the politics of the anti-Mafia movement in its home country. (Schneider and Schneider, '94) They trace the role of feminists, and women generally, in the struggle to oppose the Mafia, and the shifting positions of the Left, agrarian interests, the judiciary, and the Church.

At times the Mafia has filled a power vacuum, when weak government was unable to enforce contracts and protect its citizens from banditry and other wrongs. In this sense it can be seen as a kind of grass-roots government. Providing protection puts it in competition with government, and along with its relatively new found prosperity through drug trafficking, places the Mafia in an unambiguously criminal role.

Always the question arises, is the Mafia peculiarly Sicilian, or a general phenomenon that occurs when the circumstances are right? And if the former, what aspects of Sicilian life lead to promoting this form of quasi-governmental and criminal activity? The authors mention the male culture of acting to right supposed wrongs, and how this fits in with Mafia ideology. They discuss circumstances when an attack on the Mafia is seen as an attack of Sicily itself. They also document the major local anti-Mafia movements. This is a balanced and insightful discussion of the various political concerns surrounding the Mafia issue in Sicily.

Jane and Peter Schneider note in passing the observations of other scholars to the effect that present day Russia has many of the features of Sicily in the nineteenth century. Federico Varese takes up the frightening extent of corruption and crime that is present in Russia as it moves from socialism to a market economy. (Varese, '97) He places particular emphasis on share ownership in the newly privatised companies.

There is no general practice of issuing share certificates, and instead ownership is logged in share registers. These are difficult to monitor and subject to corrupt manipulation. It is just one example of a lack of legal infrastructure necessary for the support of a market economy. Varese refers to the suggestion of the American economist Rudiger Dornbusch that Russia take over the commercial law of some country such as the Netherlands or Finland. Not having done this, there is great uncertainty about the law, with a bewildering variety of overlapping and often contradictory edicts.

Varese identifies three features that are essential for the working of a market economy. These are defined property rights, the possibility of earning income from property, and deterring crime against property. With taxation at various levels of government at intolerably high levels, the incentive to bribe or otherwise avoid paying is overwhelming. In this circumstance, few people can turn to the courts to enforce agreements, as most people have too much to hide. Other forms of enforcement are used, leading to a Mafia-like system. A violent culture emerges with violent death between four and five times more likely in Russia than in most industrial countries. (p. 587)

What is missing from the picture presented by Varese is the possibility that illegal activity was endemic in Russia prior to the transition to a market economy. Perhaps a functioning black market was needed to oil a system that otherwise would have been subject to massive failure. A repressive central government kept this within certain bounds. With the end of communism, a reasonably organised illegal structure had both a head start and a vastly increased scope for action. This would be an additional explanation of the rampant crime and corruption in Russia.

The Politics of Corruption Cleanups

Crimes committed by members of the government of a country are particularly disturbing, given the role of the government in upholding the law. This form of corruption is has the added aspect of being systematic and organised. The public are victims of a conspiracy from the top. Usually the public sees itself as being helpless in the face of a corrupt government. If the situation is to be addressed, the attempt at reform typically comes from the government itself. The presence of corruption is acknowledged and a cleanup is proposed. It is an interesting question for political science as to the circumstances which lead to a corruption cleanup. What are the motivations, and what form does the cleanup take?

The theory of cleanups tends to follow the general assumption that governments act to strengthen their political position. Depending on circumstances, one might be keen to discredit the previous regime, or to reduce popular discontent. Kate Gillespie and Gwen Okruhlik have investigated the circumstances of cleanups in the Middle East and North Africa. (Gillespie and Okruhlik, '91) They concentrate on cases where the pressure for cleanup was internal to the country, rather than coming from other governments or international organisations. The usual pattern is one of scandal followed by cleanup. The authors consider twenty-five Middle Eastern and North African countries over the years 1970 to 1986. The main source they use is news items in the *Middle East Economic Digest.* This was supplemented by material from *The Middle East Journal, The Wall Street Journal* and *African Research Political Series.*

Gillespie and Okruhlik identified twenty-four cleanups, none coming after an election. Iran led the pack with three cleanups over the period. Those with two were Iraq, Libya, Ethiopia, Sudan, Algeria and Egypt. The literature of the subject tends to suggest that cleanups follow coups. The idea is that the cleanup serves the two related purposes of helping to justify the coup, and as a means of weakening potential opposition. However, this study indicates that for these countries at least, cleanup after a coup is not nearly as common as cleanups done by incumbent governments, with six of the former and fourteen of the latter.

The researchers found that cleanups done in some desperation as a last ditch attempt to hold power are unlikely to work. They can get out of control and provide ammunition for political opponents. Sometimes cleanups occur because the corruption is widely perceived to exclude most of the public from sharing in a degree of prosperity. Then the pressure for cleanup is likely to come from an opposition, be done with some haste, and target high level officials. Cleanups that follow coups or revolutions help to divert attention from economic and other problems, and are a means of neutralising particular opponents. But for the majority of cleanups, done by governments in power, the target is middle range and low level officials of the government. Whether or not cleanups generally achieve their stated objective is another matter. They do suggest that even with little or no democracy, governments depend to some degree on the support of the people, or so the researchers conclude.

Violations of Environmental Law by Firms

Regulation of the impact of firms on the environment is growing in scale and complexity, especially in the United States. The Environmental Protection Agency of necessity relies on firms to report on their activities that affect the environment. Central to this reporting activity is the Toxic Release Inventory. Prior to 1986 there was very limited requirement on firms to provide public information relevant to their environmental impact. This changed with the Emergency Planning and Community Right-to-Know Act that was passed by the House of Representatives by the narrowest possible margin of 212 to 211 votes.

Section 313 of this law requires firms with over nine employees that manufacture, or engage in the use of, more than certain specified quantities of any one of over three hundred listed substances must report to the Environmental Protection Agency how much of each substance they transmitted to the air, water, land, or to disposal plants each year. Beginning in 1989 the Agency has made the data public. This is the Toxic Release Inventory. Reporting is a big undertaking, estimated to cost American firms about half a billion dollars in the first year, and about a third of a billion dollars every year thereafter. By 1991 over twenty-three thousand firms were filing reports. But many firms required by law to do so were not filing.

John Brehm and James Hamilton have studied this legislation in the context of the political science principle/agent literature — the theory of how a principle, in this case the government, gets an agent, in this case a firm, to perform certain acts. (Brehm and Hamilton, '96) Substantial evidence suggests that about one third of the companies that are obliged to file reports are failing to do so. The authors set out to measure and explain non-compliance in the state of Minnesota using exactly those sophisticated modelling and statistical techniques that are rare in political science. Minnesota was chosen for the experiment because the State's Emergency Response Commission had received from the National Enforcement Information Services Center a list of 3,400 'facilities', the unit of enforcement, who had not reported. These were followed up in detail, eventually resulting in the discovery of 165 facilities that should have filed. Brehm and Hamilton related this exercise to a Dun and Bradstreet list of firms for Minnesota.

Facilities fall into one of three categories: those that file; those that fail to file and are caught; and those that do not file. This last group contains both legitimate non-filers, and facilities that should have filed and were not caught. The authors attempt to explain where a facility winds up using county figures on such matters as unemployment and voting behaviour of the county, including the percent voting in an environmental trust fund referendum. These factors, along with considerations like the cost of filing, were intended to predict what a self-interested facility would do given the conditions prevailing in the county in which it operated.

This is a brave an impressive investigation, and a brief description does not do it justice. As it happens, the results in many cases were not statistically significant, and in some cases were inconsistent with the theory. One feature that came through strongly was the likelihood of smaller facilities not filing. The authors concentrate their main effort on attempting to distinguish between intentional violation of the law, and simply being ignorant of it. They interpret the results as giving support to the 'ignorance' explanation, as small facilities might have less knowledge of what is required.

There are obvious problems with these conclusions. It could be that the cost of reporting is more significant for smaller facilities. And as the authors point out, there is very little history of detection and the fines incurred, so the wilful, or rational evasion strategy may not have had time to emerge as a consistently statistically observable phenomenon. Certainly Brehm and Hamilton have been extremely inventive, and energetic, in amassing potentially relevant data and constructing a model to analyse them. But the conjectures linking ignorance, as one possible explanation of illegal non-reporting, and evasion as another, to the explanatory factors are very indirect, and possibly easily swamped by other considerations.

The fact that size is more strongly associated with illegal non-filing than unemployment or voting patterns does not get us very far. This study has other important payoffs. But one thing the authors and we want to know is whether or not the responsible individuals in the facilities who violated the law knew they were doing that. It is hard to say that as a result of this investigation we have much more information on that point.

Some Politics of Policing

Two authors have taken up the politics of policing in the United Kingdom. E.M. McLeay concentrated on the exercise of discretion by the police, and the police as an interest group in society like any other. (McLeay, '90) Les Johnston discussed the importance, and growing importance, of private policing. (Johnston, '92) It must be said that both papers are barely on the border of scientific investigation. They are more like lists of topics for future study. McLeay starts from the observation that the police have a unique amount of coercive power. Second, there is the discretion of the police. In an impressionistic manner, McLeay compares police action on mugging, rural public disorder, rape, and wife-battery with the action taken on racially motivated attacks. The exercise of discretion is inevitable in a police force. It would be impossible to lay down rules for action in all circumstances. The way police use this discretion is not necessarily bad according to McLeay. He sees the police as responding to public pressures, but slowly and in their own ways. The third factor leading to political clout for the police is direct access to government decision-making, mainly through the Home Office.

Les Johnson makes the point that not all activities which we normally think of being 'policing' are done by the public sector. Private interests set up all sorts of surveillance. Functions ranging from protecting cash deliveries to bouncers at clubs, and the use of private 'minders', or bodyguards, take over responsibilities that are normally thought to be those of the police. Of course, the police are meant to be working in the interests of everyone in the country, and private 'policing' serves particular interests. Johnson is undoubtedly right in suggesting that private policing raises issues about the proper role, and accountability of both the official police and their private counterparts. Beyond noting this he does not provide much detail. Johnson is especially interested in international security firms that operate in more than one country. Here again, we can imagine special problems for national governments. Exactly what these are and what might be done about them is not discussed. Neither Johnson nor McLeay make much use of theory or of data. But they do draw attention to an area full of researchable political questions.

The Crime of Pornography

Crimes with no victims, other than the perpetrator, present a special problem for political science. Here the law is operating largely to protect people from themselves. There are other aspects, not unlike blasphemy laws, which include protecting ordinary citizens from the knowledge that others are behaving in ways that are deeply offensive to many in the community. There also are possible side effects of the proscribed activity. It could be that pornography induces criminal sexual behaviour. Of course, it is also the case that it may be a substitute for attacks on others.

If the community decides to pass laws forbidding the smoking of marijuana, for example, it is fairly clear what it means to transgress that law. Laws against pornography have no such natural interpretation. For that reason they are often framed in loose terms, such as forbidding circulation of lewd material, without specifying what is lewd. Another common device is to forbid sexual material likely to cause offence to most of the population. When the law is framed in this way, it falls on the courts to decide in particular cases whether a certain book or picture, for example, is in violation of the law or not. In a famous case, Justice Stewart granted that he could not define obscenity, and defended his decision with the observation, "But I know it when I see it.". Timothy Hagle quotes Justice Stewart in his introduction to examining United States Supreme Court decisions on pornography. (Hagle, '91, p. 1039)

The decisions of the court in the matter of obscenity are either 'restrictive' or 'not restrictive'. This means, they either uphold the decision of the lower court in allowing a state government to restrict circulation of some material, or may ban it outright. The court may decide that the material is not obscene, but nevertheless uphold the decision not to allow it to be broadcast during the day, for example. Hagle examined all obscenity and pornography cases decided by the Supreme Court beginning with the Warren Court of 1953 and ending with the Rehnquist Court of 1985. There were 107 such cases.

Hagle employed three kinds of explanatory factors in attempting to explain the decision of the court. The first had to do with the media used to convey the alleged pornography. These were print with illustrations, print with pictures, photos, movies, live sex such as in topless bars, and spoken material, either recorded or live. The conjecture was that the more graphic the material, the greater the impact, and the more likely it was to fall foul of the law. The second consideration was whether the material was only available on payment.

Previous decisions have indicated that the Court wishes to protect people who do not want to be exposed to lewd material. If they have to pay for access, that should give adequate protection. The third factor is simply the decision of the lower court. The Supreme Court decides which cases it wants to hear, and is more likely to accept a case where at least on first impression it feels that the lower court made a mistake. Hagle adds a fourth factor, namely, whether the case originated in the South of the United States.

In true scientific form, Hagle runs a probit (yes or no) statistical regression with the decision of the Court as the dependent variable. The most important factor was the decision of the lower court. Next came whether the case originated in a Southern State. Finally, paid access had some influence on not upholding restrictive decisions, or reversing unrestrictive ones. The author makes some attempt to explain the failure of the media variables to have a discernible influence on the Court. He suggests that they might be too narrow. However, using broader categories does not change the results. Hagle remains open to both the possibility that the media may not matter, and to the possibility that this influence is too subtle to capture with his methods. One picture may not be like another.

Reversing the decision of the lower court was a dominant factor. The Court reversed 23 of the 27 non-restrictive decisions of the lower courts, and 67 of the 80 restrictive ones. If you want to 'explain' the decision of the

Court, in the sense of predicting the decision it will take, knowing the decision of the lower court gets you most of the way. Of course there is a problem here. We are not getting insight into what influenced the Court. To do that we would need to know why the Court decided to accept the pornography cases it did accept, and why it rejected others. By comparison, the significance of paid access is more understandable. The Court believed in protecting unwilling recipients, and was reluctant to prevent mutually agreed transactions in lewd material, whatever form it took. It is interesting that the emphasis is on the consumers. The greatest victims, and those most in need of protection from themselves, might be the producers. But this is not considered in this article.

Hagle tends to play down the significance of cases coming from Southern States in adding to the explanation of the decisions of the Court. He points out that nearly ninety percent of the cases coming from the South had restrictive decisions in the lower courts, as against seventy percent for the cases not originating in the South. But this leaves entirely open whether the Supreme Court is in general more inclined to reverse restrictive decisions, more inclined to select restrictive decisions from the South, or whether Southern courts are more likely to be in error in the eyes of the Supreme Court.

With questions still open for research, I would not like to lose sight of the fact that with sufficient ingenuity and care, relatively objective methods can be used in the study of even the most subjective of questions, like what factors lead a court to restrict certain material on the grounds that it is pornographic. As the author says, maybe in fact the media does not matter, or maybe we need other methods for determining how it influences the Court. Hagle had especially challenging decisions to make, particularly in coding the media categories. He refers to a case brought against a newspaper for publishing a "sex poem" in one issue, and a picture of a nude couple embracing in a later issue. In order to improve the reliability of the coding, Hagle had each media decision made by two independent observers. My guess is that this was sufficiently well done. Further progress might well depend on analysis of how the Court selects its cases.

Chapter Six

MIGRATION

INTRODUCTION

Human beings have a great tendency to stay put. They also are much inclined to make big moves, and then stay put. Neither tendency is at all surprising. Most people have to work, or rear children, or to get educated. Most work, most rearing, and most education all benefit from being in one place. Habit and social life also contribute to living in one place, at least for a substantial block of time. Migrant cattle farmers in East Africa take their work and their social life with them as the move, and so in one sense they remain in one place. One hears about the jet set. But probably most of them have a base, or two, from which to make forays. Even retired wealthy individuals tend to stay put; not counting holidays and trips to visit relatives. On the other hand, for some people this natural tendency to stay in one place is disrupted by the need to escape from disaster, and for other people by the advantages to be gained from living in a new location.

The motive for a big move is often a positive one. Another place may hold much greater prospects for higher income. This is typical of the quantitatively dominant form of migration from rural to urban areas. International migration, often combined with rural to urban migration, also has a predominantly economic motive. Of course, there are negative, or 'push', incentives to move. The main ones are war, and being a victim of prejudice or natural disaster. These push and pull factors combine in an endless variety of ways to produce migration.

It normally is easier for any one person to move when people from the same family, or merely the same background, have moved before or are in the process of moving. This is in spite of potential hostility from the host population when large numbers come from another place. Noticeable numbers have the double effect of creating a more familiar environment for the migratory, and arousing hostility from the indigenous population. The arrivals can be seen as economic competitors and as the bearers of an unwelcome culture. The immigrants and the traditional population may both see each other as having one or more undesirable characteristic such as a different religion, manners, language, work ethic, sexual code, public behaviour and degree of loyalty to the host country. In addition, the two groups may have one code of conduct when dealing with members of their own group, and another when dealing with the outsiders.

A neighbour of mine in Wales confessed to me one day that his wife "was not from around here." She came from Catbrook, a Welsh village about five miles away. I came to the United Kingdom from New York City in order to study. I never anticipated that I would stay on. An expert in aeroplane maintenance works in Saudi Arabia knowing that after a four-year tour, carefully planned, he and his family can return to Yorkshire with the capital necessary to start a business. Many of the people I trained as economists in Ghana are working abroad, but building homes in their villages and expect to return to them. An Iraqi Jew in London wisely decides not to return, but sees himself as a Middle Eastern person forced to live in London. What is 'migration'?

The fact that we cannot define migration in a clear and unambiguous manner is of no importance. When and if we eventually run into a problem because we use one word to cover a variety of events, then we must do something about it in order to solve the problem. But if we do not have a problem, it seems silly to me to get exercised about the definition. It is sufficient for the purposes of enquiry that roughly speaking we know what we are talking about. And this typically has to do with voluntary movements of fairly sizeable numbers of people, over a limited period of time, who intend to remain in the target place. They see themselves as migrating, and are seen as immigrants by the people who came to the host place sometime before them. For a particular case of migration, it may be highly debatable as to the extent to which these individual conditions are met. Some conditions may not be met at all, and yet we may want to group the case as being an example of 'migration'.

Social scientists have published some fifty articles in professional journals in the 1990's on the subject of what they identify as migration. I will draw on about half of these in the discussion to follow. This gives a working definition of migration. It is what these scholars write about when they call it migration. In the previous discussion of crime, the chapter was organised according to social science discipline. What does economics have to say about crime, sociology, and so on? In this chapter the organising principle is by substantive aspects of migration: the reasons for migrating; attitudes of host country people towards migrants; controlling immigration, and four other headings. In no case do more than three of the five social sciences have anything to say on a particular topic. Sometimes only one discipline has something to say on a particular topic, and sometimes one study addresses more than one aspect of migration. Migration, like crime, is an interesting topic in its own right. Please forgive just a little reminder that it is only the surface topic. The main topic is what the social sciences are like as they address what is a popular social issue among journalists, politicians and much of the public at large.

Social science, like all science, addresses problems and mysteries. If there is a problem, there is likely to be a mystery. If we knew all about it, whatever *it* might be, there is much less likely to be a problem involved. In natural science there are a lot of mysteries, such as the scale of the universe, which in the ordinary sense, are not problems in the lives of most people. The mix of 'problem' and 'mystery' varies across science, with sometimes the one being dominant and sometimes the other. In general it is probably fair to say that social science is initially mostly problem driven, and the problems generally bring us face-to-face with mysteries. If that is the case, what is the problem about migration?

Looking ahead one might hazard the guess that the central problem of migration has to do with conflicts of culture. Clearly migration is not the only source of cultural conflict, as Coca-Cola and MacDonalds will testify. But it is one source. When people move and tend not to be culturally distinguishable, there is unlikely to be perception of a problem on the part of those who were there before the migrants arrived. There may still be a perceived problem for the arrivals. Culture, and the question of race — which always involves an element of culture — seems important to the migration problem story. Where anthropology was surprisingly quiet on the topic of crime, with migration it comes very much into its own. Culture is primarily the province of anthropology, and of sociology, and together these two social science subjects make up about sixty percent of the literature on migration.

THE REASONS FOR MIGRATING

As a logical matter, the dominant reason for migrating could be economic advantage, or a non-economic advantage such as a better climate, or freedom to practice a religion. The third possibility is that migrating may make little economic sense, or non-economic sense, and be motivated by some irrational impulse. There was a strong presumption among most social scientists that those migrations which are mainly due to the 'pull' factor can most often be explained more accurately by the desire on the part of the migrants to have a chance to earn a higher income.

This perfectly sensible view appeared to face a serious challenge with the huge move off the farms and into the cities in virtually all less developed countries, especially in the years after the Second World War, but continuing up to the present day. The challenge to accepted theory came from massive unemployment in Third World cities. This lack of work was, and is, accompanied by open and obvious suffering on the part of migrants on the streets of the cities, and other public spaces. It was argued that if people left modest incomes on the farm and in the village, only to become unemployed and destitute in the city, the move to the city must be caused by a combination of unrealistic expectations and a desire to be close to the seat of modernisation.

Scholars began to wonder if the earlier rural to urban migrations in what are now the high income countries were also driven in significant part by irrational motives. However, in 1969 the case for a rational economic explanation of migration in less developed countries was made in an influential article by M. Todaro. (Todaro, '69) The essential core of his argument was that migrants are rational gamblers. They risk unemployment in order to have a chance at a higher wage. If people in general are risk neutral — indifferent between one pound for sure and a fifty-fifty chance at two pounds — it makes sense for them to move to the city as long as the expected wage, meaning the actual wage times the chance of getting a job, exceeds the rural wage.

A large and still growing literature continues to explore many aspects of rural to urban migration. Among the issues are questions as to why employers in the cities pay wages that are higher than necessary to attract workers. This is sometimes addressed in institutional terms, rather than through straight market explanations. Reasons such as union pressure, minimum wage legislation, and politically sensitive foreign owned firms are advanced, which I tend to find unconvincing. Alternatively, the higher wages may be due to a wish to reduce labour turnover, or to elicit better performance. People have to be paid enough so that they do not go off to another job with the skills they have acquired, or with the tools of the job hidden under their shirts for later sale.

There is a question as to why one has to actually be in the city in order to join the queue for a city job. Maybe being there improves the chances of securing a city job, compared to waiting in the village to get the call. It also may be simplistic to see rural to urban migration as a single move. There may be a series of moves through transition settlements, as well as chances for employment in the informal sectors of urban life. Other research concentrates on the family aspect of migration. It is not a decision taken on one's own. The family may improve its information and chances by sending a representative to the city, and may be able to provide some support for the person they send. This person may seem to be worse off, when seen to be sleeping in the city street compared to sleeping in a rural hut. But that may be more a matter of appearances.

The economists George Borjas and Stephen Bronars have constructed a theory of family migration which they apply to immigrants coming to the United States over the period 1970 to 1980. (Borjas and Bronars, '91) American law on immigration favours family members. The authors note that seventy percent of the legal immigrants coming to the United States from 1981 to 1987 held entry visas which were sponsored by their relatives living in the United States. (p.123) The central tenet of their theory is that migration is a family decision and is taken so as to maximise family income. This can have results quite different from a theory of individual movement. If the cost of splitting up the family is prohibitive, people might be forced to move who would earn more by staying, or prevented from moving, although as a single individual it would pay to move.

In this theory, or model, it is assumed that workers have individual skills that might be highly rewarded in the country of origin, or in the United States. Family income in the country of origin depends on the average income level and the differential for skill earned by different family members in that country. Similarly, that family's income in the United States will depend on the average there and the differentials earned by different family members there. It could be that a particular skill is highly paid in the country of origin, but earns little in America. In which case, the migrants will tend to be people with less skill, or what the researchers call 'negatively' selected immigrants. If the differential for skill is high in America, then the immigrants will tend to have above average skills and be 'positively' selected.

This research had to deal with formidable data problems. The relevant information had to be extracted, to the extent possible, from the United States Census. This involved identifying every household with at least one immigrant. As the Census occurs every five years, what went on in the intervening years was inevitably lost. The authors only can know about immigrants living in the family household at the time of the Census. Apart from its relevance to their theory of family migration decisions, working with the data threw up a number of trends which were not particularly relevant to their core idea, but interesting in themselves. For example, the proportion of immigrants in the 1975 to 1980 cohort who had relatives in the United States prior to immigrating ranged from 44% for the Philippines down to 9% for the United Kingdom. This proportion can change quite dramatically comparing the 1970 - 1974 cohort with the 1975 - 1980 cohort. For most countries it went up over time, from 28% to 40% for Mexicans for example, with slight declines only for Canada and the United Kingdom.

Borjas and Bronars only look at male immigrants of working age who had jobs in the year prior to the Census, apart from those who were either self-employed or in the armed forces. Immediately they run into difficulty. It seems that married immigrants had less education than single immigrants do, and earned twenty-five percent more. Efforts were made to look at the wages of men who married shortly after arrival, but nothing very conclusive comes out. The model implies that single immigrants will earn more than married immigrants will if there is 'positive' selection, and less if there is 'negative' selection. How the figures turn out cannot provide a test of whether the theory is right or not. It can only suggest which type of immigration is dominant. If we hold on to the theory as being broadly correct, then the data tends to suggest that negative selection is dominant. As the authors point out, the strongest evidence for the validity of the theory of family migration decisions comes from the proportions of immigrants who are sponsored by, and live with, family members.

The economics approach of Borjas and Bronars does not take any account of the chances of getting a job. Instead it concentrates on wage differentials. Most economists working in the Todaro tradition have put job prospects at the centre of their studies, especially when studying rural to urban migration. Economists Timothy Hatton and Jeffrey Williamson apply the Todaro reasoning, with its emphasis on wage differences on the farm and in the city, combined with urban unemployment, to migration behaviour in the United States over the fifty years from 1890 to 1940. (Hatton and Williamson, '92) During this period the difference in the real wage ratio comparing farm and city started with the rural workers getting about 70% of their urban counterparts, rising to near parity, and falling to something like half at the end, with big fluctuations in the middle. The data problem of comparability of urban and rural figures has to take account of such factors as the cost of living in the city, perks to farm labourers, and seasonality in on-the-farm demand for labour. Doubts can remain about accuracy, but a serious effort was made to generate comparable figures for rural and urban wages.

In an elaborate statistical exercise, the authors examine three competing theories of the movements, and persistence, of the wage gap. The first, attributed to Evert Hagen, holds that the growth of urban industry and the associated demand for labour is too rapid for the slow pace of migration to eliminate the differential. A second theory, associated with Arthur Lewis, sees institutional differences between the country and the city as permanent sources of difference, but on its own, this theory cannot explain movements in the gap. The third idea is the Todaro view that workers migrate to raise their expected wage, and this will result in urban unemployment.

To test which theory fares better in explaining the amount of migration, and both its responses to, and causes of, wage differences; the authors relate the rural demand for labour to agricultural prices. The rural wage is explained, in the sense of statistical association, with reference to rural demand and the urban wage. Room is given in the analysis for rises in the size of the urban labour force from foreign labour, and these increases tend to reduce migration from the farms.

The urban wage is not explained in the model. It is simply taken as data. A rise in the urban wages has an ambiguous effect on migration to the cities. Two opposite responses may occur. All things being equal, a rise in urban wages increases the move to the cities. But all things are not equal. The higher wage reduces the demand for labour in the cities. Where the higher wage induces migration, the higher unemployment acts against it. Which force will dominate on balance depends on whether the response of employers in the city to the wage rise is slight or rather large. Hatton and Williamson undertake a number of statistical investigations, none of which are entirely and explicitly consistent with economic theory. They are very suggestive. The conclusion is that a migration theory which was designed to account for the rise in urban unemployment in Third World countries works pretty well in explaining the wage gap in the United States over a period with rapid rise in non-farm activity, and a steep decline in employment in agriculture.

There is one point on which this research is surprisingly quiet. When the Todaro model is applied in less developed countries, it is assumed that the rural wage can be secured with certainty. We are dealing with largely self-employed, family organised agricultural production. Unless a person has committed some grave infraction of the normal rules of behaviour, rural work is assured. Leaving rural unemployment out of the picture in the United States over this period would seem to be rather a different matter, and potentially to be quite serious for the analysis. Families may lose their farms, and finding employment on other farms would hardly seem to be guaranteed. If staying put is not an option, migration will either be to the city, or to some other rural area, which is likely to be, or quite plausibly could be assumed to be, as badly off as the one a family is leaving. Hatton and Williamson have made a brave attempt to apply an important theory. Taking my suggestion and allowing for rural unemployment might have had the effect of complicating matters, but leaving the explanation of why people move more-or-less intact. We cannot be sure.

The most extensive effort to explain why people migrate was done by the sociologists Douglas Massey and Kristin Espinosa. (Massey and Espinosa, '97) Their work was designed to account for both legal and illegal migration of Mexicans into the United States. It also focused on second trips to America, and whether migrants chose to settle there, or return to Mexico. Some use was made of published data, as we shall see, but the heart of the study was nearly five thousand interviews carried out in Mexico during the winter months of 1987 to 1992.

Interviews were conducted in twenty-five communities in the states of Guanajuato, Nayarit, Jalisco, Michoacan and Zacatecas. The goal was to interview 200 households in each community, and on the whole they succeeded. They also followed up leads from these interviews and interviewed another five hundred selected individuals living in the United States. The basic approach of this study is to determine peoples' circumstances by asking questions about their particular characteristics. This information is related to what people actually do. Do they migrate — once, twice, and do they stay in America?

Massey and Espinosa have in their sights five related but different theories intended to explain why people migrate. The first of these they call 'neo-classical economics', which they take to be the view that the wage gap is the main determinant. Potential migrants compare the wage at home and abroad to determine the benefits, and subtract the cost of moving. If the benefits exceed the costs, the individual attempts to migrate. This rather simplistic model is reasonably consistent with how economists analyse the problem, particularly when the chances of getting a job are very high. Pure economic theory would be inclined to take account of all the costs and benefits and assume that Mexicans, like everyone else, maximise some function which depends on many things, including wage income. In practice empirical work in economics can usually be described as the authors have done, whatever the pure theory would suggest.

Suffice it to say that the 'neo-classical' model does not come off very well in this study. Standard studies done by economists typically draw on published figures for wages. By conducting their interviews, Massey and Espinosa had figures on the earnings of particular individuals in Mexico, and what they could expect to earn in the United States, or did in fact earn there. Interestingly, the payoff to Mexicans from educational qualifications when they go to America tends to be small, especially if they cannot be documented. Most wind up in such jobs as "busboy, maid, dishwasher, gardener, factory worker, and agricultural laborer". (p. 948)

It turns out that the statistical relation between wage rate differences and migration is not strong. The results are somewhat different for legal and illegal migrants. For legal immigrants the expected wage differential had no effect on a first trip to America, a second one, or eventual return to Mexico. For the illegal immigrants, it did relate to the first trip, but only weakly. There is some indication that experience and skills acquired in America add to 'human capital' as it is called, and increase the chances of taking another trip, and not returning to Mexico. This is consistent with the neo-classical view that migrants move to where their abilities are more highly rewarded.

Massey and Espinosa give some attention to 'social capital theory', which emphasises the importance of networks of friends, business contacts and family members in the decision to move or to stay, and having moved to possibly stay in America. The data give convincing support for the importance of social capital, but are not revealing as to cause and effect. The concept lumps together issues of information, insurance, and obligation. In the end, the authors do not make big claims for the theory. This is a good decision, not because there is nothing to it, but because it is not well worked out, in my view.

Two other ideas that receive very limited support from this investigation are the 'segmented labour market theory' and the 'world system theory'. The two theories have something in common. Both see the market for labour as being an international market, with the former emphasising demand for labour in the high-income countries, and the latter emphasising global capitalism. These ideas have more the flavour of being other ways of stating what we want to explain, rather than being explanations. They also tend to address the general phenomena of migration more than the question of why one person migrates and not another.

The most unusual feature of this enormous survey is the support it gives to what these sociologists call the 'new economics of migration'. They attribute the concept to the economist Oded Stark and others. Essentially it is what is called a 'missing markets' theory. In one smoothly working, integrated market, earned income could be translated into any form — consumption, financial assets, and physical assets. The ease of doing so will be less than perfect in any actual situation, and the theory holds that restricted, or missing markets, are a main motive for migration. "Interest rates, not wages, appear to be the key macroeconomic factor determining the course of Mexico-U.S. migration. As they go up, circulation within the migration system accelerates: more Mexicans leave for the United States to gain capital, and more migrants return to Mexico to invest what they have saved." (p.987) As a general conclusion, this may be pushing both the data and the theory overly hard. It does work for farmers receiving the right to work land under the *ejidos*, or land reform system. These migrants have the land, but needed to acquire the capital in order to work it.

This is a rich, if disorderly, piece of scientific work. A great variety of insights are produced. Over forty different factors are used in trying to explain this migration. The researchers conclude that there is a consolidation process going on between the two economies, and this drives the international movement of labour. Acquiring skills and building networks further reinforces the benefits from migrating. They are critical of American policies which inadvertently produce incentives to migrate, though it is difficult to see how these could be avoided, and the authors make no suggestions. What does seem very probable is their view that efforts to control migration will be costly, sometimes brutal, and pretty ineffective.

In contrast with the Mexican case, where the official American policy is one of discouragement and containment, responding to a deliberate policy of attracting workers can be a reason for migrating. The sociologist Daphne Phillips has documented the efforts of hospitals in the United States to attract nurses to that country. She attributes the growth in this practice to increased commercialisation of the health services in America, and the pressing need to control the cost of providing these services. (Phillips, '96) The evidence for active recruitment is straightforward, namely, advertisements in the local press, and meetings organised by agents of American hospitals in the Trinidad Hilton. Potential migrants were offered "compensation packages" that were deemed to be attractive.

There is a long history of nurses trained in the Caribbean going to work in high-income countries. This is not the only low-income area which is training nurses, only to see them leave and work elsewhere. When it comes to choice of foreign country, it is more common for nurses from Trinidad and Tobago to migrate to the United Kingdom. There are strong historical ties between the two countries, and academic collaboration means there is automatic accreditation. More recently, some Caribbean nurses are leaving the United Kingdom and going to work in the United States. The departure of nurses from Trinidad and Tobago has placed pressure on hospitals, and in addition, there was a strike by nurses in 1990. (p. 110) Along with the 'pull' from America, Phillips argues that there are 'push' factors due in part to IMF pressure on government wages — the government is the main employer of nurses — and the general tendency to penalise the wages of women.

The author did a survey of a stratified sample of 10% of the population of 3,500 nurses. It was intended to identify the main sources of discontent. These were spread across a wide range of issues, including such factors as night duty, security arrangements and staff/patient ratios. The items which attracted the largest percentages of nurses who were dissatisfied were opportunities for specialisation and adequacy of materials. This suggests strong attachment to the profession. The survey found over 83 percent of those in the sample liked nursing as a career. But a slightly higher percent "indicated they would migrate". Over a third of these chose the United

States as the intended destination, with a fifth choosing the United Kingdom and a fifth choosing Canada.

Phillips gives favourable mention to three policies aimed at reducing the outward flow. One is to raise the status of student nurses; a second is to make them contribute to the cost of their training; and a third is to require them to apply for hospital jobs in Trinidad and Tobago, rather than getting these jobs automatically. This policy package does not follow from the survey undertaken. One might think the last two would be more likely to encourage migration. Perhaps a better policy would be to require nurses who emigrate to reimburse the government for their training.

The survey also does not provide evidence for Phillips' conspiracy theory that, "The application of IMF policies in several areas of the Third World has deliberately served the interests of 'foreign' multinational corporations...", including those in the health sector. (p. 125) Nevertheless, the study provides a graphic picture of one kind of migration. Whether the recruitment efforts in the Trinidad Hilton are due to competition between United States hospitals, and only affect which hospital migrating nurses go to, or whether they raise the total outflow of nurses, would be an interesting research question.

Professional sportsmen and women are also migrating from low-income countries, as well as moving between developed countries. Whether this migration has similar consequences for those left behind, like those caused by the migration of nurses, may be doubted. But being in professional sport is for some people a cause of migrating, and this migration also raises research issues. People like myself, who do not follow a sport which absorbs the attention of much of the population, such as football in the United Kingdom, are sometimes mystified by the loyalty and identification the fans demonstrate for what they think of as 'their team'. This attachment would be a little easier to understand if the team members came from the same general area as the fans. But increasingly this seems to play a very small role in how teams are perceived. It is rather more the case that an area has a team that goes forth and does battle. The fans are pretty well indifferent as to who is in the team. The important thing is victory for what they think of as their side. Joseph Maguire discusses cultural identity issues of this kind as one of a number of possible research topics in sport migration. (Maguire, '94)

Professional sport leads to an international market for players, with the more prosperous teams able to hire players from anywhere in the world. The rights of workers in this sector is another one of the research areas proposed by the sociologist Maguire. To the outsider it might appear that these players are rewarded well for their efforts, but increasingly the contracts, and other practices common in a number of sports, particularly team sports, are being challenged in the courts. The author suggests that the attractions of professional sport, which necessitates moving to a foreign country, may come at an emotional and psychological cost which is not immediately apparent to those making the move. He also draws attention to possible subtle effects on less developed countries that loose their sporting heroes to the advanced countries.

Maguire ends by citing the history of the English Amateur Basketball Association, which formed in 1936 and held control of the game through to most of the 1960's. But over the years from 1972 to 1988 the league grew from six to fifty-two teams. The centre of gravity shifted from domestic amateur players to ambitious international players. The game itself shifted from being a participant's game to being a spectacle, with all that this implies for sponsorship and television appearances. The author sees this as having to do with the Americanisation of sport, and no doubt basketball is a particularly good example. Whether the United States has much to do with European commercialisation of football needs to be established. The author maintains that sport migration occupies a place once held by "...artists, musicians, poets and scholars...". (p.453) With sporting events being a major form of community activity, and a source of individual identity, displacing artists and intellectuals, more understanding of the effects of sport migration has the potential for making a significant contribution to both sport policy and to wider national policies and aspirations.

THE EXPERIENCE OF IMMIGRANTS IN THE HOST COUNTRY

We can see from the previous discussion that almost all the investigations of the motives for migration concentrate on economic advancement, at least with regard to the English language journal literature of the 90's. The anthropologist Mark Moberg is an exception in pointing out that over three million people in Central America were forced to migrate by political violence, with most of them going to neighbouring countries. In his survey of motives, one in four immigrant said they came to Belize for political reasons. (Moberg, '96, p.425) We will return to this aspect of his study when we take up the topic of refugees. Our concern here is with what happens to the immigrants in their new country. The experiences of migrants when they arrive in the host country may be disappointing and possibly tragic, even if the move to the new country was the best option open.

Moberg's research, done in 1993, concentrates on men working on banana plantations in the Stann Creek and Toledo districts of Belize. The context is essential to understanding the situation of these foreign workers, who make up virtually the whole of the workforce on plantations. Belize was a former British colony, and as such has close ties with anglophone West Indies. The Afro-Belizean population has resisted integration with Central America. Its identity as an Afro-Caribbean nation is now felt by most of the traditional population to be under threat from the Hispanic immigrants, who outnumber them for the first time in the history of the country. (p. 425)

Over the decade 1980 to 1990, the Hispanic population rose by just over seventy percent. The anglophone population actually fell in numbers slightly due to emigration. It is possible that there are now more Afro-Belizeans living in the United States than in Belize. (p. 426) The 1991 Census in Belize gives rough indications of country of origin, but is unclear on the issue of minors and undocumented immigrants. The figures suggest that three quarters of the immigrants were from three Hispanic countries; forty percent being from Guatamala, twenty-two percent from El Salvador, and ten percent from Honduras. A survey in 1993 of farm workers showed that thirty-four percent were from Guatamala, thirty-two percent from Honduras and twenty-five from El Salvador. The native Belizean farm workers were less than ten percent of the total working on these farms.

Moberg's study of the plight of immigrant farm workers in Belize is based on two kinds of information: a survey of 160 household heads working on the banana plantations, and observation combined with informal conversations. It is the latter which reveals the very poor conditions of these workers who struggle to survive in a highly concentrated industry dominated by the multinational Fyffes. The more indigenous population is not inclined to distinguish between different nationalities, and calls all immigrants "aliens", or uses an unflattering term, *panias,* meaning Spanish. (p.425) The disorganised and often illegal immigrants have lost the benefits which the union (the UGWU) secured for Belizeans. These included farm transportation, medical benefits and special clothing. Competition for jobs has resulted in low pay. (427)

Not only do Belizeans dislike the immigrants, but also the different nationalities carry the memories of war between the home countries over to the new setting. Moberg reports some chilling incidents. The hostility on all sides is accompanied by economic hardship. The author quotes a worker from Honduras. "Look at how the people live here in their little shacks. Here we have no water, no light, no doctor...and every year, we work more and more to earn less and less." (p.433) These in depth looks at the lives of immigrants do not come from the survey as such. They are due to anthropological observation, and they paint a disturbing picture.

Immigrants suffering at the hands of other immigrants, while being at the bottom of the social and economic ranking, is not uncommon. Garden City,

Kansas, a fairly rural community, has experienced rapid growth, due in part to the arrival of the IPB meat packing plant. Working at the plant is not well paid, is arduous, and is looked down on socially. The plant is a major employer of immigrants. Housing shortage and the low cost of mobile homes have led to the development of two trailer courts; the larger East Garden Village, and the smaller Wagon Wheel court. The anthropologist Janet Benson has observed the lives of the mainly immigrant residents of these trailer courts. (Benson, '90) In the summer of 1987 she lived ten days at Wagon Wheel with a Vietnamese couple, both employees of the meat packing plant. After that she stayed with various Vietnamese families for short periods. She rented her own mobile home in East Garden Village in the summer of 1988. The following summer she stayed with a Hispanic family. Hispanics were the dominant immigrant group, followed by Vietnamese, with small numbers of Laotian and Cambodian immigrants.

Benson's research draws heavily on statements from her informants. These build up a picture of two rather fragile trailer court communities, quite isolated from the wider world. Trailer court living in itself implies low social status, as does working at the IPB plant. The different ethic groups have their little sub-ghettos in the courts, and little help is given across ethnic lines. Children are sometimes bullied by children from another group, and when they do play together, this seems to have little effect on the parents. Being divided, the immigrants are an ineffective pressure group. Responsibility for dealing with such problems as burglary, fire, sanitation and traffic is divided between an indifferent local government, and the owners of the courts who find their profits to be disappointingly low. Socialising is very limited. The most that one hopes for is to be left alone. "I just stay in my house. Do my own thing. But I do make neighbor watch...Anybody I suspect I call the police. I do that, but I do not talk to them. I think there is no need to. We know each other. If I see this gentleman, this Laotian over there, I just say 'Hi'. That's all we talk. But I do watch his house." (p. 381) This is a report from one of the few Chinese people living in the courts. Benson concludes that in spite of the various immigrant groups having in principle much to gain from making common cause, the existing segregation from both the wider anglo community, and within the immigrant community, is going to continue well into the future. She attributes this in part to the importance of kinship ties over freely formed interactions, particularly on the part of less educated Vietnamese and Laotians immigrants coming from rural backgrounds.

Aihwa Ong is an anthropologist who takes the analysis of the experience of Asian immigrants in the United States to philosophical levels of abstraction, while maintaining an important role for scientific insight. (Ong, '96) As is customary with feature articles in the journal *Current*

Anthropology, half a dozen anthropologists comment on her observations, her arguments and her conclusions. These scholars, and others Ong writes about, study the processes of adjustment, settlement, acceptance, assimilation, identification and belonging, along with the opposites, or lack of these, in the experience of Third World immigrants coming to the First World. Complex interactions of race, culture, and economic position are postulated. Ong defends a concept of "cultural citizenship" which encompasses all of these aspects. She can be read as asking the question, has migration been a success for the immigrant? What factors bear on the kinds of outcomes that we observe? In a long and complex paper, Ong argues the case for keeping race as an element in the discussion. Exclusive reliance on a concept of culture as determining self-image, and the way one is perceived by others, is mistaken.

It is hard to imagine serious disagreement with this position. The anthropology commentators on her work do not do so, and instead ask for clarification of some connecting arguments, or disagree with subsidiary aspects of the discussion. The basic point is accepted. There is also general agreement with the proposition, attributed to the work of Foucault, that becoming a cultural citizen involves both self-motivated actions and choices, internal adjustments if you like, and effects coming form the community. These later effects cover a huge range running from the workings of national institutions down to the behaviour of neighbours.

The author, and some of the commentators, do not hesitate to draw on their own experiences, at times, as evidence for their points of view. Ong is a woman from Malaysia who came to New York as a student, and was quickly caught up in the Vietnam protest movement. She mixes personal observations with reports from people she has met. For example, she discusses the cultural conflicts of immigrants from Cambodia who were very poor and dependent on welfare.

A number of Khmer families were receiving money earmarked for assistance in raising children, and these cheques went to the wife. This had the effect of making the husbands feel inadequate. They wanted control over the welfare cheque, and this led to family conflict. Of course, the same could be said about a number of white Protestant families with long histories of living in America. Ong notes this. Her point is that Cambodian women feel that on balance it is better to maintain the male dominated family system. She quotes an informant. "There are many cases of wife abuse. Yes, everyone gets beaten, myself included. But sometimes we have to just keep quiet even after a disagreement...I don't want to call the police or anything...I just shed a few tears and let it go...the men still think more of themselves than of women. They never lower themselves to be our equals."

(p. 743)Undoubtedly the work is deeply felt and makes interesting connections.

One of the commentators was David Wu, who returned to the University of Hong Kong after doing graduate work in Honolulu. He concludes, "Ong may have presented an oversimplified model to explain the process of cultural citizenship in the United States that cannot accommodate all aspects and variations of the subject-making experience of Asian immigrants, but her fundamental points deserve attention and elaboration." (p.756) I see this work as having elements of social science while being philosophical in two senses. It has to do with the inherently philosophical enquiry into what is the good life. At the same time, It operates in the speculative, or initial and initiating, phase of scientific enquiry which naturally draws on philosophical predispositions.

One could hardly imagine a bigger contrast with the work of Aihwa Ong than that of the economist Brian Bell. Far from philosophical speculation and an almost unbounded scope of enquiry, Bell wants to document the wages that immigrants earn in the United Kingdom compared to natives, note changes in these relationships, and offer some explanations. (Bell, '97) Discovering what happened is not a simple matter of looking up the figures, as like must be compared to like. Immigrants and natives with skills that are scarce and in demand will earn more than other workers will. For the purposes of this study, skill is equated with education, the latter being more readily observable. The author uses the twenty General Household Surveys published over the years 1973 to 1992.

The number of immigrants in the United Kingdom is remarkably similar to the number in the United States — 5.9% for the U.K. and 6.1% for the U.S.A. Over the thirty year period 1960 to 1990 their share in the total population grew similarly by 2% for the U.K. and 2.5% for the U.S. (p. 333) Domestic policy and other factors resulted in significant changes over time in where immigrants were coming from when they entered the United Kingdom. Earlier years favoured the Commonwealth, and later years the European Continent.

The biggest statistical challenge in determining the influences on wages of immigrants is separating out differences attributable to the cohort who arrived, and the effects of assimilation over time. This is done with 'pooled regressions' which simultaneously take account of comparisons across individuals at a point in time, and changes over time. Bell concentrates on the experience of black immigrants, and on the influence on their U.K. wages of educational attainments and experience of immigrants prior to coming to the United Kingdom.

The crucial finding of this study is that black immigrants, especially from the Caribbean, with extensive work experience abroad lose out dramatically when they come to the United Kingdom. Their wages do not do justice to their abilities. The data suggests that this disadvantage diminishes over time, but does not disappear altogether. Those male workers with ten years' prior experience initially earn 28% less than comparable native workers, and those with twenty years' prior experience earn 34% less. These differentials decline to 11% and 17% respectively. (p.342) Black immigrants who enter the labour market in the United Kingdom with no prior experience earn more-or-less the same wages as their native counterparts.

White immigrants in the United Kingdom tend to be rewarded by the labour market for their prior education and experience. Indeed, there is a striking puzzle in that immigrants from Europe in the 1970 to 1979 cohort with no prior experience, but twelve years education, earned 30% more than their native counterparts. Bell suggests that they may have abilities which are not measured in these statistical exercises. However, the initial wage advantage declines over time and eventually disappears. This is mysterious. Do they assimilate and lose their special ability? The author hints that maybe the more able move on to other countries, presumably the United States. It is unclear whether or not this distorts the statistical finding. He suggests that there be more research on how the year of entry effects the movement of immigrants' wages over time.

Economic returns are far from being everything, and many observers believe that immigrants generally tend to have poor mental health. One could think of a comparison with the population of the host country, or with the population they left behind, and with the counterfactual of what their mental health would have been had they stayed. The social psychologists Regina Pernice and Judith Brook studied the mental health of British, Southeast Asian and Pacific Island immigrants in New Zealand, itself an "immigrant country". (Pernice and Brook, '96) Their method consists of attempting to form representative samples of each of the three groups, identifying demographic and other factors about the individuals in the groups, and then statistically relating the individuals to their mental health. If an association can be found between a characteristic and a mental state, particularly an adverse state, there is a presumption that the one caused the other.

A sixteen-item questionnaire was used for the study, with the usual demographic questions on age, education, sex and marital status. There were questions about job satisfaction, and whether or not the job was similar to that in the country of origin. Other items covered housing accommodation, friends and relatives in New Zealand, income, and knowledge of English. There were even items about fulfilment of spiritual needs, along with length of stay in New Zealand, and how one spent one's leisure time. Mental health was assessed using a shortened version of the

Hopkins Symptom Check List. (Hesbacher and colleagues, '80) This was supplemented by a structured interview to help with the questionnaire items, and particularly aimed at measuring the experience of discrimination. Two regressions were run. One related anxiety to the potential explanatory factors, and the other was for depression.

Pernice and Brook found no effect from demographic factors on mental health. This was a refutation of the their hypothesis that, "...demographic characteristics...should be related to...symptom levels..." (p. 513) One might wonder why there was no difference between married and single immigrants. What they did find was a "crucial" role for discrimination in causing anxiety and depression among the Southeast Asian and Pacific Island immigrants. This is in line with similar research in other countries. When it came to the British immigrants, discrimination played no part. For them being unemployed was a major factor. Eighty percent of the British immigrants with serious emotional distress were unemployed. Half that proportion of the Pacific Islanders was unemployed. Another strong association the authors found was between poor mental health and spending a good deal of time with one's own ethnic group.

The issue of causality is particularly troubling in this research. Even with discrimination, it is possible that people with poor mental health are more likely to attract adverse responses, which may or may not be examples of undiluted discrimination. Feeling discriminated against can also be a symptom of poor mental health. However, the contrast between the British immigrants and the others on the question of discrimination does lend support to the theory that discrimination causes poor mental health in the victims of it. The unemployment story is less persuasive. Being anxious or depressed, or both, can make it harder to obtain work. And when it comes to spending one's time with one's own ethnic group as a *cause* of poor mental health, the authors are rightly uncertain as to the directions of cause. Discovering the facts about mental health is always difficult. This study helps, though it does not compare overall health levels of immigrants to other groups.

Only two pieces of research in the 90's studied the outcome for immigrants moving from one less developed country to another. We have seen the results in Belize. This second case provides a far more cheerful story than the other, with a fascinating twist in the tale. A popular view nowadays is that it is healthy in psychological, political and social terms to keep memories of the past alive in the present. Where one came from matters. People should be aware of, and celebrate, their roots. The official American ideology of the melting pot is in retreat in much of the world. This may be because the level playing field which it implies has failed to materialise. But whatever the reason, attachment to one's origins is encouraged.

Much academic thinking is in accord with the popular view, and sees communities which can trace their past and are actively conscious of it as having an advantage over immigrants who cannot, or choose not, to look back. The anthropologist Janet Carsten studied Maylay immigrants and their recent descendants living on the island of Langkwi. (Carsten, '95) At least for this group, her findings go against the popular view, and the academic view, about remembering.

Carsten explains that Langkawi is an island off the west coast of Malaysia and is part of the Kedah State. Her fieldwork concentrated on a fishing village called Sungai Cantik. She interviewed 260 adults. The hope was that these subjects were representative of the village as a whole. It turned out that 48 were not born on the island. Among the 212 who were born there, another 48 had one or both parents who migrated to Langkawi. A number came from mainland Kedah, or from other states of Malaysia. "Significant" numbers came from Thailand, and there were representatives from Java, India, and Hong Kong. By any standard, this is a substantial and varied immigrant population. There is also long history of migration. Of the 164 people in the sample who were born on the island and had parents born on the island, 44 had grandparents on either their mother's side or their father's side who were not from Langkawi.

The author reports that very few people could trace their family trees more than two generations, and more to the point, had little interest in doing so. The Acehnese from Sumatra were probably among the founders of the village. This group has a generally respected reputation for military prowess, religious piety and learning. Yet the villagers who knew they were descendants of the Aceh appeared to attach no importance to this. Other descendants were unaware of the connection, and when informed of it regarded it as being of no significance. Carsten was particularly struck by the response that people made when asked where their neighbours, or others in the village, came from. They did not seem to know, or to attach any importance to it.

This research strongly suggests that the people of Langkawi place a lot of emphasis on creating kinship. "The past is to a considerable extent one of diversity, but the future can be projected as one of similarity and kinship." (p. 329) The village headman told the author that the people in Sungai Cantik "mix easily". His comment confirmed her central finding when he remarked that "people don't dig up their past". Carsten urges her fellow anthropologists to think more about systematic forgetting as a positive part of creating a community. One cannot detect in this report any of the adverse experiences which characterise many other studies. Moving from one Third

World country to another may be a part of the explanation, though very adverse experiences from such migration are far from unknown. Carsten maintains that on this island, "...forgetting is implicit, gradual and unmarked — its effects are...more hidden." (p. 331) This should be seen in a positive light as part of one way of making a successful community.

ATTITUDES TOWARDS IMMIGRANTS

Migration is unlikely to be without difficulty. Movement within a country may generally be easier for the migrants than international migration. When all three hurdles of rural to urban movement, one country to another, and from a less developed to a developed country are involved, the move may often be particularly difficult. We see from the studies above that an important source of difficulty is prejudice on the part of the indigenous population. Not surprisingly, social scientists have devoted considerable effort to studying this phenomenon.

The sociologist Lionel Cantu writes about Mexicans in Midtown, Iowa. (Cantu, '95) Expansion of a food processing plant led to hiring first illegal, and then more legal Mexican workers. The story is rather like the one that Janet Benson tells about immigrant workers in Kansas. Prior to the arrival of the new plant, the community in Midtown numbered 1,200, was white, and homogenous. People knew each other and knew who did and did not 'belong there'. Cantu interviewed a Mexican worker who sensed being watched by the local community. One woman who found the town both peaceful and beautiful, nevertheless was aware that there were "...a lot of people who don't like how we Mexicans are." (p. 405) The eight people interviewed for the study provide graphic evidence concerning a minority workforce who are needed economically but rejected socially. In so far as adverse feelings towards immigrants are explained, the implicit idea seems to be that a small homogeneous community resents any intrusion from people who are different.

In passing, Lionel Cantu makes some reference to "Proposition 187". This was a law passed in California in 1994, which excluded illegal immigrants from welfare benefits, public health care, social services and education. The social psychologist Wendy Quinton and her fellow researchers used support for the law, and opposition to it, as a means of investigating the formation of prejudicial attitudes. (Quinton, '96) In essence, they considered three possible factors leading to support for the law: having a right wing, authoritarian personality; reliance on stereotypes; and attitudes towards one's own in-group, or 'collective self-esteem'. The authors see their work as establishing that support or opposition to Proposition 187 was mainly associated with prejudice against illegal immigrants. This is different from the view that people not paying taxes should not benefit from the state, or the view that this law would discourage illegal immigration, which in itself might be a good thing.

Quinton and her colleagues began with an initial group of 231 university students. The final sample actually used for their surveys contained 92 Latinos and 79 Caucasians. There were 60 men and 111 women. Being students, their earnings tended to be around $10,000 per year or less. Some earned more. This study made use of both off-the-shelf questionnaires and one designed by the authors. To measure right-wing authoritarianism they used an up-dated set of questions originally devised by Altemeyer. (Altemeyer, '81) Respondents were asked if they agreed with statements like, "Once our government leaders give us the 'go ahead', it will be the duty of every patriotic citizen to help stomp out the rot that is poisoning our country from within.", or disagreed with statements like, "There is absolutely nothing wrong with nudist camps." (p. 2221)

To measure stereotypical belief about illegal immigrants, the authors made a list of eight positive characteristics like 'intelligent' and 'likeable', and eight negative characteristics like 'dirty' and 'uncivilised'. The students were asked to estimate the proportion of illegal immigrants, legal immigrants, and non-immigrants who could be described by each of the characteristics. Collective self-esteem was measured by a combination of the Multigroup Ethic Identity Measure (Luhtanen and Crocker, '92) and the Collective Self-Esteem Scale, (Pinney, '92). The idea here is to distinguish between people who place a great deal of importance in terms of self-image and identity on their membership in a group, and those who do not. The 'group' typically is of a religious or ethnic nature, but may take other forms.

The result of this study by Quinton and her colleagues is a curious mixture of subtle and more obvious points. For Caucasians, right wing authoritarianism is associated with both stereotyping and collective self-esteem(CSE). All three of these factors lead to support for Proposition 187, the law excluding illegal immigrants from state provided benefits. For the Latino sample the results for 'right-wing' and 'stereotyping' were much the same as those for Caucasians. But for collective self-esteem, the results were the opposite of those for the Caucasians. Latinos with high CSE tended to vote against the law, whereas Caucasians with high CSE voted in favour. The Caucasian vote might be expected. The authors feel they can explain the Latino vote by respondents identifying, or not identifying, with the group the law is attacking, which is fair enough. Presumably the Caucasians who vote against the law do so for other reasons than identification. The authors believe that, "Caucasians are a self-conscious, collectivistic political force in this country." (p.2220) One hopes that this is not an example of stereotyping.

Agustin Echabe and Jose Castro have studied the nature of prejudice against immigrants in the Basque country. (Echabe and Castro, ' 96) These social psychologists were interested in uncovering some significant details in the structure of the attitudes the dominant majority hold in their perception of newcomers. They administered a questionnaire to 393 subjects living in the Basque area. The sample contained roughly equal numbers of men and women, and the group had an average age in the mid-thirties. A third of the subjects were students, a fifth housewives, and the rest were distributed across a variety of jobs. The choice of subjects for their survey was a bit unscientific. The authors were not able to construct a stratified sample. However, they were quite pleased that their study did not rely exclusively on a sample of university psychology students, which is the norm in so many investigations.

Their particular concern was with how a policy of closing the border to immigrants would effect the perception of immigrants. On the one hand, by reducing the competition for jobs and other sources of threat, it could result in a more favourable attitude. On the other hand, by appearing to give an official legitimisation to prejudice, it could result in a less favourable image of immigrants. As it turned out, a critical factor is whether we are talking about immigrants from Third World countries, or immigrants from other European countries.

The method Echabe and Castro employed was to include over fifty questions in their survey of the kind, "Immigrants take jobs away from us", and, "I will accept an immigrant as my friend". (pp. 345 - 347) Most of the questions called for scaling on a scale of 'one' to 'five', with one being complete disagreement, and five being complete agreement. The questions were grouped under various headings meant to capture, among other features, the attitudes the subjects held, what gave rise to those attitudes, and the policies towards immigrants which the respondents favoured. A concerted effort was made, using a multivariate analysis of variance, to discriminate between the kind of policy the subjects favoured when thinking about immigrants from Third World countries, compared to immigrants from European countries.

Where European immigrants were seen as "intelligent, clean and hard working", Third World immigrants were comparatively more "friendly, generous, open and good". (p. 349) A fairly sharp result seems to emerge on the hypothetical effects of a policy of closing the border to immigrants. The Basque respondents anticipate that as a result the immigrants now in the country will see themselves as receiving less sympathy and less respect, and consequently will feel more *despite* towards the native population. The authors repeat his archaic term 'despite' a number of times. The respondents think that as a result of closing the border, the Basques are likely to feel more fear, distrust, contempt and rage towards immigrants, and have less sympathy towards them. Along with these negative reactions, the suggestion of closing the borders appears to result in more emphasis being given to attributing the causes of immigration to adverse conditions in the source countries, particularly political corruption and lack of opportunity. In itself, these results give some support the "deligitimisation" effect of a policy of closing the border. At the same time, keeping open frontiers to immigrants was seen to lead to more conflict between the local population and immigrants, and to a greater willingness to support anti-immigrant movements.

A good deal of research has centred on the idea that people like to hold what they think of as consistent views. Contradictory positions result in what is called 'cognitive dissonance'. This is an unstable state of mind, and it tends to be resolved one way or another by adjusting one of the inconsistent positions. Gregory Maio and his colleagues have examined the role of this kind of ambivalence in attitude as it effects perceptions of immigrants. (Maio and colleagues, '96) An ambivalent attitude means that an individual holds both negative and positive views of a certain group. The authors refer to a variety of studies along these lines, including work on attitudes towards African-Americans on the part of the White majority in the United States. Maio and his researchers studied the effect of ambivalence on attitudes towards Hong Kong immigrants in Canada. Their basic conjecture was that people holding ambivalent attitudes would be more inclined to change their views in response to strongly worded new information than people who were less ambivalent towards immigrants.

They worked with a rather small sample of psychology undergraduates — 73 female and 40 male students. Apart from the familiar problem of using psychology students to represent attitudes in the wider population, great care was taken to measure the attitudes the students held towards oriental people, and the degree of ambivalence in their views. For the latter, the subjects were asked to give a score of -3 if they viewed Orientals negatively with respect to a particular characteristic, and +3 if they were positively inclined. If all the opinions were the same, ambivalence is zero in the formula used. With twelve characteristics, total ambivalence would occur when there were six scores of -3 and six of +3.

The next phase of the experiment consisted of the participants reading one of two made up versions of what appeared to be an editorial from a well known paper. One version was very favourable to people from Hong Kong, describing them as hard working, polite, and friendly. The other version added the word "somewhat" to the description. Similarly, another statement described the Hong Kong immigrants as sharing the values of Canadians, with the weaker statement saying they shared "a few" of those values. In the de-briefing all the manipulation done in the experiment was explained to the students. Before revealing the trick, the final phase involved measuring attitudes towards Hong Kong immigrants.

The key point of this study by Maio and his colleagues is that for ambivalent students there was some association between the version of the made-up editorial they read, and their final view of immigrants from Hong Kong. For the students who were not ambivalent, which version they read — the one that was strongly favourable or the one where praise was heavily qualified — made no difference to their final judgement. There are a number of possible explanations for this result. One is that people with ambivalent attitudes have an underlying desire to resolve their feelings one way or the other, and therefore attend to information which could help them to do that. Using the results of the final set of questions about immigrants from Hong Kong, the authors also calculated a new ambivalence measure. Those initially ambivalent students who had read the 'strong' made-up editorial were less ambivalent, whereas those who were ambivalent and read the 'weak' message were just as ambivalent after reading that version of the editorial. One wonders what the results would be if the 'strong' version was actively hostile, and the 'weak' version was only qualifiedly hostile. Given the apparent ease of changing peoples' opinions, it may be just as well that this was not tried.

DO IMMIGRANTS 'FIT IN'?

It is generally agreed that when immigrants arrive in a host country they have certain obligations towards the people living there. They may also be thought to have a more abstract duty towards the new country. There is much less agreement as to the specific nature of these obligations and duties. Most countries have formal rules as well as informal expectations. These rules may include matters like an obligation to learn the dominant language, and a willingness to serve in the armed forces. Some countries have an expectation that new arrivals will eventually adopt all the behaviour patterns common in the host society. Other countries may place only minimal pressure on immigrants, and allow them to live for an indefinite time in a way that is quite separate and distinct from the practices of the majority. Almost no one is willing to be taken over by immigrants, and see their country transformed by them into something alien.

Both of the papers on 'fitting in' discussed in this sub-section are by political scientists, which is interesting in itself. Rodolfo Garza and his colleagues wanted to determine the extent to which Mexican-Americans support the United States core values of patriotism and economic individualism. (Garza and colleagues, '96) They begin by quoting Thomas Jefferson and his fears of the potential consequences of an influx of large numbers of foreigners who might not share American values. These immigrants might, "...warp and bias its [the national policy's] directions, and render it a heterogeneous, incoherent, distracted mass..." (Fuchs, 90) These Jeffersonian worries are echoed today by Senator Alan Simpson and ex-Governor Richard Lamm, who see the 13 million Mexican-Americans in an unfavourable light. In addition to being numerically significant, Mexican-Americans are quite well organised politically and able to support selected candidates for public office. Simpson and Lamm are not alone in fearing a threat to values that are widely held in the United States. Their views find some support in a poll conducted by the National Opinion Research Centre in 1990.

As the authors point out, it is entirely possible for a group in society to have a rather different culture than that of the majority when it comes to such matters as linguistic habits, food preferences, dress style and so on, and still share the basic values of the majority. The two should not be confused, though it is likely that they often are. In this study Garza and his fellow researchers compared Mexican-Americans to 'Anglos' in terms of patriotism and belief in economic individualism. It was conjectured that the views of Mexican- Americans on these two matters would be influenced by their degree of 'acculturation'. This is taken to depend on whether or not they were born in the United States, and whether English or Spanish was dominant, or whether they were bilingual. Native born Mexican-Americans with English as the dominant language were taken to be highest on the six level acculturation scale, with foreign born and Spanish dominant individuals being lowest on the scale. A second categorisation was made according to 'ethnic consciousness'. The 752 members of the Mexican-American sample who identified themselves as being white were held to have low ethnic consciousness. Those who referred to brown colours or Latin American origins were classified as having high ethnic consciousness. A sample of 456 Anglos was drawn from the same Primary Sampling Units as was used for the Mexican Americans. (pp. 338 - 339)

Garza and his colleagues measured patriotism with two scales: one reflecting love of country, and the other addressing pride in being American. Support for economic individualism was measured by asking the respondents to place themselves on a five-point scale, first with respect to jobs, second housing, and third income. The end points for jobs were the statements, "The government should provide jobs for everyone who wants a job" and at the other end, "It is up to each person to get his own job". (p.

342) Similar options were offered on housing and income. The statistical analysis also included demographic variables of religion, income, age and gender.

The inclusion of the demographic valuables proved to be crucial to this study. When these variables are not included, it appears that Mexican-Americans are both less patriotic than Anglos, and less in favour of economic individualism. This is particularly strong for those Mexican-Americans with high ethnic consciousness. The degree of acculturation had a similar effect, with the native born English dominant Mexican-Americans being closer to Anglos on both scales. However, when the demographic variables are included, all this changes. We get a totally different picture. Now neither acculturation nor ethnic consciousness effects the support Mexican- Americans give to economic individualism, and they are indistinguishable from Anglos in the degree of support they give. Mexican-Americans are equally in favour of economic individualism compared to Anglos. Much the same is true of patriotism. Ethnic consciousness has no bearing on it. At some levels of acculturation there is little difference in the degree of patriotism of Anglos and Mexican-Americans, but at some levels the Mexican- Americans are more patriotic.

The striking result is that Mexican-Americans as a group are less patriotic and less in favour of economic individualism than Anglos, but that is because as a group they differ in demographic characteristics. Comparing like to like in terms of religion, income, age and gender, there is no significant difference between the two groups. Being a Mexican-American in itself results in no difference compared to Anglos in support of economic individualism, and leads to greater patriotism. Why is this?

The authors suggest that economic individualism may not be a uniquely American philosophy. It may be equally strong in Mexico. There is no expectation there that the government will help with housing, income or jobs. Garza and his colleagues hazard four explanations of the equal or greater patriotism on the part of Mexican Americans, which could be investigated by other researchers. First they refer to studies showing a decline in respect for government on the part of Anglos, and this can carry over to diminished love of country and pride in country. Second, they note the emotional impact of becoming a citizen of a new country, and suggest that this could have some lasting effect. The other two reasons seem to me to confuse an explanation with what we are trying to explain. The third has to do with a reputation for patriotism, and the fourth refers to a poll where Hispanics, most of whom were Mexican-Americans, agreed that defending the United States from criticism is a mark of the true American. Whether or not these last two arguments make sense, this is an important study which illustrates the need for care in statistical investigation when one wants to isolate the effects of a possible causal factor like nationality.

The political scientist Dorren McMahon and her colleagues have examined the voting behaviour of people migrating between the north and the south in the United Kingdom. (McMahon, '92) Their main conclusion is that migrants do fit in, and tend to adopt the voting preferences of the host community. With a large net movement from north to south, this tends to favour the Conservative Party, who were much stronger than Labour in the South, at least during the period up to the time of the study. The fundamental problem the researchers face is isolating the effect of migrating on voting. Crudely put, a person may move and change their vote from Labour to Tory, because the move led to a higher income, or some other factor, and the income change, or the unspecified associated factor, led to a change in voting. The fact that their new neighbours also vote Tory, and have done so for some time, may be irrelevant. On the other hand, the main factor causing a change in voting may be the political allegiance of the neighbourhood. Ideally, we want to compare voters who are alike in all respects except that the one migrated and the other did not.

This research uses data from the British Election Studies of 1987, with comparisons to elections in 1964, 1974 and 1979. These surveys were done through face-to-face interviews which asked questions about where one lived, how one voted, and how one's father voted. There is also information on the father's class and the education of the person interviewed. The study distinguished between moves from north to south, or vice versa, before one began working, or during one's working life. Large differences emerge comparing those voters who migrated with those who did not, but whether the move was from north to south, or south to north, was not associated with striking differences.

Doreen McMahon and her colleagues note that in the United States, migrating from place to place has little effect on voting. The statistical results for the United Kingdom for the 1987 election are very different. Voters who migrated to the south are more likely to shift their vote away from Labour than those who stayed behind. The same is true of people who migrated to the north. They are more likely to shift their vote to Labour than those people who stayed in the south. The strength of these effects appear to be about the same, though the statistical significance of the shift parameter for those moving north is less due to there being many fewer voters moving in that direction. When there are small numbers involved, the possibility of any result coming about by chance is greater. The finding of an effect from migrating applies both to intergenerational effects, and changes in voting during a single individual's working life.

The authors recognise that the information at their disposal does not allow them to eliminate the possibility that other factors than moving may be causing the change in voting behaviour that we observe on the part of movers. Perhaps no amount of information could do that. Exactly how migrating might cause a change is not addressed at all. There may be an unconscious imitation effect at work here. Or people may be consciously striving to fit in, one aspect of that being adopting the political views of their new neighbours and the sentiments of the community they have moved to. McMahon and her fellow researchers consider four possible explanations of the observed tendency to change voting in the direction of the target area majority, other than the effect coming from the migration itself. One of these is that migrators are more likely to be homeowners, for example, and homeowners are changing their votes. As we said, this kind of selective effect is possible, in spite of what has been done to control for it.

A second factor in vote change might be social mobility. Maybe the migrants are on the way up, and are moving away from strong involvement with a union. It is true that the inclusion of a class variable into the analysis weakens the shifting power of migration, but only slightly. The idea that migrators are socially mobile upward is not consistent with the observed tendency of those moving north to shift to Labour more than those not moving. Indeed, including class in the analysis actually raised the measured effect of migration in the south to north direction. The third point has to do with the dominant voting behaviour in the particular initial and terminal location. There are Conservative areas in the north and Labour areas in the south. The authors reject this idea on the grounds that most people were moving to a similar voting environment to the one they left. This does rather beg the question of the scope to the environment which might be putting pressure on voters. Travel to work may take one to a different environment than where one lives. Finally, the authors consider tactical voting. Labour voters moving south may vote for the candidate most likely to defeat the Conservative candidate. In the north this might be the Labour candidate in most cases, but less so in the south. The data are consistent with some effect from tactical voting, but the study concludes that a strong effect from migrating itself is present.

This effect is a new one for the United Kingdom, and was not present, or present to a much smaller degree, in earlier elections. This is a nice example of the problem of changes in the subject matter of social science. Do voters who move tend to shift their vote in the direction of the majority where they arrive? For the 1987 election the answer broadly is 'yes', and for the 1964, 1974 and 1979 elections the answer broadly is 'no'. Perhaps there is a general tendency in more recent years towards conformity, and the effect of migrating on voting is just one example of increased fitting in. It is an interesting subject for research. If there is more conforming, is that because of television, higher rewards to acting like others, bigger penalties for being different, or something else?

STAY OR RETURN?

Very often the decision to migrate is in principle reversible. A number of the studies we examined indicated disappointment with the outcome of migration, and hostility to immigrants on the part of the host population. Moberg's study discussed above of Latin American immigrants in Belize working on banana plantations illustrated both disappointment and local hostility. As part of his survey he asked whether these arrivals planned to return home ultimately, or to settle in Belize. About a third answered that they will return home permanently. The Salvadorans were most likely to respond that they planned to return to their home country, and the Hondurans the least likely. It is unclear whether the differences depend on push factors initially leading to migrating, and different estimates of favourable change in the home country that would permit a return, or to some other factor. Refugees are usually thought of as people who would like to return home if they could. We will take up this topic shortly.

Following Eugenia Georges and Nina Glick-Schiller, Moberg conjectures that a simple view of migrants as either staying or returning ignores the modern trend towards 'transnationalism'. (Georges, '90; Glick-Schiller and colleagues, '92) The transnational migrator keeps up contact with the country of origin through trips back home, fairly frequent communication, sending money back, and a state of mind which encompasses both countries. This feature of keeping allegiance and active involvement in both societies is sometimes seen as a new way of understanding migration, and other writers see it not just as a matter of understanding but in fact as something new compared to earlier migrations. Whether this is really something new or not, as Moberg suggests, is debatable. But certainly communication and travel are relatively cheaper and less time consuming compared to earlier periods, so we might expect to see more use of them.

Massey and Espinosa, whose work on the motives for Mexican migration to the United States we examined above, pay particular attention to the factors that appear to influence return migration. Their work indicates important differences between illegal, or undocumented immigrants, and legal immigrants. They use their huge statistical base to calculate the odds that an immigrant will return to Mexico in a given year. They followed 1,600 undocumented immigrants for a total of 8,400 'person-years', and over 600 documented immigrants for 4,700 person-years. Some of the data lends support to the transnational approach, but there remain some fairly clear influences on a decision to return permanently. For both groups the more work experience and the more family members in the United States, the less the chances that an individual will be a return migrant. Legalisation increases the influence of a wife and children on the decision to stay. Being married increases the likelihood that illegal immigrants will return to Mexico. Owning land, and to some extent a home, also increases the odds on going back. Whether the migrant comes from an industrial or agricultural area has no effect of the decision to return, but returning to a poor area is more likely than to a more prosperous area. This paradoxical finding may be due to acquiring a nest-egg, which will be more significant in a poor area, as a motive for migrating in the first place. This is supported by the somewhat unexpected fact that higher rates of inflation and higher interest rates in Mexico encourage return migration. Changes in relative wages and changes in the intensity of preventing immigration into the United States had no effect on the decisions to return.

IMMIGRANTS OR REFUGEES?

No doubt there are physical, real world, aspects to being a refugee. It can also be very much a state of mind. Of course, states of mind are as real as torture chambers, but they cannot be observed in the same way. And even if they could be observed, through brain-imaging for example, they can change through internal mechanisms. In the opinion of the anthropologist Madawi Al-Rasheed, Iraqi Assyrians living in London were strengthened in their collective self-image as refugees by the Gulf War. (Al-Rasheed, '95) He traces the history of Assyrians driven out of the Hakkiari mountains in Turkey, and living a precarious minority way of life as Christians in Muslim Iraq. They have a tradition of refugee status and are inclined to carry it with them.

Al-Rasheed bases his research on this history, combined with lengthy interviews with three members of the London Assyrian community. The first is a woman who came to London with her husband, both on student visas. There was no element of being forced out of Iraq. Part of her concern is for relatives who are subject to persecution like that of the Kurds, but not receiving the same publicity. It is this treatment of relatives and fellow Assyrians in Iraq which causes her to think of herself, and all Assyrians in London, as refugees.

The second case study is that of a businessman who has managed to bring fourteen relatives into the United Kingdom under the family reunion rubric. There appears to be a legal and emotional advantage to invoking the refugee image in dealing with the authorities. However, there is genuine feeling as well. "We came to Iraq as refugees and we leave as refugees." (p. 25) The third person to be interviewed stayed in Iraq in the army, while most of his family had left the country. He felt prejudiced against in the army, and eventually left to join his family in London. He is active in a political party in exile which promotes the concept of an autonomous Assyrian enclave in the north of Iraq. He has a self-image as a refugee which is directly related to his political interests. This research maintains that minority status in the country of origin is central to the concept of being a refugee instead of being an immigrant. One need not be a victim of violence oneself, as long as there is a history of discrimination in one's reference group.

There was no shortage of victims of the war in Bosnia that began in 1992. It is estimated that in the first two years 30,000 people died and about one million people fled their homes, most becoming refugees in a great variety of countries. Before the outbreak of hostilities, Muslims in Bosnia lived in harmony with their Christian Croatian and Serbian neighbours. Intermarriage was not uncommon. The anthropologist Fran Markowitz notes that many people identified themselves as Yugoslav, with less emphasis on their regional or religious identity. (Markowitz, '96) In line with action taken by many states, Israel offered to take in 100 people trying to flee the country. This offer was readily accepted. The Muslims did not feel it odd to go to a Jewish state. Among the attractions of Israel was the policy of accepting entire families, rather than just women and children as was done in some refugee camp.

Markowitz followed the fortunes of seventy of these refugees who were settled at a Kibbutz called Beit Oren which is in a remote location. Here they led a fairly normal life. There was regular education for the children, and work for both men and women. The men were mainly involved with aspects of forest work, and the women managed the individual homes assigned to each family. The state of Israel provided some subsidy in the form of rent on accommodation, but this was not very significant and all the families actively maintained themselves.

These refugees were technically on tourist visas. After one year they were urged to follow the usual path of immigrants, a path that led ultimately to citizenship. These Muslims in Beit Oren had no desire to do so. The fact that the subsidy on their rent would go had nothing to do with it. Nor did it matter to them that they would be free to settle anywhere in the country, and take up any employment they could secure. None of this was central to their situation. However well they were looked after in Israel, there was a clear intention to return to Bosnia as soon as this became a practical possibility. That is the main point. Living in a kind of "limbo", to use Markowitz's word, was exactly what these people needed and wanted. Over the period from June of 1993 to August 1994, Markowitz made a number of visits to the eighteen refugee families. Her conclusions are based on numerous conversations, many of which are reported in her article. Towards the end of her investigation, about half of the Bosnians had left for countries closer to Bosnia.

Israel has a long history of receiving refugees, and well-developed policies for maintaining family units and for integrating new comers into the country. Markowitz sees the help extended to the Muslims as successful in the sense of preserving morale and sense of worth. Representatives of this group appeared on television thanking the people of Israel for their hospitality. The author argues that allowing these families to remain in limbo, rather than encouraging full integration, contributed to the success of the operation. While many refugees want to integrate, some have other needs. Commitment to Israel was not consistent with the self-image of this group. Markowitz maintains that a policy of temporary status, for as long as it was needed, would help to "...prevent cultural clashes and social problems..." for many groups of refugees escaping the ravages of war. (p. 127)

CONTROLLING MIGRATION

Very few, if any, countries are willing to allow free entry on a long-term basis. Even the most welcoming, such as the United Kingdom and the United States, experience intense political debate as to the desirable overall level of immigration, and who should be admitted. From time to time, attention moves from country of origin to people from particular economic categories. Issues of race, and fear of being overwhelmed by foreign cultures, hover in the background. Some countries put blocks on emigration. Repressive regimes worry about a mass exodus, and many more countries do not allow individuals to leave who they see as posing a threat to national security, or as being potentially embarrassing if allowed to leave. Wealthier countries strive mainly to keep people out rather than keeping them in. The United States Immigration and Naturalization Service (INS) has the responsibility for patrolling the border. Among other duties, they are charged with apprehending and dealing with illegal immigrants.

The anthropologist Josiah Heyman has studied the work of the INS in policing the border with Mexico. (Heyman, '95) The officers and others doing this work are pictured in his study as a kind of bureaucratic tribe. There is no hope that they could ever have the necessary resources to keep the border secure, or be allowed to employ the methods that would be needed to do that. The wave of people attempting to come into the country illegally is huge. In 1989 the INS agents caught nearly one million Mexican trying to come into America illegally. Most of those who are caught agree to return to Mexico voluntarily. It is assumed that the majority of them will try again the next night, or some other night. Catching illegal immigrants on the border with Mexico is a kind of hopeless task.

Heyman provides many telling details about the attitudes and behaviour of the people working on this border control operation. The INS has to decide how much in the way of resources to devote to this task, and what strategies to use, including the suitable levels of force to employ. There is a lot of discretion involved and difficult decisions to be made. The author attempts to structure his investigation by relating the information provided by border control agents and people working with them to a concept he calls "thought-work". It is not entirely straightforward to see how this concept knits together the rich volume of material Heyman has collected. One interpretation would be that the "thought-work" in the minds of agents involves an overview of what is going on, and this amounts to a philosophical position covering both beliefs about the consequences of actions, and value systems which can judge, or rank, different outcomes as being more or less desirable. The "thought-work" conjecture appears to hold that the overview, or 'philosophy', of the agents will influence particular decisions taken on the ground.

The other anthropologists commenting on this article by Heyman find it to be a compelling and convincing picture of the interactions between the Patrol Agents in Charge (PAICs) and the Mexicans trying to cross the border. For a person who knew little or nothing about this world of hunters and hunted, the study offers a graphic and informative picture. When it comes to the "thought-work" conjecture, most people would not only agree, but take it to be self-evident. As a general proposition, the assertion that the views people hold influence what they do can hardly be contested. The idea gets more bite when it relates thought to action more specifically. Heyman may be suggesting that a common strategy is to address complex problems by using simple ideas. "Thought-work" tends to be superficial. The anthropologist Ronald Cohern makes this interpretation. (p. 278) Scott Whiteford and Manuel Chavez see these 'simple ideas' as linking day-to-day work to national values and priorities. (p. 282) An illustration of this would be efforts to separate illegal immigration from drug smuggling. The anthropologist Don Handelman made reference to a Jack Nicholson film about patrolling the Mexican border which emphasised the difference between evil smugglers and good illegals. (p. 281)

It could be that while providing a graphic picture, Heyman's work does not go much further than the Nicholson film. Handelman also suggests that the film may have had an influence on the PAICs Heyman interviewed. These are legitimate criticisms. But as a general point, and a powerful one, Heyman agues that wide discretion is common in many bureaucracies. They are not simply agencies carrying out the policies that are established by others. There is scope here for anthropologists to study the views and resulting exercise of power by the community, or 'tribe', which is a bureaucracy.

Enforcing immigration policy is an enduring problem for most democratic states. The political scientist James Hollifield sees this as the ultimate test of the strength of the state. (Hollifield, '90) He is particularly interested in the success enjoyed by France, which is believed to be a 'strong state'. The vulnerability of the French government to direct action protest may challenge the view of it as a strong state, but that is another matter. For this study, how policy is formulated, and the possible influence of Jean-Marie Le Pen and the National Front on the government, is also set to one side. The structure which Hollifield has in mind is the following. Both government policy and the actions taken by various interest groups in society exert an influence on market conditions. In turn, the interest groups and the market conditions influence the way in which policy intentions become policy outcomes. For the author, the definition of a strong state is one where the intentions of government policy are largely realised in the final outcome. Neither the objectives of particular interest groups, nor the conditions prevailing in the market are able to deflect policy outcomes very far away from the original intention of the government. Put in this rather abstract way, it is not perfectly obvious what is being argued, but in the context of controlling immigration it becomes much clearer.

The central facts for Hollifield's study are the amounts of immigration into France over the years 1946 to 1987, and the number of foreign workers employed in France over the period 1967 to 1979. There are huge swings in the number of immigrants coming into France to take up permanent work. The flow of seasonal workers and immigrants coming into the country to join their families varies much less. Broadly speaking, there were about 32,000 immigrants a year taking up permanent work over the period 1946 to 1955. For the period 1968 to 1973 this figure was over four times higher at about 134,000 immigrants per year. And still later, 1974 to 1987, the annual figure for immigrants taking up permanent employment in France was down to something like the early post-war figure at about 28,000. The crucial, if somewhat stylised 'fact', was that immigration was suspended in 1974. As always in these matters, there is complication. Some efforts to reduce immigration came before 1974. Certain special kinds of immigration were still allowed, and Mitterrand promulgated an amnesty for illegal immigrants at that time.

Total employment of foreign workers in France rose from just under a million in 1967 to 1.4 million in 1973, with rises in every year. In 1974, the total fell by 1,400, and continued down every year to 1.2 million in 1979. On the face of it, we have good evidence for what Hollifield calls a strong government. It set its goal in 1974 to reduce the number of immigrants taking up permanent work, and both the flow and the stock of foreign workers suggests that the government was successful in achieving its objective. However, there may be other factors at work. The reason for the policy change in 1974 was serious economic decline. So we may ask, did the number of immigrants coming to France to take up permanent employment decline because that was the policy objective set by the government, or did it decline because France was now a less attractive prospect for immigrants seeking work?

The author uses two statistical equations to get at the answer. The first equation relates annual immigration to immigration in the previous year and the ratio of labour supply to labour demand in the previous year, as a measure of excess demand. The two other explanatory variables were the extent to which employers initiated visa applications, and a 'yes/no' variable as to whether the restrictive policy was in force or not. For the years before 1974 it was deemed not to be in force. The second equation is exactly the same, except that what is being explained is total foreign employment rather than annual flow. The results show that for both measures the policy variable had no effect on the immigration of permanent workers. If you knew what the economic conditions were — the relative demand for labour in the market — and the ratio of employers' to administrative applications, you could predict both annual flow and total numbers of foreign workers employed. Whether a restrictive policy was in force or not had no discernible effect on either the annual flow or the number of foreign workers.

Hollifield offers three possible explanations for these results. The first is that contrary to popular opinion, *i.e.* popular opinion as he sees it, France is not a strong state. For a strong state, the policy objective would be achieved, and as far as this evidence goes, the policy exerted no influence on its intended objective. The second explanation is that economic forces dominate in the flow of immigrant workers, and even a strong state will find it difficult to implement its policies in this area. There is a clandestine element to the immigrant labour market, and this combined with the economic muscle of employers makes policy in this area almost impossible to enforce. One suspects that the third idea suggested by the author may not have been put forward entirely seriously. It is that the government did not really intend to restrict immigration. A reserve army of foreign workers is in the interests of employers, but the government does not want to appear to support that. Being secretly in league with employers, it chose not to enforce its stated policy. Like the author, I set this to one side. There is another possibility which the author does not raise. It always is important to ask if one of the other explanatory variables is masking the effect of the restrictive policy. The obvious candidate for that is the ratio of employers' to administrative applications. It would be worth some statistical manipulation to eliminate this possibility. It also could be that in spite of slack economic conditions in France in 1974 and the years just after, immigration would have been higher but for the policy, due to equally poor economic conditions in the countries immigrants wanted to leave. Be that as it may, interesting evidence of the difficulty of enforcing immigration policy, different from that from anthropology, is provided by this study from political science.

Chapter Seven

THE FAMILY

WHAT IS A FAMILY?

The concepts we use in thinking about the elements that make up society tend to have this curious feature of combining subjective and objective characteristics. The concept of the individual — a basic and popular component for analysing society — is exceptional in being a pretty objective and unambiguous element. Combinations of individuals are also elements that make up society, and these are both real, in the sense of being observable, and at the same time are subject to interpretation.

Some concept of the family is universal in human society, but the content of this concept varies greatly from place to place. The most common way of producing and rearing children is in a family. But children can be conceived apart from any permanent association and reared in institutions. The birth of a child is neither necessary nor sufficient for there to be a family. However, the notion of the family as an institution for the production and rearing of children is central to all concepts of the family.

In most societies there is a legal concept of the family. It is not unusual in family trees — the structure of associations and progeny— to distinguish between legitimate and illegitimate associations and offspring. While the legal interpretation of the family will usually coincide fairly closely both with the generally held view of legitimacy, and with the views of those who see themselves as the members of a family, this need not be the case. The law may hold that someone is a member of a family who feels no attachment and has nothing to do with the other family members. Others may see themselves as being 'family' who have no attachment through bloodlines or marriage.

Couples may have no children through choice, or through an inability to reproduce. The union may be legally sanctioned or not. The law may or may not treat them as a family, and they may or may not see themselves as a family. How far a family stretches out from a particular couple to include distant relatives can have a legal scope, a traditional scope for a particular community, and an emotional or subjective meaning to the family members. The rights and obligations of family members may similarly vary depending on whether we are considering laws, generally agreed customs, or actual behaviour. Great variation can also be found in the degree of permanence which is expected, legally required, and practised in families.

While the 'breeding unit', to speak crudely, will most commonly involve one man and one women, polygamy has some currency. Polyandry has much less, but does exist. With modern technology, many variations are possible as to where the egg and the sperm come from, and who actually carries the foetus to birth. In a number of wealthier societies same sex couples are striving for legal recognition as families, including the right to rear either traditionally adopted, or somehow 'engineered', children.

What is a family in one community or country might not be seen as a family in another community or country. And again, the difference may be legal, conventional, or accepted by the participants or relevant non-participants. Having acknowledged all this variation, there is much in common across most of the world in what is meant by a family. Variation is part of the story, and a widely held common concept and a set of common practices is another part.

Among social scientists, anthropologists like Duran Bell have been particularly concerned with formulating a definition of marriage as the heart of a family. (Bell, '97) Bell argues against the approach taken by E.K. Gough, which emphasises the legitimacy, or lack of legitimacy, of children as resulting in the defining characteristic of marriage. He tends to reject this way of defining marriage on the grounds that while it is a common test, it is not a universally valid test. Instead, he proposes that "socially supported" access to women is the key. Other anthropologists like Michael Burton are troubled by the way Gough sets up the relationship solely in terms of the rights of men, or expectations of men, when it comes to sex. Bell sees the key distinction as between spouses and lovers. Most anthropologists applaud his efforts to say what is a marriage, and by extention, what is a family. But for the most part they are doubtful about the enterprise of seeking a universal definition, and worried about imposing a 'western' view on a world with great diversity.

WHO CARES?

Broadly speaking, there are four reasons why the state has to take an interest in the concept of the family. The first and most obvious has to do with enforcing the contracts which being part of a family entails. There are disputes in the event of family break-up, and obligations while the family is intact. Inheritance is subject to legal regulation. In order to carry out its legal obligations with respect to families, the state needs a clear notion of what is a family, and what enforceable contracts, explicit or implicit, this entails.

Individuals take part in the wider society, but so do families. In some ways they take part as a unit. Typically the family is an economic unit in which the distribution of income and wealth within it is not determined by market mechanisms, or other external allocation mechanisms, which prevail outside of the family. A good deal of research has gone into how resources are divided in families between those working outside the family, those working inside, and those not working. Most states try to take a hands-off view of allocations within the family, either for practical or ideological reasons, and treat the family as a self-regulating economic unit. Taxes fall on families, and benefits are redistributed to families. Central to carrying out many of the welfare activities of governments is the particular concept of the family, which the state employs. These and other interventions in families are partly conditioned by the views the state holds as to what families are actually like, and what they should be like.

A civilised society is likely to take upon itself some concern for the more defenceless and vulnerable members of society. Part of the function of families is exactly this — to look after those who cannot look after themselves. But the state has to play a role. Some people needing help do not have a family to look after them. And people who are in families are not always fairly treated. The weakness of women, and their sense of obligation to the children, may be exploited. The children themselves may be treated in ways that fall below the minimum standards the society sets for them. The third reason for state concern for the family is the need sometimes to go beyond taxing some families and supporting others, and engage in more specific interventions on behalf of vulnerable family members.

The fourth reason for state concern is related to the third, but different. It has to do with the idea that the family, whatever that is, is critical to the psychological and emotional health of the society. 'Family values' is a shorthand for a society in which we recognise and act on our obligations to others out of a sense of rightness and pleasure in a just society. In particular there is the shaping of children, which sometimes happens entirely outside of families, but quantitatively rarely so. Of course children in families are subject to influences from television, other leisure influences coming from outside, the neighbourhood, friends and so on. The immediate influences of the parents are there as well, and often these are believed to be the most important.

Whether or not the state is right in thinking that it can effectively promote policies which will impact favourably on family life is another matter. From time to time governments have attempted to encourage better family life through taxation and welfare measures, as well as through exhortation. Setting an example occasionally calls for penalising public figures, particularly public figures in government, whose behaviour is seen to denigrate family values.

ORGANISING THIS CHAPTER

A large social science literature has focused on the family. There are practical reasons for this in terms of informing various aspects of public policy. There also are inherently interesting questions which have attracted the attention of researchers who see the family as an important, and often puzzling, grouping in society. The variety of family arrangements is interesting in itself. What causes it, and what are its consequences? How do arranged marriages, for example, compare in various ways to marriages negotiated by the eventual participants?

The previous two chapters grouped the reports on research according to social science discipline, in the case of crime; and by aspect of the subject, in the case of migration. This chapter follows yet another method and is organised according to the kind of information, or knowledge, the social scientists are attempting to provide. A few words are needed in order to explain this kind of arrangement. We might begin with the category which groups together articles which are intended simply to record the 'facts'. But as is discussed in earlier chapters, what is a fact is not as straightforward a matter as it might seem at first.

One thing a fact is not is an explanation. I am troubled by statements of the kind, "It is a fact that the riot was caused by the shortage of bread." The speaker here is using the term 'fact' to refer to a true, or correct, explanation. Facts are not in principle as involved as explanations. They are brutes, like this stone weighs ten pounds, Clinton was President of the United States, and my dog has fleas. People are free to see for themselves and to check up on the facts. I use the phrase 'in principle' because as a practical matter it may be very hard to check up on the facts. For example, it has been asserted as a fact that one of the moons of Jupiter has a surface of ice which covers a sea sixty miles deep. Nevertheless, facts are out there. They can be observed, or at least are the kind of thing that could be observed.

In any one scientific investigation, some thing or things are the facts which that investigation is attempting to discover or explain. 'The world is getting warmer' is a factual statement. It may or may not be correct. In the end there will be some observations which will convince most observers that it is happening, or is not. The element of an ultimate sensory test is important to the concept of a fact. This test may be very complex, as in observing the speed of light, for example, but it is in the end a matter of what our eyes, or ears, or other senses tell us. In many cases the readings on the instruments which our senses observe are related to the natural phenomenon of interest in very complex ways. For the purposes of the current discussion I am calling those facts which are readily open to sensory investigation 'direct facts'.

Using this terminology, I might refer to the fact that Mr. Right, of a specified address — there is no doubt about who I am talking about — is six feet tall, is married, is left handed, and so on. These are direct facts. We know where to go and what to look for in order to see whether these are the facts or not. Serious disagreement is most unlikely. Mistakes are possible. I neglected to note that last year he was divorced. Show me my error, and I adjust my view of the facts.

'Mr. Right is unemployed' is what I call a contextual fact. If it turns out that he has a job with the secret police and has kept it a secret, it is not a fact that he is unemployed. Similarly if he is a novelist working for himself, it would be odd to say he is unemployed. The same holds if he is retired, or never wanted to work or needed to work. It could be argued that the assertion that Mr. Right is married is a contextual fact. However, there are certain observations that could be made which on balance suggest that it is a direct fact. The borders between kinds of facts are not sharp. By contrast with the contextual fact that Mr. Right is unemployed, Mr. Right is in prison is a direct fact. We do not have to know the context to see that this is a fact, or is not a fact, as long as we can agree what a prison is.

'The population of the United Kingdom is fifty-five million' I call a compiled fact. 'Two million men and women are unemployed' is another compiled fact. Reasonable disputes about complied facts are quite common and understandable. It may not be easy to resolve such disputes, and often is not necessary to do so for the purposes of a particular scientific inquiry. The relevant fact might be that unemployment is higher today than two years ago. For some problems and investigations, how much higher may not matter.

Finally, we have the category of 'stylised facts'. These are assertions about the world which the author believes to be generally true, and may be held to be true by most people, but are not actually observed or measured. They play the role of facts for the sake of the argument without being investigated. This typology of four kinds of 'facts' is neither exhaustive nor unambiguous. But it is helpful in grouping the kind of work that social scientists undertake when they study the family.

So much for facts, for the moment. Identifying causes, or what is the same thing, suggesting explanations, takes a number of forms. An explanation which is not precise, but does hope to pick out the more relevant factors and give some idea of how they fit together, I call a 'casual theory'. The world is getting warmer because of rising amounts of CO_2 in the atmosphere, is an example. Such a theory could be refuted by certain facts, but is usually consistent with a broad range of facts. Often formulating and investigating casual theories is a necessary prelude to more precise explanation. Unambiguous statements of how the elements of an explanation fit together and a precise formulation which is typically capable of mathematical expression is usually called a model. To continue the global warming example, a model might specify the actual temperature associated with given quantities of CO_2.

Research undertaken on the family may concentrate entirely on formulating a casual theory, or going further and formulating a model, leaving it to other researchers to take up the task of relating the theory to the facts. This is 'abstract' theorising or modelling. Alternatively, if facts come into the investigation, they may be used to determine the plausibility of the theory or model. We speak of the study as using the facts to test the theory or model. However, facts may enter in other ways than as tests of theories.

The structure of the investigation may be very much inclined to see some version of the model as being broadly correct, but is concentrating on how important the particular effect under investigation is for the problem at hand. Sex education in schools will result in fewer unwanted pregnancies, is a theory. The critical question might be 'how many fewer'? This is often called measurement as opposed to testing. The border between the two is blurred. Both involve precise relations between facts and theories.

It is not easy to do justice to the variety of ways in which observations — compiled or direct — and explanations can be brought together. Some important investigations consist of teasing out valid general statements from the facts. This inductive investigation is intended to find significant relations. These relations are taken to be causal in nature. We infer that something is causing something else from the fact that they generally go together. In order to test whether there is an actual causal link between two phenomena we may look for common factors causing both, and try to rule out a number of plausible explanations of the association other than the direct causal one.

Statements of the kind "making divorce difficult leads to more murders of husbands by wives" I call high order facts rather than explanations. The reason for this is that while there may be a causal element, it has not been spelt out. For the moment we have established the fact of association, but have not been able to go beyond that. I realise that attempting to catalogue the different types of knowledge different studies provide leads me into deep water. Certainly not all studies can be easily classified. An indulgent reader will take the distinctions illustrated in what follows as rough and ready. Particular social sciences tend to concentrate on certain kinds of knowledge. I hope that the groupings I employ show meaningful differences between disciplines.

DIRECT FACTS

It is extraordinary to think that in 1911 there were 700 divorces in England and Wales. Seventy-five years later there were on the order of over one hundred and fifty thousand divorces a year. The growth in divorce is greater in Britain and Denmark than in other European countries, but the trend can be seen in most countries. To think of families exclusively as a stable relation between a man and a woman and their children, where neither partner has been divorced, is not a realistic picture of many families. The anthropologist Bob Simpson is of the view that divorce can disrupt "patterns of social continuity", but can also create important new links between people. (Simpson, '94) He sees a need for knowing the facts about the consequences of divorce, and sets out to find them by reporting on three family situations where divorce has played a major role. He does not explain how he found his examples.

His first example centres on a man called Steve — names have been changed to protect privacy. Steve was a teen father. He sees his son from that encounter from time to time, but never lived with the mother or had "any permanent relationship with her." (p. 834) Later he married Kath and they had two daughters. After that marriage ended in divorce he kept close contact with the girls. Then he married Karen. She had a daughter which she was raising as a single parent. In effect Steve became the father of that girl. Karen and Steve then had two children, a boy and a girl. Steve sees himself as the father of all six children. He feels he gets on well with all three mothers. He sees his ex-wife fairly regularly, and sometimes sees the mother of his first child. Other members of the family take different views. Karen's parents see themselves as having three grandchildren, while Steve's parents see themselves as having six grandchildren.

Samson contrasts this relatively peaceful and positive picture with the tale of Stephen Thomas. After Stephen's divorce he had custody of his daughter Sharon. When he married Sally, she in effect became mother to Sharon. Stephen and Sally had two of their own children together, Andrew and Dawn. However, Sally found it difficult living with Stephen because of his violence and financial irresponsibility, and eventually left taking Dawn and Andrew with her. There followed bitter wrangles over visiting rights. Eventually they got divorced, and after a time both stared living with new partners who themselves had been divorced. It would seem that the final blow to Sally's relationship with Stephen and Sharon came when she had a son, Michael, with her new partner. Her daughter Dawn from the previous marriage wanted nothing to do with Stephen, but Andrew was more uncertain, and tended to feel that he had two fathers. In spite of this, the author is undoubtedly correct in seeing the new relationships as displacing and wiping out the past. New nuclear families are formed, and the children who overlap more-or-less have to, or want to, adjust to that.

In a way, the most 'grown-up' story is that of Sue who had three children from two previous marriages, both ending in divorce. She began an affair with Stuart, who was married to Rachael and had three children from that marriage. The relationship with Sue eventually took over, and while separating, from his three boys was very difficult for Stuart, up to a point, a new equilibrium eventually developed with everyone accepting everyone else. The six children, so it is reported, get on very well, and the adults have good interactions. A major problem for all of them was the sheer physical distance between the homes of Sue and Rachael. A great advantage was the abiding support from friends and relatives that the parties to this upheaval had during the transition.

The author takes the opportunity of reporting these three tales to advance a number of speculations and observations about family life today. There is some suggestion that more affluent participants in marital shake up will settle into more comprehensive relationships as opposed to setting up new exclusive nuclear relationships. However, there is no attempt in this research to establish general principles of that kind, or indeed, of any other kind. The main goal to see what are the direct facts about divorce. If a family forms and stays together throughout their lives, Samson feels that the members of that family will tend to give similar reports of the marriage. With divorce, all sorts of differences of view are possible. There may be little meaning in a search for a 'true' story of the marriage. The three cases reported may or may not be representative, but they are the facts of the cases for the three examples.

CONTEXTUAL FACTS

Many observers see the institution of marriage as being under some kind of threat in many Western countries. While this may be true in some places, it does not seem to be the case everywhere. The anthropologist John Knight characterises Japan as being an "all-marriage society". (Knight, '95) The Japanese phrase is kaikon shakai. A number of social changes have made it increasingly difficult for men living in rural areas to find mates. It would seem that a number of changes are contributing to increased involuntary bachelorhood. The growth of urban culture and greater mobility of women in moving to larger towns and cities appears to be a basic factor. Men whose occupations tie them to rural areas cannot follow the women. And the women, so the phrase goes, prefer to marry downstream — hanayome wa kawa o kudaru — moving from a more rural to a more urban way of life. This implies that many women are prepared to remain single and wait for a suitable husband.

In this context Knight documents a number of responses to the growth in the number of unmarried men in their thirties from seven percent in 1970 to twenty-five percent in 1990. In 1989 farmers from Akita in northern Japan travelled 750 kilometres on their tractors and held up central Tokyo with a protest against the lack of brides. Another response, which is better described as a compiled fact that the author is providing, is the existence of 5,000 private marriage brokerage businesses. He mentions that firms like Mitsubishi and Mitsui have in-house consulting and dating agencies to help their employees to find mates.

Knight draws our attention to another 'direct fact' which has its meaning in the context of the difficulty many men experience in getting married. He points out that the corollary of women being unable to marry appears to be less of a problem. This is either because they are more prepared to wait, or is actually just as much a problem, but they suffer in silence.

An organisation called the "International Marriage Association" ran an advertisement urging men to consider foreign brides. The virtues of these women, and their similarity to Japanese women, are emphasised. Along with this carrot, the ad uses the stick of ancestor worship to encourage men to look abroad. The ad raises the spectre of dying without producing any child to provide worship. This suggests that the function of ancestor worship may be to promote stable families, though the author does not make the point.

Local governments in the rural areas have also been active in urging men to consider foreign brides. This is not an easy undertaking in a country that strongly emphasises ethnic and racial homogeneity. The publicity employed by both commercial and governmental marriage facilitators tends to stress the racial and cultural similarity of women from Thailand, for example, and the argument that personal characteristics which might make it difficult for a man to find a Japanese bride would count for less, and maybe not at all, when it comes to a foreign bride. It is common for local governments to provide financial rewards both to couples who marry and to successful matchmakers. Knight reproduces a publicity photo of a couple being presented with a free honeymoon trip to Hawaii by the head of a regional co-operative. The expression on the face of the bride to be suggests that the trip might not be compensation enough.

Knight concludes his presentation of telling facts in support of the view that marriage is much prized and not always easy to achieve in Japan by making some general observations. He sees the drive towards modernisation and away from the feudal legacy in rural areas as the most important contributor to a solution of the tensions surrounding marriage, and other tensions in Japanese society. This involves a new awareness that the views and preferences of young women, often ignored in the past, have to be taken into account. These conclusions seem reasonable but they are not derived from his facts in any systematic way. The main contribution of the study is the facts which it reports and the meaning they take on in a context of intense pressure to marry.

COMPILED FACTS

Researchers who simply gather facts do so before a backdrop of ideas and concepts to which these facts might later prove to be relevant and suggestive. It is not a random or haphazard activity, but nor is it prompted in a clear and explicit way by specific theories. The social psychologists Pedro Solis-Camara and Robert Fox wanted to find the facts as to whether parenting practices were the same or different comparing mothers with young children in Mexico and in the United States. (Solis-Camara and Fox, '95) Unlike the direct facts sought by Bob Samson above, their aim was to take a representative sample, and compile the facts of the case that would be true of the entire population.

It could be that differences in the culture of Mexico and the United States would show themselves in the way mothers brought up very young children. Or it could be, as the authors supposed, that the task of rearing small children is so totally demanding that there is not much room for variation. Whether the facts went one way or the other would not cause investigators to reject one theory or favour another. Instead, it would be a relevant landmark for future research. The authors expected there to be little difference, not because of a specified theory, but because that was their hunch and it also was the opinion of a respected authority.

The sample of sixty-nine Mexican mothers was randomly drawn from day care centres in Guadalajara. Sixty-nine Caucasian American mothers were similarly drawn from a large sample of urban families. The goal was to have people from both countries who were alike as much as possible, and differed only in being from the two different countries. This objective appears to have been met. Both groups of mothers had twelve years of formal education. The Mexican mothers were on average slightly older, but the statistical properties of the two groups in terms of marital status, age and number of children, and husband's occupational status were remarkably similar.

The mothers in both groups were asked to fill in the one hundred item Parent Behavior Checklist (PBC, Fox, '94) This survey is divided into three parts covering parental 'expectations'; approaches to 'discipline'; and what are called 'nurturing' activities. Mothers with more than one child were instructed to single out one child for the purposes of the questionnaire. They rated each item on a four-point scale from it being not at all the case, or something they disagreed with, up to being very much the case. A typical item for expectations is, "My child should be able to feed him/herself". A representative discipline item is, "I yell at my child for spilling food". Nurturing has to do with activities like playing with the child or reading to it. (p. 594)

Extensive statistical analysis was done on the answers. No difference could be found in the mean scores for Mexican and United States mothers. Using country of origin had no explanatory power in accounting for the results. Only one minor difference was found. Older Mexican mothers produced higher discipline scores compared to younger Mexican mothers. For the American mothers it was the other way around. But this is a quibble, and other studies suggest that the results for Mexico may not be representative. The over-riding result was that there was no difference between the two groups.

Of course, this is as seen from the mothers' perspective. They may be inclined to say similar things, but act in different ways. Maybe the children have different experiences. We are also dealing with relatively high income and well educated urban families. The common experience of industrialisation may be eliminating, or masking, cultural differences. Perhaps less educated groups might be less similar. Whatever the case, we have a compiled fact for this group of people which is of some interest.

Measuring parenting is a pretty subtle undertaking. But even counting the number of households, or families, in an area is not without its difficulties. The anthropologists Richard Wilk and Stephen Miller argue that traditional census taking imposes apriori notions that can result in misleading quantification. (Wilk and Miller, '97) In particular, they worry about the assumption that each individual is a member of one and only one household. They began their work by observing over a hundred "domestic units" in the Afro-Caribbean Creole community of Crooked Tree in Belize. This was done in 1990. Their investigation led them to construct a four way breakdown of household members: (1) those sleeping in every night; (2) part-time residents with another residence; (3) occasional visitors, especially for holidays, who contribute financially; and (4) those with an economic relation to the household who do not sleep there.

The authors maintain that using only the first category when taking a census gives an under-counting. They feel that Crooked Tree is under-counted and as a result gets less public money than it merits. Of course, on this argument, all areas are under-counted. It would be interesting to know if some areas are more under-counted than others are. In proposing a new way of compiling the facts, guidelines are needed for making comparisons between places.

STYLISED FACTS

The political scientist Jane Lewis describes the shifting pattern of parental responsibility in the United Kingdom, with references to developments in the rest of Europe and the United States. (Lewis, '96) She makes the case that what the state can and should do to protect children is much clearer than what it should do, or conceivably can do, to promote traditional family values. She concludes that legislation in the United Kingdom, along with popular attitudes and the stances of the major political parties, have taken on board the changed nature of families to a great extent.

Of course, there are worries about the burden that unmarried mothers can place on the state. And there are worries about how children develop in single parent families. Having said this, a new ethos is emerging which Lewis calls "A new parenthood contract". (p. 92) This contract allows much more variety in the sexual and emotional relations between people, and is open to different ways of rearing children. Much of this is positive in its interpretation of the new laws and the changing culture they reflect. But there is a "missing link", namely, adequate protection of children. (p.98) "...the position of children has deteriorated significantly during the 1980's." (p. 99) The author believes that more state help is needed, and that this will complement rather than be a substitute for individual effort.

Lewis is giving us the facts about families in the United Kingdom in recent years. These are not direct facts in the sense of reports of things observed, nor are they compiled from statistical information. Her implicitly political analysis and prescription — gently understated and calmly observed — is essentially an exercise in stylised facts. A picture is put together of what the world looks like in one important aspect. The facts come from long exposure and sensitive reading of events. They can be challenged.

Roy Parker's work on the role of the state in protecting children from the actions of unsuitable parents is another example of the use of stylised facts in a political science analysis. (Parker, '86) He motivates his work by referring to a recent case of a child who died after being returned to her parents under a system called "home on trial". Over the past century in the United Kingdom there has been an almost total shift from voluntary associations to the state when in comes to taking over the responsibilities of parents, either on a voluntary or a legally required basis. Along with this shift has gone an increased sense of professionalism on the part of social workers.

In the 1950's success in dealing with a child was judged largely by the proportion of children who went to foster homes. (p. 311) The main political factors which have led to more scrutiny of the decisions of local authorities are held by Parker to be increased activity on the part of the parents' rights lobby and a more vocal and effective black lobby. He feels that the only strategy for decision-makers that can help them in their dilemma as to when and how to intervene is more variety of policies according to circumstances.

It comes as no surprise that most of the social science investigation of families concentrates on problems. The psychologists Laing and Esterson in their book on families tried to find normal families. The concept proved to be illusive, as did the subjects. Still it is both meaningful and fair to concede that the bulk of social science interest has focused on problems. One of these is teenage pregnancy. The current example comes from the political scientist Deborah Rhode who brought the method of stylised facts to bear on the politics of this problem in the United States. (Rhode, '93) Her concise and interesting history of attitudes and policies suggests that the issue of young women getting pregnant was hugely less of a problem in the past. This had a lot to do with the limited opportunities for women generally. There is also the contention that women become fertile at much younger ages nowadays, and the period of dependence is considerably longer. Adolescence itself is a pretty recent concept. Rhode also suggests that for many young women, having a baby out of wedlock in their late teens — and this is when most of the pregnancy occurs — may be quite a reasonable development for many young women, depending on their circumstances.

None of this is meant to imply that there is no problem of teenage pregnancy for many young women and their families. The author notes that the rate is much higher in the United States than in other industrial countries. She attributes this in part to the political divide in America. Conservatives are characterised by the author as having mainly moral and fiscal concerns. Sex before marriage is held to lead to the "erosion of traditional values", including those of financial self-reliance. For liberals, the problems associated with teen pregnancy have more to do with dangers to health, disruption of education, and lowered socio-economic status. However, even in the stylised characterisations the author provides there are puzzles of interpretation. Conservatives, she claims, worry about "financial self-sufficiency", while liberals worry about "reduced employment opportunities". (p. 651) It is not obvious what the difference is between that part of the distinction.

What does seem clear in Rhode's analysis is that puritanical attitudes towards sex both obscure the problem and complicate addressing it. Discouraging sexual activity and going light on sex education, on the grounds that it promotes pre-marital sex, may have a lot to do with the unusually high rate of youthful pregnancy in America. The author suggests policies which could help. Some call for sweeping changes in social attitudes. Others call for a more responsive and varied approach to sex and related education. How to bring these changes about is not discussed. The author feels that while some important aspects of the issue are understood, a great deal is not known, and she pleads for more research. An example would be learning more about how to promote responsible sexual behaviour.

The political scientist Nancy Fraser has undertaken a major analysis of the welfare state in America based on stylised facts. (Fraser, '94) "We are currently experiencing the death throes of the old, industrial gender order...the crisis of the welfare state is bound up with these epochal changes." (p.592) She contends that there has been a decline in the number of full-time jobs that would enable a breadwinner to support a family. Work now tends to be temporary and part-time. Along with this change, we can observe fewer and later heterosexual marriages, and an increase in divorce. She also refers to "new kinds of domestic arrangements" pioneered by gays and lesbians. All this calls for large changes in the provision of welfare and the means of protecting people from the new uncertainties.

Fraser attempts to compare how two concepts called the 'universal breadwinner model' and 'caregiver parity model' fare in addressing such goals as fighting poverty and equality of respect. The first has to do with recognising women as equal participants in the workforce. This calls for a number of reforms in the workplace running from eliminating sexual harassment to creating secure and high paying jobs for women. She grants that this is far from "present realities", but is still interested to see how it shapes up in dealing with welfare related needs. It does well on addressing poverty and exploitation, but poorly on leisure-time equality and forcing women to adopt men's roles. "The female half of the couple has simply disappeared." (p. 605)

The alternative approach of caregiver parity aims to keep different roles, for the most part, for men and women, while removing the penalties currently associated with the activities usually performed by women. This means receiving equal pay and status for childbearing, rearing and housework. Again, Fraser concedes that this is far from reality at the present time. It differs from the universal breadwinner approach in bringing about a better outcome when it comes to leisure-time equality and avoids some of the problems that come from simply trying to make women like men. It does worse when it comes to marginalising women and securing equal income for them. A useful framework is suggested for evaluating welfare proposals, and a case is made for issues of gender as being central to welfare reform.

HIGH ORDER FACTS

High order facts are usually about possible relations between two compiled facts. Scott Coltrane has done a fascinating study of the relation between the status of women and the role of fathers in child rearing. (Coltrane, '88) The date of publication falls a little outside my chosen decade, but it has to be included because of its breadth and energy. In one central respect the study illustrates a distinguishing feature of empirical sociology. Advanced statistical techniques are used to determine whether or not the status of women, comparing one society with another, tends to be higher when fathers take a more active role in rearing children. The use of off-the-shelf measures of both 'status' and 'an active role' is more typical of social psychology. And the sample Scott uses of ninety non-industrial 'traditional' societies is more typical of anthropology. However, the nature of the question asked, and the basic structure used to answer it, enables one to identify this investigation quite clearly as a piece of sociology.

Some studies, and even some unusually good studies, can be reported in relatively few words. In other cases, and this is one, a succinct summary cannot do justice. Nevertheless, I am going to cut to the core proposition and how it is investigated. While there is rich variety of theories which attempt to explain why men dominate in the economic, political and social life of most societies, the most pervasive explanation is that women have to give birth to and rear children, and this prevents them from taking up more active roles outside the family. If this explanation is correct, it might follow, loosely, that if the culture was such that fathers put comparatively more into raising their children, women could, and therefore would, play a larger role in the more public realms.

The basic data for this analysis comes from a study done by M. Ross in 1983. He in turn was drawing on what is known as the Standard Cross-Cultural Sample of non-industrial ethnic groups compiled by Murdock and White in 1967. Coltrane also draws on Ross' measures of the role of women in the public life of these societies. Measures of the importance of fathers in child rearing come from a study by Barry and Paxson done in 1971. Using chi-square and other statistical measure the author finds his central association. "Societies with close father-child relationships are significantly more likely to afford women a role in community decision-making than societies with distant father-child relationships." (p. 1072) This broad statistical result is fleshed out with pages of detailed discussion of similarities and differences in how this works in different cultures.

Coltrane is persuaded that when men take a more active role in raising their children, spending more time with them and being more affectionate, this has a number of good consequences, including a fuller role for women outside of the home. The obvious big rival theory to the one favoured by this author is the possibility that societies differ in the extent that they possess some general characteristic we could call male domination. When male domination is high, women have a small role in public life, and fathers spend little time with their children. It is not the case that the time and affection devoted to children in itself affects the public life of women. Coltrane attempted to test this rival theory by multiple regression. He correlates the public life of women with both measures of male domination and the role of fathers in child rearing, and finds a significant independent effect from the latter.

This research leaves open the mechanisms that result in the observed differences across societies. The author leans towards the view that personality development is key. If women are involved in public life, young men develop in ways that lead them to take more of an interest in their own children. These experiences in themselves then influence how men in later life relate to women in the public realm. Of course all this is conjecture. Coltrane suggests lines of enquiry that could be revealing, and he speculates as to whether these effects can be seen in industrial societies.

The distinction between high order facts and the testing of theories turns in part on the intentions of the investigator. One researcher might want to test the theory that more alcohol consumption at football matches leads to more crowd violence. A second researcher might want to establish the high order fact that matches where more alcohol is consumed have higher rates of violent activity. The test-of-theory versus high-order-fact distinction also turns on the extent to which the relation in question is linked to other theories, or is simply drawn out of a hat, however plausibly that might be done. If it is a 'stand alone' proposition, we are more likely to classify the research exercise as a high order fact. But clearly there is plenty of room for disagreement. A fascinating case, which is not easy to classify, is the work of A.R. Gillis on the relation between husbands murdering wives and wives murdering husbands, or domestic homicide, and the ease of obtaining a divorce. (Gillis, '96) This is a far-reaching and detailed statistical analysis of data from France over the years 1852 to 1909.

As Gillis points out, a large amount literature is unable to decide whether, "...marital dissolution is more of a stimulus or a safety valve for familial violence." (p. 1274) Clearly betrayal and desertion can lead to a violent response. Alternatively, no legal way out of a dreadful marriage could also lead to desperate measures. Any investigation of which tendency in fact dominates must deal with the problem that this relation between marriage law and violence is embedded in a most complex environment. Many social changes are going on simultaneously over the period of the data. These include the changing role of women in society, a rise in individualism, greatly increased urbanisation, and a general decline in violence. The challenge for the researcher is to separate out the influence of the changing ease of divorce and its effects on domestic violence from all the other social forces at work. For example, more people living in cities is associated with both higher rates of divorce and separation, and with lower rates of murder.

The choice of France over this period is partly determined by the unusual availability of statistics on crime. These are probably the best for any country, and include important information on the kind of homicide committed, particularly whether it was premeditated or spontaneous. The author works with annual data on crime and on divorce and separation. These come from the Comptes générale de l'administration de la justice criminelle and Annuaire statistique de la France. (p. 1281). Gillis gives a lot of attention in his handling of the data to responses that take time. The immediate effect of divorce might well be different from the effect in one year's time. Another great problem in separating out causes, perhaps the single most serious issue, is the general decline in violence over the period. Attempts to control for this involve including the general rates of violent crime in regressions relating domestic violence to divorce. The results do suggest that some of the decline in domestic violence is indeed due to, or related to, the general decline, but still leaves ample room for the negative effects of separation and divorce on murders by spouses, especially when it comes to men killing their wives.

The economic conditions of the country also have an effect on violent behaviour. Lacking any figures on unemployment, Gillis uses bankruptcy figures as an indicator. There is some tendency for murders motivated by adultery on the part of wives to decline when economic conditions are hard. It is unclear whether the actual amount of adultery goes down, or it is of less concern to husbands when they are struggling to survive economically. The overall effect of including bankruptcy in the regressions is to strengthen the negative relation between separation and divorce and domestic homicide.

In this study the author uses the actual volume of separation and divorce as the causal factor, and strictly speaking is not using the ease of obtaining a dissolution of a marriage. Other factors than the ease of ending a marriage might be causing changes in the amount of separation and divorce. There was a major change in divorce legislation in 1884. Gillis conjectures that this liberalisation inflated the subsequent figures for a time due to the backlog of applicants, and might not cause a comparably large reduction in the number of murders. To take some account of this change in legislation, a dummy variable for 'before' and 'after' is included. This has little effect on most of the findings, but it does reveal one important new relation. It more than doubles the strength of the negative impact of ending marriages on murders by wives that were motivated by adultery.

The final twist in the tale is the finding that the ending of more marriages is associated with more murders that are not of spouses. It is almost as if a murder was going to happen— for a married couple, one or the other has a pretty good chance of being the victim. But if the marriage is over, someone else may be killed. This is a simplification. For example, infanticide goes down dramatically with greater divorce and separation. On balance, while there is evidence of some extra murders of other than spouses, the net effect ending marriages is a reduction in the total number of murders.

After careful weighing of the evidence, Gillis concludes that, "If marital dissolution actually eased domestic violence, it may have done more for wives than for husbands as potential victims, especially when adultery was not involved." (p. 1297) Men murder their wives more than the other way around. The research suggests that men are less inclined to fear their wives. It offers some possible explanation of why wives are more inclined to seek divorce than their husbands. The author is cautious about generalising to other times and places.

Noraini Noor has uncovered a high order fact relating to women's well-being. (Noor, '95) Her study compares the influences of family life and work experience on the women in her study. 124 professional women, largely academics but including some doctors, accountants and solicitors, took part in the investigation. They were contacted through the Oxford University Women Tutors' Group and by drawing on employed ex-students of Exeter College in the University of Oxford. These women made up the highly educated portion of the study. The other part of the study was made up of secretaries from Oxford, very few of whom had degrees, though most had done GCE 'A' levels. The use of two dissimilar groups of employed women was central to this study of the effects of family conditions and of work conditions on women's well-being.

This exercise draws heavily on various off-the-shelf questionnaires that social psychologists use to measure a number of factors that potentially result in positive or negative emotional outcomes. Well-being was evaluated using the Oxford Happiness Inventory developed by Argyle, Martin and Crossland in 1989. Distress was measured using the General Health Questionnaire (Goldberg, '78). In addition, "negative affectivity" was measured using the Neuroticism part of the Eysenck Personality Questionnaire (Eysenck and Barrett, '85). These can be thought of as the 'output' measures, or put another way, as the consequences. The 'input', or causal factors for this study were the roles that women played in the family and in work. They were determined from a variant of the Baruch and Barnett questions and assertions on role attributes. For the job, negative aspects were work overload and tedium. Fairly obvious representative aspects were "having too much to do" and "lack of challenge". Positive features were work autonomy and the rewards of work, represented by questions including "hours fit your needs" and "good income". (p. 104)

Turning to family life, the researcher directed attention to the relations the subjects had with their partners and to the experiences they had as mothers. Positive examples of the former were statements like "good companionship" and "able to go to partner with problems". Negative items included "problems in sexual relationship" and "conflict over housework". For the role as mother, representative positive items were "enjoying doing things with them" and "the love they show". The negative side included "problems with their schooling" and "feeling trapped or bored". (p. 105) The subjects were asked to respond at two points in time, December 1991 and August 1992. The first date had to do with what they felt about work and family, and the second date had to do with well-being.

Noor subjected the large amount of data generated by the questionnaires to extensive statistical analysis consisting mainly of correlating outcomes with inputs in a range of ways. Rather strong results come out of the study. None of the family factors could be shown to influence, in the sense of enable one to predict, well-being or its absence. What shines through in the analysis is the importance of work overload in leading to distress. And here the two groups of women showed strikingly different responses. For the professional women, overload had a very small negative effect on well-being. But for the secretaries it had a big effect. It must be kept in mind that the study is controlling for demographic factors and attempting to isolate just the effects coming from the partner, being a mother, and work experience.

This study is significant in casting serious doubt on the widely held view that the satisfaction of women stems mainly from their lives as members of families. Work experience is held in much popular discussion, and in some social psychological studies as well, to play a very minor secondary role. The author has done a great deal to challenge that view, and to suggest that women's work experience matters far more in their well-being than had been previously acknowledged. The study further brings to light an interesting difference between more qualified women doing what would typically be agreed to be more rewarding work, and women in more routine jobs. The latter are markedly less able to cope with work overload. It would be interesting to see a comparable study for men.

Augusto Palmonari, Erich Kirchler and Maria Pombeni have uncovered an important high order fact regarding the importance of family relations for the emotional development of teenagers. (Palmonari and colleagues, '91) They worked with a large sample of 1,600 male and female youths with an average age of sixteen. These subjects came from three Italian cities, Bologna, Campobasso and Vicenza. The main objective of the investigation was to see how peer group relations and family relations contributed to the process of coping with the well-known stresses of adolescence.

An important aspect of the enquiry was finding out, through questionnaires, to whom the subjects turned and discussed their problems when under some pressure. Statistical analysis allowed Palmonari and his colleagues to group the respondents into four categories. Some had low identification with both their fellows and their family. Others were high on one but not the other, and the fourth category contained those youths who identified closely with both their peers and their family. Seven types of problems were specified in the study including conflicts with friends, frustration at school, and lack of life-values. (p. 389) The youths reported on a twelve-point scale how frequent and serious each of the seven potential sources of problems was. They evaluated the usefulness of talking with someone on a five point scale, and 'yes' or 'no' answers were elicited as to whether the problem was solved and whether this was a long-term solution.

The data suggest quite convincingly that the young people who do best, on their own evaluation, are those who are able to relate closely to both their peers and their family. There are young people who can only feel close in the family, and then there are those who are somewhat estranged from their family, but have good friends and good relations in informal street associations or more formal clubs and organisations. Some have neither. But those who can draw on both sources have a clear advantage. There is some indication that men draw more benefit from support of friends and family than do women. It was also found that the support is more helpful for "relational" and personal problems than school related problems like delinquency.

CASUAL THEORY

The political science researcher Vicky Randall has a theory of why there is poor provision of day-care facilities in Britain. (Randall, '93) She starts from figures on the provision in Britain compared to other European countries. There seems little doubt that these provisions are meagre. For example, for children between three years of age and school age, only Portugal compares to Britain in offering provision for about one-third of children. The other countries cover twice this proportion, or considerably more. Why is this?

Randall offers two explanations. The first is that providing day care facilities is redistributive, and Thatcherite Conservatives, dominant at the time of the study, are hostile to this. There also are sources of hostility from political interests who are not in agreement with Thatcher. On the left we can see male dominated trade unions that are unlikely to give a high priority to providing these facilities. They are more concerned with preserving male interests than facilitating female employment.

The second factor is what the author calls the "ideology of motherhood". This tends to the view that the family should not be a concern of state action, and can be hostile to encouraging women with children to enter the labour market. It could be argued that these are stylised facts as much as casual theory. Taken as general theory, we may worry about its validity. After all, there are conservative governments on the Continent, as well as traditional views of the role of women in raising children, and yet they provide more day-care facilities. I would not want to argue the methodological point strongly. What is clear is that along with a few statistics, the research draws heavily on beliefs about the facts of political life in Britain and weaves them into a casual theory. There is nothing wrong with this as an approach in general, and the application here to the vital question of day-care provision is enlightening.

MEASURING EFFECTS

It is often maintained that in less developed countries a major motive for having large numbers of children is the security they provide in old age. Not a great deal has been done to determine whether children do in fact contribute significantly to their elderly parents when they grow up. In order to provide some information on this question, the economist John Hoddinott has examined the transfers from sons and daughters to their parents. He conducted a survey of households in the Lao area of Kenya, which is west of Nairobi. (Hoddinott, '92) There is a good deal of theory, going back to Gary Becker, which argues that even totally self-interested children will reduce their consumption for the sake of the family income if a later transfer to them when they inherit can more than compensate. A later version of this theory due to Bernheim, Shleifer and Summers postulates that parents care about their own consumption, the help they receive from their children, and the consumption of their children. (Bernheim and colleagues, '85) In the spirit of Becker and what is called the "rotten kid theorem", the children care only about their own consumption and the level of care they find it in their interests to provide for their parents. In this theory the threat of disinheriting can be used by the parents to induce a higher level of transfer from their children. Hoddinott's work is more inspired by this theory than a formal test of it. His main goal is to measure the extent of the transfers.

The author collected data on sources of income from 160 households, with roughly half of them being elderly, and half not elderly. For the older households, transfers of money from their children made up a third of their income. For the rest it amounted to only five percent. And nearly ninety percent of the elderly households were getting money from their children. The proportion of income coming from children did not vary a great deal comparing the better-off households to the less well-off. Hoddinott also collected detailed data on help given in the form of eight different tasks like fetching water, cooking and going to market. A large amount of this help came from daughters living in the household and from the daughters of sons.

Dividing the sample of elderly households into two groups, those who received more money and help from their children, and those who received less, indicated that having more children, particularly sons, was a positive factor. Another factor associated with receiving more from their children was having more wealth to leave as inheritance. Whether these parents manipulate their children into helping them more, or whether the better-off families have better educated and higher earning children who can afford to give more financial help to their parents is unclear. The small sample size, and other complications, calls for caution in applying these figures to theoretical debate. But apart from any test of theory, measuring the extent to which children are a source of old-age security in Kenya does appear to be convincingly carried out.

The sociologists John Logan and Glenna Spitze have undertaken a similar measurement exercise intended to determine the significance of family connections in urban communities. (Logan and Spitze, '94) Some urban theorists expect local communities to become less important when moving about the city is easier. People will choose their friends and interactions, it is suggested, on the basis of personal preference rather than physical proximity. The authors randomly sampled residents in the Albany-Schenectady-Troy metropolitan area. 1,200 adults over 40 years of age took part in one-hour interviews. Questions were asked about family members living in the neighbourhood and elsewhere, and about help in shopping, errands, housecleaning, baby-sitting, and so on. Detailed information on all types of interaction, including visits and phone-calls, with relatives and with others, was collected.

Logan and Spitze find that the number of relatives living in the neighbourhood typically is small, but that between fifteen to twenty-five percent of interactions are with this group. The neighbourhood emerges as more important than many other writers have suggested. Their study does find that this is less true for white compared to non-white residents; less the case for better off compared to less well-off residents; and similarly for more urban compared to more rural neighbourhoods. While there are these differences, "Urban sociologists, in our view, can benefit from a reconsideration of the extent to which local community networks are founded on kinship ties, even today." (pp. 472 - 473) The data was collected over a six months period starting in September 1988.

ABSTRACT MODELS

Returning to the topic of teenage motherhood, it has been argued that if abortion is easier to obtain, there will be fewer teenage mothers. This has a kind of common sense appeal. While not every pregnant teenager will avail herself of abortion, more will do so if it is easier to obtain. 'Easier' should be thought of comprehensively as including social attitudes, financial costs, emotional costs, and future prospects. On the other hand, it could equally well be argued that teenage women are more likely to risk getting pregnant when abortion is an easier option. The result would be both more pregnancies, and a smaller proportion of this larger number of pregnancies going to term. And so the effect of making abortion easier could go either way as regards the resulting number of teenage mothers.

The economists Thomas Kane and Douglas Staiger have developed a model of decision-making which they hope captures the main elements in this teenage mother debate. (Kane and Staiger, '96) As in most such exercises, very strong assumptions are made which make it possible to construct a precise model of what is going on. Once the model is understood, there is no room for judgement or interpretation. A key element in the work of Kane and Staiger is the assumption that sexually active teenage women can only obtain information about the degree of commitment of their partner once they become pregnant. They assume that the girls have one partner, and when they become pregnant they ask him if he will marry them or not. With a certain probability he says 'yes' or 'no'. The model assumes that this probability varies from one woman to another, and is known to each woman in advance.

The model assumes that young women are utility maximisers. In effect this means that they attach a value to the various outcomes of their actions and choose the action that leads to the highest expected value among the outcomes open to them. It is assumed that all women attach the same values to outcomes. They differ from one another in two ways: the probability that their partner will marry them if they are pregnant; and the cost to them of an abortion.

An absolutely crucial part of the model is how they rank the outcomes. It is assumed that not getting pregnant carries a utility of zero. This just gives us a convenient baseline. Any number could have been chosen for this outcome. The other outcomes are scaled with reference to it.

Significantly, giving birth in wedlock is given a value of 1. This is a terribly strong assumption. That some teenage women would prefer to get married and have a baby, compared to not getting pregnant and not getting married at that stage in their lives, is plausible. That all young women are modelled by the authors in this way gives crisp theoretical results, but these conclusions may not reflect the actual goals and behaviour of teenagers very accurately.

I have fewer problems with the assumption that having a baby out of wedlock carries a negative utility, as does having an abortion. Which of the two has the larger negative effect will depend in the model on the individual cost of abortion a woman faces. All women are assumed to attach the same negative utility to an out of wedlock birth. Just to summarise, there are two factors which vary, comparing one teenager with another. These are the chances that her partner will say 'yes' to marriage if informed that she is pregnant, and the cost to her of an abortion. Then there are three factors which are common to all young women: the cost of a birth out of wedlock; the utility attached to not getting pregnant; and the utility of having a baby in wedlock. These last three outcomes are listed in ascending order of utility.

The model then implies that every teenager will be in one of three possible positions. Those with low chances of getting married, as they measure it, will not risk pregnancy, unless the cost of abortion is very low. A non-linear relation separates those for whom the very low cost of an abortion leads to a risk of pregnancy, in spite of poor marriage prospects, from those who will not choose to get pregnant. Then there are those women who will get pregnant and will not have an abortion, regardless of whether their partner says 'yes' or 'no'. And then there are the teenagers who will get pregnant, and if their partner says 'yes' will become mothers, and if he says 'no' will have an abortion. For them the cost of an abortion is less than the cost of an out of wedlock birth.

The model could aspire to more realism by allowing for varying degrees of risk of getting pregnant as against a decision one way or the other. It is often the case in modelling that this extra realism comes at a cost in terms of complexity, without any extra insight into the problem at hand. So what does the model say as it stands? It says that some teenagers will not get pregnant. Some will, and will carry their baby to term, with or without getting married. A third group will get pregnant, and with a certain probability get married and have the baby. The rest of this group, those who do not marry, will have an abortion. If the proportion who marry is designated as 'P', the proportion in this group who will have an abortion is 1 – P. In one sense, this is fair enough, and so far not very enlightening. The model says that there are four possibilities: not getting pregnant; getting pregnant and having the baby out of wedlock; getting pregnant and having the baby in wedlock; and getting pregnant and having an abortion. Options 'five' and 'six', if you will, of getting married without being pregnant or getting married and having an abortion are not of interest to the topic of teenage motherhood, which is taken to be the special problem of teenage sex.

Now we come to the crunch issue. What does the model predict when we change the one policy instrument in our command, namely, the cost of having an abortion? The authors argue that the model implies that a small change in the cost of abortion mainly moves some teenagers from getting pregnant to not getting pregnant. The number of teen mothers declines. A large increase in the cost of abortion shifts some teenagers from abortion to out of wedlock births. This raises the number of teenage mothers. For the model to be fully automatic, and not to depend on "the authors ague", the effects of large and small changes in the cost of abortion will depend on the precise distribution of teenagers across the options of varying marriage prospects and varying costs of abortion.

We might also wonder whether it is possible to vary the costs of abortion, including emotional costs, while leaving the costs of an out-of-wedlock birth unchanged. But there is the model, take it or leave it. In fairness, while I have used the Kane and Staiger study as an example of modelling, the authors do a great deal of empirical investigation, concentrating on data for the United States. They find that the distance pregnant teenagers have to travel to obtain an abortion, the main measure of costs used in the study, has little effect on out-of-wedlock births. The number of in-wedlock births from teenage mothers tends to fall with small increases. This is consistent with the model. No doubt the last word has not been said. Hopefully this is an example of one model eventually leading to a better model.

The economists Amy Farmer and Jill Tiefenthaler have undertaken a revealing exercise in pure theory to explore the possible effects of shelters on the welfare of battered wives. (Farmer and Tiefenthaler, '96) The fact that many women return to their husbands after spending a brief period in shelter has led a number of police officials, psychologists and social workers to feel that the provision of shelters is a failure. The authors feel that this is a mistaken view, and the existence of shelter accommodation, and occasional brief use of it, may reduce the amount of violence that some women have to endure. The intuition behind their argument is not difficult. Shelters may increase the chances that women will leave, and enable women to credibly threaten to leave at lower levels of violence. In brief, the existence of the option of going to a shelter changes the relation between husbands and wives without women necessarily actually exercising the option.

It is one thing to suggest an argument and another to provide a formal model. When we come to allowing for different types of women, bluffing, and guesswork on the part of husbands, intuition easily gets left behind. The model may or may not give a very accurate picture of what is going on. Thinking through some possibilities carefully does suggest potentially significant effects. In order to carry out their analysis, the authors make some stark assumptions. No attempt is made to explain why some men might want to batter their wives. It simply is assumed that the more violent they are to their wives, the more utility they gain. There clearly is some level beyond which they might not want to go, but if all the action takes place below this level, we can ignore the upper reaches and simplify our modelling task by doing that.

It is also assumed that husbands care about their own consumption, and get some benefits from the marriage. A crucial issue is the utility of being in the marriage compared to being single. It is assumed that the wives' utility depends on their consumption, the benefits of them to marriage, and is negatively affected by violence. The greater the amount of violence they experience, the greater is the negative effect.

It is assumed in the model that the women know whether they are at their threshold and on the point of leaving, or will not leave. The men do not know the situation of their wives. If marriage is preferable to being single, men will either adopt the level of violence that will just keep in the marriage women with a lower tolerance, or go for the level that keeps in the marriage women with a higher tolerance. Their violence level will never go below the former or above the latter. Whether they choose the softer or the harder strategy depends on their appraisal of the probability that the wife will leave if the harder, more violent behaviour is adopted.

The existence of the shelter has no effect on the women who are at the point of leaving if the level of violence goes up. It does raise the possibility of claiming to have a lower tolerance of violence on the part of women who in fact will stay in the marriage. They can threaten to leave, and even go to shelter for a brief period, but this strategy comes at a cost. There is the disruption itself, and if the bluff does not work, the husband may adopt a higher level of violence. The model involves three probabilities. One is the probability that the wife has a low or high tolerance for violence. Another is the probability that a wife with a high tolerance wife will bluff. And finally, there is the probability that the husband will respond to bluffing by calling the wife's bluff, or what the authors call a "tough" response.

The authors prove a number of points in the set up they have devised. Being convinced of the validity of the claims of the authors can only come from following the mathematics of the argument. The reader is invited to do so. Short of that, we may note that if there is something to the motivations and categories that Farmer and Tiefenthaler suggest, there may be important and unexpected results following from the provision of shelters for battered wives.

A key finding of the paper is that there are winners and losers from the provision of shelters. Some women are able to raise the belief in their husbands that they will leave, or may leave, and this reduces the level of violence that the optimising husband will wreak on this wife. Others will pay a price for being caught at bluffing and experience more violence than if the shelters were not there. What is clear and interesting from the model is that it is wrong to judge the success of shelters by the length of time wives stay in them, and the proportion of shelter users who return to their husbands. The existence of the option in itself may have the effect of lowering the amount of violence in marriages where, for one reason or another, husbands have a taste for it.

The way marriages form in the first place has been studied by many social scientists. Abstract theory developed for seemingly unrelated purposes has played a part in characterising the pairing that goes on in marriage. This is an interesting example of how formal theory invented to study one phenomenon can be applied elsewhere. The theory goes under the name of 'matching models'. It has been applied in labour markets, where employers and employees have to search for each other and make decisions as to whether or not to enter into long-term relations. Ken Burdett and Melvyn Coles have applied matching theory to the marriage 'market'. (Burdett and Coles, '97) Surprisingly complex interactions are possible, even with severely simple assumptions. For example, the authors assume a single number, readily seen by all parties, characterises each man and each woman. The higher this number, the greater the return to a partner who accepts them in marriage. They meet randomly, and observe the other person's number, while knowing their own. If both decide to pair up, they leave the scene together. If one or more rejects, they go back into the pool. The model allows for both death, permanent departure, and for new entrants. Not all entrants wind up married.

Heavy-duty mathematics is required to understand the workings of this system over time. Seven pages of intense mathematics follows in an appendix to the main body of the article. The article itself carries the argument forward in the formal terms common in economics. The central conclusion of the analysis is that there will emerge bands, or intervals, or as the authors call them, 'class partitions', in which men and women with given levels of desirability will form marriages. These will be equilibrium states that persist. Many different partitions are possible which are all equilibrium bands, once established. A possible line of future research which Burdett and Coles suggest is to model a matching problem where the participants are born with a certain level of attractiveness, but can invest in themselves in order to improve their attractiveness.

TESTING THEORIES

A number of psychologists and other researchers have suggested that mothers going out to work has negative effects on their children, especially on very young children. The sociologists Toby Parcel and Elizabeth Menaghan have undertaken a large-scale statistical investigation which tests this theory. (Parcel and Menaghan, '94) Theirs is one of several studies that draw on what is called the National Longitudinal Survey of Youth. The NLSY started in 1979 with a sample of twelve thousand American youths between the ages of 14 and 21. Annual interviews were conducted to gather information on the marital and fertility experiences of this group, along with their education and employment. By the year 1986 over half the women in the original survey had become mothers. Their children were tested for their cognitive abilities and for behavioural problems. The authors worked with two samples. The first had 768 mothers. It was made up of employed mothers with a child living with her, aged between three and six years old. The second sample of 526 mothers simply dropped the three-year-olds because they were not assessed for behavioural problems. Where there was more than one child, the youngest was taken for the purposes of the study.

The mental ability of the children was measured using the Revised Version of the highly regarded Peabody Picture Vocabulary Test. It tests for comprehension of standard American English by asking the subjects to point to the one out of four pictures which best fits the word spoken by an interviewer. The test for behavioural problems was a modified form of the Child Behavior Check List. (Achenbach and Edelbrock, '81) The mother is asked to indicate the extent to which her child displays relatively minor problems such as aggressive behaviour, or depressed and withdrawn behaviour.

The employment history of both parents, or stepparent if the biological father was not living with the child in1986, enters in both a quantitative and a qualitative way. The data reflects whether the parents were employed in the first year of the child's life, and average employment over the next three years. Work is graded according to occupational complexity. This last factor proves to be important in the study. It has to do with whether the work is of a very routine nature, and is heavily supervised. It also turns on the actual content of the work. Unfortunately, the authors do not explain exactly how the index of complexity is constructed.

Parcel and Menaghan are reporting on a large and complicated investigation. It is not easy to do justice to their work in any brief summary. What can be said with some confidence is that more careful investigation gives little comfort to those who believe that working mothers have an adverse effect on either the cognitive or behavioural development of their children. This is especially the case if there is not a huge amount of working time and if the mother is working in a 'complex', or better paid, occupation.

Having to take any job in order to make ends meet, and pursuing it for long hours is not in the interest of the children. A moderate amount of work of interest to the mother, on the other hand, is found in this study to contribute positively. There is an exception in the case of mothers with poor employment prospects. Being at home rather than working may contribute to verbal ability, though it has no discernible effects on behavioural problems. Another interesting finding is that fathers being under-employed in the early years is associated with behavioural problems in their children, and too much overtime work on the part of fathers has some negative effects on verbal ability.

So many factors are at work here, including in this study the education of the child's grandmother, that what is being tested has to be looked at especially carefully. The simple view that work outside the home on the part of mothers is clearly bad both for the cognitive and emotional development of children is refuted. How work of both parents interacts with many other features of the family situation in its impact on the development of children is only partly understood.

A very different example of testing theories can be found in an attempt to explain the existence, where it occurs, of marriages with several husbands and one wife. Polyandry is an unusual form of marriage. It runs against the simple biological fact that men can in principle have far more children than women. Anthropologists have advanced four conjectures to explain polyandry; (1) very harsh physical conditions leading to an environment where more than two adults in the nuclear family is advantageous to producing more surviving children; (2) where men have to be away for long periods due to long-distance trade, herding animals or at sea; (3) an imbalance between the number of men and women; and (4) special inheritance regulations. The imbalance theory requires some accompanying explanation for female infanticide. The inheritance argument has the problem of treating the rules as exogenous. One might have thought they would be a response to some causal factors along with polyandry.

The anthropologists Nancy Levine and Joan Silk attempt to test some of the theories using data collected from the Nyinba people, a culturally Tibetan people living in north-western Nepal. (Levine and Silk, '97) In this community, polyandry is fraternal. The oldest brother marries and brings his younger brothers into the marriage. Three husbands is regarded as ideal. The authors quote some data from a study by Cook and Cook to the effect that polyandrous marriages among the Ladakh people in Tibet have just over five children, where monogamous marriages there result in three children. This lends some support to the notion that in some circumstances polyandry 'works'.

The authors refer to a study done in 1983 which found that about half of the polyandrous marriages among the Nyinba were still intact. Sometimes a second wife is brought into a polyandrous marriage. This is called a conjoint marriage. If a man leaves the marriage, he is called an "active partitioner". The man left behind is designated a "passive partitioner". Younger men are inclined to leave because only the oldest brother is producing children and tending to monopolise the wife sexually. They may wonder when their turn will come, and how old the wife will be when that happens.

Levine and Silk surveyed 137 men and found that those who stayed in the original marriage, which was a stable marriage, had on average 1.78 children. But a number of men broke away. The active partitioners had few children in the original marriages. The average was .45. The men left behind when a marriage broke up typically had one child, on average. But the active partitioners had on average three children. The central proposition which they test with their data is the theory that harsh conditions lead to polyandry. They feel that two observations refute this theory. One is that poor men sometimes actively partition. The other is that their data show roughly equal economic success for polyandrous and monogamous marriages.

There is a problem here as to whether we are trying to explain why particular people in a society that allows polyandry choose to adopt that form of marriage, or whether we are trying to explain why the society condones that form. My reading of the Levine and Silk data is that it is relevant to the first proposition, but not to the second. The authors also concede the possibility that past history may have led to polyandry, and cultural momentum keeps it going.

In addition to exploring the causes of this practice, they are interested in explaining the observed instability of these marriages among the Nyinba. Without providing formal tests, the factors they emphasise in accounting for the breakdown of polyandrous marriages are too many brothers, and too large an age gap between them. There also appears to be an influence from the number of children, and who biologically fathers them. The authors suggest that in some other polyandrous cultures, such as those in Oceana, no particular account is taken of who is the father. That would tend to lead to more stability. Among the Nyinba account is taken of the biological father, and the authors conclude that this is one of the factors working against polyandry in that society.

What leads to satisfaction in marriage? A large number of studies suggest that in one form or another the sense that there is some kind of fairness in the relationship leads to more satisfaction. Several interpretations of the concept of equality in marriage have been employed. Closely related, and in some circumstances the same thing, is a concept of equity. A number of researchers emphasise the notion of the 'deal' that partners are getting. Are they putting in a lot and getting little out? The social psychologists Nico Van Yperen and Bram Buunk have tested the theory that equity leads to satisfaction. (Yperen and Buunk, '90) Among several other issues, they explore the possibility that the causality may go the other way. Perhaps people who are dissatisfied with their marriage, for whatever reason, tend to see it as inequitable. The research makes a serious effort to deal with that possibility. The central proposition under test is that lack of equity through not getting a fair return out of the marriage, or getting more than one's share, both lead to dissatisfaction. Getting less than is equitable is held to lead to more dissatisfaction than getting more than is equitable.

The authors worked with a sample of 259 couples who they recruited from an advertisement in a newspaper. Eighty-six percent were married. The others were cohabiting. The mean age was thirty-nine years, and on average the couples had been together for fourteen years. Three-quarters had children. The participants were asked to fill in questionnaires individually, and not to discuss them with their partners until after they had posted them back. A year later there was a follow up questionnaire. The response rate to the first questionnaire was 94 percent, and 66 percent of those couples returned the second questionnaire. The purpose of the second questionnaire was to shed light on whether equity leads to satisfaction, or whether the causal lines run mainly the other way, and satisfaction leads to equity.

Yperen and Buunk used their knowledge of related work, plus informal interviews, to identify 144 "exchange elements" in a relationship of an "intimate" nature. These were things like concern, sociability, sex, security and many others. A seven-point Likert scale allowed the respondents to indicate their view over a range from an extremely negative contribution to no contribution and through to an extremely positive contribution. They were also asked to indicate on a seven-point scale ranging from "this applies much more to me than it does to my partner" up to the opposite. The first part enabled the authors to identify the more important elements, and the second to see who was perceived as getting more of the returns on balance, taking each element one-at-a-time.

Two other sets of questions were administered. One was intended to measure equity as whole, not specified through a number of elements. This single item, devised by Hatfield and colleagues in 1990, offered a seven-point scale which ranged from "I am getting a much better deal than my partner", up to equality, and on to "my partner is getting a much better deal than I am." (p.294) Next came a set of eight questions which were intended to measure satisfaction. These were devised by Buunk ('90). They include statements eliciting agreement or disagreement with propositions such as, "I feel happy when I'm with my partner" and "My partner irritates me". (p. 295)

The results were quite interesting. On the single shot Hatfield measure, most of the respondents felt themselves to be equitably treated. For those who felt otherwise, men tended to see themselves as getting more than their share, and women tended to see themselves as getting less. Looking over the year to the second survey, there was no change in the overall response of women. But a smaller proportion of men saw their relationships as being equitable, with departures in both directions. Some men shifted from equitable to advantaged and others from equitable to disadvantaged.

The authors do not discuss the possibility that there may be a sampling effect here. Possibly men who feel that there has been a change in the relationship when it comes to equity are more inclined to send in the second questionnaire than those who see little change over the year. Turning to the breakdown of items that are important in the relationship, there was very little difference in the choices made by men and by women. Commitment, pleasant to be with and leading an interesting and varied life were the top positive factors. Suspicious and jealous, unfaithful and addicted to alcohol were the three strongest negative factors.

It turns out that the relation between the single global measure of satisfaction and the possible components of satisfaction is near to non-existent. The authors contend that the global measure is not the sum of the individual factors. For example, frequently women felt themselves to be disadvantaged when reporting on individual items, but saw the overall relationship as being equitable. The authors suggest that perhaps the overall report is made in comparison to how women see things for women generally, while the individual items are absolute rather than comparative.

Fairly sophisticated statistical procedures were employed to determine the direction of causality — equity leading to satisfaction or satisfaction leading to a sense of equity. The research lends some support to the conclusion that equity leads to satisfaction, rather than satisfaction leading to a sense of equity.

The social psychologists Warren Miller and David Pasta have investigated the relative influence wives and husbands exercise over a very intimate decision, namely, the kind of contraception to use. (Miller and Pasta, '96) They conclude that the answer depends on which type of decision that has to be made; the choice of a method, or whether or not to use the method. It also depends on the kind of contraception that has been selected. One could classify this enquiry as uncovering a high order fact. 'This is how decisions are made and implemented by husbands and wives.' Alternatively, we could regard the Miller/Pasta investigation as testing the theory that wives have the major influence over contraception use, at least in the United States. I am inclined towards the latter classification because the decisions under investigation are held to be related to broader interconnected theories of the influence of gender on decisions. The authors argue that the dominant role of women in contraceptive decisions is widely believed, but not often subject to empirical test.

Working with the telephone directory for the San Francisco Bay area, the researchers put together a sample of 200 married couples with one child, and two hundred with no children. All participants were fluent in written and spoken English, and had not been sterilised. In all cases the wife was not pregnant, and aged between eighteen and thirty-nine. Interviews were conducted in the subjects' homes, or the offices of the researchers, and use was made of postal questionnaires. There was an initial interview in 1989, and more interviews one year, two years, and three-and-a-half years later. The study concentrated on three contraceptive methods; oral contraceptives, diaphragms and condoms.

The investigation concentrated on finding out how regular the couples were in employing the methods they used. For example, at one end were wives who never failed to take a pill, and at the other extreme those who missed more than two pills, more than twice a year. Couples were also asked about how confident they were in their ability to use the chosen method of contraception, as well as how satisfied they were with it, using a five point scale from 'very dissatisfied' up to 'very satisfied'. The respondents answered all questions in private. Included were questions about whether they would like to change methods, on a scale from 'yes', 'uncertain', to 'no'. If the answer was 'yes', they were asked what method they would adopt. They were also asked what their spouse felt about changing method. Finally, Miller and Pasta elicited information on the ease of communication they had with their spouse on matters of contraception, and how much disagreement there was over the method to chosen.

The researchers generated a huge amount of data that was used to analyse the factors relating to the choice of contraceptive method, regularity of use, decisions to change, and actual behaviour. The first point to emerge from the study is a difference between the choice of method and the use of a method once chosen. While they did find a slight separate influence of the preferences of wives on changes in the method used, in general it was couples who made decisions, and to assume that these matters were dealt with by wives alone was mistaken. Another interesting finding had to do with how the role of individual preference and perceived preference of spouses varied according to the method under consideration.

When it comes to condoms and diaphragms, husbands place great emphasis on the preferences of their wives, while wives take their own and their husbands' preferences as being of equal importance. Not unreasonably, confidence in the method currently used, and the desire for change, depends on who has to employ the method. Wives who are confident in the husbands' use of condoms, and husbands who are confident about their wives' use of diaphragms, are unlikely to want change. When it comes to condoms, husbands tend to give equal weight to their own and their spouses' preferences, while wives give no weight to their husbands' preferences.

The researchers present convincing evidence to refute the theory that it is mainly wives who determine contraceptive practice. This area of decision-making in families is complex. There are different stages involved in formulating and implementing plans of action. What happens between husbands and wives also is sensitive to the method of contraception under consideration. This study is confined to a rather narrow socio-economic group. They were mainly white, educated, with an average annual income of $71,000. It remains to be seen how practices and attitudes vary across other groups, but the simple view of wife dominated decisions fails to meet the test for the sample of couples under consideration.

Chapter Eight

MONEY

THE PRICELESS INSTITUTION

The invention of money ranks with writing and the wheel as one of the great enabling discoveries of mankind. Complex social organisation would not be possible without it. Co-ordination of the activities of large numbers of producers and consumers requires more than the institution of money, but would be impossible without money. Like those other great inventions, one cannot point to a single inventor. Once a society reaches a certain level of complexity, people begin to use mechanisms of exchange which we today can recognise as money. This happens without pre-meditation or conscious planning. The use of money is both more ancient and more widespread than the use of writing. To this day there remain societies without writing, but none without money.

Barter, or the exchange of one product or service for another, exists on a relatively small scale along with money in all societies today. Avoiding taxes is one of the motives for steering clear of money. There are other motives, some of which have to do with risk. The institution of 'sharecropping' for example, means that the landlord is paid in the form of an amount of produce from the land, rather than in a monetary rent. These and other barter arrangements are not particularly restricting in settings where the use of money is widespread. Even if a limited number of transactions are done through barter, almost anything a person acquires through barter can be exchanged for money at a later stage.

Money creates what is called a generalised claim on society. It does not entitle the possessor to a particular product or service. The claim can be exercised at any time, or any place, and for any thing available in the market. Many people hold some of their wealth, if they are fortunate enough to have some wealth, in the form of money. This facilitates day-to-day purchases. Large purchases, like a house or a car, will typically require selling some other asset, such as a different house, or some paper assets like shares or bonds. Often it will require borrowing, with a promise to deliver money in the future. When we say that the Queen of England has a billion pounds, we do not mean literally that tucked away in the palace is a huge pile of pound notes. Indeed, very wealthy people may have a negative net cash position, and owe some money. Lenders are not worried because they know that these individuals hold assets like buildings, land, boats, paintings, and so on, that can be turned into money if necessary. Money not only co-ordinates exchanges, it is a way of measuring the wealth of institutions and individuals.

Interestingly, there is no comparable measure of power. We cannot say that an individual has so much wealth, and so many units of power. People with money often acquire power, and people with power often use it to acquire money, or what money can measure, which we call wealth. If we could quantify power the way we can quantify land, or cigars, and if there was an open market in power, then it would fall under the measuring rod of money. We could add up the power of an individual, along with the wealth that person held in the form of race horses, bank accounts, and so on, and come to a single figure. Anything on which we can put a money price, and can potentially exchange for money in a market, can be added to other things to form a total measured in money. Power does not fit either of these two requirements. There are no quantitative units of power, and there is no open market where power may be bought or sold.

This chapter is about money. Hearing that phrase, people are inclined to jump to the false conclusion that the chapter is about rich people and poor people, and about the factors that determine the income and the wealth of people. For some, the phrase even suggests that the chapter might be about how to make money. These are all interesting questions, but not the current subject matter. This chapter is about the institution of money as a social phenomenon. In the same way as in other chapters, the work of social scientists in the 90's is reported. Very little of it addresses the technical institutional arrangements of national and global monetary systems, though some is of that kind. Most of the articles making up this chapter explore the ways in which people respond to the existence of money.

ORGANISING THIS CHAPTER

Unlike other chapters, where there is an attempt to give equal weight, or something approaching equal weight, to all the investigations of the various topics which took place over the last decade of the century, this chapter highlights a single article from each of the social sciences. The other articles are simply mentioned and treated briefly as part of the group of research done under the respective headings. The reason for emphasising a single work is to make room for something which has been rather neglected in the other chapters. That 'something' is connectivity. Going back to the concept of science which is discussed in outline in chapter two, the connected nature of scientific ideas is crucial. I suggested the image of a giant structure which is worked on by many investigators who modify a bit here or there, or add a bit here or there. Scientists come and go. No one understands the whole structure of science, or even a large section of it. The structure grows and changes over time. Few individuals affect more than a tiny portion of the whole. An important point is that the ideas which make up the structure are related, one to another.

The reports in other chapters endeavour to be informative of the work undertaken, but are light, or just plain silent, on how that work relates to other work in the discipline. If we were to look into the relation between each of the studies reported and the disciplines they fall under, we would see that some of these relations are explicit and unambiguous. Others are looser and much more in the way of being suggestive. It would not have been practical to examine how each study related to its discipline. Time, space and patience simply would not allow tying in each article discussed with the wider literature of which it formed a part.

To do that 'tying in' at all comprehensively would amount to writing something approaching a full description of each of the social sciences. Some things could safely be left out, but much would have to be included. It is feasible to show how one article in each subject relates to the investigations which surround that article. This is an important way of looking at social science, and this is the chapter where that approach is attempted. Why under 'money'? This approach could be applied to any of the topics, and money is as good a place as any.

There is a danger in this approach of highlighting a single article. I have to choose one. For the other chapters, I just report what went on. As here I must exercise some judgement, it can reasonably be asserted that I made a misleading choice. It could be maintained that choosing a different article to emphasise would show the subject in a very different light. I hope that is not the case, or not to a great degree. I certainly have tried to select the articles I feature with the goal of presenting interesting and not unrepresentative connections to other work in the area. This other work will almost entirely come from research done before 1990. Researchers in the 90's enter the structure of knowledge as they find it, and endeavour to improve it in some way. Some of the relevant ideas in their different areas have been part of the structure of the discipline for some time. Others are relatively new.

I do not intend to give a critical overview of how the articles I have selected for a more extended treatment relate to other knowledge in their fields. In some cases a critical overview would involve tracing important connections which the author or authors either failed to mention, or had escaped their attention. To do this would call for a very comprehensive knowledge of each of the social sciences. For the most part, I simply draw on the researchers themselves to elaborate on the relevance of their work. It is quite common, if not universal, for researchers to indicate the motivation for their work. They explain how it either corrects, makes more precise, re-organises, or extends past work. In other chapters I have played down this aspect, but here one article from each discipline is given a fuller treatment, the key theme of that elaboration being connections to other parts of the discipline.

ANTHROPOLOGY

Tibetan refugees living inf Nepal have adopted a way of promoting saving and investment which serves the same underlying purpose as is done by banks in more advanced industrial societies. The institution is not unique to Nepal. Similar alternatives to banks can be found in many pre-industrial parts of the world. In Nepal they go under the name of *Dhikuris*. Ram Chhetri in his article of 1995, which we will examine in some detail, suggests that it is likely that the term comes from combining two Tibetan words — *dhu* which means wheat, and *khr* which means rotate. (Chhetri, '95) In making this suggestion, he is following the work of the anthropologist Donald Messerschmidt published in 1978.

Dhikuris are quite clever institutions which vary one from another, even in Nepal, but have a common underlying logic. A group of a dozen or so members agree to pay in a common fixed amount of money every month. Each month the total, less certain deductions, is made available to one of the members of the Dhikuri. Who among the members of the Dhikuri gets the money each month is determined by bidding. This is the person who agrees to the largest amount of deduction from their payout. They get the remaining money for that month once the agreed deduction has been subtracted.

At the end of the process, there is a surplus made up of the deductions taken out each month. The last member of the Dhikuri to get any money, who paid in the agreed subscription each month and never took any out, gets all the money remaining in the Dhikuri. For this member, and possibly other members at the end of the process, the investment is financial. Money is paid in each month in anticipation of a net increase at the end. For other members, joining the Dhikuri is a way of raising capital for a business venture — possibly starting a retail business, or maybe buying cattle.

Not all of the deductions agreed to by the early beneficiaries of the scheme wind up as interest on the investments of later beneficiaries. There are some administrative expenses that have to be met. This is a highly idealised description of the process. There are complications which arise from a fairly common practice of paying in other assets than money, and there are methods of dealing with late payment and possible default.

Ram Chhetri has undertaken his research well aware that many scholars have studied this form of capital formation in less developed countries, and a fair amount of previous work has even been done on the Nepaleseian form of it. Among this latter group is the work of Beatrice Miller in 1956, Shirley Ardener in 1964, Michael Vinding in 1984, and Donald Messerschmidt already mentioned. Turning to other countries, Carlos Velez-Ibanez (1982) and Donald Kurtz (1977) have studied the workings of this type of institution in Mexico (1982); David Wu in Papua New Guinea (1974); and Alice Dewey in Java (1964), among other works in these and other countries. So how does Chhetri's work, more recent than the others, relate to the investigations undertaken by them?

Basically, Chhetri sees his work as adding to the case study material already available in other studies. His claim is that while we have some observations of this important monetary institution, more reports are necessary if we are to have a deeper understanding of why they come about, what purposes they serve, and how they are modified to better meet the particular needs of different groups of people. Chhetri refers to two anthropological theorists. Clifford Geertz writing in 1962, and Shirley Ardener mentioned above also writing in the '60's provide the basic definition of this institution taking the name of Dhikuri in Nepal. They differ somewhat in the significance they attach to the institution. Geertz sees them as helpful in making the transition from a primitive to a more prosperous and sophisticated society. In his words, they are an educational force for turning "peasants" into "traders". It would seem that Ardener goes further and gives these monetary institutions a more important role, both in facilitating the transition from a more self-sufficient agrarian economy to a more interdependent commercial economy, and as a viable alternative to banks.

Ram Chhetri takes these two writers to task and argues that their perceptions of the dhikuris and related institutions leaves us with much that we need to know. We know that they are common, but are they universal? Does every society produce such institutions when in transition from a traditional to a more modern form of organisation? And he also asks if these institutions pre-date the transition phase? Perhaps they are useful on-going features of many peasant societies, and while they have come to the attention of scholars particularly interested in transition, they may have an important history, and indeed a future, apart from transition.

It is doubtful if Chhetri's research in itself answers either question. The goal of seeing whether this type of institution occurs whenever a society reaches a certain developmental phase probably calls for an unrealistic amount of effort. More case material could be useful. But however many confirming cases were turned up, there might be other examples, which we have yet to find, where dhikuri-like institutions did not flourish. This suggests that the question itself might not be very helpful. Determining whether or not these institutions are helpful, or "adaptive" in Chhetri's word, for societies at various phases of change, or of stability, is a more feasible goal. His own investigations bear on this question through the mechanism of providing more examples.

His first example involves a group known as the Loba people. They have the culture of Tibet and live in a Himalayan region of Nepal called Lo Manthang. He reports that there is a Dhikuri that has members who are quite scattered geographically. Some are in the large centre called Pokhara, which is about one week's travel time away from Lo when going by foot. Even more significantly, one of the two "guardians", or central administrators of the Dhikuri, was from Jomsom which is the district headquarter and some distance away from Lo.

Unlike most Dhikuri which are regarded as typical and were reported in the earlier anthropological literature, the membership in this example is not from a single occupation. It stretches across "community/ethnic boundaries". (p. 450) Given the risk of default, Chhetri sees this as evidence of a relatively wealthy Dhikuri made up of members with economic relationships that are far from local. It would not include the less well-off Lo people who have their own Dhikuris, and would have been the dominant kind of Dhikuri to be found in Lo in the past. In this new version, the payout occurs twice a year and is determined by lottery rather than by auction. The use of lottery rather than auction seems to be of potential interest, but is not discussed by the author.

The second example is entirely traditional in being small scale, having face-to-face members, and following the broad outline I described initially. It involves Tibetan refugees living in the Tashi Ling settlement of Pokhara.

In effect it involved two Dhikuris with seventeen members each. Payouts occur every month with the order determined by auction. In his research, Chhetri was able to observe nine of the seventeen eventual rotations. This is in contrast to Dhikuris among the Napali business people in Pokhara. They make inputs up to twenty times the size of the monthly payments of the refugees. Not only that, they often are members of several Dhikuris at the same time. This range of social, economic and ethnic groups using the institution contrasts with earlier work and is certainly of interest.

The author's final example is a bit different. He describes a system of depositing money and making loans organised and run by people engaged in forest products. Unlike the dhikuri, this form of credit union does not involve a fixed number of "rotations". In principle there is no end to the arrangement. Loans tend to be for short periods, sometimes related to ceremonies and rituals, and to medical needs. Rates of interest for such a scheme run by the Mangaltar Village Development Committee are on the order of 50% per year. Another Village Development Committee in Naya Gaun Deopur is reported as having a large total fund managed by a five-man committee and charging 30% interest annually. It would seem that this type of arrangement could be done by banks, and a lower rate of interest would be changed.

Chhetri leaves somewhat open the question of why these arrangements outside of the banks have the success that they do. He suggests that they may be precursors of banks. "Banks may owe their origin, development, and existence to some kind of traditional economic orgainzation similar to the RCAs (Rotating Credit Associations)." (p. 452) His conclusion is that the scale of operation and the amount of knowledge the members have about each other helps to address the problem of default in a way that banks, which are large and impersonal, are less able to do. He also sees these arrangements as cementing and fostering community and occupational solidarity. Finally, as a practical matter, banks tend to be in cities, and 90% of the people in Nepal live in rural areas. When getting about is difficult, local institutions have a great advantage.

It would be a mistake to see this research as applying only to Nepal. The examples come from there, but part of their significance as anthropological research stems from the way they provide additional instances of practices found in many other places. As said above, these practices are held by the author to be adaptive, which can be interpreted in two senses. The dhikuris, and other RCAs, adapt to the various circumstances faced by different types of members. They also are adaptive in that they perform functions which contribute to the well-being of their members.

In the rest of this section, I would like to briefly summarise five anthropological studies dealing with different aspects of the implications of money for social relations. Two of these are specifically concerned with money and the status of women. The Grameen Bank in Bangladesh is a quasi-governmental organisation that makes loans to poor people. It operates in about half of the villages in the country and has two million female members. Sidney Schuler and Syed Hashemi have undertaken an ingenious study to determine the effect of the Bank on the use of contraception by women in Bangladesh (Schuler and Hashemi, '95).

The culture in that country can be very repressive of women in all aspects of their lives, and keep them very much under the control of men. One consequence of this lack of access to contraception is a very high total fertility rate of an average of seven births per woman in the 1970's falling to five, which is still high, in the 90's. This fall is due in part to the presence of 28,000 workers who visit women in their homes and facilitate the use of contraceptives. The study by Schuler and Hashemi works with a sample of 1,300 women and makes comparisons between those who are members of the Grameen Bank and those who are not, also taking account of whether they have been contacted by a contraception worker. The data clearly show an independent influence on contraception use due to a woman being a part of the money economy.

In male dominated societies, which in varying degrees describes the entire world, it can be very difficult for women to have a degree of independent economic activity. Geraldine Moreno-Black and Lisa Price report on the importance of "gathered food", in contrast to farmed food, for some women in Thailand as a means of coming to the market. (Moreno-Black and Price, '93) Gathered food is wild food, or food from nature. It covers a wide range from small animals and insects to various plants, seeds and berries. The great advantage of this source of marketable commodity is that little or no capital investment is required in order to take part. A farm needs prior investment, and if men control all of the capital, this precludes women from any role other than being inputs of labour. However, a trip to the wild may result in some finds that can be sold in the market. The statistics on 100 Thai women in 1988 show that while there is a lot of variation, in general they earn significantly more from this activity than would be possible as paid labourers.

Frank Fanselow argues that anthropologists tend to see all bazaars as more-or-less the same, and this approach covers up an important distinction. (Fanselow, '90) This is the contrast between trading in relatively homogeneous goods, such as tinned products and manufactured cloth, and once-off items, often produced by cottage industry. The former, so Fanselow suggests from observing the Kalakkadu bazaar in southern India, results in a relatively open money economy. Records are kept and the normal institutions of banks and courts can be invoked. The latter depends critically on trust built up among the participants in the often long chains of exchange involved in bringing these heterogeneous goods to the bazaar. The kind of documentation which banks require in order to make loans is not available. Financing is done through moneylenders and trade credit. It is not documented or observable to outsiders, including tax collectors. For the more standard and familiar products which are traded in the bazaar, this form of hidden money economy is not the case.

I conclude this section with two interesting examples of resistance to the money economy. Marc Olshan reports on the efforts of the Amish in New York State to cope with changed economic circumstances. (Olshan, '91) As with Amish communities in other parts of America, their basic goal is to be as self-sufficient and separate from the rest of America as they can. However, the traditional reliance on farming as a means of generating the minimal cash surplus required is becoming less and less possible. Their culture rules out earning wages by being employed outside the community, except as a very last resort.

A number of Amish communities, including the one under study, have gone for the strategy of operating shops to sell cakes and other food items to the outside world, along with craft items such as toys. This implies social interaction, and dropping some of the aloof manner which is generally associated with being Amish. The author concludes that these shops and the resulting closer links to the money economy will have consequences. He sees these as reducing, "...their ability to perpetuate the values of an agrarian society...", but does not see it as a threat to their separate identity. (p. 378)

Ahmen Al-Shahi has edited material by the anthropologist Peter Lienhardt on the Islamic inheritance system known as *waqf*, particularly as it is practised in Zanzibar. (Lienhardt, '96) From this complex report, rich in detail, I single out just the feature that money cannot be made waqf, only property. As a form of trust, this institution would appear to go against the teaching of the Prophet Muhammad which holds that individuals should not exert an influence after their death. An exception is charitable activity, particularly in support of a mosque. That property can enter into this kind of contractual arrangement, but not money, is similar to the Islamic position against interest, and in favour of equity investment. The prohibition against interest means that one cannot borrow for consumption, such as financing an obligatory family ceremony. This relieves people of the burden of having to put on an excessive show. Property, rather than money, yields its benefits over time, and cannot be squandered the way money can. Lienhardt ends by noting that the income from waqf cannot normally be used for maintaining a grave. He quotes 'the commentators' as saying, "The dead are passing into dissolution and the repairing of their tombs is not appropriate to them, though we should except the repairing of the tombs of prophets, learned men and saints." (p. 106)

POLITICAL SCIENCE

The Maastricht Treaty was agreed in December of 1991. It called for a change in name of the organisation of member states from the European Community to the European Union. This symbolic step accurately reflected larger moves towards integration, both planned and agreed. The most important element in the Treaty was the agreed intention to move to a common currency for Europe. There is reason to believe that the key participants in the meeting were running ahead of many perceived national interests, and ahead of opinion among large sections of the general public in all member countries.

Michael Baun has a theory of why leadership in France and Germany, key players in the European game, were keen to move to monetary union at that time, in spite of the ambitious nature of the program and the risks which advocating it entailed. (Braun, '95-96) The significance of his approach to an understanding of these events rests in part on how his contribution relates to other somewhat rival approaches to understanding Maastricht. In addition to providing a different interpretation of a particular event, it suggests modifications in the structure of political theory.

Baun works with a distinction between 'high politics' and 'low politics'. This distinction has to do with, "...broad considerations of national security and advantage [compared to] technical solutions to domestic economic and social problems." (p.624) Undoubtedly there are borderline cases. Even low politics deals with matters of great importance, both to governments and to large sections of their populations. High politics has to do with decisions that are made infrequently and often are about great alliances, or possibly entering into a major war. Braun classifies Maastricht as an example of high politics involving France and Germany. Other member states were more-or-less willing participants in events they could do little to control. We will come to how this researcher uses evidence to support his position. First we have to outline the structure of his argument, and how it contrasts with other interpretations of events.

One view of Maastricht, which Baun calls the political economy view and identifies with the work of Robert Keohane and Stanley Hoffman, emphasises global competition. That view holds that there is strength in unity. An integrated Europe could be a more effective economic competitor with the United States and the Pacific Rim countries. Large projects such as the development and manufacture of civilian and military aircraft, for example, are beyond the capacity of individual countries, but could be undertaken by Europe as a whole. It could be argued that multinational firms, or groups of them, could and would exploit economic opportunities without the cover of political union. But perhaps union makes projects which cross national borders easier to undertake. Another consideration is the role of governments, in partnership with the private sector, in many economic ventures. A framework for co-operation could make certain ventures feasible, such as putting satellites in space, which could not be undertaken without it.

The neo-functionalist view of political events is another theory which Baun tends to challenge. This view is increasingly popular among researchers and has its supporters as a way of understanding Maastricht. He identifies this approach with the work of David Mutimer and Jeppe Tranholm-Mikkelsen. Neo-functionalists are inclined to see political change as following an inherent logic. They lean towards a view of inevitable developments that respond to historical circumstances. Monetary union is a progression from the removal of trade barriers, which was important in the first stages of the Community. It was on the cards, so to speak, once some momentum had been generated in the direction of a European political entity.

Baun does not completely reject the political economy view and the neo-functionalist view of Maastricht as providing motives for a common currency for Europe. Both views have something to contribute. There is a well-known history of plans for monetary union which resulted in the European Monetary System in December of 1978. Nevertheless, the rival theories have an essentially 'low politics', or business-as-usual flavour to them. Baun's research supports a very different theory. It holds that there was a crisis in the relations between France and Germany. The tensions were sufficiently great so that there was some danger of wiping out most of the progress in European co-operation that had been made up to that time, and worse, a real possibility of increasingly sensitive and hostile relations between Germany and France. This, in Baun's opinion, is the central explanation of what drove the delegates to Maastricht and to the actions they took there. It is a different view from the political economy and the neo-functionalist views. In taking this position Baun is doing a bit more than simply claiming that some observers were mistaken in their views of a particular event. Their mistake has a systematic component to it. They fail to note that there are circumstances in the affairs of nations where 'business-as-usual' does not apply.

Many politicians, and political scientists, see the 'German problem' as central to understanding the movement for European unity. The largest and potentially most powerful European state must not become a threat to the other countries. Of course, Germany itself has an incentive to be seen as a friendly and co-operative force in Europe. So all of Europe, and particularly France, the second largest Continental country, are involved in the need to achieve some kind of parity between member countries. The key to developments leading up to Maastricht, according to Baun, is German unification. Bringing the two Germanys together enhanced their power. This would have been true at any time, but coming on the heels of, and being a part of, the collapse of Communism added two extra complications. A common outside enemy was disappearing and American involvement in Europe was likely to decline. However much it may have been resented in some quarters, this American involvement had been a factor leading to parity among European states.

Essentially there were two strategies that France, and other concerned nations, could adopt. One was to oppose unification. The other was to tie Germany ever more closely to a structure of common interests and common decision-making. The first was tried in a half-hearted way, and not seriously pursued because it was at best a delaying tactic. The weight of history, political logic, and underlying fairness were not consistent with permanently dividing the two German nations. And better to be a friend of unity, than a defeated opponent. This led to a need to accelerate the process of European unification as the only feasible strategy for living with an enlarged Germany on a basis which minimised the threat of domination from that country. This is the essence of Baun's theory of events, and how it departs from other interpretations in the literature.

Baun supports his theory with historical evidence of beliefs and intentions which come from published statements by important political figures. He refers to Chancellor Kohl's repeated assurances that German unification was entirely consistent with European integration. As evidence of threatened opposition to German unification, he discusses President Mitterrand's trip to the Soviet Union in December of 1989 and the statements issued at that time. Mitterrand also upset Bonn by visiting East Germany. Another tactic for worrying Germany culminated in a joint press conference Mitterrand held with the Polish President and the Polish Prime Minister regarding the Germany/Poland border. Baun characterises the German response to these actions by France by referring to a variety of statements which all tended to confirm German intentions to move to more involved forms of political and economic integration. However, monetary union aroused opposition in the German Central Bank, and this was something Kohl had to deal with in order to make the German support for integration appear to be credible. The author takes us through newspaper reports along these lines which provide quite a body of evidence in favour of his theory.

This research offers a clear and plausible theory to contrast with other theories. The author follows this up with certain kinds of evidence in support of it. Perhaps it would be possible to put together other quotations and reports of actions taken that would cast doubt on Baun's view of the political forces that led to Maastricht and the drive for monetary union. He describes the political arena as involving only France and Germany as major contenders. He sees a rush to more integration, risking leaving popular support far behind, as a means of staving off a major political crisis. As a scientific investigation, the ball is now in the other court, or courts, to suggest why this interpretation and the evidence put forward in support of it, are less persuasive than it appears.

Baun points out that some knowledgeable people, not necessarily social scientists, had a different take on these events. Margaret Thatcher felt that more European integration would strengthen Germany's influence in Europe, in contrast to Mitterrand's position, and this contributed to her antagonism to Maastricht. (p. 610) She opposed 'deepening' of the union in the sense of adopting formal agreements on more matters, especially a common currency, and instead pushed for a 'widening' in the sense of more members of the union. This difference of opinion about how to contain Germany is still consistent with Baun's view of Maastricht as being essentially an exercise in maintaining the Franco/German accord after German unification.

Turning now to a quick look at other relevant work on money in political science, we may note in passing that Peter Lange takes a rather different view of Maastricht than that taken by Michael Baun. (Lange, '93) Admittedly he is concentrating exclusively on the Social Protocol. This is an undertaking to assent to decisions by a qualified majority of members, instead of unanimity, on a range of social legislation that would be binding on all members. "Why Did They Do It?" Lange asks. (p. 5) It certainly is worth exploring why countries voluntarily surrender some sovereignty. In principle, the same question could be asked regarding the common currency. Baun answers his question solely with reference to France and Germany. Lange looks at all the member countries and concludes that they were willing to bear a short -run cost in return for what they believed would be a long-run benefit. Baun is silent on the motivation of the other countries, which leaves his theory unconnected to an important part of other theory about European integration.

The remaining four articles on the politics of monetary systems are about managing existing national systems, rather than about making basic changes in a system. Motoshi Suzuki undertook a statistical study of the political pressures leading to more inflation or less inflation. (Suzuki, '93) He uses annual data for fifteen advanced democratic countries over the period 1961 to 1986. Standard regression methods combining the data for all the countries over the period was used to test five popular theories of the causes of inflation. He finds that a left ideology exerts a positive independent influence on inflation, along with an effect from increases in redistributive government spending. The independence of the central bank is a major factor in controlling inflation. Whether or not unions are heavily involved in the political decision-making process seems to have little effect, and the same is true of the timing of elections. The author makes clever use of data generated by other researchers to put together a solid empirical test of five popular theories of the politics of inflation.

William Coleman looks at the way the banking sector organises itself in the United States, United Kingdom, Canada, France and Germany. (Coleman, '94) He proposes a framework for determining whether or not the economic importance of the sector is translated into political power. The method is essentially comparative. It relies heavily on examining the institutional structure in each country, and at the same time makes a stab at quantifying the potential for the exercise of power.

The structure Coleman proposes starts by asking how much competition exists between organisations which represent different kinds of banking activity. He measures this by comparing bodies which compete for members to the total number of bodies. The next consideration is how much resources these associations have which represent banks. This includes considerations like the size of the permanent staff. The third consideration has to do with the links between representing bodies, or what he calls "building horizontal bridges". (p. 38) Finally, he looks for what he calls a peak association, or a body which integrates the other bodies. Canada and the United States lack such structures, but Coleman finds them to be important in Germany and France. Some attempt is made to see whether the differences between countries have discernible effects. In this study this is secondary to marshalling revealing institutional material. However, he does conclude that the United States has a particularly uncoordinated banking sector and this has contributed, so we are told, to the slow pace of banking reform in that country.

Managing an economy is not a mechanical or purely technical matter. Many decisions have to do with the monetary system, including matters of money supply, interest rates and exchange rates. Governments have a range of objectives and a number of instruments at their command which can be employed in a variety of ways in order to achieve, or attempt to achieve, their objectives. Richard Jankowski and Christopher Wlezien have used pooled regression techniques in an effort to determine the importance of the political component in the decisions of governments. (Jankowski and Wlezien, '93) They use quarterly data for nine OECD countries over the years 1967 to 1983. This is a highly technical study, and only a broad-brush picture can be given here. While difficult for the non-specialist to follow, this is an important paper in the political science literature.

The authors direct particular attention to behaviour around election times, and they try to see if governments on the left try different economic strategies compared to those on the right. The regressions they run relate the use of policy instruments to the economic conditions the countries face. There is no attempt to determine how effective countries are in solving their economic problems. That matter is left for other researchers. In effect, they are asking what will a government of a particular political persuasion do if its economy is in a particular condition and an election is pending.

The main finding of Jankowski and Wlezien supports the notion that there is some political component in the actions governments take. This will not come as a surprise to many people, though the authors claim that a significant number of observers tend to deny it. They conclude that, "...left governments tend to use fiscal policy and exchange rates together, alternatively or in some combination, for general stimulatory purposes." (p. 1075) However, it is not easy to see from their statistical analysis that governments on the right act more consistently in the long-run interests of the country. The researchers are aware of difficulties in the data and the methods employed, and urge caution in interpreting these results.

I will conclude this section with a brief discussion of an outstanding paper on decision-making in the Federal Open Market Committee of the United States Federal Reserve System. This body exerts the critical influence on monetary policy in America. There tends to be a high degree of consensus among the members of the FOMC, but there is room for dissent. George Krause has looked at the pattern of dissent over the years 1967 to 1990 in an effort to measure political influence coming from the President of the United States and bureaucratic influence from within the FOMC. (Krause, '94) There are twelve members of the FOMC, seven of whom are appointed by the President for 14-year terms. These are the Board of Governors. The other five members are regional bank presidents, chosen from the twelve bank presidents who are appointed by the twelve regional Federal Reserve Banks. The president of the New York Federal Reserve Bank has a permanent seat on the FOMC. The other four RBPs rotate annually.

Krause uses the published data to test three conjectures. The first is that the greater the number of members appointed during a president's term, the more consensus there will be. The second hypothesis says that the more members appointed by the same party as that of the president, the more consensus. The third says that the greater number of members appointed during the tenure of the current Chairman of the FOMC, the greater the consensus. It is interesting to see that the data reject the first and third hypotheses when we combine dissents by Governors and by regional presidents. But when the two are examined separately, there is some support for the first conjecture, that is, presidential influence. But this is small in magnitude compared to influence from the Chairman. In addition, we see support for the 'same party as the president' explanation of the amount of dissent.

In general, both internal influence coming from the Chairman, and external influence coming from the president, act on the Board of Governor members, and not on the regional bank presidents. There is also a plausible pattern of dissent depending on length of membership. New members are reluctant to dissent. As they become more confident, they tend to exert a more independent influence. And as still more time goes by they tend to get socialised into the system and to dissent less.

SOCIAL PSYCHOLOGY

Emma Boustead and five colleagues have written a two-page study which operates at the nitty-gritty level of the money system. (Boustead and colleagues, '92) These researchers studied the relations between the physical appearance of coins, their actual values, and the perception of their values. Social psychologists tend to write short articles compared to other social scientists, but three authors per page must be close to a record. The tradition of brevity is admirable. The reason for it has to do with the experimental and empirical nature of most of their work, with research reports giving summaries of findings, and leaving it at that. This study harks back to work done in the 1940s and the 1980s.

In the United States, for most of the past century, the five-cent coin was larger than the ten-cent coin. Given a choice between the two, very young children choose the larger coin, presumably being unable to imagine that the authorities would use a physically smaller coin to embody a larger value. Two researchers, Bruner and Goodman, writing in 1947, demonstrated a corollary of this phenomenon and showed that children tended to perceive more valuable coins as being bigger than their actual size.

Writing in 1981, Lea investigated the effects of inflation in the United Kingdom on the subjective value of coins and the effects of these valuations on perceptions of the size of coins. In effect, Lea is drawing on an underlying general tendency to equate larger size with more value. The decimalization of British coins provided a natural experimental opportunity in that coins had different names before and after decimalization. Lea found that when coins were referred to by their old names they were estimated to be physically larger than when identified by their postdecimalization names. This was attributed to inflation having reduced the value of money. An alternative explanation, not explored, might be that small amounts of money, which coins represent, mean more to people earlier in their lives when they typically deal in only tiny amounts compared to later in life when notes represent the major units of concern.

It is always useful, where possible, to compare what people say with what they actually do. Furnham reported experiments in 1985 where innocent subjects either picked up, or left in the street, coins that the experimenter had placed there. His found that there was a linear relation between the probability of a coin being picked up and its actual value. This is a reasonable finding, and one which is in line with a straightforward concept of rational behaviour. If there is some cost associated with stopping to gather up a small amount of money, the larger this small amount is, the more likely it is that it exceeds the cost of picking it up. But here is where Bousted and her colleagues enter the picture. Regardless of the true value, rational action will depend on perceived value. The decision to stop and pick up a coin is likely to be taken at high speed, and perceptions of what is down there need not reflect the actual value of the coins lost in the streets.

The Boustead team was given some help from 'nature' in that there were two five-pence coins in circulation in the United Kingdom in roughly equal numbers in 1990. Both were silver coloured. The old five-pence is 23.5 mm in diameter and the new coin is 18 mm in diameter, and less than half the weight. The experiment also involved the copper coloured two-pence coin which is 26 mm in diameter, and the silver coloured ten-pence coin which is 28.5 mm in diameter. The researchers placed ten of each coin, one at a time, at a busy point on the sidewalk and watched what happened. This was repeated in a quieter part of town. We are not told which town this is. Presumably the authors feel that this would not significantly effect the results, but that is something which could be tested.

The tricky part of the experiment is to determine whether the passers-by saw the coins or not. It is a different matter if the coin was left because it was not seen, as against seen and left. Two observers viewed each incident. If they were uncertain whether or not the coin had been seen, they removed that person from the results. In effect, the experimenters are making the assumption that whether the coin is 'seen' or not is independent of both its physical nature and its value.

The results for the busy neighbourhood and the quiet neighbourhood were not significantly different, so the researchers report the combined figures. The statistic of interest is the ratio of coins picked up to the number seen. The proportion picked up was .20 for the two-pence piece; .33 for the old and larger five-pence coin; .19 for the new five-pence; and .58 for the ten-pence coin. Compared to the results found by Furnham five years earlier, fewer coins were picked up in this new study. He found that .61 of two pence coins and .73 of five pence coins were gathered in. The authors attribute to inflation the greater tendency today to leave coins that have been seen. Of course, higher incomes is another possibility. As they point out, exact comparisons are not possible due to weather differences and other local factors, but the size of the difference is striking.

The newer study generally tended to confirm the earlier results that more valuable coins are more likely to be picked up. The one exception was the new five-pence coin which though smaller, was exactly as valuable as the old five-pence, and less likely to be picked up. The difference was statistically significant, with less than one in a thousand probability that it was due to chance. Boustead and her colleagues concluded that even for adults, there is a residual tendency to let size, "...effect the perceived value of a coin." (p.143) They do not discuss an alternative view that the old coin may be more familiar to pedestrians. The new coin might be seen as a washer, or some other glinting item. Perhaps the main risk in picking up generally is that it might turn out that one could be seen to have made a silly mistake.

Turning now to four other social psychological studies of money, Richard Lynn also referred back to Furnham in his explorations of sex differences in attitudes towards money. (Lynn, '93) Furnham's work only applied to Britain. Lynn wanted to look more broadly, and was able to persuade universities in twenty countries ranging from Abu Dhabi, Hong Kong and Iceland, to New Zealand, the United States and Yugoslavia to take part. Of course it is not perfect, but he was able to get together a pretty broad range of cultures. In each country roughly 150 male and 150 female university students were asked to fill in off-the-shelf questionnaires on competitiveness, valuation of money and attitudes to savings.

The bottom line is that men score overwhelmingly higher on all three than women. The two main exceptions, Transkei and Hong Kong, are put down to having small proportions of women in universities, and so the ones who are there are highly self-selected. Lynn also found statistically significant correlations between the three possible pairs: competitiveness and valuation of money, the most significant; competitiveness and saving, the least; and valuation of money and attitudes towards saving in the middle with thirty-four out a possible forty correlations, twenty for men and twenty for women, being significant. The author sees the results as possibly due to the underlying factor of competitiveness. He does not discuss the possibility that men tend to be cast more in the role of the breadwinners, and therefore may attach greater importance than women to what is more their responsibility.

Pocket money for children probably has a number of functions, including educating them into the money economy. N.T. Feather has done a study of 133 two-parent/two-children families in Adelaide. It is aimed at exploring a wide range of considerations that motivate the practice of giving pocket money to children. (Feather, '91) His method involved an elaborate questionnaire survey of both fathers and mothers. Each parent rated thirteen reasons independently. These included conforming to general practices in the community, teaching children responsibility in using money, strengthening the family unit, and as a more efficient way of meeting some of the needs of children. Separate off-the-shelf questionnaires devised by Rasinski (1987) and Gorsuch (1983) were used to determine the values that the parents adhered to. The motives for providing pocket money were found to be related to these values.

Among the many interesting findings it emerged that more money was provided by parents who placed more emphasis on 'communal' values and social welfare. This is in comparison to families that placed relatively more emphasis on matters related to the work ethic. Interestingly, older daughters were given particularly small amounts of money by parents who emphasised the motivation of independence in giving pocket money. Mothers tended to emphasise the needs of children more than did fathers. It would appear that the income level of the parents was not brought into the study. This might well correlate with the values held by parents, and in that way the author might be attributing to 'values' causal influences that are in fact due to income levels. This is just a possibility.

Michael Santos and his colleagues did an interesting study of how a strange request for money might break into a normal, habitual or automatic response and have more success in turning a 'no' into a 'yes'. (Santos, '94) This social psychological study is only tangentially related to money, but as that is the medium employed, it can legitimately be included here. In essence, people posing as beggars asked passers-by for a low, but unusual amount of money, seventeen cents; other people asked for a high and unusual amount, thirty-seven cents. As a control, passers-by were asked for a low, but typical amount, twenty-five cents, or a 'quarter', and a typical high amount in the phrase "can you spare any change". Care was taken to avoid bias in the people approached for money, and to disguise the beggars. The experiment took place in California, and, incidentally, the money collected was given to the Santa Cruz AIDS project. The odd low request worked 42.2 percent of the time, compared to 30.6 percent for the low typical request.

The authors do not seem to worry about the low 'typical' request being for more money than the unusual request. The high strange request was exactly as successful as the low typical request, namely, 30.6 percent of the time. The high typical request, which is rather different in being open ended, worked 15.3 percent of the time. In spite of these possible weaknesses, the authors do have a point when they argue that an approach which "disrupts a mindless 'refusal' script" is likely to be more successful. (p. 762)

We can conclude this section by taking note of a study by J. Wober and his colleagues on the impact of television in Britain on the European elections of 1989. (Wober and colleagues, '96) This investigation is only slightly concerned with money as an institution. The researchers were able to hook a ride on the Broadcasters' Audience Research Board survey of 4,000 television viewers. Fitting in with a project basically intended for other purposes limited the usefulness of the information, but gave a wide coverage. One of the questions asked was, "There should be a single European money system replacing pounds, francs, marks and the rest." Thirty-five percent of the respondents agreed with this statement. Forty-four percent disagreed, and twenty-one percent were unsure. The initial intention of the research was to find a direct effect of television on the likelihood of voting in the elections of representatives for Europe. None was found, and this applied equally to those viewers who emphasised news and current affairs programmes in their viewing. Perhaps one could infer that television also had little impact on opinions about the common currency. The study also suggests that the press had more of an influence on political opinions generally.

SOCIOLOGY

In what we tend to think of as primitive societies, it is not uncommon for different kinds of money to exist side by side. One kind of money may only be used for a particular purpose, and no amount of an alternative kind of money will be acceptable in its place. Sometimes the distinction turns on who can use each type of money. For example, there may be separate money for men and for women. When it comes to modern money, the dominant image is of a neutral, or purely instrumental view of money. Viviana Zelizer takes an alternative position and explores the symbolic and meaning laden aspects of money in its modern form. (Zelizer, '89) An example is what happens to money when it enters a household. "Domestic money thus shows the limits of a purely instrumental, rationalized model of market money, which conceals qualitative distinctions among kinds of money in the modern world." (p. 369)

The author sees her work as relating to other work which views money in a purely 'utilitarian' manner. Max Weber is sited as one of many writers who placed emphasis on money as a leveller. Nothing is special. Everything can be brought under the same measuring rod. Karl Marx was one of the theorists who characterised money as an important factor in alienation. Money helps to make relations between people purely objective and functional. It takes out the personal. Zelizer identifies five features of what she calls the classic interpretation of money. The first is to see money in purely economic terms as the tool for market exchange. Second, there are no differences between kinds of money. The third feature is a sharp distinction between pecuniary and non-pecuniary values, with money being 'neutral'. While neutral, money draws more and more aspects of life into "the web of the market". Finally, the classic view rejects the idea that values can impinge on money itself.

There is some room for interpretation as to how Zelizer's work relates to the 'classic' view of money. Is she correcting or modifying currently accepted elements in the structure of knowledge, or is she filling in neglected gaps in that structure? The writers she sites come from mainly from a century or more ago, and were concerned with social criticism of capitalism in particular. Money is a handy peg on which to hang arguments that go well beyond the institution of money. Socialist organisations and peasant society also depend on money. One could summarise her position as saying that there is more to money than purely economic considerations.

I believe she is right in that contention, and that sociologists have tended to stay away from money as a topic because of a narrowly economic view of it. For example, at the time of writing there is not a single article in an English language sociological journal on a common currency for Europe. Yet attitudes and alliances with respect to the Euro in Britain appear to have more sociological content than economic content.

A case can be made that Zelizer is correcting existing theories of money. I am more inclined to the interpretation that she is adding to other theories of money which simply do not concern themselves with the considerations she emphasises. In contrast to the 'classic' position, she adds five propositions of her own. The first is that money has a role outside the market and is subject to social influences. This leads to distinct kinds of money. Her third proposition re-states the argument by seeing the 'classic' view as unnecessarily narrow, rather than wrong. The fourth point is to blur the distinction between "utilitarian money and non-pecuniary values". Finally, she asserts the importance of "extraeconomic factors" in how money is used and how it functions.

So far we have talked about the possible connections of this work to existing work without saying what it is about. The heart of Zelizer's work is an analysis of married women's money in America over the period 1870 to 1930. This is done through brilliant use of an incredible variety of sources.

These range from the public and official — U.S. Department of Labor reports — to the private and personal — household budget studies. In between come the home economics literature and popular household manuals. The author draws on etiquette manuals and women's magazines, including letters to the editor and advice columns. Other sources include news articles and editorials in the *New York Times,* as well as legal casebooks and court cases. This is qualitative research at its best. Elements that would at most be suggestive on their own, go much further when combined to producing a convincing picture.

"The battle over the purse strings was regulated by notions of family life and by the gender and social class of its participants." (p. 353) The basic feature of domestic money was that while the wife had a right to support, this was a completely vague right which did not entitle her to anything other than what her husband chose to give to her. (p.356) Zelizer reports many moving tales of extreme brutality. Emma Mongomery managed to save a little over six hundred dollars out of household money over 25 years of marriage. When the marriage broke up, this money was deemed to belong to her husband who had taken no part in efficient management of the household.

Wives were commonly forced to desperate measures such as padding bills, shoplifting, and pinching money from their husbands. One husband caught his wife in the act by putting rat-traps in his pockets at night. In this case the courts upheld his right to do so. Later decisions in other courts upheld the right of wives to go through their husbands' pockets looking for change "if he fails to provide for her properly". (p. 360)

In 1909 *Good Housekeeping* magazine discussed what was believed to be a typical case of a husband earning $300 a month who gave his wife $50 to run the household. But while the correct amount was hotly disputed, the principle of a regular allowance for wives had much support. Such social arbiters as Emily Post favoured an allowance, which is a regular specified amount, over an arbitrary transfer of dole money. However, the discretion of wives over what they could do with an allowance was greatly circumscribed.

By the end of the 1920s there is evidence of a significant minority of couples adopting joint bank accounts rather than allowances. The latter was increasingly seen as making the wife financially subservient. The picture is rather different in working class families, where the wife often was handed the wage packet and allocated money to her husband. It is easy to see in this more discretion for working class wives than actually existed. The intense financial pressure meant that everything was going for basic needs. Interestingly, a study of working class families in Chicago in 1924 revealed that most wives under estimated their husband's earnings. Where women were able to earn something themselves, the author reports on strict conventions as to how this money was regarded and how it might be used.

So what is the upshot of all this? "In the case of married women, their money was routinely set apart from real money by a complex mixture of ideas about family life, by a changing gender power structure, and by social class." (pp. 367 - 368) A convincing case is made that domestic money is not well understood as being purely instrumental. It is a special kind of money. As such it is one among other examples of social influences on how money is allocated and used, somewhat separate from the neutral use of money in a broader market.

We can now report briefly on three sociological studies of money which appeared in the '90s. This brave little band is about all that can be found. There are broad 'think pieces' and possible research agendas discussed in sociology handbooks and textbooks. But actual reported research is thin on the ground. However, what is there is anything but thin. In contrast to the micro method of Zelizer, Bruce Carruthers and Sarah Babb provide a macro analysis of the controversy between those who favoured a pure fiat money, not convertible into gold, the "Greenbacks", and those who wanted a return to the gold standard, the "Bullionists", after the American Civil War. (Carruthers and Babb, '96) The war created financial chaos. It left the government heavily in debt. At the time there was no government monopoly on the issue of money. This was done by many independent banks in the various States. The case for a single national currency and a central bank was strong. But the nature of this new currency, far from being taken for granted, was a subject of national debate.

There are a number of themes to this debate. One has to do with a Bullionist argument favouring a 'natural' as opposed to an 'artificial' form of money. Another has to do with the alleged non-neutrality of the monetary system. A system based on gold would favour the established, East Coast, wealthier holders of gold over the rural and Western interests, or so the Greenbacks argued. Another area of debate, exactly like current thinking, is that in the long-run easy credit is inflationary and any gains to increasing the money supply are illusory, short-run, and eventually have to be paid for. Much attention was also paid to the national debt, and how the kind of the monetary system adopted would distribute the burden of the debt to different parts of American society.

Carruthers and Babb believe that these debates between the advocates of hard and soft money had some tendency to follow lines of economic self-interest. This rational approach has to be tempered in three ways: (1) when the actual self-interest of various sectors of society is a bit unclear, and alliance with one view or another may have important non-economic repercussions; (2) what the authors call the "rhetoric" of persuasion can be important in itself; and (3) the debate may be about matters that have relatively little to do with the substantive content. The authors claim that at bottom what was at stake was a contrast between viewing the economy as something objective, natural, and in that sense inevitable, and alternatively seeing the economy as man-made, arbitrary, and capable of a variety of valid forms.

When any social system is working well, particularly the monetary system, it has a kind of transparency which removes popular interest in it. In times of upheaval, what normally is taken for granted suddenly becomes controversial. As the authors put it, "Political rhetoric plays an important role in both exposing and repressing...the social construction of important economic institutions. That economic value is a social construct may be a sociological truism, but on this occasion such a claim was taken up by common people in a political challenge to the status quo." (p. 1582) Here we have a revealing example of a popular debate that engaged wide sectors of society. For a time, the Bullionists won the argument. But eventually convertibility was restricted to international dealings between central banks, and finally it was dropped altogether, giving complete victory to the Greenbacks.

Heiko Schrader has undertaken a comparison of the development of monetary institutions in India and Indonesia. (Schrader, '94) Like some anthropological investigators, this sociologist looks at the role of moneylenders as precursors of, and facilitators of, modern banking. They also are seen as coexisting with banks by playing a role in economic development by providing capital where banks find it difficult to operate. The author draws a distinction between indigenous banks and the adoption of Western banking practices. There is some ambiguity in the assertions as to whether there is a kind of ahistorical logic in what can be observed, or whether local conditions exert important influences. Schrader believes that with minor exceptions, the kind of indigenous money lending banks that existed in India did not occur in Netherlands Indies. The author offers two explanations for this contrast. First, India was more of an integrated economy and more heavily involved in international trade. Second, the British colonial rule was more liberal and encouraging to enterprise, while the Dutch rule gave less scope for private capital. And in any case, so it is claimed, estate production of spices, for example, was not capital intensive. While there is interesting detail in the references given, the broad argument is not easy to follow.

Finally, we have a paper by Nigel Dodd on the sovereignty of nation states over the control of monetary systems. (Dodd, '95) He examines the alleged challenges to sovereignty that come from financial deregulation and from offshore markets. The study goes forward through detailed examination of monetary developments in the United Kingdom, Japan and Germany. Dodd concludes that the view that these developments are best seen as threats to the authority of nation states is not supported by the facts. His argument rests mainly on evidence which he interprets as showing state support for both deregulation and offshore financial activity.

A sceptic might suggest that these were unwelcome events which were somehow forced on states, who did give support, but only grudgingly, when forced to do so. This alternative view would hold that on the whole nation states did what they could to minimise developments that were inherently unwelcome. The author makes it hard for the sceptic to take this view as he skilfully relates recent events in the countries under investigation. The paper has a wider agenda in forcefully illustrating the extent to which all economic activity, including the monetary system, is embedded in a social context. A free, unregulated and atomistic market simply does not exist. The money market, like all others, cannot take place outside of what we could call a sociological environment.

ECONOMICS

It is only to be expected that economists would devote more effort to the topic of money than other social scientists. There must be over two hundred articles in economics journals on this subject for every one in each of the other social science journals. The discussion above aimed to be fairly comprehensive in its treatment of money in the '90s by the other four social sciences. The reader will be relieved to learn that this section is highly selective. Only a tiny sample of studies will be discussed. Like the other sections in this chapter, the economics section begins with a fuller treatment of a study which illustrates connections in the structure of scientific knowledge. It is followed by brief reports on some investigations chosen on rather personal grounds, yet in the hope that they convey fairly the kinds of things economists do, as well as tying in with some discussions above.

The most obvious and prominent feature of money is its role in facilitating exchange. Each of us produces at most one or two things, and consumes thousands of things. And most of the things we consume are themselves produced through a huge number of exchanges involving labour, energy, materials, equipment and ideas. This bewildering variety of transactions is essential to an advanced economy and is made possible by things exchanging for money, not for other things. Amazingly, until recently no one has managed to provide a fully specified model of this basic function of money, its role as a medium of exchange. A little description is pretty easy to provide. I have just given one. The literature abounds with more comprehensive descriptions. Isn't that enough? What more do we need?

No, it is not enough, if we are to build scientific knowledge. What we need is an explicit statement of money as a medium of exchange which does not rest on intuition or informal conjecture. We need that in order to link up to other structures of understanding of how things work. The promise which integrated explicit understanding holds is eventual deeper understanding and along with that, some likelihood that we can improve the design and management of the money system. So when economists ask why do we have money, the question is not as absurd, or as easy to answer, as might at first appear. Of course, money has many aspects and roles, or functions. Medium of exchange is one of these, and in good scientific fashion, a one-at-a-time approach might succeed in modelling this feature.

It usually is the case that the first model is only a first step. Improving it is a natural and on-going part of the scientific endeavour. Without the first model, of course, we cannot have improvements. I think it is fair to say that economists were not very troubled by not having a model of the medium of exchange aspect of money. People say you do not miss water until the well runs dry. But it is also the case that the loss from not having a way to cross a river may not be appreciated until a bridge is built. When a model of monetary exchange did appear, it was exciting. Part of this was probably due to the missing bridge effect, and part of this was due to the sheer weirdness of the model, or so it seemed. But the more the model was looked at and understood, the more natural, not to say inevitable, it appeared. There is some formidable mathematics in the original. I hope to convey the guts of the model without being stopped by the techniques which the authors, with very good reason, chose to employ.

The first issue to address in thinking about this core paper by Nobuhiro Kiyotaki and Randal Wright is the familiar question of unrealism. (Kiyotaki and Wright, '89) Some of the initial strangeness of their analysis comes from the blatant use of assumptions that clearly do not hold in any actual application. There is much that could be said on this issue, and anything approaching a full discussion would take us too far afield. Suffice it now to note: more realism might result in more complexity with no change in the underlying message; the severely stripped down nature of the analysis highlights the crucial mechanism; and there is an element of subjective preference in whether the tale, however far from natural realism, is found to be enlightening.

It is easy to get wrapped up in the mechanics of the argument and lose the point of it. The authors set out to develop a model in which a medium of exchange is not imposed, but emerges endogenously through the behaviour of agents who are not co-operating to bring this about, but are simply acting in their own interests. "...a critical factor in determining if an object can serve as a medium of exchange is whether or not agents believe it will...the use of money necessarily involves strategic elements and certain aspects of social custom." (p. 928)

Immediately we can see that this analysis is tightly linked to a large body of work in the analytical structure of economic investigation. The authors employ what is called a 'matching model' in which people randomly come together in pairs and have the option of trading or not trading. This is a widely used device in economic theory, which we have seen above in the study of family formation, for example. The agents in the current analysis behave in ways that are normally employed in economic theory. The authors make assumptions about the behaviour of their agents which involve taking it for granted that, like themselves, the other participants in the economy have goals and work to achieve them. This is no 'stand alone' piece of work, but one which is clearly integrated with existing theory. It adds to, and takes up a place in, the structure of economic knowledge.

However, like much of economics, the links, or connections, to the broader body of economic theory are based on convention rather than on empirically grounded findings. This is an important consideration. Random, pairwise matching is a common assumption in economic analysis. So is the kind of rationality attributed to the agents in this model. This method of approach has the effect of linking up economic enquiry into a tight structure much like that which is more common in natural science. So far so good. The trouble is that we are dealing with a self-contained world. The relevance of this world to particular applications is never easy to establish. Nevertheless, the insight provided by Kiyotaki and Wright is impressive, and with this little aside, we can turn to their model of the exchange function of money.

We will see as we follow the analysis that the agents in this model sometimes accept in trade a commodity which they will neither consume nor use in production. They accept it because it can reasonably be expected to improve their well-being through future trades. That is a commodity money. The authors also explore some implications of fiat money, which is money with no inherent value.

The authors specify exactly how all the relevant features of their 'world' operate. For example, time is 'discrete', meaning that there is an endless succession of moments when agents come together, as in the ticking of a clock. The agents live forever and there is an infinite number of them. Part of the mathematical sophistication of the investigation comes from the need to treat issues of infinity and probability in a consistent manner.

Kiyotaki and Wright assume there are equal proportions of three kinds of agents. They each produce one kind of good but consume a different kind among the three goods in this economy. This is crucial. No one is able to produce the good which they consume. Each good can be stored, and only one unit of one good can be stored at a time. Goods are stored at a cost, with one good being the most costly to hold, one in the middle, and one the least costly.

Now we assume that agents randomly meet up in pairs. If an agent is fortunate enough to acquire through trade the good he likes to consume, he consumes it instantaneously in that discrete moment of time and simultaneously produces another unit of the good he is capable of making. So, at every point in time, every agent is holding one unit of either the good they produce, or a good they have traded for the one they produce. The good they are holding cannot be the one they consume, because, as stated, they instantaneously consume that good. It is interesting to note that as we only have one-for-one exchanges, the price of every good is in effect fixed at 'one'. Here is a model of money in which inflation is not possible. In spite of that weakness, which has been addressed in later models, the tale is fascinating. We now have to consider what will be the strategy of our hypothetical agents when they are faced with opportunities for trade.

As there are an infinite number of people out there, one third of the time, on average, each agent meets one like himself. These two can never make a mutually beneficial trade, so we can ignore that meeting. They just wait for the next discrete moment of time, and hope to meet someone different from themselves. There is discounting in the model, meaning that current gains are more important to individuals than gains in the future. The authors have to derive what happens when a type '1' person, 'type' referring to the good they get utility from consuming, meets a type '2' person, 2 meets 3, and 3 meets 1. The central point of the exercise is that it can be shown that in certain circumstances optimising individuals will trade, even taking on a higher storage cost item, because it improves their chances of acquiring the good they like to consume. Such a trade means that the commodity is acting as commodity money.

Depending on the relative size of the storage costs, discounting and the utility of consumption, there may be what the authors call a 'fundamental equilibrium' in which the traders always prefer to hold lower storage cost items if they cannot make a trade leading directly to consumption. A 'speculative equilibrium' occurs when the relevant values are such that it pays some agents to take on a higher storage cost item because it increases the likelihood of consumption in the future. Part of the complexity of the model comes from the fact that all agents are making these calculations looking at other agents and assuming they are informed of the probabilities and costs, and adopt trading strategies which are optimal for them.

With a fundamental equilibrium, type 2 agents act as middlemen, and use good 1 as a medium of exchange. When type 2 meets type 3 he will acquire good 1 and give up 3. This gives 2 the possibility of trading good 1 for good 2 when he meets a type 1 agent holding good 2. The story gets a bit more complicated with a speculative equilibrium. Now we have the additional feature that agent 1 — remember agents are named after the good they consume — will acquire good 3 in trade when given the chance. This raises his storage costs, but increases his chances enough of a future trade that will give him good 1 to consume so as to more than compensate for the higher storage costs. Now both goods 1 and 3 are acting as commodity moneys. Only the commodity which can be stored at a price between that of the other two goods, good 2, does not act as money.

I will re-state all this in more intuitive terms shortly. Meanwhile, it should be mentioned that the story changes slightly if instead of type 1 agents producing good 2, as above, they produce good 3, and so on. This is not just a rotation of labels. The configuration is not the same as in the first example, because the relation to storage costs is changed. In this case the fundamental equilibrium — where no agent acquires a good through trade which he will not immediately consume, unless it has a lower storage cost than the one he is holding — both goods 1 and 2 become mediums of exchange. In the speculative equilibrium, goods 2 and 3 become commodity money.

Let us back away from this complexity and see what is going on. We have three kinds of agents who meet randomly and have the opportunity to trade. All agents only consume one type of good, and only produce a different type of good. The goods have different storage costs. All agents try to maximise their net benefits from consumption, taking account of the storage costs. They know that there are an infinite number of agents out there, one third of each type. And they know that all agents have this information and are acting in their own best interest. These assumptions lead to mutually beneficial trades in some cases where one party acquires a good which he will not consume. In other words, agents are treating a commodity as if it were money. They acquire it not for its own sake, but to facilitate future trades. So here we have the exchange function of money emerging from the model. The authors have achieved their goal in a way that ties in completely with the existing structure of economic theory. Agents have preferences, and they think ahead making realistic assumptions about the behaviour of other agents. They choose strategies that will maximise their utility.

As a final step, Kiyotaki and Wright introduce the possibility of acquiring fiat money instead of holding a commodity. The authors show that this generates more utility than being confined to commodity money. Now there are fewer goods being held, but more trades leading directly to consumption taking place. More of each good is produced and more of each good is consumed. What there is less of is the storing of goods, with the attendant costs, in the hopes of future trades leading to consumption. A highly stylised and unrealistic model leads to the use of commodity money, and fiat money if it is present in the economy, by agents who are simply programmed to act rationally. They produce one thing and consume something else. They can store a commodity which they cannot consume, and storage comes at a cost.

These are likely to be the elements of any 'money as a medium of exchange' story. They need not be put together exactly as has been done here. But here they have been put together in a completely explicit way, and all the possibilities worked out. Later models addressed issues like the behaviour of traders evolving in such a way as leading to the choice of a particular national currency to act as an international currency. The choice of an international money emerges endogenously and is not imposed. Other models addressing other issues have been developed along these lines. What at first appeared to be a strange way of modelling the exchange feature of money, now appears to be the only way, provided the term 'way' is conceived broadly enough.

The Kiyotaki-Wright exercise in pure theory is likely to be of more interest to professional economists than to others. The two economics papers which conclude this chapter are also of interest to economists, but at the same time are of wider concern, as well as being topical. Willem Buiter and his colleagues argued that the fiscal requirements for joining the common currency in Europe were too harsh and likely to lead to recession. (Buiter and colleagues, '93) The criteria, which were set out at Maastricht, had four elements. Inflation in any country hoping to join should only be a little above the average rate in the three countries with the lowest rate of inflation. The authors see little harm in this principle. The second requirement of a substantial period of exchange rate stability gets little support from them, but again, is not viewed as being dangerous. The third test is for convergence of nominal interest rates to something close to the average of the three low inflation countries. The fourth criterion is that public deficits should be less than three percent of gross domestic product, and public debt less than sixty percent of gross domestic product.

There is a logic in this last requirement which calls for elucidation. Deficits are annual additions to national debt, and so the two are linked. It is a simple mathematical relation that year to year changes in the ratio of debt to GDP must be equal to the current ratio of deficit to GDP, minus the percentage change in the growth of GDP. When the debt to GDP ratio is constant, it will be equal to the deficit to GDP ratio times the growth rate in GDP. (pp. 62 - 63) With growth of around three percent, the two criteria laid down at Maastricht of three percent for the deficit ratio and sixty percent for the debt ratio are both mutually consistent and plausible.

The only worry the authors harbour is that inflation must be taken account of properly. These calculations rest on a notion of zero inflation. In spite of this, the researchers show that a single straight jacket for heterogeneous countries is dangerous. Either the criteria must be ignored, or interpreted very loosely, or harmful deflationary steps must be taken by Ireland, Greece, and Belgium, among others. The authors argue that there is nothing inherently wrong in the public lending to the government, but that having fiscal rules which apply across very different types of countries cannot be justified by reference to economic theory.

A similar theme was taken up by Charles Goodhart. (Goodhart, '96) He begins by pointing out that a single currency is a much more rigid arrangement between countries than was the gold standard. At least under the gold standard countries could adjust the relationship between their currencies and gold, and from time to time they did so. Even so, adherence to the gold standard led to tensions, and it would be reasonable to expect greater tensions under a single currency. If national currencies fall out of alignment, there is not a great deal national governments can do to avert economic hardship. Hence the likelihood of political tension.

Some see the single currency as vital to an integrated market. Goodhart argues that it "supports" the market, but is hardly necessary for a smoothly operating single market across European countries. He also suggests that periods of economic downturn will frequently be blamed on the common currency. If there was a system of "well-designed federal fiscal stabilisation" (p. 1083) it would help in keeping up enthusiasm for a common currency. In other words, Goodhart sees a case for the member countries agreeing to bail each other out in times of adversity. The argument may be correct, but it is asking a lot. The operation of a common currency will undoubtedly continue to receive a lot of attention from economists. Writers like José Viñals (Viñals, '96) and Paul De Grauwe (Grauwe, '96) have addressed matters like the convergence criteria, and whether a small number of member countries make economic sense. When it comes to monetary union, the voice of the economist can be heard as one among many.

Chapter Nine

HOUSING

WHY HOUSING?

Housing clearly has a physical component, and this distinguishes it from the other topics we have considered. In topics like migration, crime and the family there is virtually no tangible element, apart from the people involved. Housing is different. Here we are dealing with physical things. There is no great mystery as to why social science is concerned with housing. Economic considerations provide part of the reason for this interest. At a minimum, housing has to be produced and forms part of the economy. But that is by no means the only motive for studying social interactions with housing, or for that matter, with any type of material object. Everything we need or desire, from clothing to transportation and jewellery, has a social dimension and comes under the purview of the social sciences, including economics, but not confined to economics. While all products have important aspects which extend beyond economics, this is particularly true of housing.

Of course there is an element of shelter which is basic to housing. Under normal conditions, the attendant physical requirements that go along with shelter are readily met for most people in high-income countries. In addition to shelter, housing involves status, identity, security, and family structure. The places where people live tend to be important locations for work and leisure activity, all mixed in with eating, sleeping, cleanliness and storage. In general, along with food, more effort and more expenditure goes into to housing than into any other human need. For most people, housing has long-term financial implications, and social and practical implications related to where one lives. The housing decision is on a par with, and often related to, decisions about education, employment, and marriage.

Most housing has a long life, often stretching beyond the lifetime of particular occupants. The stock of housing as a whole cannot be modified quickly. Only small additions and changes can be made, relative to the whole. Sometimes big changes occur within a particular shell. A grand family home, replete with live-in servants, can become a series of small flats providing accommodation to separate individuals and families. The physical nature of the stock of housing, including its quantity, location and design can exert an influence on the people living there. Many observers claim that relatively low cost high-rise housing has profound effects on the behaviour and social interactions of the people who live in that kind of accommodation. At the same time, the kind of society and social relations which occur in a particular area will effect the design, location and amount of housing which is built. We have a co-evolutionary process, with housing influencing society, and the society influencing the way housing is used, constructed and modified.

As might be expected, the different social sciences direct attention to different aspects of housing. Social psychologists tend to emphasise the way people perceive the places they live in, and how these perceptions relate to feelings of well-being, or the lack of it. Crowding is an issue, as is the status people attach to houses. Housing conditions may be perceived very differently by the people living in them compared to the impressions of outside observers. Shantytowns in third world countries are an important example. Run-down areas of cities in high-income countries is another example.

Housing is very much in the political arena. It is taxed and subsidised. It is regulated at the physical level on matters of safety. Zoning has a major impact on where accommodation is located and the nature of neighbourhoods. Along with food, housing is a major medium for redistribution in kind from the better off to the less well off. Governmental responsibility for protection of the more vulnerable members of society — children, the poor, immigrants, victims of family disorder — relates closely to issues of housing. The contrast between the concept of 'taste' in homes, with its connotations of social structure and hierarchy, and the concept of 'style', which is more neutral, has been one among many sociological takes on the topic.

Our subject matter here is the physical structures which house individuals and families, and their social consequences and interactions. In fact many people are housed in some form of institutional setting — army barracks, schools, prisons, refugee camps, and so on. I do not consider these forms of accommodation. Nor do I discuss homelessness. Both are important topics, but are left out of this discussion of housing purely to keep the subject manageable. Leaving these considerations to one side still leaves us with a very big topic, and one, which is important to the lives of most people.

APPLICATIONS TO POLICY

In this chapter an attempt is made to highlight the policy implications of the studies reported. This is a tricky matter for a number of reasons. There often are great surprises in the way in which knowledge, which seems to have no conceivable application when it is first produced, can turn out to be very relevant at a later date. But there is a far more important point, and one which, however obvious, seems to be almost universally ignored. I will state it briefly now, and return to the theme in chapter eleven.

The body of scientific knowledge, including social science knowledge, is available for solving problems and improving matters, for those who might make use of the existing knowledge. As innocent and obvious as that sounds, public figures seem to be very confused on this point. On the one hand, there is the vast body of *existing knowledge*. On the other hand, there is *research*, which has the goal of adding to knowledge. Research is not intended to add directly to human well-being. It does that indirectly by changing disciplines. It is the cumulated knowledge from all the research of the past which is intended to help solve problems. Research affects knowledge, and knowledge is what we apply to particular issues and problems.

Admittedly, and undoubtedly, the distinction between research and applications, or what is sometimes called consultancy, is, like so many others, a blurred distinction. It is not at all unusual for what starts out as an application of knowledge to become, in part at least, discovery of new knowledge. And some research endeavours may fail in their attempts to add to knowledge, but turn out to involve useful applications, or do that in addition to adding to knowledge. Having said this, a distinction remains between using existing knowledge, and adding to existing knowledge. The distinction is perfectly clear when we move away from the blurred border between the two.

Adding to knowledge is called research. It is what scientists do, when they are doing science. Almost all of the work discussed in this book is research, yet we always have an eye on possible applications. Often what determines what research is undertaken is a perception that better applications could be achieved. Such research is primarily problem driven. The other motive for research is, of course, the mysteries which challenge our understanding, and seem to dare the researcher to find an explanation.

Like natural science, social science knowledge is both useful in solving worldly problems, and intriguing and fascinating in itself. Without any attempt to judge or rank the work in any way, I am going to divide the studies on housing into three categories according to their implications for policy. The first group will consist of papers which in my view are addressing matters which are remote from policy concerns. With this group of studies it is hard to see how governments, or other agencies, could use the material in tackling the problems they face. The second category consists of those studies where I see potential for policy application. And the third group is where the policy application is direct. For this last group, it is quite clear from the studies themselves how the knowledge they contain can be used in encouraging, shaping, or restraining action.

Putting studies in a policy category involves a large amount of judgement and discretion. A study may appear to have some policy potential for the very specific housing issue under investigation, but not to be relevant from the point of view of policy in any other application. I would not want to go to the wall to defend any of the choices made. It turns out that roughly equal numbers of studies, in my judgement, are remote, or have potential, or are directly of policy relevance. The most I can hope for is that the assignments to categories have some validity, and the distinctions between categories are meaningful and revealing.

REMOTE FROM POLICY

The Sukur people, with a population of somewhere between four and six thousand, are a small cultural and political grouping located in the Mandara highlands in north-eastern Nigeria. Their territory covers about thirty thousand square kilometres. It borders on the Cameroons, and spills over into that country. The Yedseram River supplies water to the area. The combination of high land, giving natural defence, and fertile, well-irrigated land has made this a viable living area for the Sukur. Parts of the soil contain reasonably rich iron deposits. The presence of ample wood for smelting makes iron production possible. In the past, the combination of ore and wood resulted in significant iron implement production and the export of iron products. This desirable territory has been subject to some envious challenges from other groups.

In modern times the arrival of cheap imported goods has ended the iron export trade, and even ended the production of iron implements for own use by the Sukur. It is possible that the Sukur were much more prosperous in earlier times. But this is uncertain. The area and its people have only been studied to a small degree. There is understandable disagreement about the extent of the wealth and power of the Sukur in the past.

Adam Smith and Nicholas David have studied the significance of chieftancy for the Sukur people, largely through analysis of the compound which the *Xidi*, or chief Sukur, occupies. (Smith and David, '95) They take the position that the *Xidi* is more of a secular leader who maintains his power through negotiation, bargaining, and political manoeuvre. This is in contrast to chiefs of the Mofu-Diamare principalities, just across the border in the Cameroons, whose chiefs are held to be divine right rulers, with much more in the way of religious authority.

A clear test of religious authority is responsibility with respect to rain making. Smith and David report that the *Xidi* do not have this authority. Their article is followed by nine pages of comment from ten specialist scholars. One of these is James M. Vaughan of the Indiana University Department of Anthropology. He writes that he noted in his diary on 23 May 1960, while on a field trip in the area, that lack of rain was attributed to the current *Xidi* being put in jail. (p. 464) This would appear to be a fairly knowledgeable counter view to that of Smith and David. Incidentally, Professor Vaughan posted bail for the chief.

Vaughan is not the only commentator to take serious exception with the conclusions drawn by Smith and David. But all acknowledge that this is an important study, in that it provides information on a social entity only little studied, and also because of the architectural detail. Smith and David follow a significant anthropological tradition in relating physical structures in buildings and the general landscape to social structures. In principle most scholars are prepared to entertain the idea of interactions running both ways. The structures influence how people relate to each other, and social relations influence what is built. Of course there are other influences, including climate and technology. In the present study, rather than rooms in a house, we are dealing with largely freestanding, individual, single purpose structures grouped together and surrounded by a wall. This is the home of a family, broadly defined.

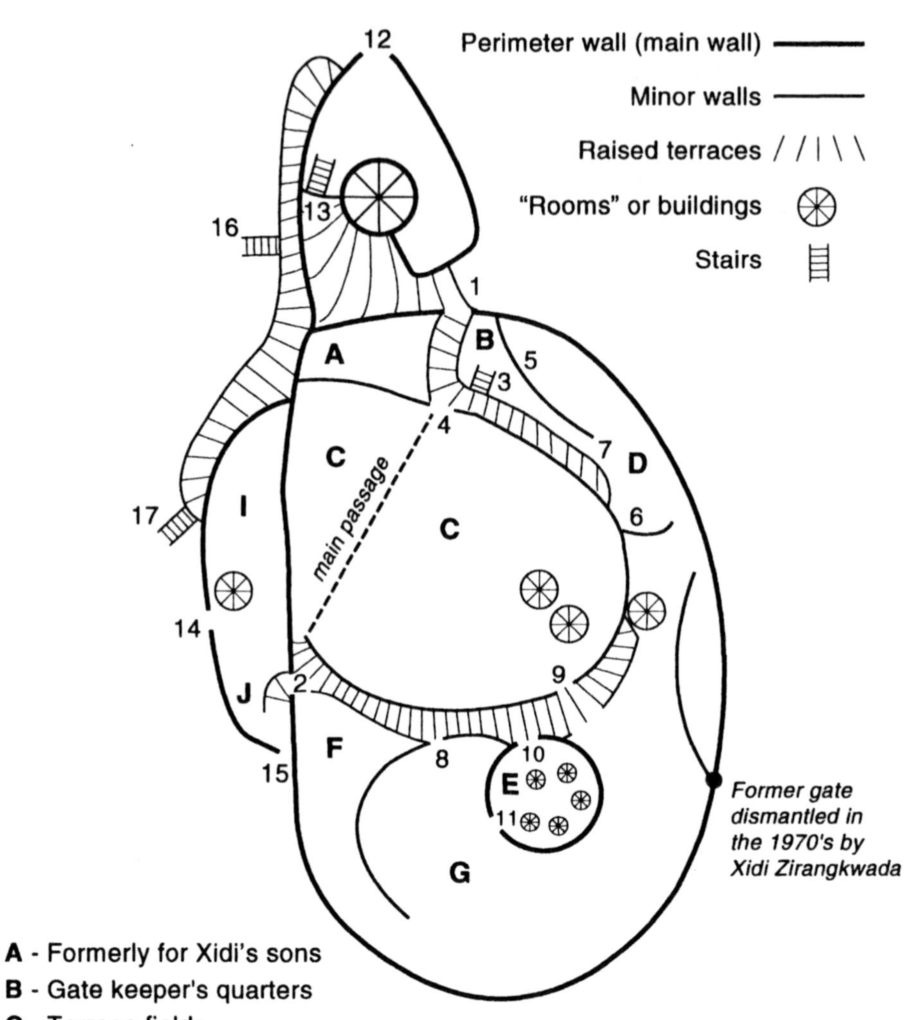

A - Formerly for Xidi's sons
B - Gate keeper's quarters
C - Terrace fields
D - Fields
E - Inner house
F - Ruins
G - Fields
H - Mbuk (courtyard)
I - Guest accommodation
J - Entrance features

1,2 - Main gates
2 - 9 - Minor gate points
10,11 - Inner house entrances
12,13 - Gates to northern enclosure
14,15 - Gates to western enclosure
16,17 - Steps to northern terrace

The chief's family lives in an inner house which is located in a much larger complex. The larger area includes the main public spaces that are used for ceremonies, negotiation, deliberation and dispensing justice. This impressive edifice is set out on the following page. The complete house, or *ghi*, the same word being used for an ordinary house, can be thought of as having four components. One is the main area which is about 1.6 acres in size. It contains the "inner house" as the second component. The two additional sections are the *Mbuk* room in the north end of the complex, and a courtyard on the western side. Both the room and this last space are important in ceremonies such as initiation and reporting of successful driving of evil influences from the land. Virtually nothing is known about the order in which the different parts of the building complex came to be built. Alas, now much of it is in dilapidation or ruin. Oral tradition has it that the complex was built in a couple of days by magical figures, which we might call aliens. Smith and David see this explanation as enhancing the position of the *Xidi,* as he is the master over a structure built by figures who were more than human. Reassuringly, the authors of this study believe it was built by humans. They think this was done in one concerted effort over a period of time, and the structure has always been more-or-less as we see it now.

The main outside wall, and the wall around the inner house, are both made from quarried stone. The minor walls are made of fieldstone. Even the main wall is in quite a state of disarray, with crevices and jagged sections which are fairly easy to climb over. The authors take this to be good evidence that the wall is not intended for defence, but rather to define social space. One might be sceptical of the contention that defence is unimportant on the grounds that even the need to scramble up may put an intruder at a disadvantage, and the wall may have been more of an obstacle a century or two ago when the wall was in better shape.

The Sukur culture attaches no significance, we are told, to the orientation of structures according to points of the compass, or put another way, according to the rising and setting of the sun. What does matter in this hilly terrain is rising and falling ground. Women are located on the downside, the easier to attack side, and men on the high side. Also, the men, and the more important people generally, are located nearer entrances, which are also often the only exits. In the typical house in the area, the entrance is marked by *maparam*, which are stone pillars. The one on the downside, the female side, is rough in appearance, and the one on the high side is more finished and is smooth. Only three of the passages in the *Xidi* "house" are *maparam*, the two entrances into the main section, '1' and '2' on the Figure, and '14', which is the entrance on the west side. The inner house is not *maparam*, which the authors take to be a symbol that the whole complex belongs to the *Xidi*

There is no doubt that the rulers of the Sukur have had a difficult time in recent years. This may well have to do with the collapse of the iron industry. No leader has lasted very long, especially compared to the nearby Mofu-Diamare chiefs. Over the past hundred years there were ten incumbents. Three were killed in office. Four were deposed, though two of these were eventually reinstated. Two abdicated. One died in office. Smith and David argue that the chiefs had a pressing need to hustle, to keep reinventing their authority, and the *Xidi* house, thought of in the large, is crucial to this activity. The main evidence the authors suggest for this relationship between the house and their power is the large number of gateways, passages, and obstacles to movement in the *Xidi* house.

> "The most startling aspect of the gateways is not the patterning in their dimensions but rather their sheer number. No fewer than 17 serve to regulate movement into, through, and around the Xidi house. Since we know that the complex was not constructed for defence, what is the purpose of this prodigious number of gateways?...Gateways, as Eliade suggested [Eliade,Mircea, *The Sacred and the Profane*, Harcourt, Brace, 1959], often have a sacred quality, marking the transition between socially constructed categories — the sacred and the profane, the public and the private." (p. 453)

The thesis is clear. The *Xidi* has dominion over a complex house with lots of entrances and passageways, and through the control of these he continually reinforces, or attempts to reinforce, his precarious hold on the Sukur society. As some of the commentators on this dense and compressed paper point out, we have no idea what the chiefly dwelling of the Mofu-Diamare looks like. Presumably they have less need to keep recreating their authority, and so might not need this kind of structure. And there are other possibilities. Over hundreds of years the Sukur building may have been modified, resulting in the current unintended form. Smith and David assert that it is a complete architectural piece and was put together as such. However, their thesis is not dependent on that. Whatever happened in the past, this may be how the house functions now.

If the building has evolved over time, perhaps that evolution has been shaped by the need for authority through complexity. Smith and David tend to reject the idea of critically examining this possibility. "Just as political trajectories follow no universal principles, spatial relations cannot be reduced to a few formulae. The articulation of power and space is far too rich and complex for such an endeavour." (p. 497) By arguing in this way, the authors tend to put their theory beyond the possibility of even weak testing.

One would expect any chief in any context to occupy a dwelling which is grander than those of his subjects. It need not be located in a complex which includes spaces used for ceremony, and in general for purposes apart from housing his family. The *Xidi* house is of that kind, however. We might ask why? Why are these other functions incorporated? And we might ask why the structure in detail is as it is? To put it in Smith's and David's terms, why are there so many gates? Few of the commentators accept the explanation these researchers suggest, in spite of general admiration for their investigation. Glenn Davis Stone of the Columbia University Department of Anthropology put their objections this way.

> "Smith and David may have more and better evidence that (1) the Xidi did and does enjoy substantial control over the Sukur's behaviour and production and that (2) this inequality is obscured and legitimated by his palace, but from this article it seems equally likely that (1) the xidi is neither especially powerful nor rich and that (2) he lives in a large and ostentatious compound which is both is family residence and a communal facility." (p. 461)

We certainly can agree that this study reports on a fascinating house. As we have seen before, anthropologists can differ markedly about basic interpretation. At the same time, it is difficult to derive any policy implications from this study, other than the general observation that houses have important symbolic aspects. Whether the history and current function of the *Xidi* house are as hypothesised by Smith and David is a different matter, and must be open to doubt.

Economists have long been intrigued by a general property of a number of markets that when prices are high and rising, the number of transactions is high, and when prices stagnate there are low numbers of transactions. On the face of it, there is no reason why more trades would occur at high prices than low prices. In the housing market, for example, would not just as many people have reasons to change houses in bad times, or times of slack prices, as in good times? If all house prices decline together, simple logic would suggest that just as many people as in good times would sell at lower prices but also be able to buy at lower prices. Similar arguments could be applied to the art market, and to other examples, where this puzzling tendency for the number of transactions to be greater when prices are high than when they are low can be observed.

Jeremy Stein suggests that an important part of the answer in the case of housing is to be found in down payments. (Stein, '96) Taking as his source of data the Chicago Title and Trust Company's Annual survey of Recent Home Buyers, Stein reports that roughly 60 percent of house sales are to repeat buyers, and over the period 1987 to 1990, down payments came from the proceeds of the sale of the previously owned houses to an extent ranging from 38 to 57 percent. (p. 381)

Following the normal economics convention, Stein assumes that agents strive to maximise their utility, which depends in part on the amount of housing they consume. Quality of housing and other benefits, such as location, are all assumed to be captured by a single measure which, for the sake of simplicity, is thought of as size. Utility also comes from consuming the other good in the model, and when there is a move from one house to another, it is assumed there is an independent gain from moving. As housing is a long-term investment, the demand for it is assumed in this model to depend on lifetime wealth.

In the absence of a down payment, the model generates an equilibrium where the number of transactions is independent of average price. But where there is a down payment, a falling price of housing creates a kind of race. More housing would raise utility for some potential buyers, but their ability to purchase larger homes is constrained by the down payment. This reduces demand, and further depresses prices. Lower prices knock sellers out of the market as well as buyers. According to the model, there is an equilibrium, with fewer transactions and lower prices. This is what we were hoping to explain. The institution of down payment, in the context of the other assumptions, does the job.

Stein suggests that even under depressed conditions it will make sense for a number of people to put their houses on the market at a price which, if realised, would generate the down payment they need for the house they want to move to. They might hit lucky. The cost of having the house on the market at an unrealistic price, called "fishing", is low. We would expect to observe more of this when the market is depressed. An almost identical situation exists for builders who need to sell off projects at prices that generate the initial capital for the next project. There is some plausibility to this theory, but it leaves nagging doubts as to why down payments do not rise and fall in a symmetric fashion in line with the general market.

An anthropological study, somewhat remote from policy but interesting nevertheless, is the work of Robert LeVine and Sarah LeVine. (LeVine and LeVine, '91) They offer a convincing analysis of the cultural and psychological significance of a traditional African house, or *enyomba*, of the Gusii people, a Bantu-speaking group of about one million located near Lake Victoria in Kenya. Dwellings are the only buildings made by the Gusii. The traditional houses are fairly easy to build, and are dotted over the land. They have no decoration, and yet are heavy with symbolic meaning. Both the culture and the building practices have changed under the impact of colonial rule, independence, and the availability of new building materials

The traditional Gusii house is round, without windows, divided into two rooms with an outside entrance to each room and an internal connecting passage. The house is made of a framework of saplings which is built by the men, and dried mud, which completes the building, is applied by the women. It has a thatched roof with a stick, or *egechuri*, protruding out of the roof. The authors make no further mention of the *egechun*; an odd omission from the discussion as this might be regarded as decoration. The house has a male side, *eero.* This side has an entrance, called *egesaku*, which is awkward, coming through the cattle pen, and is only allowed to be used by male relatives. The same term which identifies the entrance is used for the peer group of the male occupant of the house.

The female side of the house is called *enyomba.* A good deal of the structure, and the rules about use of structure, has to do with avoiding incest, and more general considerations of propriety. The men gather in these houses for beer drinking, and their rough talk is confined to their part of the house to protect the women from potential embarrassment.

For the Gusii people their houses are intimately involved in the stages of life. These stages include a stage of death and burial. Men are buried on the right side of the entrance to the room where they used to entertain. Women are buried on the left side of the yard outside their part of the house. House building marks the stages of life, and success in life, or the lack of it. Apart from the two-room house, there is a one-room hut. Men have four stages in life: during childhood they live with the mother; after circumcision and before marriage male children live in the one room hut; marriage means moving to a two room house; and burial takes place outside of the house.

Women have three stages. They move from living with their mothers directly on to marriage. The houses of married sons are a source of pride to fathers, but they are prohibited from entering them. This is another aspect of incest avoidance. Successful men tend to have more than one wife, and a house for each. Having two wives in one house is frowned on.

Beginning in the 1950s, larger houses, still on the two-room principle, could be built by using nails, and this became the standard practice. The authors assume that prior to the building of larger units, more one room huts were built to achieve the necessary separation by age and sex which the Gusii see as so vital to respectability and decorum. This seems reasonable, given the way in which these simple structures are related to the stages of life, are indicators of success, and are important contributors to preserving the rules of good behaviour.

In the 1970s and 1980s, more Gusii began building square houses with metal roofs, and separate structures for cooking. Robert LeVine and Sarah LeVine see these changes as pragmatic responses to new technical possibilities and new constraints, including the growing shortage of wood. They see culture as able and ready to be modified by practical needs. One might wonder as well if there were social changes brought about by the impact of political independence for Kenya, and more interaction outside the immediate community, which might also contribute to changes in house building. It would be interesting to know if the change in the nature of the Gusii houses was accompanied by a change in behaviour.

Moving from Africa to the 'West', the contrast between the concept of 'taste' in homes, with its connotations of social structure and hierarchy, and the concept of 'style', which is more neutral and implies individual choice, is the starting point of a sociological analysis of the appearance of homes by Ruth Madigan and Moira Munro. (Madigan and Munro, '96) Appearance includes decoration, choice of consumer durables, arrangement, maintenance and cleanliness. The study is based both on a postal questionnaire and on in-depth interviews. There were 382 responses to the questionnaire and twenty interviews. No details are given by the authors on sample selection, other than to say that the participants came from public and private post-war estate housing in Glasgow.

The intention was to avoid both high and low incomes, and to sample among people living in two and three bedroom housing. One-third of the respondents were council tenants and two-thirds were owner-occupiers. Over half the sample was made up of manual working class respondents, and one-quarter of the men in the sample were unemployed. A third of the women were in full-time employment, a third in part-time employment, and a third 'at home'. The interviews were drawn from the same general group of Glasgow residents as the postal questionnaire, but confined to households with three or more members. Just under half the postal sample were households with children. The interviews were all with women.

Madigan and Munro attempt to work with a four-way typology of styles. These are "traditional cottagey", i.e., flowers and pine; "country house", i.e., flowers and mahogany; "modern hi-tech", i.e., plain colours and black ash; and "post-modern", i.e., pastel colours and beach. The goal of the study was to shed light on the role of fashion, in the sense of the marketing and adoption of styles, in the aesthetics of homes. Going on from there the authors hoped to find the explanation of stylistic decisions in terms of family structure and social class. It would appear that this particular objective of the investigation was achieved to a very limited degree. Much of this slightly disappointing outcome had to do with the reporting of the respondents, who proved to be reluctant, or unable, to discuss their style decisions even though they clearly had made them.

It may be that explicit information was harder to elicit from the particular social and economic group chosen. And it could be there was something inappropriate in the interviews and questionnaires the authors employed. The authors put it this way. "It was immediately striking in our interviews that there was not generally a strong involvement with design...Our sample of working-class and lower middle-class households did not appear to share the vocabulary of design and style promoted so strongly in the design-conscious 1980s." (p. 46)

While an interest in style was difficult to pin down, it was clear that the people taking part in this study did care about their homes. Madigan and Munro identify the concerns as being divorced from material wealth and giving impressions of status to others, and having instead to do with, "...familial ideology — homeliness, warmth and a welcoming feel." (p. 47) They interpret the responses as placing emphasis on conformity, which seems to mean keeping a tidy and clean house, and not pretending to anything special.

There is an interesting tension here between a relaxed and welcoming home — the phrase "put my feet up" occurs frequently — and a tidy and clean home. While half agreed, and the rest were neutral, in response to the postal statement, "It is more important for the house to comfortable than tidy", an equal number agreed with the statement that, "I can't relax when the house is untidy." (p. 49) Employing principle component factor analysis, three factors accounted for fifty percent of the variance. These are described as: style and judgement attitudes; attitudes with respect to familial values and comfort; and traditional judgmental attitudes. Men are more likely to fall into the first cluster. This cluster includes statements like, "I like to have everything matching in the living room". Women are more likely to fall in the second cluster which includes the statement above and the statement, "It is more important for a house to be comfortable than tidy".

The postal questionnaire used by Madigan and Munro included twenty paired words describing the impression the respondent would like his or her house to make on other people. The pairs gave opposites as choices, and did not allow any middle ground. For seven pairs, over ninety percent of the respondents preferred the same word describing the impression they would like to make. These words were; warm, quiet, neat, comfortable, respectable, sensible, and contemporary. The authors describe these as very "modest" choices, contributing to the conclusion that this group of people, at least, wanted mainly to conform and not to stand out in any way. But we may wonder how much really can be deduced. The authors do not tell us what the rejected paired words were. Few people would want a 'disreputable' or a 'cold' house. And the choice of 'contemporary' is not easy to interpret. It would be interesting to know whether its opposite was 'old fashioned' or 'traditional' or 'customary', for example.

Madigan and Munro conclude that the concept of consumption as a leisure activity, and as a vehicle for self-expression, can be over-done. The furnishing, decorating and arranging of one's home might be thought of as a natural place for such expressions. But for many people, so the authors argue, the cost constraints, even with DIY and flat-packed assembly furniture, are too great. In addition there is usually a dominant path through time when it comes to the style of a house. Few people have the resources and energy to create their homes from scratch. One thing is bought after another, often with long gaps between purchases. So what is there at any point in time may be hard to explain or justify if it had been done all of a piece, but could perhaps be understood as a sequence of decisions.

Only one of the twenty people interviewed, a thirty-eight year old woman who owned her home, was keen to discuss style. She had put a great deal of time, energy and money into painting and decorating. It would be rash to assume that as a general rule one in twenty occupants of houses thinks about the four-way typology set out above, or in some other way takes an active stance stylistically. But maybe that is the case, and if so, it would be interesting to know how much influence this innovating minority has on the conforming majority.

Of course the places that people live usually have emotional overtones that have to do with belonging, often within a family unit, a sense of place, a sense of refuge and of identity. For this side of housing we tend to use the word 'home'. The sociologists Janet Finch and Lynn Hayes adopted an ingenious approach to examining the relationship between the physical place and the existence of a home. (Finch and Hayes, '94) Before coming to this we might note that they do rather see the home as coming from creative acts on the part of the occupants. "It offers significant opportunities for its occupants to express their individuality and their taste, through the way in which they organise and furnish it. It is therefore, in a meaningful sense, a personal creation..." (p. 418) This does not accord with the findings of Madigan and Munro. This contrast is interesting, but for present purposes it is not critical. Finch and Hayes are expressing their opinion on what makes a home. This opinion does not follow from their study. Their objective is different. Whatever leads to a dwelling being a 'home', they want to know whether a home can be inherited, or only the physical place can be inherited.

The authors start from the premise that if the home is simply part of the total, or residuary estate, it is likely that it will be sold and lose the quality of being a home. But if it is bequeathed as a separate unit, there is a possibility that the home will passed on as such and, "...become someone else's home."

The implication must be that it remains the same home, though this is not stated. The authors constructed a random sample of 800 wills. They report that in seventy-five cases, or nine percent, the deceased specified that his or her home go to a particular person. As home ownership is much more common than nine percent, they conclude that most homes enter wills as undifferentiated property. The exception to this would be if the whole estate went to a single person. In fact, this was true of thirty-nine percent of the sample. But, again, not all of these single person bequests may include a house. The data they are working with is not entirely revealing. On balance the authors conclude that it is rather uncommon for a testator to pass on their home "as a home".

Most cases of estates going to a single individual are to spouses (eighty-four percent). In the case of the seventy-five bequests of the home as a singled out item, two-thirds went to the same address as the deceased. In the cases of bequests to co-residents, two-thirds are lifetime rather than absolute bequests. The bequests of homes to people living elsewhere are all absolute. So again, the conclusion is that homes are rarely passed on as such. When this does occur, it is likely to be a spouse staying on in the house to which she, typically, made the major contribution in turning it into a home.

To study the picture from the point of view of the recipients, the authors interviewed ninety-nine people, usually on their own. The interviews showed that there is little likelihood of people moving into inherited homes if they were not living there before. Adults eventually find themselves, in their own homes, hopefully, and have no desire to move into another home, even if it was the one they were brought up in. "...in the contemporary British context a home is so strongly identified with, and symbolises, its creator that it does die with the person who created it and cannot be occupied by someone else as their home." (p. 428) This seems reasonable enough, but, more than that, has been put on a scientific basis. Whether this and other issues of 'home' versus 'house' will have policy implications remains to be seen.

POTENTIAL FOR POLICY

Quite a number of studies have explored the consequences of crowding and long-term high levels of density in dwellings. It is generally found that women are more adversely effected than men. This is widely understood to be due to women spending more time in the home and carrying a greater responsibility for the work done in homes. Women are also more responsible for the caring which goes on in the home. The idea that men may grab a larger share of limited space and other resources associated with the house, and therefore be less troubled by crowding, is not emphasised in the literature, but is mentioned occasionally. This gender difference in response to crowding is confirmed in a study of rural India by the social psychologists Barry Ruback and Janak Pandey. (Ruback and Pandy, '96) Their study is notable for the care taken, and for an interesting twist in that while women report on the effects of crowding in more adverse terms than men, they still are attracted to the idea, on the whole, of an increase in the number of people in the household.

In this study a male and a female interviewer visited a stratified random sample of mainly very poor households in three villages in the Allahbad area of India. Having secured co-operation, the man interviewed the husband and the woman interviewed the wife. These interviews were held at the same time in different places. 159 men and 159 women were asked 158 questions over roughly an hour. Some questions were not relevant to this particular study. The questions were grouped into seven sections which covered: (1) description of the respondents; (2) details about the home, including perceived changes in crowding over ten years; (3) family life with an emphasis on division of tasks and support from neighbours; (4) the positive and negative aspects of the current number of children, and whether more boys or girls, or both, would be desirable; (5) the degree of control people had over their own lives, and the control exercised by God (the majority of households were Hindu); (6) physical and mental stress including anxiety and depression, and disturbing events like the tragedy of a friend's death, or robbery; and (7) personal characteristics such as the outward going nature of the respondent, and his or her reaction to crowding. In addition, the interviewers made their own observations of the home and its significant contents.

As is common in social psychological studies, the authors draw on many standard sets of questions, adapted for the needs of their particular investigation. These off-the-shelf questionnaires include the Barrera, Sandler and Ramsey scale of social support (1981); Levenson's measure of control (1973); the Pennebaker, Burnam, Schaeffer and Harper measure of perceived physical symptoms (1977); the life events scale of Sarason, Johnson and Siegal (1978); and the Jalota and Kapoor measure of extroversion adopted from Eysenck. More detail on these sources is given on page 424 of the study.

The central variable in the study is density, defined as the number of people in the house divided by the number of rooms. In the present study this ranged from one quarter, or four rooms per person, all the way up to eight, meaning eight people per room. This measure of density calls for comment. Size of rooms is not considered. This can be acceptable if room size does not vary much from house to house. In the current study, density is positively related to number of people and negatively related to the number of rooms, as we might expect. Number of people and number of rooms are positively associated, which also conforms to expectations.

The authors contrast this relationship between rooms and people in their sample of houses with studies in North America, where density is associated with number of people, but not with the number of rooms. In North America, so they report, there is no tendency for places with fewer rooms to be more densely occupied, or places with more rooms to have fewer people per room. Their results also differ from those found in urban India, but in a different way. In urban India there is an association between fewer rooms and more people per room, but no association between number of people per household and density.

Ruback and Pandy found a lot of similarity in the answers given to questions by men and by women. They also found noticeable and notable differences between men and woman. Density was more significantly and more strongly correlated with a lower rating of the house for women than for men. This is a key result. The same applied to parts of the house where special activities take place. In addition, women were more adversely affected by lack of resources for the house than men. For example, fifty percent more women than men reported lack of privacy in going to the toilet and in bathing. Not only did women have less privacy, they also were more troubled than men by lack of privacy. Women rated their living conditions less favourably than men, and perceived less support from others in dealing with household tasks compared to men.

Men and women tended to agree on the positive aspects that their children brought to their lives. However, women were more strongly effected by the inevitable negative aspects. The general result of this investigation is that the women had a significantly less favourable view of their homes and the interactions taking place in them than did the men. However, on the specific issues of crowding and the size of the household, measured by numbers of people, women did not perceive these as being problematic. There was a clear association in the case of women between higher levels of density and greater problems with the home. For the men, this was much less the case. But when asked directly about density and its consequences, women did not see much of a connection. Multiple regression techniques which combined a number of variables in a simultaneous investigation were unable to account for this apparent contradiction. Women were even more inclined to welcome additional members to the household than were men, even though they seemed to suffer more from crowding.

Ruback and Pandey offer three explanations as to why women might be more disturbed by crowding than men, and yet wish for more people in the home. They posit that women may take more pleasure in social interaction than men. They also emerge as more extroverted than men in this study. For completeness the authors raise the possibility that women may not make the connections between the positive and negative aspects of more people in the home. They doubt the plausibility of this idea, as women have a good knowledge of factors that bear on life in the home. And finally, they suggest that though the negative aspects of crowding are felt by women, there are even stronger reasons to want more children. The familiar economic reasons of labour on the farm and support in old-age are relevant. In addition there are religious and cultural reasons for preferring more children, especially more male children. This study, and related work, has potential bearing on the kind of accommodation those in a position to influence housing design might provide.

A common feature of third world life is the move from the a rural village to a large city. This is rarely accomplished in a single step. Typically the move involves a number of stages, going from satellite settlements, squatter communities, and eventually conventional urban dwelling. Tahire Erman has done an in-depth study in Ankara, the capital of Turkey, of the housing side of these transitions. (Erman, '96) Her work concentrates on the experiences of the residents, mainly women, in both squatter communities and in high rise apartments. 105 women and 39 men were interviewed. 108 lived in squatter settlements, which are called *gecekondus*, and 36 of the people interviewed were living in apartments. This study took place in the *gecekondu* called Cukurca, and in apartment blocks near there in Bagcilar.

The author lived for five months in the Cukurca *gecekondu*. She provides a very graphic picture of community life. This involves strong social relations, as in a rural village, along with a high degree of social control. Much of the social life is between women, especially when they are working outdoors. They even enjoyed a picnic lunch in one of the incidents Erman describes. In the winter similar activity takes place in a succession of houses.

There is a troublesome contradiction in squatter, or *gecekondu,* life for many residents. In some ways it works well, and replicates traditional village life. In other respects, for many residents, it carries a negative image. The stigma attached to living in a squatter settlement is keenly felt by certain groups, such as young, second generation, women attending high school. They were not the only ones who felt uncomfortable. Some older women did their best to dress in a modern fashion, and to take a very small part in the social life of the *gecekondu*. But other women identified strongly with the *gecekondu.* For them the squatter community successfully replicated traditional ways. They did not share the values, attitudes and aspirations of the wider urban community. This group felt little, or no, contradiction in living in the *gecekondu.*

The women living in apartments, almost all of whom had come from a squatter settlement at some time, had a considerably restricted and more formal social life compared to their past. In part this is due to a somewhat random allocation of tenants to apartments. The *gecekondu* tended to reflect family and former village attachments. People did not move randomly to a squatter village or to a part of it. This was much less true in apartment living. In addition to the physical structure, apartment life is less conducive to the formation of, and encouragement of, social interaction and interdependence. There are no animals and vegetables to be tended together, and there is a real shortage of space for community exchange. On the other hand, for young men all this can be quite an advantage. They have much more freedom and independence. And to some extent women also have more privacy and independence in apartment living, though that may matter less to them. There are practical advantages in apartments. For example, so the author suggests, very young children are more easily controlled in apartments. But the practical side may not be paramount. The main consequence of moving to an apartment is greater social esteem.

While there may be nothing very startling or unexpected in Erman' study, it is important qualitative evidence concerning the major role of women in issues of housing. It poses very neatly the conflicts between physical arrangement and need, and the vital issues of image and status. The change in circumstance which is involved in moving from a *gacekondu* to an apartment in a high rise building is very great. The ability to cope with this, and the priorities people have, are shown in this study to be very dependent on the length of time spent in the new urban environment. The move to apartment housing is not a simple move to better housing. There are gains and losses on the way.

National and local government in most countries are in a position to influence many aspects of house building, including matters of style. Of course, location and space play important roles in how people respond to houses, but so does style. It would be natural to expect some difference between architects and others when it comes to matters of style. The social psychologist Terry Purcell has compared the way Australian college students doing architecture, and those doing other subjects, react to modern, or "high-style" houses, compared to conventional, or popular style houses. (Purcell, '95)

The author worked with photographs from Australia, their home country, and from the United States. Slides were shown to the students in random order. They were projected for seven seconds, followed by a ten second period with lights up to allow the students, who were paid subjects, to record their reactions on a nought to one hundred scale. They were asked to give a score to each picture of a house in terms of four different criteria. The first question was how good an example of its kind of house is it, that is, is it typical of its kind. Next came the question, how familiar are you with this kind of house. The third ranking had to do with how much the house was of interest to the subjects. Finally, they were asked to score the houses according to how much they liked them.

Architecture students at the beginning of their training reported that they were more familiar with Australian than American houses. For both countries they were more familiar with popular than modern houses, and they judged the popular houses to be more representative examples of that style than the modern houses. In spite of the familiarity issue, there was an overall tendency to rank American houses higher than Australian houses, whether popular or modern.

This is a rich body of data, and the author makes a large number of comparisons. Taking only the American houses, Purcell compared responses of architecture students at the beginning of their studies and in mid-career. He found no difference between the two groups on any of the four scales — goodness of example, familiarity, preference and interest. This result takes on particular meaning when combined with a comparison of architecture and non-architectural students. Both groups found popular style houses to be better examples of the type compared to high-style. This may well be because there is more agreement on what is a conventional house than what is a modern house. However, the architecture students found the examples shown of both types to be more representative of their types, compared to the scores from the other non-architecture students.

The key result, in my view, was that the architecture students had more interest in the modern houses than other students. They also preferred them more. No doubt we would expect that. However, what is not obvious is that beginning architecture students do not differ from those much further along in their training in these responses. The unchanged responses of architecture students during their education suggests that they are different from other students before they arrive. This information could play a role in determining the composition of committees that decide on matters of style. Exactly how it should be used would depend on what outcome one wanted to achieve.

The relations between political pressures, both internal and external, housing style, and the way people live are beautifully illustrated in a study by the anthropologist Margaret Rodman. (Rodman, '85) Her work is on people living in Longana, which is part of Vanuatu. The impact of greater wealth, more peaceful conditions and conversion to Christianity have all had marked effects on the structure and use of houses by the Longana people.

This study has close reverberations with that of LeVine and LeVine on the Gusii people which we have discussed above.

Rodman has analysed the changes in the design and use of Longana houses since the 1970s. These changes have their roots in the 1930s, when the area was pacified. Continuous struggles were common in the past, and at last came to an end. Coastal areas were made safe. New buildings were located there, and coconuts planted. Copra as a cash crop became widespread. Wild boars with prominent tusks remained an important part of the diet and the culture of this once predominantly polygamous society.

The long-standing tradition of the Longana was to build male, or *na gamal*, houses and female, or *valei*, houses. The husband proved each of his wives with a house. This had a thatched roof that reached down to the ground. It was dark and private, with a single opening. Cooking was done either in a separate shelter, or in a front portion of the *valei*. Rodman refers to these dwellings as "containers of women and wealth".

The men had a communal house. The *na gamal* is similar to the *valei*, but four times as large, with a higher roof and both a front and a back entrance. Internally the *na gamal* is divided by a series of hearths which mark a progression of status. The *na gamal*, located off to one side of the collection of *valei,* included a clearing of ceremonial significance. Women were strictly excluded from the *na gamal*, including the outside courtyard. The courtyard is an essential feature of the social role of the communal male house. Indeed, in some circumstances, the house may not yet be built, and the *na gamal* may consist only of a clearing used mainly for drinking kava by men. It is strictly off-limits to women.

Children stayed in the *valei*. Females remained there until marriage. Boys moved into the *na gamal* at puberty. The status of a leader of a sub-group of the Lugana was measured by the size of the *na gamal* under his authority, and by the number of *valei*.

The arrival of missionaries had a huge impact on Longana society. The missionaries encouraged men to live as members of a nuclear family in the *valei*. This implied an end to polygamy. In addition, they encouraged the construction of a third type of building, a church based on the design of the male house. These buildings, more recently tending to be made with cement floors and woven bamboo walls, are easier to build than the traditional *na gamal*. Men began to eat "at home", and the hierarchy of the hearths was eroded. Most important, women now entered the *na gamal* to cook, and thatching down to the ground was abandoned. One traditional *na gamal* with thatching down to the ground remained in 1970, and this one did exclude women.

In 1980 independence came to Vanuata. This engendered a new spirit of returning to customary ways. The word to describe this is *kastom* — this local expression would appear to be easier for foreigners to master than some others. With *kastom* came a renewed building of *na gamal* in the old style. There was a return to kava drinking as the fashionable tipple, instead of drinking alcohol. The design feature of hierarchical hearths in the *na gamal* was abandoned, but once again these houses became male preserves. This was not as strict as in the past. Women could enter for what the author refers to as "practical tasks". Presumably they were excluded from the social interaction of the men.

Interestingly, and rather well put, the Longana refer to ten "holes", or *buloi*, which they recognise as vessels, or repositories of custom and knowledge. Two of the 'holes' specify the many details in use of materials and proportions for building which are required for the proper construction of both *valei* and *na gamal*. The latter, as we indicated, is both the male house and a public house. The name *na gamal* literally means "coming and going". There is a kind of double, or possibly triple, meaning here. The men visit many times in the day, but the "coming and going" can refer to passage through life, and a passage through status levels. Rodman summarises the nature of the two houses as follows:

Two Logana Houses

na gamal	***valei***
public	private
male	female
activity	rest
large	small
pigs	mats
exchange	savings
passage	container
conservative	innovative

Most of these contrasting pairs are readily understandable. However, the pairing of "mats" with "pigs" calls for comment. Mats are an important part of bride-wealth, and therefore of the status of women. Mats also effect the status of the man providing them. As it happens, providing pigs also influences male status. Pigs contribute to status in the male preserve, and mats do the same in the female preserve.

Over recent years there have been great changes in the *valei*. Modern materials are becoming common. These tend to take the form of cement floors, corrugated iron roofs and woven bamboo walls. Whereas the traditional female house was uniform and not a status symbol, the new house varies a lot, one from another. Some are screened and have glass windows, painted walls, and front steps. And so we return to the question of why the one type is changing, and the other is reverting to, and upholding, tradition.

Rodman suggests that the answer can be found by viewing the two types in relation to each other. The *valei* is the locus of personal wealth. The *na gamal* represents the collective. The relation of the two has a critical role in cultural identity. "Men are linked with the earth and rootedness, women with the sky and mobility." The male house, says Rodman, embodies customary knowledge. The female house expresses wealth and female flightiness". (p. 277)

While willing to accept that there may be some truth in this explanation, other possibilities immediately suggest themselves. One has to do with the symbolic nature of the *na gamal* as a building. It has little in the way of practical function. It is for gathering, drinking, and being away from women. It could be any shape. The missionaries were right to link it to the church, another building whose practical needs are swamped by symbolic requirements. Admittedly, the *na gamal* also seems to be a male dwelling, particularly for adolescents before marriage. But this is not discussed in the article, and one can only guess about the physical requirements.

In addition to the symbolic and arbitrary nature of the building, one must also consider the role of male domination in the Longana society. These factors taken together suggest that we could divide the two buildings into the categories of 'status', on the one hand, and 'efficiency' on the other. Which would one expect to be more resistant to change over time? Which would be more likely to respond to new materials and new wealth, the male status symbol, or the place for day to day living? It seems likely that the more symbolic building, particularly as it is more of a collective, like a church compared to a home, would keep up tradition. To conclude, it could be argued that this investigation is better classed as remote from policy. On balance, I see it as having potential for policy as it raises issues often present in current policy decisions.

An economics study, where the authors see direct policy implications, and I am more inclined towards a potential implication, is the work of Jane Black, David de Meza and David Jeffreys on houses as collateral for business loans. (Black and colleagues, '96) The stock of capital in the form of housing has significant implications for the economy as a whole, simply through its size. Banks are unwilling to lend without collateral, and for many potential borrowers, their houses are a major source of collateral. The authors have examined the relation between changes in unreleased net housing equity and the formation of new businesses in the United Kingdom. They find that a ten percent increase in housing collateral results in a five percent increase in new VAT registrations. The latter is a good indicator of the number of new businesses over a certain threshold in size.

The association between the amount of housing collateral available and new business starts could come about for a number of reasons other than direct causality. The researchers took care to explore some possible sources of spurious correlation. They considered the possibility that a booming economy may both raise house prices and result in more new businesses, the boom itself acting on both variables. However, adding house prices to the regressions they used explaining new starts did not result in a significant coefficient, and only marginally reduced the effect of unreleased net housing equity, effectively dealing with this possibility. Another possibility is that better times might lower the banks' lending criteria. In this case housing debt should be positively associated with new registrations. In fact the coefficient is negative, but insignificant, tending to also eliminate this possible cause of a spurious association.

Black and her colleagues also investigate the survival rate of new firms. They note that very few of the new firms exit in times of economic adversity. They put this down to the lenders with the best prospects being the only ones to get loans. They argue that many potentially able entrepreneurs are prevented from starting new businesses because of lack of collateral. "Those who are able to surmount the entry barrier consequently tend to earn high economic rents and so can weather adverse economic conditions." (p. 73) At this point the authors move into policy considerations, but in a somewhat speculative way. The key finding of their research is the association between potential housing collateral and new business starts. We may or may not go along with them when they say they are opposed to grants because of the importance of entrepreneurs putting their own assets at risk. In addition, they see an argument for taxing human capital, and subsidising housing assets. Of course, these contentions cannot be deduced from their statistical analysis.

Some policies are easier for central government to impose on local government, even reluctant local authorities, than others. The political scientist Barrie Houlihan provides a revealing example of this difference in the area of housing policy. (Houlihan, '87) Houlihan compares implementation at the local level of national policies to sell council, or public housing, to the occupiers, with the national policy on area improvement.

The author begins by comparing a framework of analysis using a single-interest, rational-actor model, in contrast to a model with many interests, coalitions, bargaining, and the general push and shove of political life. With these two frameworks in mind, he traces out the central government success, and lack of it, in implementing its policies at the local level. The selling of council houses by local authorities was very much a local decision until the late 1960s. At that time the Labour government exerted pressure to restrict sales. With the following Conservative victory, the lead in policy given by central government was reversed, and with the Labour victory of 1974 it was reversed again. In 1980 the Conservative government made a major change with a Housing Act which gave tenants the right to buy, in principle taking the decision away from local government.

Two Labour controlled councils were particularly opposed to implementing the Tory policy of a tenant's right-to-buy. These were Newcastle-under-Lyme and Stoke-on-rent. This local frustration of policy directives coming from the centre was done through a combination of publicity and ingenious bureaucratic delaying techniques. Delays occurred at the District Valuer's Office, and further delays were provided by specially chosen solicitors. In Newcastle 1,470 enquiries resulted in only 116 sales. However, when the authority had to meet with central government, it was agreed to replace committee action with chairman's action, and after two years from the passing of the act, the Newcastle authority, as an example of a particularly reluctant council, had complied completely.

When we turn to the policy of area improvement, the story is very different. First of all there was much less local level opposition. The development of legislation for area improvement was more diffuse, compared to the legislation for the sale of council houses. In essence, the Housing Act of 1964 invited local authorities to identify improvement areas. Under the act, older houses could be refurbished and existing neighbourhoods improved. This policy is more in line with the views of Anne Power and others who are critical of big developments and large scale relocating of people. Houlihan identifies a number of reasons why this apparently admirable approach had very limited success. Some Conservative councils, such as Sefton Metropolitan Borough, were inherently unsympathetic. They favoured the lowest possible building programme and the smallest expenditure on house improvement. But even sympathetic councils were slow to react to this initiative from central government.

Part of the explanation has to do with big decisions versus detail. In his marvellous book on the planning of aircraft production in Britain in the Second World War, Ely Devons graphically illustrates the problems central authorities have in dealing with detail. Deciding how many engines or airframes should be made of the different types of fighter planes is something that can be done reasonably well by a central committee. (Devons, '50) Deciding how many spare pasts is another matter. Each plane will involve many thousands of parts. One defective part may stop an entire plane. Excessive production of parts means fewer planes and clogs up the system. Houlihan is giving us a lucid analysis of related phenomena in the area of government policy on housing.

Administratively it was not clear exactly who in local government had the specific responsibility for the implementation of 'area improvement'.

Nor was it clear what priority to give this activity compared to other needs, including other housing needs. Liverpool, for example made a good start, but in 1983 the Labour council, taking over from the Liberal leadership, re-emphasised clearance and new building rather than improving privately owned homes. So, though funding from central government was in principle forthcoming, to make use of it, officers on the ground had to make detailed decisions. Further, there was uncertainty as to whether the physical needs of the building should dominate, or the wishes and objectives of the occupants.

Stoke-on-Trent was also a Labour led council with a marked preference for new building. The authority had a large Direct Works Department with considerable political muscle. Major projects also had more attraction for the increasingly important profession of planners. Diverting funds to housing associations in order to carry out area improvement was not something either group favoured. But unlike the situation for the sale of council houses, where the Minister of Housing, John Stanley, could make clear announcements, threaten to carry out the selling policy over the heads of councils, and haul reluctant councillors on to the carpet and demand action, the very nature of the area improvement programme contained much less in the way of clear measures of successful implementation, or the lack of it. This nicely illustrates how the balance of power between central and local government can depend in part on the nature of the policy being implemented.

In a promising, but slightly wandering effort, Ingemar Elander raised the question; why has there been significantly less selling off of publicly owned rented accommodation to private owners in Sweden compared to many other European countries. Having set what appears to be a very clear goal for this research, Elander then backtracks somewhat. Two forms of covert privatisation complicate the picture, and weaken the contrast between Sweden and the rest of Europe. Private management companies have played a larger role in public rented housing, and the opportunity exists in some places, by no means everywhere, to buy an improved place in the queue for a rented place. However, there remains a difference between Sweden and elsewhere in the former's greater attachment to the provision of public rented housing.

The prominence of the Social Democratic Party and the Communist Party in Sweden is central to the discussion. This relative difference in political power compared to other countries, argues Elander, affects housing policy. There is a serious problem of causal explanation here in the obvious follow-on question of why do these political views have greater success in Sweden. Other reasons for the success of the public housing programme include its sheer size. Such a large proportion of the population live in public rented housing that it avoids stigmatising, but this too has to be qualified. Then there are well organised groups to defend social housing: the Construction Workers' Union; the union owned National Building Association; the National Association of Municipal Housing Companies; and the National Federation of Tenants' Associations. Again, why do these groupings exist in Sweden more than elsewhere, and with such good organisation and power? This takes us to the root of one problem in this kind of political explanation. It is not tautological to say that something came about because it had more political support. But it does leave the origins of that support unexplained.

The research places considerable emphasis on the ultimate objective of Swedish social housing policy. Much play is made by the author of the use of the term 'social' to refer to society at large, rather than to the weaker and more down trodden parts of society. But again, this is stated only to be qualified. "...even in Sweden [social rented housing] has been used in the municipalities as a kind of 'residual' for marginalised groups." (p. 34) Elander sees this movement toward socially segregated public housing as peaking in the 1970s. Four developments are mentioned as having mitigated the effects, or even reversed the trend. To a limited extent, more attractive inner city sites were developed. Second, parts of estates were privatised. And greater variety in the nature of homes on offer was tried, and, to a degree, was achieved. And finally, more tenant control over maintenance helps to remove stigma from public housing.

One can reasonably conclude that while there is no clear and sharp difference between Sweden and elsewhere in housing policy, there still are notable differences. Elander discusses two estates, Rosta in Orebro and the Dalhem estate in Heisingborg. The former is architecturally more attractive and now has an ageing population. The latter is more high rise, and reads much like a troubled English estate. However, remedial action through physical rehabilitation and tenants' associations have been reasonably successful in Dalham. That Sweden on balance is different from much of the rest of Europe is explained by Elander in terms of culture, political will, and political institutions.

DIRECT POLICY APPLICATIONS

Discrimination is much more likely when it comes to housing than in other social and economic interactions. Markets in themselves need not be conducive to prejudice. Compared to many other institutions, markets tend to be more indifferent as to who is participating. But housing may well be an area, like employment, where prejudice can have an important impact. Certain groups may be excluded from some neighbourhoods. It may be more difficult for groups at the bottom of the pecking order to obtain mortgages, even after fully accounting for their financial position. As a possible example of discrimination, the sociologists Richard Lempert and Karl Monsma have examined the fate of Samoans in Hawaii living in public housing, when they come before an Eviction Board. (Lempert and Monsma, '94) Their findings illuminate some problems of public housing boards generally, and raise fascinating dilemmas inherent in the concept of discrimination.

There is little doubt that Samoans, of all groups, are the most likely to suffer discrimination in Hawaii. They have the lowest income per person of any comparable group. And while Laotians, Tongons and Vietnamese do not escape from discrimination completely, Samoans were observed by Lempert and Monsma to be mentioned most frequently, and most strongly, in ways that implied prejudice. The Supreme Court ruling of 1971 in the case Griggs vs Duke Power laid down rules for protecting victims of discrimination. These rules are aimed at preventing differential treatment. Lempert and Monsma fundamentally question the logic of this principle.

The investigation begins by establishing that a Samoan is more likely to be evicted than a member of another ethnic group. The authors base this conclusion on a probit analysis of decisions of the Hawaii Housing Authority eviction boards over the period 1966 -1985. These boards tend to be informal in nature. The tenants usually are not represented by lawyers. They are questioned by the board and have a reasonable opportunity to respond. Non payment of rent is the most likely reason for any tenant to come before a board, and this is even more the case with Samoan tenants. The probability of eviction for all tenants before the boards is .326. It rises to .437, holding other things constant, for Samoans. This differential outcome seems to be rising over the period under consideration.

Drawing on interviews with prosecutors, board members, and detailed reports of the hearings, the authors feel that in the end a non-Samoan tenant with rent arrears will be treated in the same way as a Samoan, given all the circumstances and the content of the discussion in the hearing. In that sense, equal treatment, required by the Griggs vs Duke Power ruling, is satisfied. The problem comes about because of what the authors call cultural discrimination. If a Samoan were to make the same explanation of why rent was owing as any other Hawaiian, the treatment would be the same. But living in a different culture, the causes of financial difficulty, assumed to be accurately reported in all cases, are different. To be specific, the most common cause of financial problems for Samoans is sending money home for funerals and weddings. And often these events called for expensive trips to Samoa, as well as sending money. The other most common financial burden came from making contributions to the church.

Three concepts are important here: *aiga*, or the extended family; *matai*, which refers to the chief of the family; and the church. The Samoan is obliged to support these institutions. It is not a matter of choice. But because of cultural differences, the boards are not inclined to respond to these explanations of financial difficulty in the same way as they would respond to other explanations. The boards are particularly inclined to avoid eviction if the tenant, or someone in the tenet's family, has a medical problem. Another argument likely to be convincing is being a victim of theft. But the obligations of the Samoans, and the consequent explanations of why rent has not been paid, are foreign to the boards. Equal treatment might be thought of as treating people the same who make an equal effort to pay, given the circumstances. But should we interpret the circumstances from the cultural perspectives of the tenants, or from the perspectives of the boards? It is this difference which the authors identify as resulting in discrimination against Samoans in housing.

Richard Lalonde, Shilpi Majumder and Roger Parris have studied the responses of black Canadians to discrimination in housing. (Lalonde and colleagues, '95) They employed the familiar experimental technique which involves telling different stories to different groups, and comparing the responses. This study is somewhat unusual in that most social psychologists study the perpetrators of prejudice, rather than the victims of it. For those who do study the responses of victims, a basic and widely held conjecture is that individual responses are preferred by victims to collective responses. The results found in this study are consistent with that conjecture.

The authors worked with what they describe as a highly educated, black, "convenience" sample of 39 men and 33 women. The subjects were asked to read a report about a black man going to look at an apartment with a view to renting. The report stated that on seeing the apartment, the man expressed a strong wish to rent. His interest in the apartment was noted, but two days later he was informed that the apartment had gone to someone else. The continuation of this report then brakes off into three branches: one contains some slight evidence of racial discrimination; one has moderate evidence; and one has overwhelming evidence of discrimination. This last version consisted of reliable information going to the prospective tenant that the apartment was still being offered for renting, and that no black people lived in the building. The respondents were then asked to fill in a questionnaire. Two thirds returned the questionnaire. They were asked to give a score to each item on a list of eleven possible reactions to the story. A score of '1' meant they definitely would not take the action. Scoring went up to '9', meaning they definitely would take the action.

The authors tested the mean differences in the scoring of alternative choices of responses, and these were found to be statistically significant.

The following list gives the options, which were mostly drawn from a longer list prepared by Lalonde and Cameron (1994).

> Do nothing. Inform others. Seek advice from social agencies. File a formal complaint. Consult a lawyer. Take legal action. Become active in fighting discrimination. Help in organising a black rental agency. Report the event to the government. Inform the media. Organise a boycott.

The researchers undertook an analysis of variance which identified two leading responses; informing others and seeking advice. When asked for their single preferred action, one third of the respondents chose the former and a quarter chose the latter. All other options were chosen by less than ten percent of the people taking part in the experiment. At the bottom of the list, that is, receiving the least support were "forgetting about the situation" and "organising boycotts", significantly the weakest response and the strongest response. The persuasiveness of the evidence for racial prejudice in the three different versions of the story effected the responses to two of the options. Strong evidence raised the proportion preferring to file a complaint (with the Human Rights Commission), and reduced the preference for ignoring the whole incident.

This study by Parris and his colleagues clearly supports the widely held view that, for most victims of prejudice, individual action is preferred to collective action. The authors offer two explanations of why tougher actions and collective actions may not get higher votes from the respondents. One is that the tougher actions may be more costly in terms of money, time and energy. And secondly, undertaking a hard collective fight in order to live in a place where one is subjected to prejudice, even if won, may be a pyrrhic victory. Policies designed to combat prejudice in housing have to take account of the likely responses of victims.

As a place to live is the largest single item of expenditure for most people, owning a home usually involves substantial borrowing from the capital market. And while markets play the dominant role in housing in many countries, it is almost always the case that governments play a role as well. Government housing policy takes a variety of forms: tax relief on mortgage payments; rent control; state provision of housing on preferential terms; building regulation and regulation of the location of housing.

The issue of prejudice in the granting of loans on homes has received a great deal of attention, especially from economists. In the United States the Home Mortgage Disclosure Act (HMDA) generated data for 1991, 1992 and 1993, and showed that black and Hispanic applicants seeking loans were between two and three times as likely to be turned down compared to whites.

The data collected included demographic and income information, along with information on the race of loan applicants.

Sceptics, and this includes most of the lenders themselves, doubted the validity of the obvious conclusion that prejudice plays a significant part in this market. They claim that race is not a factor as such, and more information would be required in order to establish a case one way or the other. The Federal Reserve Bank of Boston attempted to obtain the necessary information by comparing additional characteristics of Hispanic and black applicants as against white applicants. A sample of just under three thousand observations was generated from all minority applicants, and a random sample of white applicants. This was done in the Boston Metropolitan Statistical Area, where minorities account for about 15 percent of the population. The data has been analysed by Alicia Munnell, Geofrey Tootell, Lynn Browne and James McEneaney. (Munnell and colleagues, '96)

It is assumed that the rate charged on loans is uniform and fixed by competition. Profits depend on this rate, which is outside the control of lenders, and on the proportion of borrowers who default, along with the costs of default. The relevant information, then, has to do with the likelihood of default and costs of default when it occurs. Where the original HMDA survey covered only the applicants race, sex, income, property location and mortgage amount, the MSA data added 38 items which were intended to cover every economic factor that the lenders in fact do consider, as well as those that, in principle, they should consider. In the study these factors are grouped under four headings; risk of default, cost of default, loan characteristics and personal characteristics.

Very briefly, and to give a flavour of the study, default risk includes items like size of the loan relative to the property value, the applicant's credit history, debt payments relative to income, and net wealth. The cost of default includes rent value and presence or absence of mortgage insurance. Loan characteristics are items like fixed or variable rates, and number of families in the house. Finally, personal characteristics are age, gender, marital status, dependants and race.

Two methods of analysing the data were employed, logit and ordinary least squares. The logit method in effect finds values for the direction and importance of each of the explanatory factors that are assumed to influence the loan granting decision. These values are chosen so that when applied together they maximise the accuracy of the prediction from the data as to whether a loan will be granted or not. This prediction from the analysis can be compared to what actually happened. In this study the result was correct in 96.3 percent of the cases. This suggests that most of the relevant factors were identified, along with the direction, positive or negative, in which they influenced the final decision. Ordinary least squares was also employed.

This method usually is more appropriate when the thing to be explained can take on a continuous range of values. It is slightly odd in this application as the dependent variable can only assume two values, loan or no loan. However, the two methods produced results which were consistent with each other, namely that race seems to exert a significant independent influence on whether or not a loan was granted.

This influence appears to be much smaller when the influence of other factors relevant to the decision to grant a loan are included. Minority applicants were found to be 18 percent more likely to have a loan application rejected than white applicants in the original HMDA study. With the additional data, black and Hispanic applicants of equal merit on other grounds were found to be 8 percent more likely to be rejected. As useful as this information is, much remains to be explained. Neither method tells us how these independent factors interact in the decision-making of lenders. They are assumed to have independent additive influences. In spite of the high degree of accuracy in predicting from the raw data whether a loan will be granted or not, there may be other variables which bear on the loan decision which have not been included.

This study finds a smaller independent effect of prejudice on housing loans than turns up in previous studies. As the authors explain, it could be that prejudice greatly influences the ability of minorities to draw on the loan market by effecting economic variables like income and unemployment history, which in turn determine the outcome of the loan decision. As a policy matter, this would suggest that affirmative action in loan granting might be one avenue for addressing the problem of prejudice. Account would have to be taken of the incentives bearing on those granting loans.

An interesting avenue of investigation, yet to be explored, is the profitability of loans to white applicants compared to loans to black and Hispanic applicants. On the assumption of profit maximisation, without prejudice on the part of lenders, all applicants would be ranked according to the profitability of lending to them and the most profitable selected up to some cut-off determined by the cost of capital. Prejudiced lenders might be assumed to have two rankings, one for white and one for black and Hispanic borrowers. Instead of equating the marginal profitability of the two types of borrowers, a higher marginal profit on loans to minorities would result. By making some robust assumptions about the relation between marginal and average profitability, this could be examined in the data.

The special housing needs of disabled elderly people has been studied by John Gilderbloom and John Markham. (Gilderbloom and Markham, '96) They undertook an impressive review of the existing literature. They also provided a detailed discussion of the American Annual Housing Survey, which appeared annually from 1973 to 1981, becoming bi-annual thereafter.

The survey provides extensive information on the characteristics of the occupants of a large sample of houses. There is evidence on both the presence of, and the desire for, such facilities as:

> Handrails. Elevator. Stair lift. Braille. Special sinks. Wheelchair usable bathroom. Easy grip telephones. Ramps. Wide doorways. Special light fittings. Push bar doors.

The analysis comes to the conclusion that the factors which contribute to greater need for these housing modifications are, living alone and poor health. In addition, men express more need than women.

From the social psychological point of view, the main interest in this study is that forty percent of the respondents with significant difficulties in everyday activities did not want to modify their houses. Why is this? Gilderbloom and Markham put forward some preliminary suggestions. The cost of modification may be seen as too high. These could be both out-of-pocket costs and costs in terms of time and energy. Modifications may be seen as lowering the value of the house, reducing the bequest that can be made to heirs. There may be an aesthetic preference which is stronger than the practical considerations involved. The disabled occupants may not trust builders to carry out the modifications effectively, and may be sceptical of their worth, even if done well.

Finally, and perhaps most importantly, the modifications may be seen as a kind of irreversible giving up. The occupants are admitting to themselves, and to others, that it is all downhill from here on. Not having the modifications is a way of not giving in to disability. This keeps hope alive, and contributes to working for improvement. An aggressive policy of 'helping' elderly people by introducing special facilities in their homes may not always be in their interests.

An elaborate study intended to see how two types of housing, mobile homes and apartments, used by low ranking military personnel living off base, effected health, marital harmony, morale and general well-being, showed very little impact from housing. Paul Paulus, Dinesh Nagar, Timothy Larey and Luz Camacho collected a great deal of data on 169 United States Army families. (Paulus and colleagues, '96) Neither the date of the investigation nor the Army base studied were identified. Both objective and subjective measures of housing quality were employed. Two-thirds of the subjects, mainly white couples, lived in rented mobile homes, and one-third, roughly equally white and black, lived in apartments.

The bottom line of an intricate statistical investigation is, "Lifestyle problems but not housing problems appear to have an influence on health, well-being, morale and harmony measures." (p. 2070) One possible explanation of little effect from two very different kinds of housing is the relatively small amount of variation in both types of housing in the subjects used in this study. We are dealing with a very homogeneous group. They all have similar work and similar income. A very interesting potential explanation of why housing appeared to have little impact has to do with choice. People are not assigned to particular apartments, or to particular mobile homes. They choose what is appropriate to their perceived needs.

This element of choice may account for why differences in housing in this study do not correlate with measures of how well things are going. That does not mean that housing is unimportant. "When degree of choice is limited, as in prison environments, fairly strong effects of environmental quality on evaluative and health related reactions are observed." (p. 2070) This reinforces the view that what matters is how the occupants see their accommodation, not how outside observers see it. If some of the military families who preferred mobile homes were in put in apartments, and vice versa, the effects of housing on well-being might be more readily measurable.

Local authority housing is the single most important element in United Kingdom housing policy. As Anne Power discusses, councils were widely believed to be the best vehicle for achieving slum clearance, and for replacing slum housing with a suitable alternative. (Power, '87) This policy consensus resulted in a series of six great waves of council house building beginning in 1918 ending in the late seventies. In addition to a controlled building programme, the Housing Act of 1977 placed a new responsibility on councils for providing emergency accommodation. Compared to the private sector, councils became much more involved in renting and in providing flats rather than houses.

Power reports that flats made up four percent of private housing and thirty-five percent of local authority housing. In her analysis, Power does not discuss the politics of the total budget for council housing, or its distribution across the country. Taking the budget as given, she looks at the problems that arose from how it was spent. Her central objective is to explain the growing disillusion with council housing which eventually extended to the Labour Party. She is also clearly interested in understanding the problems in order to find and support improved policies.

The problems with council housing are interrelated, and have an important physical dimension. Power describes the typical buildings as; "...an artificial construct of planners, aiming to unify and harmonise the built environment by creating enclaves of purpose-built housing, separate from main roads, from busy shopping centres...the desire for scale...800 dwellings or more...marooned and isolated." (p. 289) These concrete towers were not what potential tenants wanted, or even the councils themselves. The author feels strongly that they were the wrong type of building, and were located in the wrong places. Power does not go into how this allegedly tragic development came about, other than to say that, "Politicians were seduced by these "hygienic" arguments and went for the clean sweep, rather than incremental renewal." (p. 289) She does refer to Patrick Dunleavy's famous analysis of this political process. (Dunleavy, '81) Her emphasis is rather different. It is on the management issue.

The prevailing view at the time was that little management of the housing was needed, as the new housing automatically created a better environment than the slums it replaced. This was a questionable assumption. Apparently no consideration was given to the dynamic process whereby many council estates would become ghettos for ethnic minorities. The concentration of children, unemployed people, less educated and less appropriately socialised people, single parents, and so on, all grouped together created strains that could more easily be handled in a more natural, spontaneous, and mixed environment. The author argues that the heavy turnover of people, anti-social behaviour, and often poor building in the first place, resulted in a great need for management, including management of repair and maintenance.

A starting point if one wants to improve the situation is the recognition that housing needs vary so much, one household to another, and no two accommodations are the same. This calls for sensitive and varied responses, for flexibility and detailed knowledge. These are not things centralised management arrangements can provide, the point made by Devons above. The management problem appears to have been lost in the political structure. Unlike the role of the government in health and education, the Secretary of State has no authority in council housing to set and enforce standards of management.

Power concludes her analysis with an encouraging discussion of the development of estate-level management, as against management through centralisation. Objective measures of the success of local management can be found in a near doubling of repair jobs accomplished, with an average of ten jobs per worker per week on a typical estate, compared to the former rate of six per week. Other measures include a halving of the number of empty dwellings, and a reduction of the time taken to re-let dwellings from an average of fourteen weeks to two-and-a-half weeks. These objective measures of success are not the whole story. Perhaps more important is the sense of involvement and improved morale on the part of council tenants as a result of local management. The author provides a brief discussion of the costs of local management which suggests that these are no higher than with the former system of centralised management.

The concept of 'slums', the target of all public policy housing, is interesting in itself. In his analysis, Alexander von Hoffman writes about "idealistic philanthropists" and "moral reformers". (von Hoffman, '96) "They firmly believed that the slums of the city were a malevolent environment that threatened the safety, health and morals of the poor who inhabited them." (p.423) Two strands of thought intermingle here: the environmentalist view that poor buildings induce poor behaviour; and the reinforcing and self- propagating effects of a sick social nexus.

An alternative view might be that this is an unfortunate community, comparatively, and given the economic constraints its members face, the slum is the best solution. Most people would agree that if the members of the slum could command more resources, or put more directly, had more money, they would be better off. The question is what is the most efficient way of improving the life of slum dwellers. Typical housing oriented answers involve a combination of breaking up the slum community, perhaps by scattering it across the more well-off parts of cities, and by providing better accommodation.

von Hoffman outlines the responses to slums and the resulting legislation in the United States. Apart from many inherent problems with high-rise concrete housing estates, he draws attention to the distinct style, the visual impact itself, as a way of identifying the poor and the under class. He also discusses the tactic of low cost housing designed to look like middle class housing. His main point is that people were led to expect too much. "...the failures of public housing have been less in the area of housing (despite the well-publicized disasters of a minority of projects) than in the area of expectations...although few seemed to realize it, [the alleged failure] was simply that the program by itself could not solve social problems, integrate society, or usher in a new high-rise urbanism." (pp. 423 and 436)

The modern era in America begins with the Housing Division of the Public Works Administration in 1933. It lasted only to 1937. The Wagner-Steagall Housing Act of 1937 created the United States Housing Authority. It built over 100,000 units by 1942. At that point it became the National Housing Authority. The Housing Act of 1949 gave a new impetus to public housing. It did not meet its building goal of 810,000 units, but did build many houses. Coming more to the present, a dispersal policy, rather than a building programme, came out of a civil rights initiative in Chicago. Known as the Gautreaux program, the Chicago Housing Authority, with care and sensitivity, successfully relocated many residents. von Hoffman sees "housers" as being chronically over ambitious. The first Bush and Clinton administrations attempted to extend "Gautreaux" to Baltimore, Boston, Los Angeles and New York under the heading "Moving to Opportunity". Without the care of the original, these efforts have run into resistance, sometimes of a powerful kind. The delayed implementation of Gautreaux in Baltimore under the Clinton administration is an example.

von Hoffman concludes that large-scale projects, social or physical, are likely to be politically controversial. Like Anne Power, he favours flexibility and pragmatism. Also like her, he sees more hope for the future at the state level than the national level, and more hope from local government within States. Unlike Power, and without explanation, he places more emphasis on the private sector. While emphasising the market, to counter adverse market effects, he favours rent vouchers, and tax benefits such as to encourage community based non-profit housing initiatives. Just because efforts on housing have not solved all major social problems on their own, the author feels that it is important to record that many people have lived markedly better lives because of housing programmes.

Chapter Ten

RELIGION

CAUSES AND CONSEQUENCES OF BELIEF

Eileen Barker, an expert on religion, once teased her audience with the suggestion that perhaps the scientific study of religion was a contradiction in terms. She quickly stopped teasing. The phenomenon of religion can be studied scientifically. Social science is not particularly concerned with the truth or falsity of religious doctrine. Was the universe 'made' in six days, and is it five thousand years old? An honest answer from most people would express doubt about both propositions. However, there is nothing in the training of social scientists, and in the cumulated knowledge of social science, that can enable practitioners to do better than lay people with these questions. Natural science is better placed to provide answers as to the literal truth of much of religious doctrine.

It is unusual for religions to encourage critical investigation of their beliefs. Some religious propositions, those relating to god and life after death, for example, are framed in some religions in such ways that they simply cannot be investigated. Whether this is a strategy for hanging onto beliefs by avoiding all possible avenues of enquiry, or merely what the believers hold to be true, is an open question. Those versions of doctrines about god and the after-life that are amenable to objective investigation would seem to be pretty easily and firmly refuted by evidence. It may be easier to hold on to doctrines that cannot be investigated, but either way, faith, rather than critical investigation, is a feature of many religions.

Moral codes, with much in common between them, are as widespread as religion — more so, in fact, as even non-believers almost universally adhere to some moral principles. But religion is a common source of rules of behaviour, sometimes claiming to ground the ethical argument in the will of god, made manifest one way or another. The purported views of god are typically set out in an ancient text, and interpreted by appointed official experts of the religion. Philosophers continue to struggle with the nature of the feelings people have and views people hold about right and wrong. Are they arbitrary? Do they serve the needs of society? What is the content of moral codes and are we obliged to adhere to them? Again, social science, as science, has nothing to add to the enquiries of the philosophers.

Many religions have clear institutional structures. Appointed bodies have the responsibility for determining the content of doctrine. Other bodies deal with the finances of the religion in its institutional form, such as acquiring, maintaining, and disposing of property, which is often held in the form of places of worship. Money has to be raised, often from the contributions of the members of the religion, to pay officials, and frequently to engage in educational and charitable activity. Religions as institutions certainly can be studied by the social sciences. The behaviour of members of a religion can be compared to that of members of other religions, and to that of the not-affiliated portions of the community.

We can observe competition between religions, and some co-operation, and attempt to explain both. Some religions attract the better-off members of a society, and others appeal to the most disadvantaged. Given its importance in society, establishing the facts of religious affiliation, and some of the consequences, are basic tasks. Understanding causal relations surrounding religion is more demanding, but not totally out of the reach of social science. Are antagonisms between Catholics and Protestants in Northern Ireland solely due to religion, or are they related to class struggle, or historical fights over territory? The Nazis claimed they killed Jews because of their racial make-up. Did they also see a threat in their religious beliefs?

One hears phrases like, "Wall Street is his religion, and money is his God." This is almost certainly a figure of speech. But anything can be worshipped, from the rising of the sun to a chosen individual. That chosen individual may be mythical, historical, or around today. Modern religions tend to arouse hostility from old established religions, which is understandable, but also from people with no formal affiliation who can accept convents run by old religions, but would not tolerate the same institutions run by Scientologists, for example.

It is always possible to question whether a particular religion is in fact a 'genuine' religion. The motivation for claiming to be a religion may be nothing deeper than tax avoidance. As with so many social phenomena, there can be a blurred border around the territory we identify as religion.

Football clubs may have many of the attributes that are associated with some religions, such as rituals, fervour and identification. But they are not religions. Communism is not a religion, at least as I choose to use the language. It is quite clear that British Rail is not a religion, and that the Catholic Church is a religion. It is interesting that none of the many articles by social scientists in the nineties dealing with religion felt that there was any demarcation problem. In the reports below, I go along with the implicit or explicit definitions of the researchers. I have organised their work according to discipline, as in the first substantive chapter, chapter five on crime. My hope is that, having come this far, the differences between the social sciences are reasonably clear. Grouping the articles on religion according to discipline should consolidate this picture of social science.

SOCIOLOGY

It is natural to expect religious doctrine to change with the times. Views which seemed entirely acceptable in one era might look very different in another. At the same time, it is difficult for a religion to change its doctrine. The status of cherished beliefs as something divine means that adjustment calls for persuasive diplomacy, if not slight of hand. The example of controversy over women priests in the Church of England is revealing. Alan Aldridge attempts to use the concept of grid and group, developed by Mary Douglas, to explain the eventual acceptance of women priests in the Anglican Church. (Aldridge, '94)

The term 'group' refers to the sharpness of the boundary separating a particular aggregate from the rest of society. 'Grid' refers to the rigidity and extent of the internal hierarchy. Aldridge pictures the centre ground as a "power struggle" between the "accommodationist" camp who tend to be found toward the higher reaches of both grid and group, and the "exclusivist" camp, who score high on the group dimension but low on grid. The latter favour a tight knit, homogeneous, undifferentiated hierarchy. In keeping with tradition, this is a concept of leadership made up of male priests and bishops.

The two camps, accommodationist and exclusionist, have very different attitudes towards a career in the Church. Exclusionists are hostile to the concept of a career as such. They think more in terms of a sacred calling. The accommodationist camp has a mental model of people being drawn into the Church and moving on to more responsible jobs in it as they develop the necessary abilities. As the two camps share the same stance with respect to group, the author attempts to explain the different views taken on women priests in terms of grid. One wonders whether the grid concept can capture the struggle between the male dominated, sacred calling philosophy, as against the careerist church philosophy.

However tense any debate may become, an accomodationist church is unlikely to expel dissenters. It has a place for them, even if that place is not in the "centre". Aldridge sees the traditionalists as being low grid, and displaying a typical low grid response to the proposal of allowing women priests. This response includes a fear of "both conspiracy and pollution". (p. 506) The author sees the key development, which led to a vote in favour of women priests, as being the collapse of the Anglo-Catholic and Evangelical alliance. The Evangelical group moved into the accommodationist centre. Exactly why this happened, or how it relates to grid, is not clear.

The author reports voting figures on allowing women priests for the years 1978, 1984, 1987, 1988 and 1992. The trend is towards increased acceptance of women priests. The author urges caution in using the figures, as both the context in which the debate took place, and the actual wording of the motion being voted on, changed over time. Nevertheless, we can see a fairly clear picture in the votes of the Bishops being more keen, compared to the Clergy and the Laity. The attempt at using theory to explain these events is laudable. Whether the particular theory employed is up to the task must be open to question.

Grace Davie has done a large-scale study of the place of religion in Britain in the '80s. (Davie, '90) She is interested in both religious observance and in the inner beliefs that people hold. Acquiring and interpreting data on both of these is not easy. Davie sees a puzzle, or a 'paradox' as she calls it, of British religious life, similar to that in much of Europe, in that the majority profess to believe, but only a minority outwardly practice a religion. She begins her daunting survey, which can only be sketched in here, with a quote from a survey done by N. Abercrombie and his colleagues in 1970. In answer to the question, "Do you believe in a God who can change the course of events on earth?", one respondent replied, "No, just the ordinary one". (p.395) The importance of various kinds of ambivalence in religious views and behaviour runs through this investigation. Among other considerations, Davie wants to explain why religious institutions enjoyed "a higher profile" in the '80s than their numerical membership would suggest.

One might have thought that church membership would be a relatively straightforward statistic, but this is not the case. Membership is not the same as attendance at services, or making financial contributions, and can mean quite different things to different religious institutions, and to their followers. The meaning of 'membership' also changes over time. Davie is cautious about the figures, but feels that the best picture we have comes from the *UK Christian Handbook 1989/90* complied by P. Brierly. This source indicated that 15% of adults in the United Kingdom in 1987 claimed membership in a Christian church, down from 21% in 1970. England had the lowest proportion with 11%, and Northern Ireland the highest with 75%. Membership in the Church of England was just under the two million mark, and Roman Catholic membership was just over. The total membership of the other Christian religions taken together, at 2,709,014 was roughly half a million above the Catholics in 1987.

Turning to the non-Christian religions, the Jews have been holding steady at around the one hundred thousand mark. Hindus and Buddhists have had a three and a four-fold increase in membership over the years 1970 to 1987. Muslims have grown nearly four-fold to 900,000. Satanists have enjoyed over a ten-fold increase to 16,000 members. (p. 403) Membership is far from evenly spread across the country. And older, middle class women figure more prominently in membership than their proportion in the population generally.

Membership is one thing, but as Davie explains, "...nominal allegiance is the most prevalent form of religious attachment..." (p. 400) Here we find that three quarters of UK citizens have some religious affiliation, and 65% nominally adhere to a Christian religion. By far the largest religion on this count is Church of England, which can claim one in four of the adult population.

In her discussion of religious belief in the United Kingdom, Davie relies on a survey of 1,600 people in Leeds which she undertook with G. Ahern (Ahern and Davie, '87), and on the report of the *European Value Systems Study Group* (M. Abrams and colleagues, '85). The EVSSG study collected questionnaires from 1,200 people. In both studies all sorts of questions were asked about 'the meaning of life', 'attitudes towards death', 'God is important in my life', and so on. The results for the United Kingdom were similar to those for Europe as a whole; three quarters say they believe in God; about four percent are confirmed atheists; roughly half see themselves as religious people, engage in prayer, and draw strength and comfort from religion. The author appears to concur with earlier rather confusing conclusions that belief tends to be associated with "superstitious" belief, and attending church is "antithetical" to superstition. (p. 406)

The research concludes by considering the political role of religions in the United Kingdom. The first point is that it is hard to see how the spokespersons of any religion can claim to speak for the nation as a whole. In particular, the Church of England has taken stands on such matters as housing, the Falklands conflict, the National Health Service and education. (p.410) Of course, any group can enter the public debate and argue its corner. It would seem that Davie is puzzled by the apparent success of the C of E in doing this. She attributes it, in part at least, to the very Englishness of that institution, and judges its prominence in debate as being "deserved". (p. 419) In fairness, this is really an aside, but if it were to be taken seriously, it would call for investigation. Davie does make a case for anticipating greater authority of the other religions in Europe. This might be rather self- evident. On balance, I see the contribution of this paper as being more in the statistical picture it summarises than in other conclusions.

Michael Winter and Christopher Short do not entirely agree with the picture that Grace Davie presents of religion in Britain. (Winter and Short, '93) They characterise her position, in summary, as holding that the dominant pattern is 'believing without belonging'. Winter and Short suggest that a more accurate summary would be 'believing and belonging'. The difference turns on the interpretation of 'belonging'. Davie has a rather objective measure, including attendance at services and things of that kind. Winter and Short employ a more subjective concept of belonging.

The authors conducted 489 face-to-face interviews in Durham, Gloucester, Lincoln, Southwell and Truro over the period 1988 and 1990. One sample was randomly selected from electoral roles, and one was randomly selected from the Anglican Church's electoral roles. In many important respects there was not much difference in response between the two groups. Winter and Short believe that their findings for rural England tend to apply in urban areas as well. They attempt to employ a more realistic and significant concept of belonging than simply relying on official membership or attendance. While two-thirds of the people in their study did not attend Sunday service, other tests of belonging did show a certain kind of commitment. (p. 341) The evidence for this commitment, or belonging, came mainly from asking about belonging in a non-directive way, and from asking questions about turning to a minister for help.

Davie's method has the potential danger of classifying as not belonging some people who in fact have strong subjective feelings towards a religion. As it happens, most of the Winter and Short study relates to the Anglican Church. The danger of their approach is that unless someone comes out and explicitly rejects the religion into which they were born, so to speak, they may be classified as belonging. The authors quote a study by C.R. Hinings which also found high levels of belonging, but 'not belonging' was described as, "...would admit to having no denominational affiliation." (p. 640) The heart of the Winter and Short study is the answer that people gave to the question to the effect, though not generally in those words, 'Do you belong to a church, denomination or religion?' Except for the thirty-five to forty-four age group, where 84% said 'yes', generally about 90% gave a positive response to this enquiry.

In some ways more revealing is the Winter and Short investigation into whether the respondent might turn to the clergy for assistance. Around sixty percent of the general sample said 'yes' when it came to illness, marriage and bereavement. Few would turn to the clergy on financial or relationship problems. This last sits a bit oddly with the marriage answer, but as that was coupled with baptism and confirmation; it most probably has more of a ritual context. The sample of respondents taken from Church rolls showed the same pattern, but higher levels of seeking out the clergy. Of course, these are questions of principle. When asked if they had actually turned to the clergy for assistance, 26% of the general sample said yes, and 43% of the Church roll sample said yes. We would expect the 'actual' to be lower than the 'potential', as anyone who actually turned to the clergy for help would be unlikely to say they would not take that action. And some of the potentials may not as yet have had the need to avail themselves. Nevertheless, the big difference between actual and 'would you' is striking. The authors conclude with a very interesting contrast between attenders and non-attenders. The latter placed much more emphasis on the traditional qualities of the Church, and its "Englishness".

We might expect different religions to engender different attitudes on moral issues in their adherents. Bernadette Hayes has studied attitudes on morality among Christians in Britain, and made comparisons with those who were not affiliated to a religion. (Hayes, '95) She distinguishes the non-affiliated subjects between 'independent apostates', who are currently not members of a religion, but come from a family with religious membership, and 'stable independents', non-members whose families were also non-members. The religious categories employed are Anglican, other Protestant and Roman Catholic. The data come from the British Social Attitudes Survey, 1989, which used a stratified sample of just under three thousand respondents. A little over one thousand of these could be used for this exercise.

The moral issues the author studied were: attitudes towards AIDS victims; public acceptance of homosexuals; adoption by homosexuals; conventional and unconventional artificial insemination; and pornography. Along with religious affiliation, or the lack of it, a number of demographic and related variables were used to attempt to account for attitudes on these questions of morality. These other factors were:

Gender Age Education Occupation
Employed/Unemployed Political Party Affiliation.

The results show a consistent pattern of a statistically significant less tolerant, or more conservative and less liberal stance, on the part of those identifying with a religion compared to those who do not. However, though religious membership exerts an independent influence on attitudes towards moral issues, it is not the most important factor. Younger people are more open minded on these matters, to put it that way. Much of the observed relationship between church membership, or not, and moral attitudes comes about because young people are both more tolerant, and less inclined to be members of churches. Youth is not all of it. Within any age band, the members of churches are less liberal in their attitudes compared to non-members. Though the results are statistically significant, the effects of religious membership are not large. The proportion of people holding conservative views might be seven percent higher, comparing Anglicans to Stable Independents, on the issue of homosexual adoption, for example.

A related study was conducted by Nancy Davis and Robert Robinson in the United States. (Davis and Robinson, '96) Their starting point is a widely accepted view in America in political debate, and in the press generally, that America is divided sharply along lines separating religious opinions from other opinions. They question this view very heavily, and see it as a threat to a more realistic and productive consideration of a number of issues. In brief, they find significant differences between the keenly religious and the rest when it comes to family related issues of sexuality and educating children, but not on matters of race and economic issues. One could argue that the politics of "the great divide" along lines of religion can only survive by elevating the importance, and the appropriateness for political debate, of family and personal matters, as against broader political concerns.

Davis and Robinson drew on the National Opinion Research Center's Survey for 1991. This survey included 1,517 individuals over eighteen years of age, and not in an institution. A high proportion, 1,359 individuals, also filled out a Social Survey Program Module which had to do with religious beliefs. Three elements went into this part of the study. People were asked to rank their view of the Bible from being "an ancient book of fables", through to "the actual word of God". Similarly, they ranked degrees of agreement or disagreement with the statement, "The course of our lives is decided by God." The final element was a ranking on the assertion, "Right and wrong should be based on God's laws." In addition, respondents were asked to scale themselves on attending religious services. The range went from zero, meaning never attend, to eight, meaning attend more than once a week. The subjects were classified into either: one of five Protestant categories; as Catholic; as Jewish; or "other", which included no religion. Demographic variables used in the study were age, occupation, race, education, and urban/rural.

The results of ordinary least square regressions showed that those who are more religious hold noticeably different views than the less religious members of the study. They tend to: oppose the Supreme Court ruling against required Bible prayer in state schools; oppose sex education in state schools; oppose making birth control available to teenagers; and oppose sex outside marriage. There are also significant differences when it comes to gender roles. The more religious subjects favour keeping women in the home and out of politics. So far, the results support the popular view of the "great divide". However, when it came to issues of racial equality, there was no significant difference between the two groups on such matters as intermarriage, bussing, affirmative action, and so on. Even more strikingly, when it came to some economic issues, such as governmental responsibility for providing jobs, spending more on Social Security and union recognition, the religious group were in fact more liberal. There are complications and matters of judgement in employing figures on church attendance, and on religious belief, as we have seen from the Davie study above. In spite of these problems, Davis and Robinson appear to have made their point that a simple left/right political divide along religious lines is not an accurate description of the United States.

Joseph Tamney has studied some aspects of the relation between religion conservative politics in the United Kingdom. (Tamney, '94) His focus is on the efforts of the Thatcher government to encourage religious education in schools as a means of furthering conservative political objectives. He feels that this programme was part of Tory policy, and is doomed to failure. Starting with the Education Act of 1944, which made religious instruction compulsory in primary and secondary schools, Tamney traces the history of changes in the law, and the responses of educators and others. He sees Thatcherirtes as part of a Christian Right with certain distinguishing characteristics. Important among them are attitudes which favour material advance, individualism, capitalism, and the primacy of Anglican Christianity.

The author offers four reasons why pressing for religious education in schools in the United Kingdom is unlikely to advance the Thatcherite cause. First, religious education is at least in part inconsistent with the rest of education. Second, the Conservative approach to religious education is at odds with a humanistic approach which is gaining support. Third, multiculturalism is inconsistent with enthusiastically advocating market centred values. Finally, the teachers on the ground are, on the whole, not sympathetic to the Conservative programme. Tamney offers telling quotes from Thatcher. "But it is not the creation of wealth which is wrong but love of money for its own sake. The spiritual dimension comes in deciding what one does with the wealth...The truths of the Judaic-Christian tradition are infinitely precious, not only, as I believe, because they are true, but also because they provide the moral impulse which alone can lead to that peace ...for which we all long." (pp. 198 – 199) One cannot help feeling that while the author may be right about some Conservative objectives and tactics, his analysis of the likely outcomes has more to do with hope than with analysis.

Liana Giorgi used the *European Value Survey of 1981* to compare across ten European countries affiliation with institutional religions and the more subjective question of religious feelings. (Giorgi, '92) Her interest is in the growth of secular attitudes as ways of perceiving and living in the world. The work of David Martin provides a framework for the analysis. (Martin, '78) She identifies three conjectures in his work. The first is that historical events condition the path taken by secularisation. The second is that the American pattern of Protestantism, existing in an environment of separation of church and state, has different effects from Protestantism as state religion. And the third is the potential importance of the relation between politics and religion in the growth of secular beliefs and behaviour.

The EVS measured adherence to doctrine by asking questions about such things as an absolute in good and evil, and the presence or absence of a single true religion. The degree of religious devotion was measured by questions about the importance of god in one's life, and the amount of comfort drawn from religion. The author's first objective was to use the data to make three points: religiosity is not confined to the formal religions and their members; Catholics are more involved in religion than Protestants; and the decline in church influence is not the same as a decline in religiosity. A major problem with the study is the lack of information over time, which would seem to be central to the argument. In other respects, the data can be read as consistent with Giorgi's contentions.

An interesting comparison is made between the beliefs and practices of individuals, wherever located, and of national aggregates. If we characterise countries as Catholic, mixed, or Protestant, a certain pattern of differences in church attendance, and the other considerations, emerges. If we look at individuals, wherever located, as members of different religions, the differences emerge more clearly. The author sees less coherence across countries as bearing out Martin's thesis that historical factors of culture influence the secularisation process. While France is a real exception being a Catholic country with very low church attendance — only Denmark with three percent is lower — this can be explained as "...France saw the first real secular Revolution of modern times." (p. 651)

We may wonder whether this is an explanation, or a re-statement of what we are trying to explain. The figures showing variations across countries are interesting. We see high levels of religiosity in all countries, including Denmark. But support for conjectures intended to explain the figures is only suggestive at best. The framework Martin offers is more a set of observations than a theory of religious belief and affiliation.

Church membership, and religious belief generally, have been shown to be associated with matters such as family size, marriage, divorce, childbearing and premarital sex. Most religions tend to be marriage oriented, and to discourage sex outside marriage. Arland Thornton and his colleagues have used a large data set to study the relations between religion, marriage and cohabitation in the United States. (Thornton and colleagues, '92) Their work allows for effects in both directions, with marriage and cohabitation having an influence on religious beliefs, as well as influences from religious beliefs on marriage and cohabiting.

On the order of one thousand first, second and fourth born white babies were selected from the birth records of the metropolitan area of Detroit. Either the third born were not used for some reason, or there is a typographical error in the paper. The mothers of these babies were interviewed in 1962, and again in 1963, 1966, 1977, 1980 and 1985. Quite remarkably, the investigators interviewed 92% of the mothers selected for interview in 1962, and even more amazingly they interviewed 82% of the mothers and their children in 1985. This obviously expensive study had purposes in addition to the one under discussion. The children, now followed closely over the ages fifteen to twenty-three, were asked, "Have you ever been married?" and, "Have you *ever* lived together as a partner in an intimate relationship with a (man/woman) without being married to (him/her)?" Both mothers and their children were asked about attendance at religious services. In addition, they were asked, "Quite apart from attending religious services, how important would you say religion is to you — very important, somewhat important or not important?" (p. 634)

This is a truly powerful and sophisticated statistical study, and it is a shame to have to give a sketchy report of the findings, and not go into the statistical techniques employed. It is clear from the study that religious feelings and participation influence both decisions to get married and to cohabit. There seems little doubt that young people with little religion are far more likely to cohabit. It also appears that the religious stance of the parents exerts an influence. This can come from shaping the views and religious practices of the children, as well as exerting a direct independent effect. It is interesting to note that for Catholic men there is little difference in the type and frequency of unions they enter into compared to non-fundamentalist Protestants. Religion shifts them away from cohabitation. For Catholic women, the effect of religion is to slow entry into a union, without shifting the balance between marriage and cohabiting. Both men and women who are not affiliated to a religion are 50% more likely to cohabit than religious Protestants, for example.

Looking at effects running from being in a marriage, or cohabiting, on religious behaviour, the authors found a negative effect from cohabiting.

Cohabitors who had attended religious services frequently in the past tended to reduce their attendance dramatically. Those who had little involvement with religion in the past experienced no change. Entering marriage without a previous period of cohabiting had a positive effect on religious participation. There was no discernible effect either way in the case of people who lived together and then got married. Thornton and his colleagues believe, with ample justification, that their finding regarding individual behaviour can be helpful in explaining national trends. For example, in the 1960s and 1970s there was a marked decline in the marriage rate in America and a rise in cohabiting. The authors refer to other research showing that; "...the importance and centrality of religion to Americans declined [during this period] as did confidence in religious institutions and authorities." (p. 647)

Of course, people can change their religious affiliation, going from one religion to another, or to no religion. This religious mobility has been studied more in the United States than elsewhere, but rarely has the importance of gender been taken into account. Bernadette Hayes used the British Social Attitudes Survey (Brooks and colleagues, '92) for 1991 to study this phenomenon. (Hayes, '96) This survey covers a randomly selected representative sample of United Kingdom citizens over the age of eighteen. Hayes worked with five religious categories; Catholic, Mainline Protestant, Other Protestant, Anglican, and Independent. The data were mined to see if the adults in the sample had the same, or a different religious orientation in 1991 compared to that of the childhood. It turns out that over one-third the people in the survey were 'mobile', with men at 43.7 percent being more mobile than women at 32.1 percent.

Breaking the figures down by religion, 'Independent' were the least mobile, followed by Catholics, and 'Other Protestant' being the most mobile. All religious categories were net losers from people leaving their childhood religion, with all the gains going to the Independent category, meaning the non-affiliates. The next phase of Hayes' work was an attempt to identify the factors leading to whether or not a person changes from their initial identification. As the dependent variable is either 'change' or 'no change', a logit multiple regression was used with the following long list of potentially significant variables

Gender Marital status Age Education Number of children
Whether or not one changed 'class' Manual or non manual
Employed or unemployed Spouse same religion
Parents both have the same religion Church attendance of Parents
Church attendance while a child.

From this list, five factors emerge as highly significant. These are: (1) marital status; (2) being Mainline Protestant; (3) being independent; (4) same religion as spouse; (5) being male. (1), (2) and (5) encourage mobility, while (3) and (4) discourage mobility.

One does wonder what happens over time. Will the data for the children born after 1991 place many in the "Independent" category, or does the process start all over again, with the children being brought up "Anglican", "Catholic" and so on, in spite of the 'independent' decision on the part of the parents? There is some support for this latter possibility in an informal paper by Mairi Levitt. (Levitt, '95) Her work in a small Cornish town led her to feel that mothers there felt that religion was appropriate for young children, but was less so for older children. She concludes that, "The impetus to some involvement in Christianity was a desire to give their young children the religious experiences that were part of a normal childhood... while regarding committed church goers with suspicion." (p. 535)

Similar research into people drifting away from religious affiliation, this time in the Netherlands, has been undertaken by Ariana Need and Nan Dirk De Graaf. (Need and De Graaf, '96) While church membership has been very important historically in Dutch society, the rise over time in the proportion of the population who are not church members exceeds that of other European countries by a large margin. The authors report figures for Holland as follows.

Procentage of People Without a Churche	
1930	14
1947	17
1960	21
1979	42
1990	55

This can be compared with the only two European countries with over ten percent unchurched — France with 26 percent and Belgium with 15 percent. (p. 87)

Using a cohort of 653 respondents, the authors calculated the probability that a person will leave the church in the course of a year, given that they have not left before that year. The factors used to explain the probability of defection were age, parental education, parental religious homogamy, frequency of attending services, and denomination. 186 members of the sample left their churches, the largest proportion from the nineteen to twenty-nine age bracket. Parents of different faiths doubles the chances of leaving to 46 percent if one parent has no religion, and raises it to 33 percent if they have different faiths. More education contributes to the probability of leaving. The authors speculate as to whether their results would hold for other countries. However, they are confident about the Netherlands. "The continuing process of modernization and its accompanying higher levels of education, and the increasing level of religious heterogamy make the process of secularization irreversible." (p. 97) Such confidence sometimes meets with surprises.

In the Muslim world the situation is rather different from that of the Christian countries. Here we see a rise in religious involvement. There is quite a range of views among Muslim thinkers and leaders as to whether the interactions between the religion and science, democracy, modernisation and the secular society generally are to be ones of extreme antagonism, mild rivalry, or compatibility. Kayhan Mutlu is concerned about Turkey's relations with Europe. (Mutlu, '96) The attitudes common in Islamic thinking in Turkey are likely to be critical here. To document these attitudes, the author takes as his sample university students at Ankara, including theology students. He defends the choice of students for this exercise on the grounds that the youth of today are the adults of tomorrow, and university students will be among the more powerful figures in the country. The author has interesting data comparing 1978 and 1991 in terms of the degree of religious affiliation or belief, and the essentially political stance of the students regarding the role of religion in the rest of society.

In response to questions about the existence of god, heaven and hell, resurrection, and the commandments of the Qur'an, there is little doubt that we see a significant increase in religiosity among students at Ankara, comparing the responses of the earlier sample of students with the more recent one. Where just over half accepted the existence of god in 1978, this figure rose to four-fifths by 1991. To explore the wider implications, eleven questions were added to the 1991 sample. These had the objective of determining how democratic the students were in their values. Three questions were negative in implication in the sense that agreement indicated opposition to democratic values. An example would be, "Political decisions must be made in accordance with Islamic principles." Two-thirds of the students disagreed. A similar proportion agreed with the proposition, "Secularism must be continued in Turkey". (p. 356) All this leads the author to conclude that the rise in religious belief in Turkey is not a threat to democracy, and particularly that Turkey can suitably join the European Community.

SOCIAL PSYCHOLOGY

We begin this section with research in which the religious element is secondary, but still significant. Sheryl Peck has studied the cluster of views, from a 'liberal to conservative' perspective, which were held by a sample of seventy Evangelical or Fundamentalist Protestants in Los Angeles County in the United States. (Peck, '96) Her work follows on from work by F.N. Kerlinger on the consistency of views people hold, looked at from a political point of view.(Kerlinger, '72, and Kerlinger and colleagues, '76) The basic conjecture which Kerlinger entertained was that people who were in favour of 'conservative' views could fairly reliably be predicted to be opposed to 'liberal' views. When he came to test this proposition with real life subjects, it was quite convincingly refuted, and on more than one occasion. The reason he gave was that his subjects were probably too middle of the road. The consistency he sought might be more apparent if the subjects were chosen from a more extreme end of the political spectrum.

Peck chose to work with what is called a "biased sample" to see if Kerlinger's expectations emerged in that case. She felt that Evangelical and Fundamentalist Protestants, who both can be readily identified with the "new Christian right", satisfied the required extreme position. She gives a very brief description of her method, but it appears that respondents were asked to score themselves as to agreement or disagreement with a number of propositions drawn from a combination of two surveys, the Moral Majority Scale and the Moral Majority and Politics Scale. (Georgiana, '89 and Merllon and Wilcox, '86) These contain questions like the following.

Do you approve of mandatory prayer in public schools?
Should homosexuals be allowed in the military?
Would you favour decreased spending on welfare?
Do you agree that Judeo-Christian values will help solve the world's problems?
Should creationism be taught in public schools?
Should abortion be allowed to terminate a pregnancy caused by rape?
Do you agree that the government should protect minorities from discrimination?

Peck drew on the relevant literature to classify assertions as liberal or conservative. For example, "...'mandatory prayer in public school' was considered conservative, and 'homosexuals should be allowed to serve in the military' was considered liberal." (p. 642) The results of the study showed quite clearly that individual liberal items associate very closely with a widely agreed construct of what constituted liberalism, and similarly with respect to conservatism. What the data failed to support was a negative association between the liberal and conservative constructs. This fits in with the findings of the sociologist Hayes in Britain and sociologists Davis and Robinson in America.

The author offers two possible explanations of why the expected negative correlation using a 'biased' sample failed to materialise. One possibility is that while the sample, which came from church groups generally believed to be uniformly and strongly conservative, might in fact have been more middle-of-the-road and not sufficiently biased to provide a valid test of the theory. The second explanation is that the theory is in fact false when applied to the right. Peck suggests that, "...it is possible that only samples biased to the left and not to the right show a negative correlation between liberal and conservative items." (p. 644) But of course this has not been demonstrated.

A number of researchers have been interested in whether there is a relation between active involvement in religion and personality. Francis and Wilcox investigated this question working with a sample of sixteen to eighteen year old English girls. (Francis and Wilcox, '94) Using Eysenk's model of personality, they came to the conclusion that there was no relation between church attendance and prayer, as indices of religiosity, and extroversion and neuroticism. They did find a negative relation with 'psychoticism'.

John Maltby set out to replicate the results of the study by Francis and Wilcox. He worked with a sample of ninety-two female university students in Ohio. The results of this experiment are essentially the same. Prayer and church attendance, both measured on five point scales from "never" to "daily" and "never" to "once a week or more", were found to be highly correlated with each other. Personality was assessed using a shortened version of the Revised Eysenk Personality Questionnaire. (Francis and colleagues, '92) And while there appears to be no relation between either neuroticism or extroversion and religious behaviour, prayer and church attendance are significantly negatively associated with psychoticism. In terms of Eysenck's theory of social attitudes, greater concern with religion emerges as a 'tender-minded' attitude, in the tough/tender dichotomy.

Church attendance is also of interest to Michael Siegrist, but in his work the concern is with attitudes towards suicide, rather than with personality. (Siegrist, '96) An active literature centring on the work of Durkheim postulates that religion discourages suicide. Many studies have examined the possible differential effects of different denominations. In some cases the expected relation failed to be seen in the data. Siegrist suggests that crude figures of religious affiliation, without taking account of whether the person is an active participant in the religion, may be misleading. He also feels that extending investigation beyond the over represented American data can be important.

No new data gathering was required for this study, as the author was able to draw on data from a representative sample of 1,133 men and 1,096 women in West Germany conducted by G. Schmidtchen. (Schmidtchen, '92) In their study the authors are trying to account for attitudes towards suicide, rather than suicide itself. Among the many questions put by Schmidtchen and his researchers to their sample of fifteen to thirty-year old Germans was, "In really hopeless situations, I would not rule out suicide as a last option for myself personally." (p. 561) Respondents were asked to approve or disapprove of this proposition.

The subjects were either Protestants, Catholics or not religious. The first two groups were asked if they attended church "now and then" or more, or "seldom", or "never". Other independent variables were suicide of an acquaintance, gender and education. The results were that the non-religious respondents were more sympathetic to suicide, the Catholics unsympathetic, and Protestants in the middle. The church attendance variable was also significant. Those people who rarely or never went to church were more open to the idea of suicide than those who attended more frequently. Gender was not a predictor, but education and knowing an acquaintance who had committed suicide made respondents more sympathetic to suicide.

When interactions between variables were taken into account, a more complex picture emerged. For the frequent churchgoer, the suicide of an acquaintance made them more open to suicide, but for the infrequent churchgoer it made them less open. In so far as knowing someone who committed suicide contributed to a more positive attitude towards it, Siegrist entertains two explanations, and cannot discriminate between them. One is that maybe the respondent and the acquaintance shared a common culture which was open to suicide, and the fact that an acquaintance actually took that step was of little significance. Alternatively, the example set by the acquaintance might make the act seem more "legitimate".

Social psychologists like John Greer have studied the role and significance of religion in society, and examined the extent to which, if at all, there is a trend towards a more secular society. (Greer, '90) Working with respondents in Northern Ireland means that religious affiliation is particularly significant. "In Northern Ireland, a social identity is acquired by young people who are under great pressure to see themselves as members of one or another ethnic group…" (p. 579) Greer administered questionnaires to large numbers of Protestant sixth-form pupils over twenty years. The samples were drawn as follows.

Northern Ireland Sample

Year	No.of Schools	No.of Boys	No.of Girls	Total
1968	42	991	640	1,631

1978	35	1,090	781	1,871
1988	28	1,190	1,213	2,403

Questions were put on concepts of God, allegiance to denomination, gambling, sex, need to attend church, the Bible, war, and other related matters. Both girls and boys showed a tendency towards more religious belief over the years, and at all times girls were more religious than boys. The most salient finding was the complexity of the picture.

For quite a range of questions there was no significant change comparing 1968 to 1988. But a number of questions, which could broadly go under the label of religious belief, showed a significant increase, as well as movement towards more orthodox belief. And then four items showed significant decline. These were:

Helpfulness of the Bible
Churchch attendance
Private payer
Premarital intercourse

This is a fairly familiar result, which can be seen in a number of countries, of noticeable decline in the readily observable features of religion like attendance at church, combined with statements indicating more belief in religion. The author does not attempt to explain the change in sexual morality. On one reading he simply records it as a fact. "Such a change in sexual morality is indicative of a more permissive society, and the adoption of a less strict moral code by Protestant sixth-form pupils in Northern Ireland." (p. 578) An alternative reading of the data could be that young students are responding to changes in behaviour on the part of adults, while retaining, and even enhancing, religious faith, perhaps, in part, as a means of coping with the violence in Northern Ireland.

John Greer and Leslie Francis teamed up to investigate the role of "religious experience" in shaping religious attitudes. (Greer and Francis, '92) The authors do not say anything very helpful about what constitutes a religious experience. The sample in this study involved 2,133 students from the age of twelve to seventeen. Respondents are described as having had, or not having had such an experience. About one-third of the boys and two-thirds of the girls in Catholic schools indicated that they had had a religious experience. For students in Protestant schools the comparable percentages, at 31% and 39%, were lower and closer together.

An index of attitude towards Christianity was constructed from a twenty-four item Likert scale with questions on belief, prayer, church attendance and the like. The idea was to see if having a religious experience had a significant effect on religious stance. The results of regression analysis showed that if you took account of gender, church attendance, personal prayer, and belief in god, having had a 'religious experience' added little to explaining the scores on attitude towards Christianity. One might query treating religious experience as an independent variable. Would it not be more likely for the more devout students to have such experiences, or to interpret all sorts of experiences in a religious way? The causal connections could be quite complex.

As discussed above, social psychologists have searched for relationships between aspects of involvement in religion and personality traits. An interesting example is a possible relation between prayer and self-esteem. The studies so far have produced very mixed results. One study finds a positive association, one a negative association, and one no relation. Leslie Francis and Darryl Gibbs have responded to this conflicting literature with a study of their own. (Francis and Gibbs, '92). The authors work with a United Kingdom sample of 82 boys and 84 girls aged eight to eleven. Sixty-three were not affiliated, and the rest belonged to a Christian church. They used the Coopersmith Self-Esteem Inventory. (Coopersmith, '81) Frequency of prayer was measured on a five level scale from "never" to "daily".

A priori one can imagine that people troubled by low self-esteem might resort to prayer, and equally that positive relationships support self-esteem, and prayer could be thought of as a positive relationship with God. The upshot of the Francis/Gibbs investigation of prayer and self-esteem was no relation between the two. Additional work might attempt to determine why some authors found the same lack of relationship, and others found different results. It could be that the theories of both negative and positive relations are valid, but only if we are dealing with for correctly specified samples of respondents.

A large literature deals with various aspects of the relations between religiosity and work norms. Some studies concentrate on entitlement. Abraham Sagie has investigated the obligations associated with work, and the different views on this matter held by religious and non-religious workers. (Sagie, '93) He works with a sample of 102 male university students in Israel. Half were religious and half not at all. Sagie constructed what he called a Work Situations Questionnaire with fifteen questions. Respondents rated themselves on a five-point scale from minimal obligation to maximal obligation. A sample of test items follows:

Being honest with clients
Allowing non-work-related activities to interfere with job performance
Reimbursing money when prices are lowered
Using a company car for private travel

Working with a supplier who commits tax evasion
Tasting merchandise

Some of these items were classified as implying "intrinsic", or moral obligations, and others as "extrinsic", or contractual obligations. Means and variances of the religious and non-religious groups were calculated and tested for statistically significant differences. The results were pretty straightforward. "...it may be concluded that the religious individuals had a stronger sense of both intrinsic and extrinsic obligation than their non-religious colleagues did and that the difference in intrinsic obligation between the two groups was greater than the difference in extrinsic obligation." (p. 534) It seems plausible that the two groups of students would show less difference when it came to contractual obligations.

The model the author has in mind calls for a direct influence of obligation, and entitlement, on work behaviour. He reasons that the religious ethic indirectly influences behaviour through a primary bearing on obligation, and a secondary bearing on entitlement. This is in contrast to "Western humanism", which has a primary bearing on entitlement, and a secondary bearing on obligation. Three of the test examples used by the author failed to meet the general result. He attributes this to all three being extrinsic. "...the obligation norm in these three situations was based on values other than the Jewish religious ethic." (p.535) Sagie appeals to a kind of balance. If secular norms are strong, the religious influence will be weak, and if the secular message is ambiguous, the religious influence will be strong.

Social identity theory makes predictions as to how members of a social grouping will perceive the status of members of a different grouping. These evaluations are expected to vary, depending on the 'within-group' status of the person making an evaluation. Drawing on this theory, Louk Hagendoorn and Roger Henke conducted a complex study of how Hindus and Muslims in Northern India perceived each other. (Hagendoorn and Henke, '91) The exercise suffered from significant shortages of data, but did achieve some positive results. Considering a 'two status' set-up — in this example membership in the same or the other religion, and high or low status within one's religious grouping — social identity theory predicts that: (a) high status individuals will view high status members of the 'other' religion as being of lower rank than members of their own religion; (b) high status individuals will view low status members of the other religion well below low status members of their own religion; (c) low status individuals will view high status individuals of the other religion as being above the low status members of the other religion, and as being above members of their own religion.

The picture gets more complicated when there is more than one status indicator applying within a grouping. For example, some individuals may have a mixed status in the sense of little money, but a more privileged status on other grounds. The theory predicts that mixed status individuals will rank members of the other religion below members of their own religion. When there are two dimensions, such as wealth and status, the other group will be viewed less favourably than when there is one dimension. The authors attempted to test all these conjectures with data drawn from 317 high school students in Banares and Mughalserai in Northern India. Banares has a Muslim minority and has been the scene of riots. Mughalserai has a substantial low caste Hindu population and very few Muslims. It has not been subject to rioting. (p. 253)

Hagendoorn and Henke worked with questionnaires which were administered in three elite schools and six ordinary school in Banares, and six ordinary schools in Mughalserai. The students to invited to apply sixteen adjectives to high and to low status Hindus and Muslims. They were asked to judge whether the adjective was unsuitable, neutral or appropriate. The adjectives were drawn from a study of social identity done by E. Ghosh and M. Huq where they were found to be relevant. (Ghosh and Huq, '85) Taking the evaluation by high caste Hindus first, the results bear out the expectations of social identity theory. The ordering is their own group, which is high caste Hindus, ranks highest, Hindu low caste come next, Muslim high status next, and low status Muslim ranked the lowest. Exactly the same pattern, in terms of own group and other group ordering, is found with high-class Muslim respondents.

While high-ranking individuals reacted as the theory predicted, the authors found that both the low caste Hindus and the lower class Muslims failed to meet the predicted pattern. This is in contrast to what some other investigators have found. They found that lower class Muslims evaluate Hindus less positively than other Muslims. Hagendoorn and Henke see this "communalized" response, as they call it, as consistent with Islamic rejection of the caste system. (p. 258) On the 'mixed status' front, the research suggested that high caste Hindus with little money gave a low ranking to Muslims regardless of their social status. Often these results rest on unfortunately small numbers of respondents. However, the main point of the study seems to gain support. Further work is necessary, both to formulate predictions, and to test them, especially where people can be of mixed ranking, high in wealth but low in status, or low in wealth but high in status.

It is understandable that religious groups can see themselves as in some competition with other religions. Taking a different question, we might ask how religion affects views of other people who differ from oneself in ways not involving religion. Perhaps naively, and very simply, one might take it that religion would tend to promote a more caring and sympathetic view of other people, and so lead to a more tolerant stance towards gays and lesbians, for example. This is especially the case if one takes the view that sexual orientation is a matter of personal preference, and that there is nothing immoral about homosexual activity. A large literature explores the attitude of believers towards homosexuals and fails to find a generally tolerant attitude. It does appear that religions differ in the attitudes they engender, and that the kind of relation a person has towards his or her religion also matters.

Three types of relation are identified in the literature. The 'extrinsic' believer uses religion to achieve goals involving personal advantage. The 'intrinsic' believer cares about religion for its own sake. And finally, the 'quest' believer is self-critical, open-ended and questioning. These categories were developed by C. Bateson and his colleagues in connection with religion and racial prejudice. (Bateson and colleagues, '78) Randy Fisher and his colleagues conducted two experiments aimed to provide additional evidence on the relations between religion and sexual prejudice. (Fisher and colleagues, '94) The first involved a random sample selected from the Florida telephone directory. When the person answering the phone was found to be suitable, that is, an adult voter and prepared to take part, they were interviewed over the telephone by the researchers. The second study employed an eight-page questionnaire filled in by University students in Florida.

In the telephone study the respondents were told about a bi-sexual deputy sheriff who was fired because of his sexual orientation and was bringing a case for wrongful dismissal. Then they were asked four types of questions. The first had to do with the trial, such as, "Do you believe that questioning Woodard (the plaintiff) about his private sexual behavior was justified or an unwarranted invasion of his privacy?". The second set were demographic in nature — age, marital status, education and so on. The third were specifically concerned with attitudes towards gays. Do you agree that, "Homosexual behavior between two men is just plain wrong." And the final group of questions had to do with religious orientation, including denomination and frequency of attending services. (p. 519)

The data was collected from 175 women and 109 men. About a quarter were not religious. The religions represented in the study were as follows.

	Percent
Christian (reported)	8.5
Fundamentalist	2.4
Baptist	20.1
Protestant	11.2

(either) Methodist, Episcopalian, or Presbyterian	18.4
Catholic	23.1
Jewish	1.4
Lutheran	3.4

The results were consistent with those found in the previous literature. Members of certain denominations tend to be more intolerant of homosexuals than other denominations. Baptists, fundamentalists, and 'Christians' as a self-identified general category, were more intolerant. Those with some history of tolerance were treated as a single category in the analysis. They are Catholics, Methodists, Presbyterians, Jews, Episcopalians and, again, 'Protestants' as a self-identified general category. The results were quite striking. "Persons with some religious preferences(i.e., Baptists and fundamentalists) tend to be relatively prejudiced against gays, whereas persons with other religious preferences (Catholics, Jews, and many Protestant denominations) tend to be relatively accepting of gays, but generally less accepting than those who report no religious preference." (p. 623) Distinguishing between members of religions generally found to be more anti-homosexual, the frequent attenders at religious services were found to be particularly prejudiced.

The questionnaire study the authors submitted to students in Florida had three sets of questions. The first was primarily demographic, but included a question on whether the respondent had homosexual friends or co-workers. The second section was on religious orientation — denomination, seriousness, and attendance at services. It included questions aimed at detecting intrinsic, extrinsic and quest leaning and was based on Batson's investigations. The third section drew on scales devised by G. Herek on Attitudes Towards Lesbians, Attitudes Towards Gays and Attitude Functions Inventory. (Herek, '87) An additional index was constructed specifically to measure attitude towards the deputy who lost his job through being bi-sexual. There was a high degree of correlation between this index and the Herek measures.

In this part of the research, aimed primarily at the extrinsic-intrinsic-quest part of the relationship between religious orientation and prejudice, those respondents without a religious orientation were eliminated from the study. Again, the results here are consistent with earlier literature. "...prejudice towards gays and lesbians is greatest in those who describe themselves as more religious and attend religious services more frequently. Such prejudice is also positively correlated with scores on both the Internal and External scales. Only scores on the quest scale are negatively correlated with prejudice towards gays and lesbians." (p.627) The authors conclude by raising interesting questions about causality. One might infer that much of religion is not inclined to inculcate a tolerant attitude, at least when it comes to homosexuals. An alternative view might be that socially conservative individuals are drawn to religion, and bring with them their hostility towards gays and lesbians. Fisher and his colleagues suggest some possibilities for future research designed to distinguish between these conjectures. This research could place emphasis on a dynamic element tracking how attitudes change.

The last article in this section deals with a popular topic, the relationship between religiosity and attitudes towards pre-marital sex. The research of Paschal Sheeran and his colleagues follows on from a large and complex set of findings. (Sheeran and colleagues, '93) The work that came before is generally inconclusive, and sometimes contradictory, probably due to a variety of factors. A common problem is the use of university students as the subjects. In this area they may be particularly unrepresentative. Then there is the problem that any group may be reluctant to answer questions on sexual matters, and may deliberately falsify their answers. As other studies of religion have shown, there are many dimensions to religiosity. These include denomination, degree of activity, and how the participant thinks of religion.

Sex, as some distinguished figures have pointed out, is an ambiguous term. Some studies define it solely in terms of coitus. It is also the case that attitudes towards sexual activity may vary according to whether the respondent is thinking only about himself or herself, or is expressing an opinion on the views and the behaviour of others. The authors are very aware of these many problems and hope that their empirical work improves on previous investigations. (pp. 39 – 42)

The data for this study came from earlier research on AIDS which was done by many of the same investigators as the present work. (Abraham, '91) A postal survey with a 64 percent usable response rate resulted in 201 male replies, 319 female replies, and 7 failed to specify. A number of people were eliminated from the 690 returns because of being married, or either had or were expecting children. Some respondents failed to supply adequate information on religious orientation. The ages of the group investigated fell between 15 and 20 years inclusive, with a mean of 16.8 years. Sexual attitudes were assessed with six questions of the types; "It is a good idea to get sexual experience before settling down", and, "I would only have sexual intercourse with someone I was married to". Agreement, or disagreement, with these propositions was measured on a six point Likert scale. Social judgements in the sexual realm were also measured by the phrase: "A young woman (man) who changes her male (female) partner a number of times during the year is..." followed by four possible endings. These were:

Irresponsible generally popular among both sexes
lacking in self-respect attractive to the opposite sex in general.

Agreement or disagreement with each of the four endings was specified as "not at all", "slightly", "moderately", "very" and "extremely".

Another section of the questionnaire dealt with behaviour rather than attitudes. The following five questions were asked:

How many people, if any, have you had sex with in your life?
Do you think you are likely to have sex with someone during the next year?
How often have you had sexual intercourse?
How often in the past year have you had a sexual experience without having sexual intercourse?
How often in the past year have you had sexual intercourse? (p. 43)

The authors measured religious orientation in a variety of ways. First people were asked if they had been brought up "according to a religion". If the answer was 'yes', they were asked to specify the denomination. They were also asked to give a yes/no answer to the question, "Would you say that, personally, you are religious?". Next came a quantitative answer on how often they attended services. Finally, a five point Likert scale, ranging from "strongly disagree" to "strongly agree", was applied to the proposition, "Religious beliefs would influence my decisions about sex." (p. 42) Interesting alternatives to the word 'would', might be 'do', or possibly, 'should'. Of course we do not know if these alternative would have influenced the results. Just over 40 percent of the sample had a religious upbringing, with roughly equal numbers of Catholics and Protestants. Other religions were not represented enough to be statistically useful. Half the sample were virgins. While a third had fewer than three partners, one respondent had thirty partners, or at least claimed that number. (p. 43)

Earlier research by K. King and his colleagues held the view that religious attitudes are associated with attitudes about sex, and religious behaviour is associated with sexual behaviour. (King and colleagues, '76, pp. 535 – 639) The present study by Sheeran and his colleagues did not support this result. On the contrary, what the authors call the "self-attitude/self-schema" formulation of religious attitude turned out to be the best predictor of both sexual behaviour and sexual attitudes. (p. 50) It was the case that the six different measures of religious orientation tended to move together. Having a positive rating on one is likely to be associated with positive ratings on the others, and vice versa. In this sample of respondents, sexual attitudes and sexual behaviour were strongly associated, each to the other. Neither sexual attitudes nor sexual behaviour were as closely associated with religious identity as they were with each other.

Openness about sexual matters, or lack of embarrassment, was tested by eliciting agreement or disagreement on a Likert scale to the statement, "Sexual matters should not be spoken about in public." There was more agreement with this statement from Catholics than from Protestants, though not a great deal from the former. This result ran across all the findings. The relationship between sex and religion was weaker in Protestants than in Catholics.

The researchers found that personal sexual standards, and attitudes towards the sexual behaviour of other people, are correlated with each of the six measures of religious orientation the study employed, when taken one at a time. This nicely illustrates the care needed in statistical investigation. We know that the six measures relate to each other. So, taken one at a time, they will most likely relate to sexual matters in roughly the same way. However, when all six measures are correlated with personal sexual standards, for example, in a simultaneous exercise, only self-attitude, church attendance, and 'identity salience' were found to have an effect. It would seem that the other three appear to have an effect through their association with these three measures of religiosity.

Some of the results the authors found with respect to the status of 'virginal' were as expected. Church attendance, and a positive religious self-attitude, were seen in the data as contributing to remaining a virgin. However, once the effect from self-attitude is taken into account, church attendance has no independent effect. A surprising result was a statistically significant negative effect of a Catholic upbringing and remaining a virgin. "...being brought up in the Catholic tradition was not related to conservative sexual beliefs if one is not currently religious." (p. 46) When it came to anticipating having sexual intercourse, neither Catholic nor Protestant upbringings had an effect. The other religions did have a negative effect. This is a complex study, rich in implications. Like many other social phenomena, the relation between sex and religion is not simple.

POLITICAL SCIENCE

It is easy to see that political scientists have a different interest in religion, compared to sociologists and social psychologists. Gloria Beckley and Paul Burstein examined the position of religious minorities in the United

States. (Beckley and Burstein, '91) The research emphasised the concept of 'pluralism', meaning allowing the pursuit of distinct cultures, while living under the broad umbrella of American society. There is a clear tension between the issue of equal treatment, and "the right to be different". (p. 195). The authors tested two propositions. The first was that "accommodation", which relates to pluralism, is growing in importance. This opens the door to new opportunities to further the interests of religious minorities. The second proposition is that the courts have tended towards a narrow view of accommodation. This results in the members of minority religions doing poorly when they take their cases to the courts. This study focuses mainly on discrimination in employment.

The authors believe that discrimination on grounds of religion in the United States is less common in more recent years than in the 1950s. They take this position in spite of the fact that more and more cases have been filed with the Equal Employment Opportunity Commission since the Civil Rights Act of 1964. 1984 was the last year for which the authors had data.

Year	Cases Filed
1967	159
1972	1,176
1984	3,417

The composition of religious groups bringing cases throws up three generalisations. The first is that Jews bring approximately a quarter of the cases. Very few of these are brought by Orthodox Jews. The second is that a surprisingly small number of cases are brought by Catholics. The third is the large number brought by Adventists. (p. 189) The Jews and the Catholics bring more cases alleging unequal treatment, while the Adventists mainly complain about failures to accommodate. (p. 194) While these facts have some interest in themselves, the author offers little in the way of explanation as to which religions tend to go to court.

Once in court, the chances of winning are not too good when the argument is about disparate treatment. Cases based on the first Amendment Free Exercise clause, or the Establishment clause, do much better. These observations, drawn from the data, tend to support earlier work by Frank Way and Barbara Burt, to which Beckley and Burstein refer frequently. (Way and Burt, '83) Striving for equal treatment seems to be having more success than securing recognition in employment law of the special needs of certain religions, such as particular dress rules among Jews and Sikhs. The study recognises that the principles of equal treatment and of accommodation can be in opposition to each other.

The work of James Guth and John Green is concerned with the links between religious affiliation and political activism in the United States. (Guth and Green, '90) Drawing on American law, which requires reporting all donations of $200 or more to Political Action Committees, the authors constructed a stratified random sample of 5,650 contributors during the 1981 – 1982 election cycle. They got back 2,827 usable returns to their ten-page questionnaire, with its 350 questions, which is quite remarkable. The range of coverage of the questions was very great. Essentially the authors wanted to discover the extent of political activity of the respondents over the years 1960 to 1980, along with their religious affiliation. In addition, a good deal of demographic information was elicited.

Respondents were also asked to provide information on their general political position. This was sought by putting questions on: their trust in the leaders of twenty-two political institutions; which they felt were the most important political problems of the day; their closeness to certain political views; their values; their ideology and other matters. It seemed from the data that the religious left had become more active, as had the secular right, over the twenty-year period under study. The religious right had gone up a bit in activity, and so had the secular left. Looking at only the most active individuals, rather than averages, produced a similar pattern.

Guth and Green find little or no evidence that the upsurge in activism had to do with the content of political activity. What does seem to have a bearing is new sources of information, particularly television. The religious activists generally seemed to make greater use of information than their secular counterparts. The religious left appeared to be more active in their churches, but a bit contradictorily, the donors to Christian Right Political Action Committees were the most active in their churches.

When it comes to demographic generalisations, the secular donors are concentrated in the large metropolitan districts of the East and West coasts. The religious left is to be found more in the smaller cities and the rural areas. Education is important in explaining differences, with the secular donors being better educated. Liberal activists are more likely to be in the professions, and conservatives in business as owners or managers. Religious activists are more likely to work on farms or in blue-collar occupations. Conservatives are almost twice as well off economically as liberals, the secular right being the best off. Among many other generalisations we may note that women donors are far more prominent on the left.

It is not easy to know what to make of all this, or indeed what Guth and Green make of it. It does seem relatively clear that religion is not fading away as an important force generating and mobilising political goals and activities. There also appears to be movement over time. Some of this is the result of demographic changes in the composition of the population. The authors feel that in so far as there is a secular trend, this trend influences, but does not negate, or fundamentally change, the nature of religious activism. Some religious values, such as the importance of moral objectives, bring religious activists closer to the liberal and anti-materialistic positions held by some secular forces in society. There may also be a growing alliance between the more conservative and traditional religious values and the secular views that are on the right of the political divide.

Like some other observers, the authors see a significant political divide between religious and secular activists. They find the expected association between religious belief and conservatism, but in addition find a more complex pattern. Where some scholars expected the force of religion in politics in the United States to decline, others had the opposite view, and they seem to be more correct. Guth and Green make the point that what we are seeing is not a simple revival of religious influence in politics, but rather a re-alignment. "...traditionally-religious activists are moving towards the political right and less traditional activists are moving left." (p. 174) The authors work with a very large body of data. Selective results are reported, and it is not always easy to relate the conclusions to the data. It is also the case that this is an "input" rather than an "output" study of political influence. The degree to which activity is rewarded with changes in policy is not studied.

Ted Jelen set out to explain political support in the United States for people and institutions identified as the "New Christian Right", and to explain support for the Republican Party. (Jelen, '92) He is interested in the relative importance of individual characteristics in the explanation, compared to the importance of the congregation in which the individual is located. As we shall see, this relation of the individual to the group is crucial to the method of study the author employed. Jelen worked by establishing relationships with fourteen Christian congregations in a rural county in the mid-West of America. These were chosen so as to cover Mainline Protestants, as well as Evangelical, Pentecostal and Fundamental denominations, and Catholics. The study was brought to the attention of members of the congregation at services, and self-addressed envelopes and a questionnaire were distributed to 1,176 parishioners, who returned 662 usable replies.

The respondents were asked to rank twenty-three individuals and groups on a scale from one to ten, one being the most negative and ten being the most positive. The scores of each participant were averaged over the twenty-three items, and the scores on four items of interest were subtracted from the average. The author is exploring the extent to which individual views on four particular people, or groups, depart from their views generally. The four particular items were two right wing television preachers, Jerry

Falwell and Marion "Pat" Robertson, and two institutions, the Moral Majority and the Republican Party. Attitudes towards these four were the dependent variables, or what we are trying to explain, in this study.

Jelen used three independent variables, or possible explanatory factors, to account for the respondents' attitudes. The first is what could be called theological conservatism or doctrinal orthodoxy. This was calculated by combining the respondent's views on the Bible — exact word of God or folk fables — along with an opinion on the literal existence of the Devil, and the respondent's views on the description of Creation in the book of Genesis. Next, 'moral conservatism' as a factor was measured by taking account of views on marijuana, atheists, abortion, gay rights, school prayer, gender roles and pornography. With some overlap, the third element in the index took account of the respondents' views on 'liberals', homosexuals, atheists, feminists and secular humanists.

Average levels of the variables reported by individuals were calculated for each congregation as a whole, and then these were subtracted from the average for all the participating congregations. Similarly, for many of the exercises, the independent variables for individuals were used in the form of deviations from congregation means. The main form of statistical analysis was to regress attitudes to the four targets, the two television preachers and the two institutions, on the combined individual index — doctrinal orthodoxy, moral conservatism, and views of certain allegedly progressive groups — and the same index for the congregation as a whole, plus the product of the two. This comes down to attempting to explain individual stance on 'own' features, features of the group one belongs to, and interactions between the two.

At least as a first pass approximation, the author suggests assuming a one-way causal path from doctrinal orthodoxy to moral conservatism, and from moral conservatism to hostility to the groups including liberals, homosexuals, feminists, and so on. Looking just at individual level effects, the 'hostility' index is the best predictor of attitudes towards the four target variables, Falwell, Robertson, the Moral Majority and the Republican Party. The next experiment looks at the power of individual levels and congregation averages in the causal sequence. With the first two links in the causal chain from orthodoxy to conservatism, and from conservatism to hostility, both individual and context effects appear to be significant, with the latter being much stronger. This is in line with earlier work by Wald, Owen and Hill to which the author makes frequent reference. (Wald and colleagues, '88) Just to keep it straight, these results refer to effects coming from the characteristics of individuals, not the congregations they belong to.

When it comes to the influence of moral conservatism on hostility, the congregation effect is not significant. Jelen attempts to explain this by suggesting, "...that contextual effects will have an independent impact on political attitudes when the connection between the independent and independent variables is to some extent indirect...The connection between moral conservatism and affect towards cultural minorities is much simpler, requiring only that respondents perceive a connection between the 'sinner' and the 'sin'." (p. 703) This may be correct, but it does not follow from evidence.

Jelen used the three independent variables, one at a time rather than simultaneously, to attempt to explain the attitudes towards the two target political figures and the two target institutions. Here both the individual level indices and the group level indices worked well, with the exception of 'moral conservatism'. There the congregational effect is statistically insignificant, both in the case of the Moral Majority and the Republican Party.

The really odd feature in these results is this opposite effect of moral conservatism at the individual level compared to the congregational level, when it comes to the "televangelists". Jelen suggests as a possible explanation that very conservative congregations, or their ministers, might see the television right-wingers as competitors. (p. 709) The conclusion of the study is to lend support to the effects of context on political views. In this study, the context is affiliation to a congregation. At the same time, there is additional evidence of the complexity of some of the interactions between the views of individuals and the settings in which they find themselves.

Much of the discussion of religion and politics in the United States emphasises the potential of religion for dividing sectors of society from one another. Turning to the case of Senegal, and writing before more recent upheavals, Leonardo Villalon sees Sufi rituals as an important contributor to integration and the relative stability of that country. (Villalon, '94) "The country's high degree of stability, the non-involvement of the Senegalese military in politics, the relatively high tolerance of political protest and organisation, and the moves toward the reestablishment of a multiparty system starting in the mid 1970's present striking contrasts to the broad patterns of postindependence African politics." (p. 415) His explanation relies heavily on the special emphasis in Senegal on the role the marabout, or spiritual guide, in the practice of the Sufi version of Islam in that country. The Muslim religion adapts to local needs in every country, as no doubt other religions do as well. But maybe Islam is more adaptable. The author plays down the role of the worldwide Islamic revival in his explanation.

Being a marabout, or important figure with spiritual overtones, is not confined to a priestly caste. Almost anyone may become a marabout and attract followers. The largest groupings follow family lines, where a current marabout can trace back decent from earlier important marabouts. Numbers of followers is crucial in measuring prestige and importance. The more important marabouts in Senegal hold ritual festivals, typically covering two nights and the intervening day, which involve feasting, formal and informal greeting of distinguished guests from other parts of the country, an atmosphere of entertainment, socialising, sightseeing, religious spectacle and long speeches and much chanting. These events bear a close similarity to political rallies, and are held to serve the primary purpose of legitimising the social structure and hierarchy.

The author makes reference to William Miles' work along similar lines, which discusses the importance of political rallies in Nigeria. (Miles, '89) Villalon provides graphic description of the various types of festivals. They go under different names, such as maggals, gammus and siyaares. Some occur as national holiday events, and others are more local. Some leaders hold an event on the days of a big national festival for those unable to travel to the primary site. Other events occur on their own, when there is no national event. On these occasions, secular and religious leaders come to pay their respects and to the marabout, and to publicly display their own importance and authority. These Sufi rituals serve a dual purpose. They have, "...their importance both in reinforcing the internal relations of the maraboutic following and in demonstrating its cohesion to those external to the movement." (p. 429)

Villalon maintains that the organisers and the participants both gain from these rather extended and enjoyable rituals. The links to the wider political structure of Senegal are important. No longer just a private individual, having a link to a marabout, whose importance can be publicly seen, mitigates the uneven power relations between the individual and the state. It is easy to see how being a part of such an event can take an individual out of or beyond himself. "Attendance at a maggal or a gammu provides the discipline (sic, disciple) with a sense of belonging to a much larger, and more important, social order than the purely local world in which he or she normally dwells." (p. 433) Interestingly, J.M. Keynes uses almost the same words to explain the importance of attending an artistic event, such as an opera, in Western industrial countries. (Keynes, '36)

The benefits to the organisers, and prominent participants, of one of these rituals seem clear enough. "In a very real and concrete sense, the numerous religiously sponsored events in Senegal can be understood as continuous and ongoing maraboutic 'electoral' campaigns, rituals as rallies." (p. 431) The basic goal of the author is not simply to describe or account for these rituals, but to offer their existence as an important explanation of the stability and relative democratic success of Senegal as a political entity compared to most African countries. It falls to other authors to explain the more recent upheavals afflicting the country. Was Villalon wrong in his analysis? Did some change occur which reduced the importance of the marabouts and their festivals? Or did events bubble up to such a degree that they overcame practices which were sufficient for creating order in the past?

The political scientist Mark Juergensmeyer observes that the rise of the secular nation state has been challenged, especially in Third World countries, by the dramatic rise of what he calls "the new religious state". (Juergensmeyer, '95) He begins his analysis by questioning whether or not the Western secular state represents Christian nationalism in disguise. No clear answer emerges. A very succinct and useful history of both national and religious interests, their struggles and occasional collaborations, follows. The pressure for Islamic states in Iran, Egypt and elsewhere is examined. In a similar vein we see Hindu pressure in India, Buddhist pressure in Sri Lanka, and many other examples are provided.

The author appears to accept the necessity of a territory and the people living within it becoming a nation state. This necessity is based on both alleged economic requirements, and on the need for independent survival. But whether the state can function well as a religious state remains a question. Juergensmeyer feels that only time can tell. "One of the reasons why it is difficult to gauge whether the new religious state will become congenial members of the family of nations is that the few that have come into existence in recent years — such as Iran, Afghanistan, and Sudan — are still in the process of formation." (p. 387) Too early to say, is the argument.

Juergensmeyer also raises the issue of whether or not a religion taking on domination of the nation state tends to compromise religious values. One rather important distinction between the secular and the religious state is not discussed. This is the degree of homogeneity the religious state imposes on its members. The religious homogeneity is obvious. Only the "true" religion is allowed to flourish in the religious state. But the cultural domination may be equally important. It would seem that the secular state can accommodate more variety. Perhaps the struggle between the secular state and the religious state will be the great story of the coming years. This is a view which the researcher identifies with the work of Samual Huntington. (Huntington, '93) If we do have to endure this struggle, it remains to be seen whether the greater variety of the secular state, or the greater devotion of the religious state, will prove to be the more important advantage.

It is inherent in the nature of a plural society that fundamentally different beliefs must co-exist. A most intriguing and difficult matter is the allowable nature of comments on the religious beliefs of others in a plural society. Peter Jones points out that while all the participants may accept the concept of the plural society, it may not be possible to find an agreed set of rules that will govern the relations between different belief systems. (Jones, '90) What is generally taken to be the liberal position, including freedom of expression, may in fact run contrary to the views of one or more religions in the plural society. His discussion is fairly general, although the main examples come from the Rushdie affair as it developed in the United Kingdom.

Jones points out that the decision neither to extend nor to abolish the Blasphemy Law may have been expedient, but has, "...little to recommend it in either logic or equity." (p. 420) An important part of his analysis is a careful distinction between treating beliefs with respect and causing offence. An individual may take offence at remarks which in fact treat beliefs with respect, though not with agreement. And equally one may not in fact feel offence, while still objecting strongly to the lack of respect for one's beliefs. The author feels that there is evidence for the latter reaction in the observed practice of Muslims in the United Kingdom of passing around quotations from *The Satanic Verses*.

At some risk of abbreviating a careful argument too much, I see Jones as successfully challenging the idea that all of, or even some part of, a person's religious beliefs can be ring-fenced from criticism in a workable plural society. There is no obligation to accept the ground rules of a plural society, but doing so does entail tolerating objections, as a practical as well as a logical matter. In the manner of J.S. Mill, he argues that criticism must be tolerated. The various religions promote doctrines which often conflict with each other. If one is not to be prevented from expressing one's views, criticism must be tolerated.

The second big question is the issue of the "decency and manner" in which views are expressed. A thoughtful and measured discussion of why it is unlikely that god exists may be troublesome to believers, but such an expression is clearly part of a plural society. Making fun of, and strongly belittling, the views of others, while having the same content as the measured argument, might not be acceptable. Jones argues that in practice the easy separation of ideas from the mode of their expression is not possible. "If the principle is concerned more with the way something is said than with the substance of what is said, it does not run into the simple contradictions that characterise its stronger version, nor does it collide so readily with the concerns that underlie freedom of expression." (p. 436)

Jones makes an important point of distinguishing between what can be "properly condemned" and what should be made illegal. "People ought not gratuitously to vilify the most cherished beliefs of others even though, legally, they should be unprevented from treating beliefs in that way — just as people should not call for the banning of books whose content they dislike, even though, legally, that is a call they should be free to make." (p.437) Jones also briefly addresses the public order argument. This holds that even if something is legal in principle, it should not be allowed if the consequence will be violence. He rejects this argument as giving too much power to those who are willing to resort to violence, and penalises in a relative sense those who are more "stoical and pacific". There is much here which is closer to philosophy than to social science, but the application to concrete events makes the difference.

The relation of Latin American countries to the Catholic Church has traditionally been viewed as one where the Church was part of the political process which led to authoritarian regimes. More recent periods have seen a greater explicit involvement of the Church in more radical politics. This new role has tended to be one where the Church, or at least some Bishops and associated priests, identify with the needs and interests of the poor. This is quite a contrast with a stance which involves support for the traditional existing order, an order which has been authoritarian, often held in place by military government, and characterised by great inequality. Anthony Gill has a theory that this very noticeable change in significant numbers of members of the Church from support of the hierarchical regime to championing the cause of the poor has to do with the advent of competition from other religions. (Gill, '94) "I hypothesize that the Church's new stance is a strategic response to an increasing supply of religious and ideological alternatives — Protestants, Spiritists, and Marxists." His theory is an alternative to what could be called the demand side theory which draws more on "...increased desire for social justice and spiritual guidance...". (p. 404)

Gill tests his theory of why the Church responds using a probit, or two-outcome, regression. The dependent variable, or fact to be explained, is the dominant stance of the episcopacy in either opposing or supporting dictatorship. The data come from twelve Latin American countries. It would seem from the text that the dependent variable was determined by the judgement of the author. This may be perfectly obvious and reasonable, but it passes without comment.

Two independent variables are used to capture the "demand side" hypothesis. One is a "Physical Quality of Life Index", which is an equally weighted combination of life expectancy at age one, literacy rates for those over fifteen years of age, and infant mortality. The conjecture is that the Church in the worse off countries would be under more incentive to help the down trodden. Demand for reform is also quantified using an index of repression. This index was constructed by Raymond Gastil and attempts to measure the level of civil rights in a country. (Gastil, various years) The "supply side" conjecture is captured in a variable giving the percentage increase in membership in proselytising, non-Catholic, religions. The data for this measure comes from the World Christian Encyclopaedia. (Barrett, '82)

Gill reports the results of four different regressions. One includes all three possible explanatory factors together — quality of life, political repression, and competition from other religions. A second drops the 'competition', or what Gill thinks of as the supply side, explanation. The third leaves out repression, and the fourth drops the poverty, or quality of life, index. The results turn out to be pretty consistent. In all cases, only the measure of competition from other religions is significant in accounting for the stance of the Church. In fairness, it must be granted that even this factor is only weakly significant, being at the 10% level. (p. 419) However, the author sees this as clear support for the supply side theory.

In this analysis the extent of non-Catholic religions in the various Latin American countries is treated as strictly independent. It could be that countries where more of a challenge to old fashioned authority is in the air are both places where non-Catholics might be better received, and where the Church is more independent from government. That would tend to result in an apparent causal relation between the other religions and the stance of the Church where none existed. It also might be the case that poverty of the lowest groups, while dire, does not vary enough from one country to another to be picked up statistically, with inevitably imperfect data. Finally, the "demand" for a reformed Church might be there in many countries, but factors internal and external to the Church, not measured in this study, only allow it to be active in some countries. In spite of these possible problems, Gill's model of a strictly self-interested Church is interesting, and has some support in the data.

ECONOMICS

Cunning and boldness have led economists to conjecture that religious belief and practice may be influenced, and even determined, by utility maximising considerations. What this means is that one's stance towards religion is determined by the amount of pleasure or satisfaction it yields. For example, people who are doing well in the here-and-now, might be little inclined to place emphasis on rewards in the next life. Those doing very badly would take the opposite path. This has to be adjusted to take account of investments made in the past by one's parents, and in early childhood.

James Montgomery, active in this area of research, starts from a very simple model with two actions, attend church or not, and two states of the universe, god exists or not. (Montgomery, '96) This two-by-two set up yields four possible pay-offs. It could be that people generally choose what will be the highest for them, which depends in part on the probabilities. Montgomery is mainly concerned in this paper with clarifying the logic of this 'rational actor' approach. The process forces him to conclude that decisions on religion are nonrational. He leaves economists to ponder whether some decisions are made in a nonrational way, and others are made rationally, or whether, "...all beliefs are formed through the same nonrational process." (p. 446)

Laurence Iannaccone works in this tradition of analysis. One of his investigations emphasises the element of risk in decision taking on religious matters. (Iannaccone, '95) No reasonable person, so he argues, could be at all sure about the claims for salvation which different religions offer. Which is the 'true' religion? In any other investment decision, one possible strategy for handling risk is to diversify. Western religions, by which the author means Christianity, Judaism and Islam, do not tolerate this strategy. Either in, or out. Asian religions — Buddhism and Shintoism, for example — do not act that way, nor do New Age religions. (pp. 290 – 291) Why is this so?

In an attempt to solve the riddle, Iannaccone divides religions into those which are 'collective' and those which are 'private'. Collective religions emphasise the congregation and brand loyalty, or more politely, commitment. They encourage sacrifice and stigma and offer comprehensive benefits to members. Private religions are client based, encourage purchase of certain products and services, and are specialised in the benefits they offer. The author sees these two strategies for religions as ways of coping with the inherent risk their potential members face in choosing a religion. This is an interesting start, though no attempt is made to explain why religions go one way or the other.

Drawing on his earlier work, the author makes revealing comparisons across Protestant religions in America. His data refer to Northern California in 1963. Average household income in dollars comparing different types of Protestant religions was as follows (p. 293):

Liberal	10,140
Moderate	9,435
Sect-Like	8,399
Sects	6,944

The first group includes Congregational, Episcopal, Presbyterian and Methodist denominations. The more sectarian religions included Jehovah's Witness, Pentecostal, Southern Baptist, Fundamentalist and Adventist. There is remarkable consistency in the data. Average years of education follows the same pattern form fourteen-and-a-half for 'liberal', down to twelve- and-a-half. Attendance at church services rises from thirty-four times a year to forty-nine. In spite of the income going the other way, church contributions rise from 244 dollars per year to 497. The same pattern holds for the prominence of friends from the same church, rising as we go down the list, as well as exclusive beliefs, measured on a three-item belief scale.

The author sees this spread as consistent with his theory that the more the experience is collective, the more one is forced to choose a single faith. The more private the religious experience, the more one may spread the risks. "For example, one might go to confession on Sunday, consult a medium on Monday, and engage in transcendental meditation on Wednesday...Southern Baptist church members are much less likely to hold New Age beliefs than are members of more liberal Protestant denominations...""Born Again" Christians were far less likely to approve of astrology, psychic practices, or Eastern meditation." (pp. 288 and 292) There does seem to be a point here, though going to "confession" sounds like belonging to a collective religion.

A number of economists have examined religious doctrines that might affect an economy adversely, including Islamic prohibitions against interest, for example. It is interesting, and revealing, to compare the position taken by Timur Kuran with that of John Presley and John Sessions. (Kuran, '96; Presley and Sessions, '94) With total dismissiveness, Kuran puts a rhetorical question. "...why would anyone believe that Islamic economics is capable of raising productivity, stimulating growth, or reducing inequality?" (p. 438) He simply takes it for granted that the economic beliefs of Islam are harmful to the economic well-being of individuals and societies which adopt those beliefs, and presumably, that they always have been harmful. Along with the well-known objection to interest payments — a feature of much early Christian thinking — he lists as part of the economic doctrine of Islam prohibitions against the uses of indexation, provision of insurance, speculation and arbitrage.

It must be admitted that most economists would be inclined to agree with Kuran that these prohibitions are unlikely to contribute to prosperity. His explanation for their continued appeal is less likely to persuade. He argues that these doctrines are intended to be harmful, and that they are not intended to be obeyed. In this way, to be explained shortly, he sees them as serving to preserve Muslim identity.

Holding to doctrine is a part of all religious practice, and shared beliefs tend to bind people together. The mechanism which Kuran proposes whereby the economic views of Islam support the culture of Islam is somewhat special. His argument is that violating the economic prohibitions is more-or-less inevitable for most Muslims. Breaking the rules in this way induces feelings of guilt. To compensate for these feelings, Muslims act in ways which support the religion.

> "...the most effective way to make amends for transgressions against Islam is to undertake acts that carry Islamic significance...public prayer...donations to mosques...political rallies wearing clothes that symbolize Islamic piety. The upshot is that medieval economic injunctions, when revived centuries later in settings where they pose a nuisance, will have the effect not of changing economic behavior but of promoting various forms of religious participation." (pp.440 – 441)

Presley and Sessions take a completely different line. Employing a popular branch of modern economic reasoning, they argue that the prohibition against riba, the charging of interest, can be defended on economic grounds. This prohibition does not mean that entrepreneurs cannot raise capital from the market. Murdarabah, or lenders having a share of the profits, is allowed. According to the authors, Murdarabah is not quite the same as allowing limited liability equity, as it requires taking on the losses of companies, when they occur, as well as enjoying the profits. With this exception, we have a rule which prohibits debt and allows equity.

The authors argue that this arrangement is superior to allowing debt contracts because it will result in more investment and less volatility of investment. "Under a mudarabah contract the manager is left free to chose the individually optimal level of investment in each state contingent on his contractually specified level of effort. Such a contract permits a mean-variance improvement in capital investment — average investment is increased whilst inefficiently large fluctuations around this level are reduced." (p.595) In their model, the manager observes the state of nature and then decides how much to invest. With a fixed return on capital, that is, a debt contract, the manager pays the lender the same amount in good times and bad times. With an equity contract he pays less when the profits are less, and so will invest more in bad times.

In my view, there are several problems with this analysis. It is unusual to assume that someone can know the outcome of an investment before making it. Usually we assume that entrepreneurs undertake investments, and some time later "nature" informs them whether the times turned out to be good or bad for their investments. When we allow for a range of projects, some with greater risk and more potential, different mixes of financing between debt and equity will result in different choices of projects. Assuming that people know their own interests, the possibility of a debt contract will not be exercised unless it is felt to be to the advantage of both the lender and the borrower. This does not mean that only debt contracts will be undertaken. In order to show that allowing debt as one among many contracts is socially harmful, two things are required. One has to show the effect of allowing this contract on the contracting parties and those not party to it who are effected. Either rational agents freely harm themselves, a prisoner's dilemma story, or innocent bystanders are harmed. Of course, if total output rises by banning a contract, we might leave it at that. Have the authors shown this? No, because the model is an either/or model, we cannot have more than one type at the same time, and because the motive for some contracts is that the future is uncertain, contrary to their assumption.

Charles Goodhart points out that there are cultures where there is enormous pressure to spend heavily on certain family rituals, particularly weddings and funerals. The debt contract might be evoked for consumption, not production, with great hardship following, when people are virtually forced to spend more than they can afford. An equity contract cannot support consumption. Here we have a simple and rational explanation for riba. It stops borrowing for socially undesirable conspicuous consumption.

A number of economists have examined religious institutions, formal churches that is, as if they were maximising bodies, or at least, as bodies with self-interest as part of their goals. Robert Ekelund, Robert Hebert and Robert Tollison make a persuasive case that the introduction of the doctrine of purgatory by the Catholic Church in the Middle Ages can be reasonably understood as a profitable product innovation to take to the market. (Ekelund and colleagues, '92) They conceive of the church as selling salvation. The method for bringing the product to the market has what economists call an 'up-stream/down-stream' relation. Treating distinct parts of the Church as if they were firms, the authors think of the Vatican, an 'up-stream' monopolist, as creating new products which are distributed by churches lower down-stream.

The concept of purgatory is a particularly interesting innovation as is has no basis in scripture, and is not present in other religions, or splinters off from mainstream Catholicism. Purgatory gives a second chance to go to heaven and avoid hell. If a person dies without having atoned for all their sins, an interested party still on earth can make a suitable payment to the Church, and thereby release the poor sufferer from the pains of purgatory. It may seem odd that the Church would create a doctrine which lowered the cost of sin, and thereby encouraged more sinning. Ekelund and his colleagues suggest an answer. "...the Church wanted to increase its membership and/or prevent existing members from defecting to alternative religions that offered strong assurances of salvation at a lower price." (p. 7) The Vatican was a monopoly supplier of its doctrine to member churches, but there was competition between member and non-member churches. The authors offer an interesting range of historical insight, including discussion of how the revenue from the sale of indulgences was divided between the centre and the periphery of the Church.

Audrey Davidson has suggested another possible analogy between the activities of the Church, and those of commercial organisations, by looking at the Cistercian monasteries. (Davidson, '95) She sees these as being monopoly franchisees of the Church. "...franchise arrangements were used to control Cistercian monasteries, which were the dominant retailers in the salvation industry." (p. 120) In her analysis she assumes the Church was something of a monopoly supplier of salvation when and where it was operating. Salvation is a rather intangible product. The problems for the Church came from quality control, and an optimal contractual arrangement with the retailers. It achieved the latter by offering territories where each monastery would be a monopoly retailer. In return for this privilege, they paid about five percent of their income to the Church. Of course the Church had to make its input into this process. "The intangibles provided by the Church included guarantees for salvation, doctrinal purity, and a brand name which reduced search costs..." (p.122)

It is interesting to argue that as monasteries were not owned, and could more realistically be thought of as franchises. However, analogy with optimising firms only gets us so far. We could equally well say that a firm is like a religion. Where the religion is selling salvation, the firm is selling hamburgers. The advantage of the former analogy is that we probably know more about firms as institutions than about religions. The objectives of firms may be easier to specify than those of religions, though modern economic analysis of firms puts even this in doubt. However, if religions can legitimately be thought of as analogous to profit making institutions, that is a new and potentially useful perspective.

Douglas Allen is another economist who models churches as firms. (Allen, '95) In the economic world, we see a variety of firm structures. Similarly in the religious world, we see churches with different hierarchical structures. Allen attempts to employ concepts of property rights and transactions costs to explain these structures. A good deal of complex and interesting church history is employed. It is assumed that the main purpose of the structure is to prevent misappropriation of funds. "The property right approach argues that the essential aspect of a good which influences organization is the extent to which opportunism is possible in its production. Hence the classification of theology in this paper centres on the extent a particular theology allows for potentially illegitimate wealth transfers within the church." (p. 90)

Broadly speaking, Allen finds a relation between the institutional structure of different types of Christianity, and the theologies, or beliefs, they uphold. The latter are treated an exogenous. In effect, we do not explain the theology, but take it as given, and see how the institutional arrangements respond to it. Quakers have a more individualistic theology, and a more democratic structure. Roman Catholics have a more prophetic theology and a more hierarchical structure. Lutherans come in the middle, with more denominational control and a more doctrinal, or sacred-text-based, theology. (p. 102)

Aubrey Davidson and Robert Ekelund came together to provide an economic interpretation of the Catholic Churches' control over marriage. (Davidson and Ekelund, '97) They believe that there is evidence that Church policy on marriage was "observationally equivalent" to pursuing profit maximisation. The essence of the argument is that rules were established over which people could get married, and rules over when a marriage could be dissolved. Under special circumstances, these rules could be relaxed, and fees were charged for this. "By regulating and re-regulating the conditions for a valid marriage throughout the medieval period and by offering services in the form of exemptions and dispensations, the church was able to secure a strong social presence while maintaining the inelastic demand for its ultimate product and enhancing rent collection." (p. 226)

An interesting side issue, which the authors raise briefly, is the importance to women of enforcing marriage contracts. More men in positions of authority, and more women practising the religion, is true of some religions. The researchers feel that it was mainly marriage regulation that led to greater involvement of women than men in the ordinary day-to-day life of the church. Whether marriage regulation is in fact an important part of the explanation is open to doubt.

W.C. Heath, M.S. Waters and J.K. Watson have studied a different kind of relation between economics and religion than analogies with firms. (Heath and colleagues, '95) They are interested in the effect of religion on income per capita. In principle, there are a number of ways in which adhering to religious beliefs might affect economic performance. These include matters of private morality, family stability, attitudes towards work, trust and reliability, and savings behaviour at the micro level. This is to be distinguished from effects of religion on the economy at the macro level. For example, different religions can influence legislation on banning certain activities — alcohol consumption in some places, trade in erotic material — and considerations such as usury laws.

The authors do not try to minimise the complexity of possible factors relating income to religious belief. Their method was to run regressions using States of America as observations. For each state, income per capita is explained by nine variables. The non-religious variables have proved effective in other studies. The data are for 1952,1971 and 1980. One statistical approach would have been to employ a simple pooled regression analysis, in which it is assumed that the explanatory factors interact in the same way in all of the States, and do not change in their effects over time.

Instead, Heath and his colleagues used a variable coefficients model which allowed for changes in both slopes and intercepts. The non-religious variables they used were:

percent of population in urban areas
value of mineral production per capita
proportion of the population in the civilian labour force
percent of the population over 64 years of age
median years of education completed

These figures are available for each of the states for the three years under study. The additional religious variables used were:

percent Jewish
percent Catholic
percent Protestant
percent fundamentalist

The results for 1952 show no significant effect on income per person in the different States from the Jewish proportion in the state, but this factor does become significantly positive for the years 1971 and 1980. The strongest result, both in statistical significance, that is, how sure we might be that it is correct, and how large is the response, is the negative effect of fundamentalism on income per capita. The authors suggest that an illiberal atmosphere may be harmful to the economy. They also emphasise the tentative nature of their findings. This is fair enough. However, the possibility that poor people are more inclined towards fundamentalism may be a more plausible explanation of the association, even given the effort in this study to include as many factors as was practical to account for variations in income per capita across States of America.

Brooks Hull and Frederick Bold have studied the effect of church membership on the enforcement of property rights. (Hull and Bold, ' 95) At least that is what they would like to have studied. Property rights are taken to be essential to the efficient running of a market economy, and for economists tend to be the main justification for government. While the government has the apparatus of the courts, backed up by a monopoly on the legitimate use of force, there is no reason why other organisations, such as the churches, might not help in creating an orderly society in which property rights are respected. Hull and Bold build on earlier work which found a statistical relation between the amount of church membership and social order. (Lipford and colleagues, '93) They want to go beyond mere observed association and explore a theory that would link the church to property right enforcement.

It might seem self-evident that churches would encourage honest behaviour. The church gains the support of its members by offering salvation. The church helps individuals to save their souls by giving both instruction and encouragement to act in certain ways. However, just for the sake of enquiry, would it not work just as well for the church if salvation depended on socially disruptive acts? Of course, at times this has been the instruction. The Crusades are an example. But since the church is an institution of society, a social order which allows institutions to have stable existences would appear to be in the interests of the church. Hull and Bold are not satisfied with this argument, and construct a more narrowly self-interested theory of why the church promotes social order, and in particular, enforcement of property rights. Here is how the argument goes.

The church is assumed to maximise revenue, which depends on the number of members, the cost per member, and the donations to the church per member. Donations are assumed to depend on the degree of enforcement of property rights. The reasoning is simply that with better enforcement, there is a higher level of income in society generally. The proportion going to the church is relatively fixed, so more income means higher levels of donations. The level of enforcement, in turn, depends in the model on total church membership in the society, not membership in particular denominations. The bottom line is that individual churches add their membership up to the point where an extra member adds an amount to donations equal to the cost of acquiring the member, assumed to be constant. The extra revenue comes from both the donation of that member, and the larger donations from existing members, due to better property right enforcement. More members add to more enforcement, but at a diminishing rate.

Hull and Bold attempted to test their theory using county level data in the United States in the '80s. (Glenmary Research Centre, '80 and '82; and U.S. Bureau of the Census, '83) They reason that property rights enforcement cannot be observed, but the inverse of that is crime rates, which can be observed. The investigation comes down to regressing crime on church membership. The standard list of variables often used to explain the amount of crime was included in the regressions.

Unemployment - Proportion of the Population in Urban Areas
Personal Income - Expenditure on the Police - Population Density
Proportion of the Population who are White - Proportion Below the Poverty Line

Religious affiliation is measured as the proportion of the county who are members of a religion, regardless of denomination. This proportion also measures as a squared term, enabling a test of diminishing returns.

The authors feel that the results of this statistical exercise are encouraging to their property rights theory. Church membership has the effect in the regressions of reducing the amount of violent crime, crime against property, and total crime. Diminishing returns to membership is found, with the membership squared term having a positive coefficient. I am much more inclined to interpret these results as revealing a high order fact that more religion and less crime tend to go together. The link to the property rights theory, in itself dangerously simplistic, is so tenuous as to carry little weight.

But what is causing what? Unemployment is found to encourage crime. Neither income nor urbanisation were found to be significant, in contrast to many other studies. Police spending was positively associated with crime, highlighting the issue of simultaneity. Countries with higher crime rates may be inclined to spend more on the police, and would have even more crime if they did not do so. And could it not be that criminals and non-believers are both drawn to certain countries, but for very different reasons? "The results also strongly support [previous investigator's] conclusions while employing more appealing county-level data." (p. 148) With this we must agree. The earlier work used state level data. As the influence of the church is held to operate more at the community level, the county level data does seem more suitable.

ANTHROPOLOGY

Fenella Cannell has enquired deeply into religious practice in a remote village in the Philippines. (Cannell, '95) She calls the area 'S. Ignacio', presumably to preserve its anonymity. Two hundred families make up the village, which is "rural but not isolated". It is located in the Bicol province. There is a market town not far from this village of small-scale farmers, fisherman, and petty traders. All are under "severe economic pressures". Catholicism is the dominant religion, and the area has a superficially "Western" appearance.

As is common in so many places, religious practice combines universal Catholic elements with local beliefs and traditions. The author's main concern is with the nature of this combination. Do we have a superficial overlay of Catholic Christianity, or can observed practices be seen as one of, "...historical continuities in Bicolano culture..."? (p. 377) Cannell frequently refers to 'imitation' as a key concept in explaining what is going on. As I have done, she puts the word in quotation marks, indicating that it means something a little different from normal usage. I found this hard to understand, but in the end it did not detract significantly from an extraordinary and powerful tale.

The research emphasises the role of healers in the community. They deal mainly with what are thought of locally as spirit-caused sickness. The people in Bicol believe they are surrounded by invisible people. The local phrase is *tawo na dai ta nahililing*. As they cannot be seen, it is easy to bump into them, and they may take offence. A possible response, naigo, can cause disease. These spirits are capricious. They may take an interest in an ordinary person — Cannell uses the word 'pity' to describe this, again, in quotes, leading to some uncertainty in me. These positive spirit actions, or herak, may bring good fortune, but even these may have adverse outcomes, rather like excessive attention from an unwanted admirer.

Healers are closer to the spirit world than other people, and have to be careful in the way they relate to Catholic beliefs. The origin of the spirits, or tawo, is interesting.

> "When God created the world, they say, he decided to bless everything with sprinkled water, as a priest does at the end of Mass. He gathered all the people and animals together, but some of the people hid among the tree-trunks of the forests, and so they did not come within the area reached by the blessing. Hence they remained invisible." (pp. 385 - 386)

This has serious consequences for healers. At any time, they might be possessed by one or more spirits. If they stay for the blessing at a Catholic Mass, they run the danger of having the spirit, or spirits, "fixed" inside them. This means that their own soul cannot get back into their body.

The focus of the study is on the relation between the spirit world and the ordinary world. The most obvious movement from one to the other is the event of death. As everywhere in the world, this is accompanied with grief and ritual. "The first eerie wail of the most closely bereaved is heard at the moment of death itself." (p. 381) Cannell goes on to describe what she refers to as a "predictable pattern of activity" which has an irresistible momentum and orders those involved in a passive spiral of acceptance. The exception to passivity being the handling of departure, or giving up of the dead. This is an interaction of potential danger in which an exchange of “pity” must be handled with circumspection.

According to the author, the Catholic church has had an uphill struggle in Bicol in giving top priority to Christmas and Easter Sunday, the festivals of birth and resurrection. In this part of the world, it is Good Friday, the death of Christ, which remains the most significant, the most emotional, and the most involved religious event. This is entirely in keeping with the traditional concerns. It is at this point that the most amazing part of the beliefs and practices in Bicol comes to light.

In one of the homes in S. Ignacio there is a glass coffin, and in this coffin is a wooden carved figure of Christ. This figure is called the Ama, "...dressed in wigs of human hair and clothing down to underwear...". (p. 380) The author explains that some of the older women of the village are in more or less constant attendance, and will say prayers for pilgrims, the barangay, for a modest fee. The main annual event in the 'life' of the Ama is a mock burial on Good Friday.

> "...the family who own the image and shrine of the Ama, together with a large crowd of pious people and male and female healers, gently remove the clothing of the Ama, sponge him all over with perfumed water (keeping towels carefully placed over the groin as though to save the image's modesty) and re-dress him. The mixture of tenderness and proprietorship with which this is done is remarkable to see." (p. 382)

It is uncertain, according to historians and anthropologists, whether this image came from Mexico at the turn of the century, or was made by craftsmen in Manila. The origin, according to local belief, is far more interesting.

> “The image was found as a shapeless piece of wood by a childless woman who ...’adopted’ it. She ‘took care of’ the image, which began to assume a recognizable human shape, and gradually grew from child to adult. The miracles took a new turn when the Ama began to walk about in the area, recruiting pilgrims and devotees...the Ama is now said to be ‘too old’ for such energetic pursuits, but he still works miracles by healing sickness..." (p. 379)

One interpretation of these beliefs and practices would be that Western Christianity has come to a remote part of the Philippines and been modified by the people living there. The author argues that in fact what we see are rituals and beliefs with deep historical origins. The crucial elements are the spirit world and the handling of death. At the centre lies the Ama, or what is called the 'dead Christ'. This figure has a kind of life such that it can do good, and be buried every year.

What keeps all this going? In my opinion there is a need for it in the identity of the community, and in the way in which the community deals with life, poverty and death. Cannell has brought this vividly to the page in this remarkable article. "...the figure of the Ama is taken from his coffin...he is dressed as an honoured corpse, with a binding-cloth tying up his jaw. A sigh and a shout from the waiting crowd goes up...Local men struggle for a place pulling the bier...". (p. 382) Only passing mention is made of the "owners" of the figure and the shrine. The 'healers' gain legitimacy from association with the Ama. This is a poor area, and one where these practices generate not insignificant income for those who promote them. Crass to raise this? Yes, but I feel compelled to do so.

David Mosse also takes up the question of interaction between proselytising Christianity and beliefs and practices in host societies. (Mosse, '96) He emphasises the handling of caste on the part of Catholics in the Indian village of Alapuram. This community of about two thousand people is located in Ramnad district in southeastern Tamil Nadu. There are roughly equal numbers of Christians and Hindus. Mosse comes to what appears to be a rather strong conclusion. "Religious affiliation merely re-enforces existing rules of sub-caste endogamy or imposes a further rule. Religion is thus of wholly secondary importance as a principle of social organisation in this part of south India, where Hindus and Christians live as members of rural village communities primarily organised around caste rather than religion." (p. 463)

Defending this thesis requires a pretty clear theory of the place held by caste in the society. Mosse observes that Hindus and Catholics do not intermarry, and treats this as a minor point. Given the family structure of property ownership, and the lack of social mobility, it seems a little hard to accept the author's degree of dismissal of religion as an influence on social organisation, if only to take the intermarriage point.

Mosse does provide a wealth of interesting material, particularly with respect to rituals surrounding death and burial. He notes that Catholics place more emphasis of rites before death, and Hindus place more emphasis on rites after death. In keeping with the Hindus, Catholics make use of appropriate caste members for various practices when death occurs. The bottom line is that Mosse sees the Christians as living in a "dual moral world". The Jesuit missionaries set a pattern of belief and behaviour which called for adoption of the "ultimate verities of Christian faith", while living in the social world. Part of this world was, and is, caste. "...only in the late twentieth century has the Catholic church taken a decisive move against caste." (p. 476) It is not clear from the article how this impacts on Alapuram.

Proselytising Islam also faces the issue of interacting with local traditional religious beliefs. Possession by spirits is a common feature of such beliefs. Kjersti Larsen has investigated this phenomenon in Zanzibar. (Larsen, '98) With characteristic anthropological involvement, he reports on a conversation with 'Halima' and 'Nuru', while, "...slumbering on the baraza just outside their mother's house in Zanzibar Town...". (p.64) Halima was thinking about her relationship with the spirit which occupied her —a Muslim Arab spirit called Sheik Said bin Mohammed bin Hassan who was from Muscat and Jeddah.

> "...'the spirit has climbed to my head, and even though I have prepared for my spirit, I cannot always believe in spirits' ability to inhabit people and interfere in the lives of humans...' Nuru joined the discussion...'Many people live on Unguja (Zanzibar Island) all their lives without getting a spirit. This is possible because they do not believe that they can get a spirit...some people who do not believe it is possible to get a spirit, get one...Others who actually do believe that it is possible to get a spirit may never get one.' " (p. 64)

Larsen is concerned with relation between the "spirit world" and the Muslim religion in Zanzibar. He does not agree with those who speak of dini as being the realm of orthodox Islamic belief, and mila as being the realm of traditional, pre-Islamic faith. "In Zanzibar, the reality of spirits is not debated. What is debated is how humans should behave towards spirits." (p.66) The author discusses particular cases of different kinds of accommodation to the spirits, including ignoring them and relating only to God. These he sees as equally consistent with being a good and moral person.

Virtue and merit are defined in terms of Islam. Having an active relation with one or more spirits is not in contradiction with Islam. If one removes a spirit or spirits from one's life, or refuses to allow a spirit or spirits, in one's life, that is a matter of personal decision. It depends on one's life, which is to say, on one's perceptions and circumstances. "There is, in relation to spirits, no true answer in terms of right and wrong, good and evil: spirits are ambiguous." (p. 73)

Larsen argues against the view that in Zanzibar we see a world religion overlaid on traditional primitive beliefs. Not at all. "Describing the spirit phenomenon as peripheral to Islam would imply that certain local discourses are accepted as more valid than others. To women and men in Zanzibar Town there are alternative ways of being a good Muslim. Thus, what might appear as negotiations of morality should rather be understood in terms of creativity, self-construction and moral choice." (p. 74) Of course, this is evidence collected while slumbering on the baraza with Halima and Nuru, and, in fairness, talking at length with other respondents. It could be that spirits and Islam are exactly on a par, "...two different systems of knowledge where one can be invoked to explain the other."(p. 72) Or it could be, to stick my oar in, that the relationship of spirits to Islam is more like the relationship of the horseshoe to the crucifix.

Different interpretations of a religion, and indeed different religions in an area, need not have an antagonistic relationship. Bernard Formoso explains how some religious activities of the Chinese minority in Thailand helps in their relations with the majority groups. (Formoso, '96) The religions involved are Buddhism, Taoism and Confucianism. The Chinese make up less than nine percent of the population, but hold a dominant position in the economy. They normally take Thai citizenship, and intermarriage is quite common. This alleged easy accord between the Chinese and the larger Thai community is unusual. Formoso believes it can be explained largely through shared belief between the Thai and Chinese.

Both groups are concerned about the dead. Ancestor worship is important, and the dead should be disposed of correctly. Without this, they wander as ghosts, causing problems for the living, and are unhappy in themselves. The status of the beliefs that people hold about ghosts is not discussed. Are these to be taken literally, or in some sense symbolically? It would seem that for present purposes it does not matter. We are to take it that this is how they explain their activities regarding the dead to themselves, and to others.

Formoso conducted fieldwork in 1993 and 1994 in Surin City and in Roi Et in Northeast Thailand. He believes what he observed regarding the handling of the problem of ghosts is typical of the country at large. The remarkable practice which the author studied, called Hsiu-Kou-Ku, can be thought of as providing proper burial for the dead in the form of cremation. This is preceded by cleansing ceremony — mainly washing bones and done by women — and accompanied and followed by prayer, ritual movement about the city, and the placing of totemic notices.

Four groups are involved in all of this: key figures in the Chinese temple, referred to as a "cult community"; patron saints are a second symbolic element; "mediums" and Taoist priests; and the dead themselves. These are the "unfortunate" dead. For the Thai people these are persons who died young or violently, and for the Chinese they are persons who were not succeeded by sons to worship them. What seems clear is that these are the poorest people whose remains were often disposed of improperly, such as in an unmarked grave in the jungle. Finding the corpses — the emphasis is on bones — is sometimes difficult. At the beginning of a search a special paper is laid out, and if the bodies cannot be found, the paper is burned in the place of the bodies. In the event that decomposing bodies are found, they are burned on the spot.

The number of corpses involved in Hsiu-Kou-Ku is large. In a rural area it may easily come to 300 in a year. In Bangkok the number was 30,000 over the period 1976 to 1989. (p. 221) We might wonder why the Chinese, with very limited help from the Thai people, take on this task. It is a task which has important spiritual value, and probably hygienic significance as well. The author suggests that the Thai people fear the ghosts much more than the Chinese fear them. The Chinese, we are told, experience limited fear, and they feel some compassion for the ghosts. In spite of this, they do appear to resent having to deal with the problem of disposing of bodies.

The crucial thing seems to be that for the Chinese there is a kind of honour, or grace, that comes from taking on this role. It gives them a sense of importance and of being needed in the country. For the Thai, oddly enough, it simultaneously gives them a sense of superiority over the Chinese in that they can pass on a problem to them. Somehow, both groups feel superior to the other through this practice. "The Thai abandon to the Chinese their malevolent ghosts, while the Chinese...consider these a source of danger but also of spiritual profit." (p. 221) Perhaps we could go further in explaining this interaction, but it can hardly be doubted that simply being aware of Hsiu-Kou-Ku is important, in itself, for appreciating the country.

The most sensitive issues in any society are those involving sex, reproduction, and the family. Some societies are fortunate in having widely agreed and accepted principles. This is not the case in large advanced countries, where rival views on such matters as abortion, legitimacy, and rules of sexual conduct exist side by side. Controversy and debate is heightened by the new technologies of reproduction. Is surrogacy acceptable? Can it be allowed on a commercial basis? Who has claims on the child in cases of artificial insemination? What uses can be made of frozen sperm and eggs? Can embryos be used in research? The list goes on.

In the United Kingdom, the Warnock Report of 1984 intensified debate, as did passage of the Human Fertilisation and Embryology Bill of 1990. Chris Shore makes a strong case for the value of anthropological enquiry in unravelling these controversies. (Shore, '92) He identifies many strands of the debate with various interest groups, including formal religions as well as more diffuse opinions of a religious nature. This article could equally well be placed in chapter seven on the family. It is interesting that only one of the many dozens of studies we have examined could go in more than one place. But it makes certainly makes a telling contribution here.

Widely held religious views entered the debates at many points. The simple argument against surrogacy, in some discussions, was that it is unnatural and against the will of God. The case against research on embryos has a great deal to do with the Roman Catholic contention that an individual begins at conception. In his comments on this paper, Professor Ronald Frankenberg took exception to Shore, questioning the relevance of "organised religious lobbies" as having much to do with public opinion. (p.305) It is true that the research does not employ questionnaires to determine public opinion. The author makes use of what he sees as key, or telling, comments and observations. "Would questionnaires and opinion polls have provided a better source of cultural data? I think not." (p. 312)

This methodological point is quite central to the article. Shore is employing anthropology to get at rather subtle and illusive, yet powerful forces that are at work here. Professor Abrahams in his comments observes, with Shore's agreement, that, "...it may be valuable for anthropologists to point out that we are sometimes dealing with new versions of old fundamental problems and what our culture tends to treat as natural is in fact highly variable." (p. 302) Introducing sperm into a woman without her engaging in sexual intercourse, can be done with primitive techniques. The Archbishop of Canterbury set up a commission in 1948, considerably before the advances associated with the work of Professor Robert Winston and others, which recommended that this be made a criminal offence. Warnock found this practice to be ethically acceptable.

In discussing artificial insemination, Shore refers to the well-known contention that Trobriand Islanders believe that intercourse does not cause pregnancy. What it does is open up the passage for a spirit sent by the woman's ancestors to enter her and make a spirit child. Shore chides some objectors to Warnock as lacking the Trobriand insight. He paints a vivid picture of competing interests reacting to the new reproductive technologies. "The lesson from anthropology is that every society has a vested interest in controlling reproduction, and in each we tend to find dominant institutions — the church, the state, the medical profession or whatever — competing to monopolize the discourses..." (p. 301) This is a field rich in values, and while religion is not the only locus of ethical concern, Shore demonstrates that it remains an important one.

PART THREE

APPLYING SOCIAL SCIENCE

Chapter Eleven

WHAT SOCIAL SCIENCE IS

VALID GENERALISING

As we can see from the previous core chapters, each of the five social sciences has something to say on each of the six topics we have considered. This research undertaken in the nineties provides a sample of what can be found in the full picture. I believe it is a representative sample. More will be said about that shortly. On the assumption that the research reported here is representative, we can use this material to construct some valid generalisations.

As in other attempts to get at an essence, generalising comes at a cost. A generalisation is a simplification. Odd cases must be set to one side. A smooth and understandable picture has to be overlaid on a complex reality. Generalisation means throwing away information in order to construct a comprehensible summary. The loss of information in the present exercise is much the same as that which occurs in constructing theories. The test is whether or not the emerging picture goes to the heart of the matter, or whether it misleads.

Misleading or not, one inevitable result of generalisation is that information will be lost. It will be impossible to deduce chapters five through ten from what is written here. But from chapters five through ten, one can deduce the generalisations that appear here, or hopefully something rather like them. I hold no particular brief for what I am going to set out. The reader is not merely invited, he or she is aggressively encouraged to make his or her own deductions. That is why the material is set out in those chapters.

We are all tired and bored with high sounding statements about the nature of social science — what it is about, what it might be, what it should be. If we want to understand social science, or if we want to improve it, we have to work with what is there. The real question is, what is there? I hope the reports in previous chapters display this branch of science, rather like an array of spices laid out in a market in Dubai. There it is. This is the reality.

Forgive a short digression. Years ago I had a little statistical problem where I felt I needed help. Plotting the data on a scatter diagram showed that the relation between two variables was not linear, nor was it easy to see how it could best be captured in a logarithmic curve, or a logistic. We had a distinguished visitor to the Statistics Department at LSE, and I asked him how I might approach summarising my data in an estimated equation. I have never forgotten his reply.

"Why do you want to summarise and throw away information? This data is perfect as it is." Perfect, yes, I thought, but too much to take in. Without a valid generalisation, the theory could not be tested. Comparison with other findings would be nigh impossible. The attempt at simplification was necessary. However, the ensuing exchange taught a lesson and that lesson was invaluable. If you have to generalise, the correct procedure depends on the purpose of the exercise.

THE OBJECTIVES

I would like to make a number of statements about social science on the basis of the chapters that have gone before. Prominent among these statements will be a summary of the distinctive nature of each of the social sciences. That involves some consideration of their strengths and weaknesses, and how they relate to each other. There is a logic to the way investigators have carved up the field into five distinct specialisms. We will take a close look at why we have five specialisms, and not four, or six.

Practitioners in the social sciences have certain shared skills and information. The scientific study of society from any perspective involves a common objective. The test of success or failure is the same when we go to a high enough level of generality. Closer to the ground, there are different skills and techniques. This is almost inevitable. If there was only one set of skills, there would only be one kind of social scientist, apart from specialisms in subject matter. As much as anthropologists differ one from another, and the same for economists, we can broadly identify different things one needs to know in order to do anthropology, or to do economics.

So much for the inputs. What about the output? What can we expect from each of the five social sciences? When social psychologists and political scientists study crime, they both produce theories and data. In short, they generate information about crime. Typically, the information is not the same. Different subjects generate different kinds of knowledge. It will be helpful to be able to characterise these differences.

We hear a good deal these days about interdisciplinary work. This is not entirely foolish. Social reality is not confined to disciplinary specialisms. Migration, for example, has both a sociological aspect and an economics aspect, to randomly choose but two disciplines. Is it necessary for the disciplines to combine when they undertake investigation? It could be that certain problems call for combined work, and others do not. We will explore what can be said in general on these matters.

A BALANCED AND ACCURATE PICTURE?

We should be a little systematic in addressing the question of whether chapters five through ten give a usable picture of how the social sciences operate. A basic premise is that the leading professional journals in each subject publish the best work in their fields. The challenges to this proposition tend to come from scholars who have not had great success with the journals. An extreme position is to denigrate publication in any form. This is nonsense, if for no other reason than that science is a collective endeavour. No one is obliged to take part. But if you want to do science, the work must be made public and subject to criticism from other practitioners.

Of course print is not the only way of going public. For example, one cannot be sure how the World Wide Web will evolve. At the present time material is 'published' there, but much of this material is not subject to peer review. There is no editing. No test is applied as to whether the material warrants a place in the structure of science. This point has been made before, and we need not dwell on it. In contrast, a journal available on the web is still a journal. That is another matter. What about other means of publication than journals?

In the distant past, books were important vehicles for reporting original work in the social sciences. Today there is a flood, an avalanche, of book publication. In economics there are not many examples of original material that appears in this format. Instead of original work, many are textbooks. They play a role in conservatively summarising the state of knowledge. Other books bring together journal articles. Many put forward a broad thesis about how to do economics, often with a methodological slant. Other books push a particular line, such as the need to fight inflation, or reform health care provision. Often these are addressed to a wide audience, not just to fellow economists. There are some scientifically important books produced today that take their place in the structure of knowledge, along with the journal articles. There are not many of them, and they are not different in kind from the articles in the serious journals.

When it comes to the other social sciences, I am both less sure of my ground, and have some reason to feel that book publication plays a bigger role in advancing the subjects than it does in economics. From the point of view of the purpose of this book, the important consideration, or better, the niggling worry, is that the inadvertently excluded material might change the picture of social science which is present in the material I have included. That is the central consideration. Hopefully, in all disciplines, the journals are representative.

There are journals which are subject matter based rather than discipline based. Among the topics I have taken up, these journals figure prominently in housing, crime and religion. I have paid some attention to these sources, but by no means have I given them a thorough screening. Most of the articles in these journals use ideas from the discipline based journals. The test of originality, or contribution to the subject, is less forcefully applied. Rather, if an article is of potential interest to people with an interest in housing, for example, it goes in. The sociology, or economics, or whatever, used in that article may be rather familiar to specialists. The contribution to science may be small.

An important exception in the subject matter based journals is work that cuts across disciplines. It could be that an article drawing on anthropology and political science to address issues in international drug trafficking might be hard to publish in a mainstream discipline based journal. This is a possibility. However, the discipline based journals certainly do publish good work that cuts across fields, and work that goes outside the normal confines of the discipline. But the possibility remains that due to less systematic coverage of material in subject matter based journals, telling work has been missed.

The selection of topics used for this investigation could be a source of bias. Suppose that instead of crime, migration, the family, money, housing and religion, six other topics had been chosen. Consider, for example:

Tourism	Education	War
Medical Practices	Unemployment	Art

Does it wet the appetite for another volume? The topics are all interesting, and each of the social sciences has something to say on each of them. My contention is that the resulting picture of the social sciences would be indistinguishable from the one that emerges here. That is an assertion. The topics are very different. The sciences would look the same. Researchers undoubtedly do specialise. The list of contributors would have very little overlap with the present list. It would have some. My assertion rests on a lot of flipping through journals, and on something else.

Why should the sociologists who work on education be more able, or work in a drastically different way, than those who work on crime? Why should economists who study housing be different in kind or in quality from those who work on tourism? In fairness, it could be that they just happen to be significantly different, the sociologists and the economists, and their work reflects this. The fact that it is hard to come up with a reason why it might be so does not guarantee that it is not so. Yet it establishes a presumption.

In every subject there are fashions. These are driven by everything from perceived need, to new ideas that open up promising areas of enquiry. Talented people are drawn to fashionable topics, and so are less able researchers. But the same can be said about topics that are a bit out of fashion. It must be admitted that some researchers make a little corner for themselves, taking advantage of the fact that few people have an interest in their area. At the same time, there are many examples where first rate researchers have also been drawn to areas that others ignore.

I claim that any list of six areas of concern to all the social sciences, which are also big topics for society, will generate much the same picture of the five disciplines as comes from the topics I have selected. The balance may shift a bit in one or two topics. The great advantage is in running across a range of topics. It helps to average out and cut down on potential bias. What makes a discipline is not the particular topic.

In the course of undertaking this investigation, a number of people have suggested topics to me which I feel are inappropriate. They are not suitable for this exercise for one of two possible reasons. Some are not substantive topics. They are suggestions about how to go about examining substantive topics. The other suggestions seem to me to be substantive, but typically treated in a way that is either indifferent to, or hostile to, social science. This is a crunch issue in my thesis about social science. I brushed against it in chapter three. A careful look is needed now. Consider the following six topics as representative of a kind of material which is very popular, but does not belong in an investigation of the scientific study of society.

Social Theory
Risk
Postmodernism
Networks
Globalisation
Post-Structuralism

Everyone would agree that if these six topics were put through the same mill as the six I in fact did use, we would get very different results. The results would be qualitatively different from the actual six, and from the alternative six suggested above. For a start, there would be much more sociology, and a lot less of the other five disciplines. In itself that need not be an objection. In principle it might reflect the state of knowledge more accurately. But that is just a possibility in principle. It is not the case. I contend that a different picture would emerge, not because the proportions of scientific work in the different disciplines would be more accurately reflected, but because sociology is more open to unscientific work than the other social sciences. That does not mean that there is no genuine scientific work in sociology. Ample examples are provided in the previous chapters.

The writers who promote one or more of this last list of topics tend to be sympathetic to all of them. In seminars and other settings, I have observed a variety of opinions from these writers as to how these kinds of topics relate to social science. Some hold that social science is one thing, and they are doing something else. Both are perfectly reasonable undertakings, so they contend. The term 'social theory' was invented to suggest an alternative to social science. However, it is almost impossible to extract from people of this persuasion what this other thing is that they are doing. If their work does not pursue the goals of science, what is it after? If it does have the same goals, how are they advanced in a non-scientific way?

Some enthusiasts for the list above, which is far from complete, are more aggressive in the way they position themselves vis-à-vis social science. Rather than a 'distinct from, but both reasonable' line, they hold that social science is either impossible to do, or wicked and dangerous. They are not doing it, and no one should try to do it. My answer to the assertion that social science cannot be done is chapters five through ten. Social science is being done. How well and with what consequences are the subjects of this and the next chapter.

A third position maintains that there is no difference of principle. They are also doing social science, but perhaps at a different level of generality, or from a different angle. This position cannot be justified. Ordinary social science investigates matters ranging from the finest possible detail to the highest level of generality. Claims of a yet higher level of generality mean going outside the orbit of science. As to the 'different angle', there are similarly two possibilities. That angle may fall within the orbit of science, in which case it is not different from science, or it falls outside. A genuine distinction requires that it fall outside. But why call it social science if it bears no resemblance to science?

I can understand the desire to hold an academic post, or some other post that calls for a 'social scientist'. There is also a matter of funding from public and private sources. One might need the label 'social scientist' in order to qualify. These are understandable motives. We should nevertheless resist them because of the element of fraud. If one is doing work which is not science, perhaps closer to art and philosophy, why not say so? To answer my rhetorical question, there is the risk that the art or philosophy related social investigation might not be of interest to philosophers or artists. Does this possible lack of interest depend on the 'social' aspect, or the quality of the work? The lily pad approach is to say to the artists, I am doing science, and to the scientists, I am doing art.

Items like social theory, postmodernism and post-structuralism are methodological stances. They identify views, somewhat different from each other, but with some overlaps, which distrust conventional science. They advocate certain approaches to the investigation of social phenomena. They are not the phenomena. They terms refer to suggestions, foolish suggestions in my view, but suggestions nevertheless, as to how to think about society. Methods of approach are not the same as phenomena to be studied. For that reason alone they do not qualify for a place on any list of substantive topics for scientific investigation. However, the success and popularity with some poorly informed parts of the general public of these far fetched approaches is something that could be studied scientifically.

Post-structuralism is particularly interesting for the present investigation. Extreme versions claim is that all rational thought is a delusion. We are fooled if we think we can be coherent. Weaker versions hold that science, and particularly social science, is incoherent, and so can make no claims for any kind of objectivity or legitimacy. It is probably the most openly hostile stance to social science. I believe that rational argument can deal with those claims, but for writers who believe they have succeeded in debunking all rational endeavour, there is no need to deal with my arguments, or any arguments based on rationality.

The other three items, globalisation, risk and networks, have an implied methodological stance, though on the face of it they do refer to social phenomenon. The first implicitly suggests that something new and very general is at work, which includes everything from financial markets to travel and access to information. The claim of newness is simply false. All these things, including global marketing of products, have long histories. There are two issues. Have we seen a change, or discontinuity, in the nature of global interaction, or the 'quality' of it, to use a traditional Marxist term, as a result of the change in the amount of worldwide interaction?

The second issue turns on whether global interaction can be fruitfully studied as a single phenomenon, or is best studied as lots of phenomena? I see no historical break, and I see more potential for progress in breaking down the worldwide interacting phenomena into a series of separate but related topics. I could be wrong. Are the advocates of the globalisation program on to something? The answer depends on what the advocates are able to come up with. So far, the 'globalisation' advocates have given us a heady mixture platitudes and unsupported wild observations. This may sell, but it is not science.

The ‘risk’ and ‘networks’ writers take something out of context, and hope to say useful things about it. Financial risk is one thing, health risk is another. But what about risk as a topic, apart from any of these possible applications? Again, the proof of the wisdom of the strategy defining a territory is in what it discovers. So far, we get very serious sounding statements of the obvious, side by side with the obviously wrong. Of course, much of mathematics works on exactly this principle of abstracting from context. The 'risk for its own sake' and 'networks for their own sake' writers do not like mathematics. They like a special kind of prose which cannot be damaged in translation. The endeavour has little in common with science.

These last six topics would result in a very different picture of social science than the one we can derive from the six topics I actually used, or ones like them. For the reasons given above, I reject that alternative list, and argue that it is not representative of social science. There is a final possible objection to my way of going about the task of capturing 'social science'. I chose topics on which I guessed that each of the social sciences would have a good number of recent articles. That turned out to be right. They all do. But what about topics which tend to be exclusive to a single social science? Suppose the topics were:

> Exchange Rate Fluctuations - Marriage in Nomadic Societies Aggressive Behaviour and Video Games - Composition of British Cabinets - Crime and Ethnic Minorities - Pricing of Used Cars

Each of these are both more narrowly circumscribed than the topics I chose, and closer to the heartland of one or the other of the social science disciplines. One social science might have a lot to say on one topic, but the others would have little or nothing. Would that give a very different picture of the social science endeavour?

I believe that scientists are like other people. They know a little, and they work with what they know. They are pretty inflexible. They do not work one way when in the heartland of their subject, and another way when stretching out a bit. The disciplines have very recognisable characteristics. Seeing each of the social sciences doing their own thing would be one way of setting them out. There would possibly be a small problem in separating out features of the disciplines from characteristics that could be more correctly attributed to the subject matters they address. However, it would be another way of doing it. I doubt if the answer to the question 'what are the social sciences like' would change materially.

WHAT ARE THEY LIKE?

The disciplines differ in typical subject matter, and in typical methods used to study their subjects. We have to insert the word 'typical' because a wide range of work goes on in each discipline. There are times when each turns to topics that are somewhat unusual for them, and times when they use uncharacteristic methods. Statistical data, and statistical techniques of one kind or another, are common in four of the social sciences. They are unusual in anthropology. However, among the articles discussed above we see cases where anthropologists have used statistical techniques, and to good effect. There also are cases where other disciplines explore subject matter in a manner similar to that of anthropology.

Even when data plays a role in an anthropological enquiry, such as in Janet Carsten's work on Langkawi, there is a crucial element of studying particular named individuals. Anthropologists frequently give us some words in the local language. The place and people, individual people, are clearly identified. Anthropology is the social science of the specific. Where a sociologist might refer to data collected from high schools in the mid West of the United States, anthropology directs us to a particular high school. Names might be changed to protect privacy. Society is made up of particular individuals, families, clubs, and so on. Anthropology is the 'small particle' branch of social science. We are continually reminded that when it comes to the elements that make up society, no two are alike, and no two are totally different.

Anthropologists are mainly involved in description. They bring home something to look at. Physical anthropologists bring back mainly objects. Social anthropologists bring back mainly verbal reports. These descriptions have a special feature of getting under the skin of the subjects and their practices. They are not simply reports from the outside. They may tell us something about former peasants living in high rise buildings, or victims of prejudice in a trailer park, or religious beliefs in Zanzibar. This 'something' has an element of what it is like to be there, not just for the anthropologist, but for the subjects themselves.

Good political science may involve capturing the sentiments of a particular situation. This is related to but different from the sensitivity of anthropological enquiry. The political canvas is too broad to support that much detail. How do anthropologists learn to undertake this subtle form of investigation? Specialising is part of the answer. Learning a language, learning one's way around, leaning how to fit in. These call for heavy intellectual investments. There is some transferability from one situation to another, but not all that much. Seeing the work of others is a help. Interacting with other investigators is important. In the end, one has to be thrown in, and have one's findings criticised by other practitioners.

Anthropologists are well aware of their skills, but are troubled by questions of what to study, and from what angle. How to choose a particular area, and why should they find it interesting, let alone someone else find it so? As reporters of the human drama, there is little problem. An insightful report of any small scale social phenomenon will be interesting, and sometimes fascinating. The problem arises from the scientific meaning of the work. Almost always there will be some kind of explanation, as well as description, in an anthropological enquiry. We can remind ourselves of the nature of some of these explanations.

> Gifts of turtle meat are made by some Melanesians to avoid theft.
>
> Polyandry in Napal is not motivated by harsh economic conditions.
>
> A complex building helps to enforce the authority of some chiefs in Nigeria.
>
> Feeling part of a community encourages Mexican migrants to remain in Texas.
>
> The Amish turn to shop keeping because it is a means of meeting the need to enter the money economy, which is not too disruptive of their society.
>
> The Chinese minority in Thailand engages in disposing of the neglected dead according to religious requirements because it improves their status.

These explanations make no claim of wider applicability. They do not suggest that what is true for the particular community under study has is true of others. I also think it would be fair to assert, but probably resisted by some, that the purely descriptive parts of these studies are the important parts, and the causal assertions are not always to be taken too seriously. Scientists are continually looking for alternative ways to account for what they observe. The explanations being put forward may be reasonable, but they may be wrong. How much effort has been made to find out which is the case in the examples above? I would claim that a limited amount of effort has been made, and the reason for this is that the explanations are not dreadfully important, and not worth a lot of effort. Very little, other than the accuracy of the individual claims, turns on whether they are right or not.

Social science requires an arm which is capable of intimate, subtle and detailed enquiry. Anthropology gives it that arm. At present the decisions as to where to direct that searchlight are bound to be a little arbitrary. Pure preference, professorial contacts, existing literature, budgetary considerations — all these play a part. The recent arrival of the Journal of Anthropological Theory is much to be welcomed. If more structure could be put on findings, they would slot together better, and suggest the next steps to be taken in a less arbitrary way than these are taken at present.

One way for anthropologists to decide where to study, and what to study when they get there, is to avoid territory covered by other researchers. There are exceptions, but in the material above there are almost no cases where the motive for study was to extend, or challenge, an investigation done by someone else. So here we have a field of enquiry where, for all its positive advantages, three factors come together in a potentially dangerous mix. The research depends heavily on the judgement, sensitivity and subjective impressions of the researcher. Second, there is little in the way of a theoretical framework to guide the researcher. And finally, in addition to being rather more on one's own intellectually than is the case in other disciplines, one is usually on one's own in the material under study. Not surprisingly, these factors together can lead to trouble.

In only two of the many anthropological studies considered in previous chapters do two researchers report having first-hand knowledge of the same subject matter. As it happens, in both cases they offer conflicting pictures of what is going on. These differences are not minor matters. They go to the very hearts of the information we are given. In one study we are told that certain self-help groups in the Philippines grew out of village tradition. They are needed for dealing with crime in areas where the state is unable to offer even minimal protection. Another study says, in effect, rubbish, these are CIA promoted institutions, designed to fight communism, and often engaging in criminal acts themselves.

The anthropology of housing provides another example of serious disagreement. One study tells us that a certain line of chiefs in Nigeria have secular authority, rather than the kind of religious authority which credits them with being able to affect the weather. Another scholar says they are believed by their subjects to have the power to affect to the weather. This occurs in a study where the secular nature of the authority is central to the whole thesis. This is not a minor or incidental difference of view. The point of my examples is not just that scientists differ. There is always disagreement at the active research perimeter in any discipline. And of course, disagreement can also suddenly crop up, and fruitfully so, in what was taken to be settled and agreed parts of a subject. My point about anthropology goes well beyond those considerations.

Progress in any subject is more likely to occur when there is agreement about most of the facts, and the disagreements are about which are the better explanations. In anthropology there is little in the way of conflict in the articles we have examined. When there is debate, it is essentially about the 'facts' of the case. I put facts in single quotes to indicate that these facts are not simple sensory observations.

The evidence of the previous chapters strongly supports the view that anthropologists are loners. They work on their different patches. Being interested in the particular, they are most unlikely to make claims that go beyond their patches. When they do break one or the other of these conventions, disputes are likely to be about the facts. One researcher or the other got it wrong. Of course, it is better to get it right. But the consequences for the subject due to which version is right are very slight. This lack of potentially fruitful conflict is a major problem for the discipline.

There are background notions in anthropology, such as 'functionalism', meaning that what we observe serves a useful purpose, however odd it may seem to people from a different culture. This is part of the admirable non-judgmental tradition of anthropology. It is part of viewing things from the inside. But such theoretical notions do not guide research. Nor do they depend on the outcome of research. No doubt there is a danger from having an elaborate theoretical framework when undertaking intimate investigation. One might well tend to find what one was conditioned to expect, rather than what was there. Anthropology is not in that danger. It has the opposite problem.

If the kinds of things anthropologists study are truly unique, it becomes more of an exercise in a sort of timeless, or contemporary, history. But are they unique? Within hours of first arriving in West Africa, and never having read about the area, Georgescu-Rogan gave a seminar on what it is like living in an African village. African listeners to his talk nodded continuously as he struck one insightful and recognisable note after another. When asked how he managed to do this, Georgescu-Roegen explained that he was an authority on East European peasant society, and one such community is like another. The suggestion that small scale human interaction and its social structure and practices may have much in common, comparing one society with another, offers a lot of hope for anthropological theory.

The anthropology articles we have reviewed above, as interesting as they are, point to an accumulation of knowledge through more examples rather than through more powerful theory. Investigative skills are on display unlike those of the historian or the journalist. They are appropriate for what can be directly observed, and are confined to that kind of application. They are not used to study events. They are directed to general practices, on going arrangements, and continuing customs. These skills could have much to contribute to joint efforts with other social scientists. Take the tribe of central bankers, for example. A lot has been done in the study of their decision-making. But without concrete involvement, there is a worrying feel of remoteness in this work. The anthropologist Josiah Heyman, among others, has advocated directing more anthropological attention to the study of bureaucracies in their exercise of power.

It is natural for anthropologists to limit their studies to communities where they can gain direct access. Indeed, access is an essential requirement of the discipline. The club, or tribe, of central bankers might be hard to penetrate in the way that anthropology requires. Similar remarks might be made about the possible study of Colombian drug traffickers. Social science disciplines which do not require close involvement can study hard to penetrate groups of this kind. While often very useful, working from a distance limits understanding. With many topics, the close look of anthropology could contribute greatly to our knowledge. There certainly are many communities, or groupings, which usually are studied from somewhat of a distance, where access would be possible. Collaboration between anthropologists and other social scientists in these areas appears to have much potential. At the same time, by working with more structured disciplines, anthropologists might overcome some of their reluctance to develop theories of what they so scrupulously and sensitively observe.

Economics places the least emphasis among social sciences on what is actually going on inside people's heads. None of the articles we have looked at make any effort to find out. Instead, very simple assumptions about subjective states are made, and consequences are derived. We shall examine this research strategy more fully subsequently. For anthropology, what people believe, think and feel is almost everything. Social psychology is also concerned with finding out what people are subjectively experiencing, but in a very different way. Where anthropology is unashamedly and unapologeticly based on sympathetic and sensitive observation, usually by a single observer, and so providing subjective reporting, social psychology aims at objectivity.

It is interesting to ask about the characteristic subject matter of the two disciplines. For anthropology it is interacting communities. These tend to be face-to-face groupings who see themselves as such. However, a common problem and a common identity can suffice, as in the case of Assyrians living in London. Often the subject matter is remote communities living according to traditional patterns and little affected by contact with the developed world. But it can be rural workers in modern Japan, and their problems in finding brides. Anthropologists look more at life in the round of the people they study, though concentrating on a particular aspect, such as family formation where polyandry is common.

Social psychologists tend to study groups with no face-to-face interaction, such as young children in middle class families in America and Mexico. There is much less emphasis on seeing people in the round. Nor do they expect their results to only hold for the particular subjects under study. On the contrary, the more universal the findings, the better.

Social psychologists often feel uneasy about working with university students, as the findings might not apply to people before or after university, and to those who will never go to university. Student groups are usually used for investigation because of convenience. An anthropologist studying a college class would be more interested in that class as subject matter, rather than as representative of a wider body. In fact, student groups are unlikely to be studied by anthropologists because of the tradition of reporting on remote communities, and because of their temporary nature. University faculties are more likely to come under scrutiny from anthropologists, like any other professional or occupational tribe.

Every social psychological study we have seen has an important statistical aspect. Clearly this is the approved method. The type of statistical inference that is employed, and the questions it is designed to answer, both have recognisable shapes. A major influence on those shapes comes from psychology proper. That subject forms the foundation for much of social psychology. This is admittedly a somewhat insecure basis for further work. But it tends to inform much of the work we see undertaken. The relationship between psychology and social psychology calls for comment.

Psychology has important links to medicine. Much of the research aims at finding cures for emotional and personality problems. A concept of normal, or healthy psychological states is needed in order to help in the identification of pathological states. It can determine the direction of efforts to bring about change, and provides a definition of success. The focus is on understanding and treating individuals. There is a kind of background assumption in medicine that at some level all healthy individuals are much the same. This is assumed to apply as much to emotional and mental phenomena as to bodily functions.

Social psychology is the study of average tendencies, or the typical composition of responses, views and behaviour, from groups of individuals. The distinction between healthy and unhealthy plays a very minor role for this discipline. There are exceptions. Regina Pernice and Judith Brook did research on the mental health of immigrants in New Zealand. But for the most part, we are asking what are the states of mind of people out there, without emphasising the distinction between ill and healthy states of mind.

Social psychological theory makes some attempt to explain the dynamics of the views that it uncovers. Why do people think, feel, and behave as they do? In answering this question, the discipline draws on, and often modifies, past work of noted practitioners, as well as drawing on ideas from psychology proper. Of course, groups do not have a psychological makeup. Individuals do. Being part of a group, in whatever sense that may be, may well exert an important influence on the feelings and actions of individuals. Social psychologists study the nature and strength of these influences.

This discipline is more geared up to make hopefully correct statements about groups, often quite large groups, and even universal statements about mankind as a whole. For example, Richard Lynn attempted to discover differences between men and women in their attitudes towards money that cut across all cultures. He worked with a large and diverse sample of cultures, and assumed that cultures not included would not give different results.

In a world awash with psychological theories, it often falls to social psychologists to produce the facts that can test theories. Unlike the anthropologists, the choice of facts to collect is usually driven by theory.

> How much, and in what way, does the victim knowing the rapist influence perceptions of the seriousness of the crime?
>
> Does holding to a religious faith induce more negative attitudes towards suicide?
>
> How does new information influence attitudes towards immigrants?
> Why are children given 'pocket money'?
>
> Do victims of prejudice prefer to respond with individual or collective action?
>
> Do men typically benefit more than women in intimate relationships ?

There are a number of observations we may make about these kinds of questions. First, they tend to take as the prime explicanda what people believe and how they respond. Second, the views people hold are 'explained' in terms of factors with which they have strong statistical associations. Typically this 'association' has both a statistical sense as well as intuitive plausibility. That women take a harsher view of rape than do men is understandable. That juries are more inclined to believe evidence which is induced under hypnosis is a bit less so. There may be little theoretical or intuitive reason for it, but it is the case. Incidentally, that this is the case is unfortunate, as other social psychological enquiry has shown the unreliability of hypnotically induced reports.

Third, there are causal theories in the background which social psychologists relate to the observed associations. Prominent among these is the notion that people prefer to have relatively consistent views of what is going on around them. They will attempt to change awkward facts into something less awkward by adjusting some aspect, or aspects, of their belief systems, or possibly by ignoring or playing down the uncomfortable facts.

Social psychology studies the opinions that are held by large aggregates of people. What are these opinions, and why do people believe as they do? Do individuals of a certain kind, third cousins for example, tend to see themselves as members of the family or not? Anthropologists could go deeply into how these opinions work out for a particular family. Social psychologists would have nothing to say about a particular family, but would attempt to find out who is seen as 'in' or 'out' across a large segment of society. Furthermore, they would offer explanations of differences in terms of any factor that seemed to be relevant, according to some theory or other. Perhaps religion, or income level, or occupation would prove to be relevant. None of the studies we have seen simply report what people think and feel without also offering some kind of explanation.

This discipline is very empirically oriented, but consider some of the kinds of facts it hopes to uncover.

> Are people with more vulnerable personalities more likely to confess to police interviewers?
>
> How does personality relate to church attendance?
>
> Do immigrants experience higher levels of anxiety?
>
> What expectations do parents have about their children's development?
>
> How does living in a mobile home affect the sense of well-being?

The statistical methods employed by social psychologists call for measuring subtle states of mind, both permanent and transitory. Anxiety, vulnerability, ambivalence, well-being — these are elusive facts. Beliefs are inherently subtle things, however real, and they are inescapably involved in the investigations of social psychologists. One can approach them through intuitive verbal description, as in much of mainstream psychology. Social psychologists insist on measurement. We have no examples of researchers saying that something may be important for the phenomenon under investigation, but it cannot be measured. Distributing questionnaires, or conducting coded interviews, is assumed to be capable of putting numbers to anything from fear to pride, and beyond.

There are plenty of illegitimate objections to this procedure. A popular one is to argue that 'By pride I mean something different from that', whatever the definition the investigator is using. Fair enough. But specify what you do mean, and let us see if we can identify a suitable measure of it. The reply 'I mean lots of different things' is the response of a scoundrel, refusing to lay his or her cards on the table. But we must be cautious here. It is equally foolish to hold that if something cannot be measured, or we do not know how to measure it yet, it is meaningless. Social psychologists are very grown up with respect to these matters. Their goal is to take measurement as far as it can go, always being aware of potential pit-falls and limitations.

In its efforts at measurement, the discipline has two great advantages. The first comes from studying groups rather than individuals. When measurement is straightforward, such as how much does a person weigh, individuals are as easy to measure as groups. Measuring the self-esteem of an individual is another matter. The scale only has meaning with reference to some average, and is subject to large measurement error. This can lead to a situation where one is bound to be very unsure about the measurement found for any individual, but much more confident about the measurement for the group. If the behaviour of errors can reasonably be assumed to have certain characteristics, such as that small errors occur more frequently than large errors, positive errors are as likely as negative errors, and errors are independent of the size of the true value, statistical techniques can be brought to bear to make statements about the level of confidence one can have in the measurement of a characteristic of a group. Not only are these statements quite trustworthy, the level of confidence, or how likely they are to deviate from the true value by certain amounts, can be specified.

The second great advantage comes from employing standard, or 'off-the-shelf', scales rather than designing a questionnaire specifically for each investigation. This means that a set of questions, or propositions, designed to measure self-esteem, to take that example, has been used over and over in the past. There is an accumulated body of information on the responses to that set of questions. How does age, gender, income, or education, for example, influence the outcome? Furthermore, as questionnaires are used repeatedly, they can be refined. Questions which appear to be unrelated to the object of the exercise can be weeded out.

There is a sense in which social psychology, as we can see from the studies above, often has very limited social content, and in many instances could be described more accurately as statistical psychology. These statistical procedures are used to get around the problems of measuring aspects of individuals, and to test general propositions, such as that religious affiliation promotes hostility to homosexuals. We have noted before the obvious fact that only individuals, not groups or collectives, have a psychological make-up. While there probably are genetic influences on the psyche, as well as idiosyncratic random elements, social influences, one would think, are major factors. How do the features of the social environment work to shape mind sets?

The dynamics of personality formation must be one of the most difficult areas to study. It should not be too surprising that none of the social psychological studies reported above do more than hint at the effects of the social context on the opinions and emotional make-up of people. They are more inclined to go in the other direction. What is the effect of having an authoritarian personality on voting on legislation regarding illegal immigration? Social psychology relates socially significant views and behaviour to aspects of personality. These features of personality are often treated as given for particular investigations. It may be more difficult to study, but it would be intriguing to have an idea about how a society which promotes consumer activity, for example, affects personality. In fairness, there is some of this kind of enquiry, but much of social psychology is pretty remote from the causality of influences on our minds from what others believe, and how society is structured.

An interesting and distinguishing feature of social psychology compared to other social sciences is its heavy reliance on experiment. How do responses to racial prejudice vary with the strength of the evidence that prejudice is at work? This kind of question can be examined experimentally. The usual method is to give one group a hypothetical report containing weak evidence of racial prejudice, and another group, as much like the first as the experimenter can make it, much stronger evidence. The responses of the two groups as to how they choose to deal with prejudice can be compared.

These experiments occur repeatedly in the literature, and are a distinguishing feature of social psychology. Drawing on experimental evidence is admirable, but the fact that it applies so readily in this discipline has to do in part with the curious lack of social content in social psychology. Typically what is varied for experimental purposes is some piece of information. For example, different groups are given different information about the racial mix of an accused rapist and his possible victim. Another example might be giving strongly and weakly positive information about a particular group of immigrants. These variations can well occur within a given social context or structure. The experimenters are typically not asking their subjects how they would respond to different social arrangements.

There are good reasons for not asking subjects in what way they would be different people, in effect, with different views and responses, if they lived under different social arrangements, or in a different kind of society. For example, a narrative could tell one group that in your society concealed hand guns are allowed, and another group that in your society they are not allowed. The members of both groups could then be asked to score how likely they are to be a victim of a burglary. The trouble with this type of experimenting is that it is asking subjects to reveal their theory about an aspect of society. They cannot draw on immediate feelings in the same way that they can if told that the man was white and the woman was black, or the other way around, and are asked how likely is it that the woman was raped, rather than having consensual sex.

In all the examples we have seen, the broad social context is the same for all participants. Typically, the experimenter tests for differences in judgements, for example, those associated with such features as the conditions of the roads, or the time of day. It is in this sense that social psychology is the least 'social' of the social sciences. Where experiments are used, they tend to vary factors other than social arrangements. Nevertheless, social psychology plays a critical role in uncovering what people feel and believe.

The kinds of information social psychology provides can play an important role in other parts of social science. A political scientist may conjecture that voters in cities may be may be more optimistic about a piece of legislation than rural voters. An economist may suspect that low self-esteem leads to a conservative investment strategy. If they want the facts, social psychologists can provide the best available measures of optimism, self-esteem and a host of other socially significant factors. The articles we have seen suggest that the research agenda of the discipline appears to respond more to issues in psychology than to issues in other social science research.

Turning to political science, it is noticeable and remarkable that in the research we have seen that two very distinct branches of the discipline are evident. One branch might almost be described as macro anthropology. Instead of reporting on the inner workings of a small community, these researchers take the nation, or a large slice of it, as their area to be investigated. This investigation is based on something very much like first-hand knowledge. This is acquired through giving focused and sensitive attention to media reports, speeches, conversations, actions of political actors, and in other ways testing the political atmosphere.

We see this approach in the work of Leonardo Villalon, Jane and Peter Schneider, Federico Varese, Deborah Rhodes, Michael Baun, Jane Lewis and others. These researchers develop a kind of first-hand intimacy with some political situation. Like anthropologists they usually are aware of how different participants in the political process see and interpret what is happening around them. They simultaneously have to have a feel for what it is like for the various participants in the political fray, while hanging on to an objective stance on how the pieces fit together. Here is a sample list of topics which political scientists have approached through a method I am calling macro anthropology.

Public housing policy in the United Kingdom

The influence of religion on political stability in Senegal

The power of organised crime in post communism Russia

The politics of welfare provision and concepts of the family

The motives for agreeing the Maastricht Treaty

Of course these same topics can be approached through more objective and largely statistical methods. With those methods it is likely that parts of the topics would be peeled away from the broader picture. Staying with the broader picture, the more intuitive and subjective approaches have the advantage of treating topics more in the round. Actual policy debates, and the search for solutions that can be applied to perceived problems, provides the motive for investigation in political science in many cases. The relevance to policy calls for a more comprehensive treatment than work which is motivated more by scientific advancement of the subject.

At the other end of the spectrum we find work in political science which addresses relatively narrowly specified questions and uses data to find answers. It appears to be an equally common way of doing work in the discipline. Of the thirty-four articles in political science journals which dealt with the six topics I chose for investigation, sixteen based their work on an exercise in data collection and analysis. In some other cases data was used, but in a way that was incidental to the study, in my judgement, so I do not include those articles among the sixteen data based studies. There is an element of judgement involved in this classification, but it is not important in the overall result. On any reasonable count, about one half of articles in political science journals that address the kinds of topics covered here are based on statistical investigation.

While at it, we might note that the level of statistical sophistication involved in most of these studies is not very great. It may be adequate for the tasks at hand, but more advanced techniques could, and probably will, find a place in political science. A reasonable example of the kind of empirical work typical of this kind of political science investigation might be David Nice's study of different use of the death penalty in different States of America. Basic regressions are used to identify the factors, such as a more conservative ideology, which are important in accounting for differences.

The real skill and ingenuity in the study is not in statistical method, but in constructing indices of 'use of the death penalty' and 'conservative ideology'.

In order to measure the degree to which a state has a conservative political stance, Nice uses two methods. First there is a large survey, State by State, where voters self-assessed themselves as conservative, moderate or liberal. This survey was published in the Journal of Politics, 1985. He also uses the proportion of voters who voted for McGoven, a clear liberal, in the 1972 presidential election. In itself there is nothing so remarkable about this approach, but it does require a working knowledge. The explanatory factors which the study explores are representative of much work in the discipline. They do not come from an explicitly specified theory. Rather, they come from a combination of popularly held views, and informed intuition.

This discipline is based more on a common subject matter than on a shared body of theory, or on a particular set of skills. We see more variety in approach than with the other disciplines. This runs all the way from an in-depth sense of a political situation, rather 'anthropological' in feel, to the kind of statistical investigation which is common in sociology. The subject matter of political science can be defined as government, law, political processes and power. Practitioners in the discipline share a common interest in the subject matter, while adopting very diverse methods in approaching it.

Of course political science has no monopoly in the study of government and politics. Sociology and economics are similarly involved at many points. Political economy and political sociology are not readily distinguishable from political science, nor is there any pressing need to firm up the distinctions. The labels can be confusing. 'Political economy' can mean anything from less technical economics, to economic method applied to the institutions of government.

Terminology is more of a problem, if we let it be so, when we consider political science than with other social sciences. A graphic illustration can be found in A New Handbook of Political Science, Oxford 1996. I maintain that not a single article in this imposing volume is an example of a piece of science. So what is it? A heady mixture of political philosophy and methodology, is my answer. The philosophical roots of the discipline are more in evidence in political science than in other social sciences. The classics of politics are philosophical in a way that the classics of economics are not.

It certainly is the case that the foundations of economics were laid down by philosophers like Adam Smith and John Stuart Mill. Today, apart from specialists in the philosophy of economics, modern philosophers do not concern themselves with subsequent developments in economics that have sprung from those philosophical foundations. The situation in political science is different. The philosophical classics of politics did not tend to lead to a body of theory that later researchers could refine and test. They generally led to more philosophy.

As we are concerned with social science, these philosophical concerns are not evident in the studies of political science we see above. What is evident is the absence of a body of theory of government or of politics. In one respect this is a consequence of the topics chosen. Political science does have a strong theoretical wing in the theory of voting. Economists and political scientists both work in that area. However, in the topics we have examined in the chapters above, we cannot identify a fully developed set of interrelated explanations that are normally employed in the discipline.

Every society has an economy, and every society has a political structure and political processes. Political science addresses the latter. On the whole, it does not have the predatory nature of economics, because it does not have a firm and all-purpose theoretical apparatus to deploy on any front. Whether it will come to have such a body of interconnected explanations remains to be seen. For the present, it is the subject matter, rather than techniques of investigation, that remains crucial. It is clear that if we are to study society, government and politics, along with the economy, is a vital concern. Political science has the feature of staying close to matters of immediate policy concern. The discipline has the highest proportion of work which is of direct policy relevance.

Economics is the least empirical of the social sciences. Here are some of the questions that are addressed in the articles reported above using the method of pure theory. Other articles may bring evidence to bear. This is a list of questions where the researchers have chosen to approach their topics using the method of pure theory, and without any reference to statistical data, or other types of facts.

> How much should be spent on collecting taxes in order to maximise net government revenue, given the rate of taxes?
>
> Will economic competition tend to eliminate corruption in firms?
>
> Are there benefits to society from a prohibition against charging interest?
>
> Why are lower volumes of transactions associated with lower prices in the housing market and in other markets?
>
> Do shelters for married women reduce violent attacks by husbands?

No other social science is inclined to address these and other matters using the deductive method. Economists can employ this method because they are prepared to make assumptions about the goals that people have.

Over a range of circumstances, but typically not all circumstances, these assumptions generate predictions of what individual agents will do. Another part of the economic method enables the actions of individual agents to be combined into a response for the 'economy' as a whole.

I put economy in single quotes to draw attention to the last item in the list above. Here we are dealing with battered wives and their husbands, which is not normally thought of as an economy. The problem yields to economic analysis because it is assumed that the husbands and wives have certain goals, which are very simple to specify. It is assumed that both husbands and wives get some benefit from being together. Wives are better off the less they are attacked. The type of husband studied in this model is assumed to get some utility from beating his wife, and beating more yields more utility. The model makes predictions as to how shelter provision will affect wives under threat of being beating. Of course, we can reason all we want, but in the end, the answer is "out there", as they say. Among other benefits, pure theory is a way of getting a handle on what might be the answer. Better science depends on combining theory with evidence.

Here is where the propensity of economists to model is possibly a worry. Pure theory works best, in the sense of putting some restrictions on what will happen, when a small number of factors are at work. For example, in the interesting analysis of fatal encounters in disputed territories in the crime chapter, two factors enter the argument. These are the cost of loosing a fight and judgements about the chances of winning. This yields what is to me a very interesting conjecture, namely that guns make it harder to predict the outcome of a fight, and so result in more fatal encounters. Clearly there are a host of other factors that could be brought in; these include the degree of mutual support in gangs, reputation, police action or inaction, racial tensions, alternatives to controlling territory, and many more.

To take a more conventionally economic problem, firms may compete through pricing policy, the quality of their products, advertising, refunds, after sales services, and so on. Typical pure theory exercises take on board one, or possibly two, of these potential areas of competition into consideration. What will happen when they are all at work? Who knows? Pure theory is rarely very good at addressing the total picture. On the other hand, a crisp and insightful result for a part of the story is better than an unproductive chat which hopes to, or pretends to, cover the whole story.

It is possible to say interesting and potentially useful things in economics through pure theory. In the other social sciences we do not find examples of investigations of that kind. That is 'fact', for the topics chosen and for the nineties. My explanation, like it or not as I will not defend it here, is because the other disciplines lack sufficient theoretical structure to support deductive investigation. Not a single example can be found of a non-economics exercise in pure theory in chapters five through ten. However, the fact that productive theory is possible in economics does not mean that there is little empirical work in that discipline. Roughly, the breakdown above is two-thirds theoretic and one-third empirical. The summary has to be rough because most essentially theoretical papers make some reference to facts, usually of a stylised nature, and there is some room for judgement as to whether the theory in effect stands alone or is linked to evidence.

At this point we must wrestle with a familiar objection to economic theory, which cannot be allowed to pass, let alone be taken to be right, just because it is familiar. The typical statement goes that theory is one thing, but what we care about is the 'real world'. Personally, I would rather refer to the 'world'. The phrase the 'real world' suggests the existence of a world more real than the one out there. But anyhow, the really essential point is that economic theory is about the world. As it tends to deal with one aspect in isolation, which in fact never occurs in isolation, it is hard to test whether the explanation is right or not. But the fact that something is hard to test in no way suggests that it is either wrong or irrelevant. It is invariably the case that objectors to what they think of as economic theory in fact have an alternative theory in mind. Usually that alternative theory is muddled to such a degree that it cannot be specified. Economic theory, for all its worries, is the finest achievement of social science.

Having given praise where it is due, we must also note that econo-land is an odd place in the house of science. The elements which make up economic explanations link up to each other with near perfection. This is apparently a splendid realisation of the goals of science. Economics is neater than physics. However, order has been achieved at a cost. Consistency is assured by the relentless use of conventional assumptions. The awkward nature of the world out there is kept at bay. It is not so much that the air is stale, rather we see work in a vacuum. Much of economics consists of solving surprisingly subtle maximising problems. Often they look easy, but in fact have unexpected wrinkles. This is great training for the discipline, and for any social science. It is muscle building. It is weight training in the gym, fine as far as it goes, but not to be mistaken for unguarded confrontation outside of the gym.

In fairness to the econo-land discipline, we should note that the topics chosen for enquiry in this book tend strongly in the direction of microeconomics. The macro issues of inflation, growth, unemployment and the like tend to be studied exclusively by economists, so there is a bias in the way the subject is presented here. It has been suggested that macro investigation tends to be driven more by events in the world, such as quite high levels of inflation and unemployment running together for quite long periods. Micro enquiry, such as we see here, tends to be driven more by the unfolding of the logic of previous work, and this may contribute to the slightly other worldly feel to econo-land as presented here.

Now what can we make of our last social science discipline, sociology? The founding fathers, Parsons and others, had in mind establishing a full blown body of theory. It was thought that this grand theory of society would probably incorporate economic theory as a sub-section. The sociology articles we see above make it clear that no such grand edifice of theory is being employed. More likely, that grand theory endeavour has been quietly set aside in favour of other objectives.

From the articles in chapters five through ten we can discern a role for sociology which has a residual aspect to it. Questions which are not central to the economy, and are not central to the study of government, can come into the domain of sociology, more or less by default. There is absolutely nothing wrong with this. The economy and the government, however important, are far from being the whole of society. Moreover, sociologists can adopt a different take on the economy, and on the polity, than are conventional in economics and political science, and do this to advantage.

This difference in approach in sociology to what is conventional subject matter in other social sciences is part of what defines the subject. Along with this goes its concentration on 'residual' material, not taken up by any of the other social science disciplines. One way of describing this difference in approach in sociology is more objectivity and a higher level of generality than anthropology, and more concern with behaviour than states of mind compared to social psychology. It is instructive to remind ourselves of a series of questions posed by sociologists.

To what extent do people in Britain believe in their religions, and to what extent do they practice their religions?

How do religious affiliations influence moral stances of members on matters such as AIDS, homosexuality, pornography and artificial insemination?

Why do Mexicans migrate to the United States?

How does living on the street affect the propensity to commit crimes?

What are the causes of violent crime?

To what extent are 'neighbours' family members?

Do mothers working outside the home adversely affect their children?

Does making divorce difficult lead to more domestic violence?

How do fashion and marketing influence the aesthetics of homes?

What are the effects of discrimination on the allocation of public housing?

How is money controlled in families?

What accounts for the political alliances which developed in the Greenback/Bullionist debates in America?

What are the effects of foreign sportsmen and women on host countries and on source countries?

Immediately we see that the subject matter of sociology is more diverse than that of the other social sciences. This means that it requires a longer list of representative studies to capture the flavour of the discipline. It is clear that almost anything can come under the scrutiny of sociology. It also is clear that there is no common framework, or theoretical stance, that is common to the various investigations. One could go further. There is almost no theory, in the sense of general explanation, which can be drawn on and employed in individual studies.

The first nine of the thirteen investigations listed above are statistical studies. Most are quite large scale in the sense of lots of observations, and sometimes also large in that many explanatory factors are combined in a study. This is pretty representative of a large part of sociology. Four-fifths of the sociology articles we discuss in the substantive chapters above are statistical in nature. The authors hope to uncover ‘the facts’, often in the sense of 'compiled' facts, as defined above. How many Catholic Church members are there in the United Kingdom, and how many members of the Church of England? This type of work is essentially a difficult exercise in counting. It calls for care and fine judgement.

Other 'high order' facts go beyond counting, and examine associations between social quantities. Kposowa, Breault and Harrison relate violent crimes, and crimes against property in the United States to such factors as the ethnic makeup of counties, urbanisation, unemployment, poverty, education, and at least ten other factors. They work with over two thousand observations. There is a theory in the back of all this, namely that there is a culture of crime which is important in some areas. As it happens, the data does not support that theory. The important point is that we cannot find a structure of linked explanations here. The best we might do is to establish that there is a strong association between crimes against property and density of population, if there is such an association.

A good deal of sociological investigation is statistical and of this kind. Data is analysed to see if there is a relation between, say, unemployment and robbery in the United States. We might find that areas with more unemployment have more robbery. Intuition might support such a relationship on the basis of economic need, and such notions as the devil plays with idle hands. In a way, this is much like the statistical work done by economists. And indeed there are overlaps. But we can crudely distinguish between typical examples of the work from both disciplines. An economist is likely to specify the goal of an individual. He or she will assume that people behave in such a way as to attempt to achieve their goals, taking account of such matters as the chances of getting caught and the cost of being caught. A relatively small number of variables will enter into an explicit theory of individual behaviour.

The sociologist will have similar thoughts in mind, but is unlikely to specify the objectives of individuals formally. Often quite a number of variables enter the analysis. Rather than an explicit theory, there is a fishing exercise hoping to turn up statistically significant associations. The economist is very much inclined to assume that deep down all people are the same. Broadly speaking they have similar objectives, and rationally figure out how to achieve them. In this approach, individuals only differ in their circumstances, and possibly in the information at their disposal. The sociologist is much more inclined to entertain the view that certain identifiable groups, such as young men, ethnic minorities, new arrivals in the country, products of split homes, and other such considerations can bear on the likelihood of committing a crime. Exactly how these possible factors relate to each other is left unspecified.

WHY FIVE DISCIPLINES?

A quick thumbnail sketch of the five social sciences would go like this. Political science, economics and sociology cover the main aspects of society, partly because anything not in the first two can be fitted into the third. Anthropology studies the inner workings of small groups, the building blocks of society, and social psychology studies what people are like in terms of their mental states and opinions. Traditions of investigation and intuition determine what observations might be relevant to particular studies, except in economics where a body of theory dominates. Compiling and analysing statistical data is the main method, except in anthropology, and often not in political science.

Is there anything we could readily cut out, or subsume under another discipline? Another way of putting this question is to ask if the questions one of the disciplines is asking are the same or similar to those of another discipline. The result from the sets of questions we see above is a clear negative answer. The politics and economics of society must be on the agenda, and while overlapping and interacting, are sufficiently distinct to support traditions of investigation. And clearly society is more than its politics and economics, and this must be studied as well. At the same time, the study of families, communities and 'clubs', broadly interpreted, as well as the psychology of the people making up society, must be part of social science. The existing five would all appear to pass the tests of being distinct from the others and addressing important aspects of society.

These arguments are by way of logical defence of the existing divisions. There also are practical, or pragmatic defences that could be made. Social science is different from natural science in a number of ways, one of which is that we are continually observing society. Social scientists do a good deal of conscious and unconscious empirical observation. They do not all emphasise and observe the same things. Not surprisingly, economists observe prices, while political scientists take in elections, and other means of changing governments. Sociologists are quick to see the significance of mobile phones for teenagers. No one person can concentrate on it all. Having the different disciplines tends to divide up these observational undertakings.

In a similar way, subjects have their histories, their literatures, their current themes and developments. It is interesting to see the fate of many well-trained mathematicians who see the elementary nature, for them, of some of the mathematics used in economics. A number in this position have wrongly deduced that they can easily contribute to the field. Economists are inclined to listen to them for awhile, particularly if they are touting what is to economists an unfamiliar technique. But more often than not, nothing comes out of this in terms of economic insight. The mathematicians may have the techniques, but without being immersed in a subject, it is hard for even skilled technicians to bring about advances in it.

The case for fewer social science subjects appears to be easy to refute. We seem to need them all. What about the other side? Do we need more disciplines? If so, it is not because of subject matter that falls outside the purview of all the existing disciplines. Partly because of the partly residual nature of sociology, everything in society in principle has a place where it is studied, or can be studied.

One could make a fancy argument that phenomena can go unnoticed until a subject springs up to study them. This is a bit like claiming that men did not see the stars until astronomy came along. As a logical matter, one has to concede that there may be important blocks of potential subject matter that no social science has investigated, or is naturally geared up to investigate. There is no way of showing that that is not the case. On the other hand, until someone walks into the room holding out this subject matter for us to see, we can agree that there does not appear to be a case for more disciplines based on hitherto ignored social material.

The case for more disciplines has to be based on a re-organisation of subject matter and investigative techniques in a new way which will lead to better progress in understanding. There is one candidate out there for this treatment. We could call it the discipline of institutions. Institutions are formal and informal arrangements for organising functions and activities. Marriage is an institution. So is a central bank, an army, a football league and a limited liability company. Social behaviour and activity are conditioned by existing institutional arrangements. Social science attempts to explain behaviour and the activity that takes place, given the institutional set up. It also attempts to explain why the institutional set up is as it is.

There is no separate and self-contained social science of 'institutions'. Each of the social sciences works on the nature and the consequences of the institutions within its field. If institutions have a great deal in common, having political scientists explain the existence and structure of political parties, and economists explain the same for firms, might be wasteful and inviting duplication of effort. The 'institution' discipline could try to account for the rules of the game, so to speak, and economics and political science could be left with studying the progress of the games. If the institutions can usefully be studied as entities in themselves, without too much concern for their settings, which is another way of saying if they have a lot in common, this is an attractive proposition.

In my view firms are sufficiently different from armies so that the discipline of institutions is a non-starter. The institutional arrangement is so much a part of each separate subject as to preclude the specialism of institutions. Subjects like management science and operations research are the disciplines of institutions, but from rather special perspectives. They tend to be more involved in consulting than in scientific investigation. Improved performance and greater efficiency are important objectives. This is not quite the same as explaining the existence and role in society of various institutions.

It is conceivable that a discipline of institutions could develop that revolved around a set of coherent principles with sufficient explanatory power to be able to help in understanding economic, political and other social institutions. I doubt if this will happen, but you never know. A number of investigators nowadays place high hopes on concepts like chaos, complexity and catastrophe for providing important insights. Of course, we need all the help we can get. My contention is that this help, when it comes, and in fairness it must be said that some has come, will supplement existing disciplines rather than constitute a new discipline. The formal argument for this contention is much the same as that for institutions. A class of subject matter has to be found to be similar in hitherto unrecognised ways in order to justify or promote a new social science discipline.

INTERDISCIPLINARY SOCIAL SCIENCE

From time to time, some of the organisations which fund social science research favour interdisciplinary work, rather than research within a single discipline. This view is often shared by senior academic administrators, and by some researchers. Many different factors come into this debate between those encouraging discipline based enquiry and those favouring interdisciplinary work. It has to be admitted that some of the fuel for this fire comes from considerations such as empire building, sitting uncomfortably within a discipline, distrust of specialists, divide and rule, and simple ignorance. There also are valid reasons for involving more than one discipline in a research project.

We have to distinguish two different applications of the interdisciplinary approach. The first combines the separate insights from more than one discipline in addressing a question. The second aims to produce a new kind of research where specialists from more than one discipline undertake work together which is different in nature from the work done within their disciplines. This is an important distinction. The first says, in effect, here is what social psychology can tell us about betting on horses, and here is what economics can say on the topic. The two only come together because they are in a single article or volume. Each in itself would be just as meaningful if presented on its own. The second type of interdisciplinary enquiry cannot be separated out into its components. It is also hard to find examples of it.

In the studies above, one or two combined insights from more than one discipline in a significant way. The work of Douglas Massy and Kirstin Espinosa on migration of Mexicans into the United States combines economic and sociological enquiry. And it can be argued that the analysis of the Greenback and Gold backed money controversy by Bruce Carruthers and Sarah Babb cuts across disciplines. The same could be said for Kenneth Meier's work on drug abuse laws in America, with its political, economic and sociological aspects.

Has Meier reached professional competence in all three subjects, or is the level where the mixing takes place pretty accessible to a well trained and disciplined mind? It is no criticism of Meier to hold that it is the latter. While there is more than one researcher in the other two examples, both come from the same discipline, and the outward look, while deserving of full credit, does not require especially deep understanding.

Some topics call for at least a nodding familiarity with another discipline. Any research effort which laid claim to some degree of comprehensive coverage would probably have to incorporate at least three disciplines, and maybe all five. But when do we need a full and comprehensive coverage of a subject? We do not need it for the purposes of science. We do not need it to advance knowledge. At the moment of writing a black cat is being affectionate to the point of molesting me. Suppose we want to study this cat, or even cats in general. Do we have to study all aspects? Must we bring in all the biological sciences, plus the psychology of cats, their chemistry, and so on? While all these aspects are interesting, they need not be studied at once, or together. Progress can be made, and this is fortunate to the point of being the door that opens the possibility of science, by dividing up the field.

When it comes to policy, or applications of social science, the picture can change significantly. To take a classic example, a floating exchange rate may make good sense for a less developed country from an economic perspective. Yet any government contemplating such a move would be well advised to examine the politics of such a move. The politics, in turn, may depend, at least in part, on sociological considerations.

There is some evidence that people respond to economic incentives when making decisions about marriage, numbers of children, education and saving. Many would see it as a legitimate goal of government to encourage responsible rearing of children, including insuring that they attend school. Exhortation is often tried by people in power. We might want to know how effective it is. Alternatively, we may want to know how effective are incentives provided by such measures as taxation and subsidy, or prison, and how they might best be employed. Inevitably, more than one social science comes into such an exercise. And now the hard question. Do they enter in an additive way, one added to another, or is combined knowledge called for which is not fully present in the individual disciplines on their own?

There are two aspects to answering this difficult question. We must have an idea as to whether the findings of the disciplines occasionally contradict one another, or whether they illuminate different parts of the subjects. If they contradict each other, by which I mean that the importance of a causal factor is held by one subject to be significantly different from that held by another, one of he subjects is wrong. That is all there is to it, provided they have a common concept of 'cause' and 'importance'. If they have legitimately different views of these two things, then there is no actual contradiction, only the appearance of it. The conflict can be resolved by specifying what the subjects are saying more clearly.

In the chapters above we see the five social sciences all addressing the same six topics. I do not believe there is a single case where the findings of one subject contradict those of another. Where there is conflict, practitioners within a discipline are disagreeing with each other. Of course this is perfectly healthy. There often is a kind of dialectic, or adversarial phase, in the development of knowledge. The lack of contradictory findings across subjects is a somewhat surprising finding of this investigation. In principle, it could be that conflicting views from one subject compared to another are common. In fact, I claim, on the basis of the evidence above, they are almost non-existent.

Rather than outright conflict, we can find cases of research bias. Investigations into the causes of crime provide an example that goes to the heart of this situation. The sociologists Augustine Kposowa, Kevin Breault and Beatrice Harrison use multiple regression techniques to attempt to explain variations in the amount of violent crime. They use a large range of explanatory variables which are largely demographic in nature. What is the ethnic composition, age, divorce status, and so on, of the county? No reference is made to policing, the chances of getting caught, or the penalties imposed in different countys. On the other hand, the economists Harold Brumm and Dale Cloninger relate violent crime to ethnic and other demographic characteristics, but include the intensity of policing and the severity of punishment. There is clear subject bias, if you will. The economists take a cost and benefit approach to crime, and the sociologists see crime more as an outcome of pre-determined roles, to put it crudely.

It would be a mistake to see these as contradictory approaches to crime. All researchers agree that all sorts of things influence the amount of crime taking place in a county, or other region. The question is how important are the various influences, how do they interact, and what do you choose to investigate in a particular study. My reading of the studies we see above is that the discipline of the researcher tends to influence the choice of explanatory factors to be investigated. This is not the same as having rival theories of what determines the amount of crime. I am trained to see the effect of age on crime, and you are trained to see the effect of policing on crime. We both agree that both affect crime.

A very important part of being scientific is breaking problems and mysteries down into manageable bits. This is one of the functions of disciplines. They make the first divisions, and particular researchers make further divisions. Looking at different aspects of housing, for example, is not the same as having contradictory views about housing. The case for more interdisciplinary work cannot be based either on the need for completeness, or to resolve conflicting explanations. The former, or something approaching it, may be needed for, or just helpful to policy, but not for advancing the disciplines. The case based on resolving conflicts fails because it is hard to find any. What remains?

I suggest above that there does seem to be some potential gain from bringing anthropological and social psychological work to bear on the other three disciplines. We can elaborate a bit on that. Economics in particular has a connected body of theoretical propositions. On the whole the connections do not lead to reliable propositions about the world, but to a self-contained body of interesting conjectures. Social psychology and anthropology could facilitate certain links to more substantive aspects of social reality. There are many problems where this would not apply, but some where it would. At the same time, this process of integrated work would give more structure to anthropological enquiry, and help to move social psychology more towards societal considerations and away from a purely psychological orientation.

THE ECONOMICS 'TAKE-OVER'

Many economists, who feel that matters outside of economics can be of interest, favour improving knowledge in these areas through an economics 'take-over'. There are a number of sides to this proposed take-over. First comes a general presumption in favour of developing formal models for whatever is being studied, be it elections, marriage, education or any other social event. A close second is the view that these models should include a notion of maximising agents — people with goals who take actions in an effort to go as far as the constraints they face allow them to go in achieving their goals. Third come a number of methodological tricks or stratagems. These include: ignoring history; employing concepts of equilibrium, or explaining what we see by where the system is headed; looking at one aspect of the problem at a time.

A more brutal and institutional aspect of the take-over is to suggest that all social scientists be trained as economists. Economists would then be turned loose on all aspects of society. Similar methods and approaches would be used as currently dominate in economics. As silly as all this sounds, there are times when it is a tempting proposition. What times? During or after a weak seminar by a practitioner in one of the other four social sciences. There are instances where just being more organised, better trained, and dare I say it, smarter, gives enough of an advantage to the interloper. But as a general strategy for social science, it is a poor idea.

Most of the case against the economics take-over is implicit in what is said above. The point about informal empirical inputs can stand a little amplification. Social science, for all its disadvantages compared to natural science, does have the advantage, for those who can realise it, of its investigators living day-to-day in an observational laboratory. Physical scientists rely on experimenters for their facts and tests of theories. Looking around does not give much information about atoms. But looking around does give information about social reality. One cannot attend to all of it, and as I argue above, a discipline helps to organise observations of parts of it. A monopoly of economic perspectives would tend to result in missing a good deal of what is to be seen out there.

The measurement and investigative skills of social psychology cannot be acquired in passing. It takes full-time effort over a lifetime. There is no hope of economists doing that. The case for anthropological enquiry is a little harder to make, but real nevertheless. The articles in chapters five through ten provide the best evidence. In my view, they are almost all the product of sensitive and well-trained researchers. This assertion can best be tested, and perhaps can only be tested, by reading what they have to say.

There is too much institutional material in political science for the subject to be swallowed up by economics. And the macro anthropological skills of the political scientist cannot easily be acquired. The biggest flaw in the economics take-over programme is not its effects on the other four disciplines, but the effects on economics itself. The discipline needs to break a little free of its own success. It has to be more open to evidence. The facts are rarely used to limit the range of enquiry to the extent that they might. Traditional assumptions play that role, and that is not the same thing.

As one might expect in a huge intellectual undertaking like economics, all sorts of things are tried, and all sorts of things go on, in spite of the grip of the mainstream. There certainly are looser, more speculative parts of the subject. Interestingly, over the past fifty years there have been great gains in understanding. Hosts of new ideas are moving through the subject today that were hardly there thirty years ago. And where did these new ideas come from, the rigid and convention bound central core of the subject, or the looser, less mathematical periphery? Surprisingly, it is the former that has yielded the new ideas. Unfolding the logic of economic investigation continues to yield results. The 'take-over' would bring this aspect to other subjects, but it would shut off, or at least play down, other avenues of enquiry. Economics needs to be opened up to these approaches. Leaving economics more on its own through a take-over of the other social sciences would hurt economics.

HOW ARE WE DOING?

I am not sure that it is even possible, or meaningful, to make an overall evaluation of the social sciences. How do you compare the work, and to what? Having said that, it is important and informative to try.

It is clear that quantitatively, and in terms of intellectual muscle power, economics stands apart from the rest. This is because of an earlier start, compared to the other social sciences, and because of a ready demand for the ideas being produced, and for people trained in the subject. There may also be something in the subject matter itself which promotes scientific development. Economics has a more obvious applied side than the other social sciences, and ultimately this fuels the development of the subject. The sheer number of undergraduate and graduate students; the economists in government and private firms; the volume of researchers in universities and elsewhere, all cumulate to a large intellectual effort. In the last chapter we discuss the potential for application in the other social sciences.

The other outstanding observation which follows from the many articles discussed above is the dominant position of the United States in social science. If we take the section above on migration, half the articles making it into this study, intended to be comprehensive of the major English language journals, are about migration into the United States. The rest of the world gets an equal number of studies. It can be pointed out that migration is of particular interest to the United States, a country founded on migration and continuing to be a major destination for immigrants, but migration is an important factor in much of the world.

There is a natural tendency for social scientists to write more about their own countries than about other places. But this is only a tendency. We can see from the work reported above that he largest proportion of research on European monetary integration, for example, originates not from Europeans, but from American social scientists. The domination of social science by the United States applies both to what is studied and who is doing the studying. It is likely that the same picture of dominance applies to natural science as well. America has led the world in sheer quantity of university education and conjointly in research, both research in universities and outside universities.

The consequences of American domination are much greater for social science than for natural science. Obviously, most of the subject matter of the latter is universal and not country specific. There is no physics of Holland, or of the United States. But many social considerations are country specific. The American economy has features which are distinct from that of Brazil. Questions of law enforcement, family welfare, and the problems of foreign workers, race relations and the aged differ from one country to another. This suggests that more social science research is required, and that its heavy concentration in one place has adverse consequences.

Looking at chapters five through ten above, I think it is possible to form some judgement, however tentative, on the amount and state of social science investigation. These chapters cover the professional journal work for more than half a decade, typically from 1990 to 1997. That a high proportion of the articles on such broad topics as migration, religion and housing can be included in chapters of moderate length strongly suggests that the sheer quantity of investigation is small. One could hope that these are but small additions to large and well-established bodies of knowledge. How likely is that with disciplines of one hundred to two hundred years existence? With the knowledge explosion, most of the development is recent. It seems hard to avoid the conclusion that very little work has been done on crime, money and the family, for example, apart from the work of economists on money.

A number of impressions can be gathered from looking at the broad picture. An inescapable one, as I maintain, is that there is not much social science about. A handful of articles in professional journals is all that can be found on what are central issues. This is particularly distressing in an area where we believe that the subject matter itself is subject to change. Social science knowledge is time dependent. The nature of religious affiliation and belief, and the consequences of this for individuals and for society is an important consideration. It is a big and pressing issue. Who can claim that an answer found for the period 1920 to 1950 in any country whatsoever is likely to be reliable information for the present? This raises a big issue about the scientific status of social science. If the findings are not fairly general, indeed only apply to the restricted sample studied, and if they are not going last for some time, is this science?

We like to think of scientific knowledge as building on the past and continually refining and improving itself. The current investigation shows some evidence of this with respect to social science. Given the need to continually investigate what may turn out to be new social interactions, significantly different from those of the past, how can social science be building on past knowledge? Part of the improvement lies in the standard of investigative technique. It is now common- place to apply explicit modelling and sophisticated statistical enquiry where it would have been rare, if at all, to do so in the past. The cumulation of study does lead to more productive research, even if the findings cannot be relied on not to change with time.

It is more than a little generous to describe social science disciplines as deploying sizeable bodies of interconnected explanations. Economics can make that claim, and we will come back to that. One cannot say the same for sociology, anthropology or political science. Either it is too soon to expect much in the way of pieces of theory that fit together in a way that can generate a rich body of implications, or it is in the nature of these subjects to afford little opportunity to do that. A third possibility is that certain traditions of research have not been sympathetic to explicit theoretical conjecture. If it is only a matter of time before theory emerges, one can only hope that the wait will not be too long. More interesting is the possibility that there is something in the nature of the subject matter of social science which rules out a large role for interconnected explanations.

It is interesting to speculate that a range of phenomenon exists which resists the interconnected explanations common in the rest of science. This is the old claim of devotees of the paranormal. We can be sure that human society is not paranormal because nothing is. So why is there so little connected theory? One form such theory would take would be to provide predictions as to how society would respond to different changes in policy. This means knowing what lots of people would do, and how their individual responses would combine to produce a general outcome. Perhaps these considerations are enough to give an answer to our question.

Individual responses depend on the genetic endowment and on the full history of each person up to the time of the policy change. The general outcome of the policy depends on all the individual responses and the myriad ways in which the responders relate to each other. Clearly the potential for variety is enormously great. Of course, this potential might not matter. There might be a few robust principles that organised the potential variety into regular and predictable outcomes. While the social sciences are quite new, they have been around long enough so that it is highly probable that strong and reliable responses would have been detected. For anthropology, political science and sociology it will be necessary to build up much more in the way of particular observations. Hopefully, some degree of carry over from one case to another has emerged and will continue to emerge. Gradually, more interconnected theory can be developed.

Economics achieves its impressive structure of interconnected ideas by employing a conventional and simple set of propositions. Being conventional does not make them right. Being simple comes at a cost. And analysing effects one at a time in isolation means that it is very hard to know how important each effect actually is. This would be hard enough to measure if effects were constant and not dependent on context. Consider the willingness to risk a lethal conflict, as is analysed above. The need to establish a macho reputation may be important, and can be studied. So can the effect of revenge activity by other gang members; group reputation may interact with personal reputation; conventions about when to fight can have an effect; so can territory; availability of medical treatment, and so on. The economic method is not consistent with putting all these and other factors to work at the same time. This structure of interconnected theory has been achieved to some extent by high degrees of simplification.

Political science and sociology have tended much more to work with less explicit theory, and to lean more heavily on a much wider class of acceptable evidence. That does not mean that they have no theory. Early stages of the process of theory development can be seen throughout social science. Taking political science as an example, the left-right spectrum can be and is employed as an organising and explanatory factor. Kenneth Meier uses differences in the balance of liberal and conservative views across American states to explain differences in drug laws. David Nice uses the same concept to explain differences in the use of the death penalty. This familiar political divide can prove to be a useful organising principle. It also is something that we want to explain. Work is progressing in political science which attempts to account for the prevailing balance of left and right, such as the research of Jon Hurwitz and Mark Peffley on the political agenda. Doreen McMahon and her colleagues also undertook work attempting to explain the political climate. Other examples include the work of James Guth and John Green relating religion to political stances.

How people form political allegiances relates to questions of national identity, among other things, and we have seen examples above where a theory of identity is emerging in the work of Garza, Falcon and Garcia on Mexicans in the United States. Other themes in political science include the concept of a strong or weak state, as is exemplified by the work of James Hollifield on France. The theory of strong and weak government is also employed at more local levels of government, as can be seen in the work of Ingemar Elander on housing in Sweden. These are examples of commonly employed theoretical structures. Clearly it is possible to make too much of the lack of connected theory in social science.

Though not strictly driven by theory, the collection of data by social scientists is not done in an arbitrary manner. The material we have reviewed provides ample evidence of shrewd and purposeful enquiry. The collection and examination of data is rarely if ever motivated by the need to perform a critical experiment which will unequivocally determine the direction of theory, yet it is certainly far from being a random or haphazard process. Theoretical notions, or frameworks, are guiding enquiry, though not determining it in a precise manner. And as the facts are found, compiled and analysed, the framework of theoretical background is expanded and refined. A structure of science is being built, much as in natural science, but not out of such rigid and enduring material.

The studies we have reported show how difficult it often is to find the social facts. Statistical information is rarely compiled to serve the needs of scientific investigation. It serves other purposes, usually to do with the administrative responsibilities of government. Social science often has to make do and manipulate the data in ingenious ways to uncover the required facts. Simply getting the facts is important scientific activity. We should not limit our understanding of what is science to the situation where practitioners operate with an explicit and unambiguous theoretical base.

Because we all live in society and are observers of it, the very serious effort needed to uncover the facts is often greeted with the cry that we knew that all along. If I told you that migration to the city from farms in America tends to speed up when economic opportunity in urban centres is greater, you might well say we knew that all along, and hardly needed all this effort to confirm it. If I told you that migration to the city was pretty steady, and went on regardless of economic conditions, you might also say you knew that all along. Please do not take offence. It is just that social propositions like United States mothers and Mexican mothers are parenting their young children in much the same way, often seem plausible, while their opposite also seems plausible. Finding out which is the case is important, and often a thankless task. Even in rare cases when there appears to be only one acceptable view, having it established in a more reliable fashion is a service to knowledge.

Perhaps enough has been said about the more objective matters regarding the journal literature in the social sciences in the nineties. It is time to hazard a judgement. Do we see an impressive body of knowledge? Is there a large body of material of a high standard? First of all, there is not that much of it. Roughly speaking, the period of observation is not the whole decade, but mainly from 1990 to 1997. Even if we call it half a decade, it is remarkable that a summary of all the articles on big topics like crime and the family can be reported in a chapter of reasonable length. Of course all the monographs, books and special reports are important, and we have not looked at these. But the journal literature is the natural home for serious independent scientific enquiry. It is a vital link in the scientific establishment. When we turn to see how many studies of migration or religion were published over a significant slice of the history of social science, the answer is not many.

The social sciences are new, and are expanding rapidly. If the quantity of journal quality work in recent years is something on the order of five to twenty articles from a single discipline, and maybe fifty to a hundred studies altogether from social science on subjects like money, excluding economics, and housing, the conclusion is inescapable that we have remarkably little work done in the social sciences compared to any reasonable estimate of what needs to be studied. Granted that this is a very shaky area, and granted that we have looked at six topics among a possible two hundred, or two thousand, I do not care, the amount of work on major topics is pitifully small.

The point has been made before, but needs reinforcing now, that social science knowledge is inherently less enduring than that of natural science.

No one could argue that we did not need much research on crime in the nineties because research in earlier periods tells us much of what we need to know, or simply might want to know. I maintain that there was not much scientific work on crime in the past either, but even if there was, can we be sure that it would give reliable answers today? The answer must be 'no'. Technology changes, life expectancy, income levels, the composition, location and sizes of populations change in unprecedented ways. Who can say how these developments effect crime without undertaking new studies?

Reading through what the social sciences have to say on major issues one sees a picture of tiny rays of light trying to illuminate a fast darkness. Here I define 'darkness' simply as areas not investigated scientifically. That may be too strong an image. Even if we have pitifully little scientific knowledge on the consequences of adopting a common currency, there is a lot of comment in newspapers and on television. Various people are held to be experts, and anyone can have an opinion, a vague idea about what sharing a currency does to an economy, so maybe science is just one part of the knowledge input into any social question. But scientific knowledge is better than the other sources. It is more reliable, and it is capable of being improved, through the systematic effort of many researchers.

One could ask how important it is to have better knowledge. We will return to this question in the last chapter. The point now it that like it or not, worry about it or not, the fact is that there is not much social science about, given the many potential areas for study. Not only are many topics essentially left unexplored, those that have been studied typically occupy just a few researchers. A single draw of a standard filing cabinet can easily contain all the articles published by social scientists in their professional journals on the six major topics we have considered, excluding again economists writing on money. If there was a lot of social science, quantitatively speaking, how we thought about it and what we might want to do about it would differ radically from what is in fact the case.

Now is the time to have a stab at the most difficult question of all. How good is the work social scientists are doing? A Nobel Prize winner once remarked that economics has yet to have the benefit of a first rate mind. It has no Einstein, no Beethoven. I guess that is right, and probably no other social science has a Darwin or a Newton in its past or present. There may be a good reason for that. Maybe the difference between what a talented and hard working researcher can accomplish and a genius is not very great in the current stage of social science. It has also been noted that geniuses like to work on hard and solvable problems. It may be tough to get the answer, but at least you know when you have done it. Social science offers few if any challenges of that kind. The reason lies in all that we have discussed before.

In a word, the structure of explanations is not sufficiently developed or sufficiently firm.

The relative need for painstaking and ingenious uncovering of the facts is greater in social science than in natural science. It may not be the chosen work of the finest brains, but it is more than enough challenging for those just below this exalted level. Some of the work we have seen above has hints of this very impressive kind of scientific work. I could point to my preferred studies, and try to convince you. I will restrain myself. Let us say instead that there are a few studies where surprising ingenuity has been at work in finding evidence relevant to some question. There are occasional cases where statistical investigation has gone beyond the all too common application of standard techniques in a relatively uncritical fashion. One can see a lot of competence in offering explanations and setting out a framework of analysis. But there are few if any startlingly original explanations.

There are quite a few cases where one could imagine a reasonably intelligent person being pointed at the problem, or stumbling on it unaided, and producing work of similar quality with only a few months training in the area. The exception to this is work requiring statistical analysis. But even here, there is more application of standard statistical packages in an uncritical manner, perhaps adequate to the job at hand, but perhaps missing an important opportunity, than one would like to see. There are quite a few other cases, particularly in political science and sociology, where the line between scientific investigation and ordinary journalism is a fine one. There are other cases where a scientific style, or gloss, is tedious, and one would have preferred honest journalism.

One of the amazing things about scientific work is that much of it is just 'work' in the sense of not being intellectually more demanding than what most non-scientists do for a living. One suspects that in natural science there are honest workers who are not capable of either great ideas or the skills in exposition of the science popularisers, but who still do meaningful work. Yet, having said all that, one feels that in much of social science, the 'discipline' to draw on that word, is not present to the extent that it is in subjects where a lot of mathematics has to be mastered, or a great deal of theory understood, or facts mastered, or all three, in order to play at all.

To do useful social science may require more sensitivity, more detachment, more maturity, more judgement than is needed in much of natural science. I just do not know. I doubt very much if it requires more, or even as much raw intelligence as natural science. The mere fact that most of social science, apart from economics, and the more statistical parts of social psychology and sociology, is an open door to lay people must say something. It would appear that one can read and comprehend most of anthropology, political science and sociology as readily as one can read and comprehend a demanding novel. That may have an element of appearance. It is not easy to measure the insight of an anthropologist reading a piece of anthropology compared to that of an outsider.

Being difficult, of course, is not an end in itself or something to be desired. Just the opposite. Being simple and comprehensible is the goal. In much of natural science it cannot be easy for the outsider to understand, or even the insider, because of the complexity of the structure of ideas that has been built up over the years. Whatever else one might say, much of social science lacks this degree of development of structure. But it is a matter of degree.

As I have argued elsewhere, what makes something science is not success, or method, and certainly not difficulty, but the objective of finding explanations. The goal is understanding. It is a goal shared with many non-scientific undertakings, but pursued in a somewhat different manner. Consistency of argument, being open to criticism, and willingness to accept evidence make up part of that difference. There is lots of very ordinary, and let us face it, very weak social science to be found in chapters five through ten above. But it is science. We see examples of a collective endeavour aimed at understanding. The researchers accept the ultimate test as being beyond his or her control. It is to be found in evidence. What matters is getting closer to more powerful and more accurate explanations.

The social science establishments have almost everything in common with those of natural science. They take the form of university departments and professional associations. They have similar conventions for ranking individuals and validating contributions to their respective fields. Now and then, social scientists have tried to be recognised by august natural science establishments. On occasion they have been denied entry. There is a noticeable tendency for the natural science establishment generally to look on overtures from social scientists with suspicion. In one or two cases distinguished mathematicians have held that the mathematics employed by social scientists was bogus in some way.

There is nothing in the training or experience of mathematicians to enable them to see whether a particular mathematical model of inflation, or of violent crime, is a valid use of formal techniques. Being a nuclear physicist offers no special advantage over the lay person in contributing to non-proliferation negotiation. Being a specialist in international aspects of political science does confer an advantage. We should not take too seriously the views of natural scientists on social science.

I resist the idea of providing a 'bottom line' on social science. The picture is too complicated for a one-sentence summary. Social phenomena are being investigated in a scientific manner. Chapters five through ten illustrate this. There is some work. There is not a huge amount. The problems faced by social scientists are daunting. The results of their efforts are mixed. Scientific views of social matters are the best views we have. How this knowledge might be employed in public decision-making is the subject of the last chapter.

Chapter Twelve

SOCIAL SCIENCE AND PUBLIC POLICY

SOCIAL SCIENCE AS APPLIED KNOWLEDGE

The intention of this book is to put down a marker. It says 'this is social science'. To me, and to many others, this is a perfectly natural and uncontroversial statement. But to a frighteningly large number of people the existence and nature of social science is a matter of dispute, or this branch of science simply is being ignored. It is clear that society and its problems can be studied, and are being studied, in a scientific way. Those who doubt this, or worse, those who do something unscientific and pretend it is social science, are wrong and are doing a serious disservice to mankind. This sounds grandiose, but there is no other way of putting it. The adverse consequences of denying and confusing research can affect everyone, however remote they may be from centres of social enquiry. Alternatively, this branch of science can be used to improve the lives of people generally.

Whether a particular piece of knowledge will prove useful or not is often subject to big surprises. My guess is that research on the origin of the universe is unlikely to provide immediate benefits to poor people, or rich people, if it comes to that. Still I support such research. A full account of my reasons would take us too far afield. A careful analysis of how much resources should be put to such research, as against searching for treatments for, or prevention of, AIDS, for example, would take us even further field. A partial account of why we should support additions to knowledge which are unlikely to yield immediate practical benefits would go something like this.

The practical, or applied, benefits of knowledge come out of that great structure of ideas, explanations and information that make up science. More than anything else, it is the ability to draw on that complex of ideas which accounts for the difference between the way two-thirds of all people live today and the way all people lived in the past. It is a sad commentary that there are large numbers of people yet to benefit from scientific advance. I rank this as the number one issue for all of us, though the effect is on a minority. To put it most crudely, and most irrefutably, science is the reason why many people live to be eighty-five and beyond, where most people did not live beyond forty in times when science was less developed.

The best defence for working on apparently esoteric research projects with little prospect of useful application is that additions to knowledge are not isolated from the rest of the structure. This means that the structure as a whole grows and improves along with particular advances. Strengthening the structure through improvements anywhere adds something to the power of the whole. There are other defences of difficult to apply research that have to do with knowledge for its own sake, and they are strong arguments as well.

While conceding the case for better understanding regardless of applications, much of social science is not of that kind and is precisely aimed at providing potential improvements in public policy. In comparison, much of natural science is more remote from applications and it is hard to imagine how it will lead to improvements in practical terms. Work on continental drift and on the fossil records might be examples. By contrast, knowing more about the aspects of society which we have seen illustrated in the chapters above has the potential of contributing to improved lives for many people, here and now. Understanding more about areas like the family, immigration and crime is obviously and directly applicable to current human needs.

SOCIAL SCIENCE COMPARED TO THE ALTERNATIVES

It is not uncommon for people working in the social sciences to feel that they know very little compared to what needs to be known. This can be quite discouraging. There is a cure for this problem. Talk to people who are not social scientists. Even very intelligent people from the arts and from the natural sciences typically hardly know where to begin in addressing social issues. I strongly recommend to any social scientist that feels depressed about the achievements of our endeavours to talk with ordinary folk, such as politicians, journalists, or police officers. If these are not part of your social network, neighbours, people at parties, and members of your health club will do just as well. Social scientists are so familiar with the benefits of a scientific understanding of society that we are inclined to take it for granted. We tend not even to see it, like people living in beautiful mountain areas who no longer see the view.

Many people, and perhaps most people, who are not social scientists, have opinions about social issues. They may politely concede that a lifetime spent trying to understand interest rate policy, or reform of the voting system, has to be respected. However, when push comes to shove, they typically place more reliance on their cherished opinions than on any argument or evidence from experts. One can actually admire this self-confidence, and take some pleasure in that at least people seem to care about social issues. But at times I wish I worked in an area like quantum mechanics, where lay people are less likely to have any opinions at all.

It is especially in social matters that this curious phrase, "I'm entitled to my opinion, or he or she is entitled", can be heard. Hardly anyone would deny a person the right to think what he or she likes, and to express his or her thoughts in suitable circumstances. People have rights to think what they like about what powers the sun, for example, and how far it is from the earth. They can think what they like about how embryos develop and what determines the sex of a creature. Who would deny people the right to an opinion on why the sky appears to be blue, and why the moon goes through phases? In short, people have rights to opinions, even if they are false, absurd and uninformed opinions. People need not rely solely on their intuition, but they have every right to do so if they choose to.

I see no difference in principle between holding an unscientific opinion about what makes a rainbow and taking a guess on the likelihood that a convicted murderer released from jail will murder again. Of course people are free to reject science. They can do so from a knowledgeable position, or without having the foggiest idea of the nature or content of science. If people are in a responsible position, such as setting the interest rate, or determining investment in public housing, that is a different matter. Responsibility generates an obligation to take informed decisions. Voting in elections on the basis of hunch or instinct may not select the best candidate, but to do so is a right. Ignoring social science, when done by people exercising power over others, is not defensible.

We may be more sure about what causes rainbows and how they work than we are about the political and economic responses to taxes on petrol. In the same way we may be more sure of the time and place of an eclipse, but less sure about whether we will be able to see it because of cloud cover. Some science allows us to be pretty sure. Other scientific information is the best we can get, but not very reliable. The undoubted fact that much of social science provides information that is far from certain to be right does not mean that it can justifiably be ignored. The obligation on decision-takers is to be aware of the best information which is available, regardless of the absolute quality of that information.

Let me agree straight out that this chapter is highly speculative. As I say, the purpose of the book is to present social science. But I do not want to take my leave without making some comments on actually applying this branch of science. My speculations lead me to feel that social science is used much less than it should be, if the goal is to make the best decisions that we can make. A partial exception is economics. It does tend to be used more than the other social sciences. I will try to make a case for more use of social science, and hazard some guesses as to why this is happening at a slower pace than it could do, and should do.

ECONOMICS AS APPLIED SOCIAL SCIENCE

Fifty years ago in the United Kingdom, people critically responsible for economic policy, as well as those responsible for making technical inputs into policy decisions, were more likely to have degrees in history or classics than in economics. This is no longer the case. It is now widely and generally accepted that when it comes to matters such as controlling inflation, or financing government activity, economics is the undisputed source of information and economists are everywhere to be seen. In the United States this process began a little earlier, and the process has gone a little further. The Employment Act of 1946 established the Council of Economic Advisors, and enshrined in legislation the dominant role of economics in the appropriate range of governmental activity.

Similar developments have occurred in some of the rest of the world, but by no means everywhere. It might as well be admitted that part of the rejection of social science in the form of economics has to do with the objectives of rulers who are primarily interested in their own advantages, such as personal wealth and staying in power through any means. To such leaders, the potential of economics to improve their economies has little appeal.

Looking around the world, it would appear that there are quite a number of self-serving rulers, and other betrayers of trust, who exercise power. As common, and as wicked, are rulers who exploit their positions of power, this probably accounts for a relatively small amount of the widespread failure to use economic knowledge which we can see in many parts of the world. Friends of the ruling group and political allies who unfortunately have no knowledge of economics often fill posts that require economic expertise. In principle, they have nothing against social science. It just does not occur to those leaders and their chosen advisers that there is scientific knowledge out there that could be employed.

Those people who exercise power and want to adopt a scientific approach to social matters need to identify qualified social scientists. A Ph.D. in economics will not guarantee a sufficiently good grasp of economic matters to warrant a post in policy making. Some very talented researchers are too specialised and too uninterested in policy to do a good job. They may be poor at weighing up the risks and potential benefits of alternative courses of action. A top flight grounding in economics is a necessary, but not a sufficient, qualification for influencing or exercising economic decision-making, with a reasonable probability of some degree of success. Maturity, level headedness, experience, along with the ability to seek criticism and advice all play a part. Policy makers are team players, and not everyone works well with others.

The best way of improving the chances getting a Volcker into a position of economic decision-making is to have a large economics establishment in the country. Peer evaluation done by the economics establishment is the best guide to identifying individuals with the ability to draw on economic science directly, and through assistants. It is also the best guide to finding people with the other important characteristics that a good economist must have, along with knowledge of the subject. There is nothing unique about this suggestion. Commercial airlines send pilots to do check flights on other pilots. They do not send shareholders, passengers or nuclear physicists.

Finding the right social scientist, including the right economist, is best done through the relevant establishment. As it happens, only a few countries have a sufficiently large economics establishment to perform this screening and evaluation process. For the rest it is necessary to go outside the country, even if the objective is to find the best national for the job. Smaller countries, and those lacking a reliably large establishment, can tap into the establishments in larger countries who do have informed researchers and practitioners in universities and in public and private policy making.

Establishments, including intellectual establishments, like to extend their influence, and typically have some concern for the well-being of people. Both of these factors work in favour of countries genuinely seeking good social science. The economics establishment is usually ready to help with suggesting an economic adviser, and similarly for the other social sciences. My advice to any government that has taken power by force, or by getting elected, and wants to institute economic policies that will raise income in the country generally, is to consult actively and broadly with the economic establishment. This 'club' can readily be found by seeing where the most able students want to do their Ph.D.s. This applies to the other social sciences as well as to economics.

I suggest 'active' and 'broad' consultation because while I have some faith in a consensus opinion, the view of a single source, even a highly respected one, a Nobel Prize winner for example, might come up with a talented technician lacking the broader base. Even good scientists can have bees in their bonnets. The qualities needed for adding to knowledge are not exactly the same as those needed for applying knowledge. Four out of five people who are asked for advice will be well aware of this, but some forget, or have poor judgement, so enquiring broadly is the best insurance against appointing to a sensitive job an inappropriate social scientist.

The person who has done the most to bring a scientific approach to public policy in economic matters is John Maynard Keynes. He himself was intensely active and energetic in both the economic science establishment and in public policy circles. He made it very difficult for people in power to turn their backs on more informed ways of addressing issues. He also directed his most well known work to the issue of unemployment. This was done when most leaders saw unemployment as the number one problem. Even if they did not fully understand his reasoning, Keynes represented what certainly appeared to be a better approach than the normal uninformed thrashing about typical of leaders and their followers.

There were two things that Keynes wrote which were widely understood, and it is interesting that both turn out to be wrong. One was the famous remark that, "In the long run we are all dead." The phrase carries a number of meanings. One interpretation is that standard economic analysis, prior to his formulations, might be true if circumstances were to hold for very long periods, but that these consequences are of no interest or relevance because they will happen too far in the future. If the problem will cure itself in time, but only in a very long period of time, who cares. Another meaning is that any adverse side effects of the policy measures he was advocating, if they exist at all, will not show up within a relevant time period.

Politicians are understandably drawn to the idea that the present is what matters. If future consequences can be ignored, that is a definite plus, and the advisor who gives that assurance is most welcome. I believe that Keynes had no way of knowing what the 'long term' consequences of what he was advocating would be, and when the 'long term' would kick in. Now a good deal more is known about these matters. Crudely put, a quick fix for the economy will unravel in months, not decades, and surely long before we are all dead. It is for this reason that many experts advocate that national central banks be independent of the political process. To varying degrees many countries have adopted such an approach. This means that the money supply cannot be manipulated to serve the perceived immediate short-term interests of the people in power.

I think it highly likely that if Keynes had not got his foot in the door, and through that opened the door to the big foot of the economics establishment, the application of scientific thinking to economic problems would have been much delayed. He had a major influence on Roosevelt, and so brought the message to the United States. After the war his influence on the World Bank and the IMF helped to confirm the role of professional economic analysis in economic affairs. No doubt some aspects of these developments can be criticised. But the advantages of applying informed economics over the alternatives are beyond dispute. Relevant criticism of institutions and their behaviour requires a good grasp of economics. Amateur criticism of economic policies and institutions is of little value.

The gains from applying social science, in this case economics, have an additional effect in feeding back on the subject. A major reason for the relative strength of economics compared to other social sciences is the ready willingness of governments, international agencies, and private bodies to make use of this branch of social science. The application of knowledge to real problems has the effect of benefiting knowledge itself in two ways. Crudely put, it means that there are more jobs and more reasons to study the subject. It also means that new questions are continually being put forward, and received ideas are constantly being tested. Resources and critical application are hugely beneficial to the development of any scientific discipline.

KNOWLEDGE CAN BE USED, OR IGNORED

Historians might suggest that I am putting too much emphasis on Keynes as a single figure promoting the application of science to society. They may be right. I just do not know. Certainly he was a factor. The other famous statement of Keynes is longer.

> "...the ideas of economists and political philosophers, both when they are right and when they are wrong, are more powerful than is commonly understood. Indeed, the world is ruled by little else. Practical men, who believe themselves to be quite exempt from any intellectual influence are usually the slave of some defunct economist. Madmen in authority, who hear voices in the air, are distilling their frenzy from some academic scribbler of a few years back. I am sure that the power of vested interests is vastly exaggerated compared to the gradual encroachment of ideas."

Nothing could be more inspiring to social scientists. But no matter how beautiful the writing, we should always ask, is it right? Science is not dependent on good writing. Of course, good writing is to be preferred. While I am at it, let me add that we should not allow scholarship to sway our judgement, or the amount and difficulty of the mathematics employed in a piece of analysis. Writing, scholarship and mathematics have all been inappropriately used to signal good science. In themselves, they are irrelevant to whether the conclusions are correct or not.

Coming back to Keynes' statement, on close inspection it appears to be a little self-contradictory. Towards the end it suggests that ideas do get taken up, but with a lag. That is not too bad, if true, and one could work on means of shortening the lag. Earlier on it suggests that current policy is usually influenced by the ideas of a 'defunct economist'. On my reading, this poor creature, the defunct economist, is someone who has been shown to be seriously wrong. Is Keynes saying that there a gradual application of better science as time goes by, which sooner or later results in solving some of our pressing problems, or are we always working with ideas that science has refuted?

Whatever Keynes had in mind, my reading of the situation is that people who are around have far more influence than those who are not around. One of the interesting features of the years after the three score and ten is seeing people who were universally admired by students and fellow colleagues, and sought after by governments when they were active, being completely forgotten shortly after they die. If Keynes is right about the influence of the 'academic scribbler of a few years back', that influence comes from his or her effect on current academic and policy practitioners. Perhaps not the very latest speculations, but fairly current ideas in the subject are likely to have the ear of the 'madmen' and 'practical' men, and those who are both.

I am doubtful about any theory that scientific thinking will be applied to social problems whether people in power are aware of what they are doing or not. If social science is to be more widely applied, it has to be promoted. There is no obvious or inevitable process that will bring a scientific approach to bear as a matter of routine. If Keynes was arguing otherwise, he was wrong.

When we turn to the social sciences other than economics, the picture with respect to applications of knowledge to real problems is pretty bleak, perhaps even dismal. It is the norm for people who should be seeking knowledge to totally ignore what is known, and instead make it up as they go along. I do not think there is a conspiracy of silence. That would be an improvement over the present situation. The conspirators would be aware that social science exists, and for reasons best known to them, conspire to keep it at bay. What we have instead is almost universal ignorance.

Some politicians and television controllers are slightly aware that there are traditions of investigation of potential relevance to their concerns. They believe this, but they also believe that they themselves are the experts. A kind of split personality prevails, and slight awareness co-exists with complete denial.

Let me take just one recent example which combines both media and politics, and is quite a typical instance of ignoring social science. A distinguished politician fronted a recent TV program on power in the United Kingdom. Who has power? What does it mean to have it? What do the powerful do with their power? There could hardly be a more studied question in social science. All of the social sciences deal with issues of power, especially political science. Yet this able politician, now acting as TV presenter, who himself had more than toyed with power, started the program by asserting that nothing was known about this subject. His line on the box was, 'let us get together and try to figure it out'. And who will do the figuring — media people, sports personalities, natural science popularisers, actors, authors, and so on. Will we use any political scientists, or sociologists, an economist, perhaps? Not a one.

Perhaps the presence of specialists on the 'power program' would have spoiled the fun. The presenter could hardly say, "A lot is known about power, but I have assembled a colourful group of amateurs, and let us see what they come up with. We will not have time to compare their ramblings to scientific findings." Obviously that is not the way to sell a program. My guess, though, is that this man of affairs genuinely believed, in half of his mind at least, that hardly anyone had ever studied power.

IS IT BETTER TO BE CERTAIN, OR SCIENTIFIC?

It is widely believed, and for all I know it is correct, that voters prefer candidates with unambiguous and firm convictions. I suspect that political scientists and social psychologists may have studied these phenomena. For less sophisticated audiences, weather forecasters say 'there will be thunder', or not. More advanced services say that there is a thirty percent chance of thunder. It would seem that politicians cannot say that we have consulted with sociologists specialising on crime, and on balance there seems to be a case for harsher sentencing for certain crimes, or the opposite. Instead they have to act as if they knew more than anyone else about all social issues, from what to do about drugs, homelessness, a common currency, financing air traffic control, where to build homes, to conflicts in the Balkans. Not only do they present themselves as actually knowing about these matters, in addition they see their opinions as being totally reliable and correct.

Typically, all questions amenable to social science investigation are addressed by public figures as if they, the politicians and the media figures, were themselves the experts. When it comers to natural science matters, such as can prions pass from infected beef cattle to humans though eating their meat, or certain parts of it, politicians readily defer to the scientists. Does living under pylons tend to induce leukaemia? Ask a natural scientist. But policy issues rarely depend exclusively on the knowledge that comes from natural science. What if people prefer not to live under pylons, or near nuclear power stations? What policies should we adopt then? The natural science information is part of the story, but only a part. Social science has a great deal to say about these matters, but it would appear that decision-makers are only dimly aware of that, if they are aware at all.

One view of what is going on is that the politicians have to pretend to be authorities, and to pretend that the truth is cut and dried, in order to be elected. Meanwhile, through think tanks and other avenues of communication, they are drawing on social science where it is appropriate. I think this conjecture is oddly both overly cynical and overly optimistic. Part of my reason for this view is that the temptation is very strong to draw on the think tank and other sources with one real question in mind. How can I best hang on to my job? And as it is my job which is at stake, and I got elected and not you, maybe I know best, even for the question 'how to stay in power'. The result is that politicians often make very selective and limited use of social science.

Many public policy issues depend on the nature of communities. It would be a more fortunate situation than we currently have if the people who deal with community issues were aware that anthropologists and sociologists know something about these matters. If policy makers were aware of that, the temptation to base policy on political bias would not be so great.

One frequently hears that the people to blame are the researchers themselves. There they sit in their ivory towers sending their findings to academic journals and not informing the public at large. This accusation is dangerous nonsense. Social science is extremely demanding work. One cannot just toss it off. A division of labour is called for. Someone has to create the knowledge, and someone has to move knowledge into application. While the researcher can play a role, it usually should be a minor role. I say 'should' because when publicising is believed to be a major responsibility, academics tend to get promoted and get resources depending on the number of times they have been on television, not on the basis of their qualities as scientists.

There are a few brilliant researchers with a talent and a taste for popularisation. Fine, let them do it. But to make spreading the word a big and inherent part of research is a good way of bringing near frauds to the top of the ladder. Writing for Sunday supplements may be very useful, but it is very different from doing social science. When administrators and fund allocators get the idea that the popular presentation is the real thing, that it is genuine research, far from promoting social science to the wider public, social science gets even further shut out from possible situations where it could usefully be applied. Attempts at popularisation take the place of social science.

We might ask, what is the role of general awareness on the part of the public of social science? There are an endless number of cases we could consider. For example, a very big and vital question is how much and what kind of crèche facilities should be provided. This has strong implications for families, for working women, and for the babies and children involved. Social scientists have done a great deal work that has the potential of improving our approach to the provision of crèches. I would argue that it does not matter very much what the general public thinks about all this. At best the man in the street might recite a few boiled down conclusions, and these will probably be over simplifications. The general public will certainly not follow the statistical investigation. Educators, people taking decisions on councils, local government figures — these are the people who should regard it as natural to turn to social science. I believe it is a mistake to place much emphasis on getting the general public to appreciate social science. That is a very round about approach, and probably will have no impact. More to the point is to directly encourage 'officials' to be more inclined to draw on scientific information.

So how should the relevant decision-takers be induced to draw on social science more than they do at present? I could hazard a few answers. Perhaps one might look at the typical educational career of such people and see what interventions might be effective. How to effectively promote the application of social science to social issues is itself a question for social scientific enquiry. Sociologists, social psychologists and political scientists could have useful things to contribute here, not as individuals, but by drawing on their respective disciplines. It does not matter what social scientists have to say off the tops of their heads, it matters what the sciences have to say. If more people trained in a social science held posts in government, that would change the culture of government and go a long way to bringing about greater use of appropriate knowledge.

SOCIAL SCIENCE AND THE LEGAL PROFESSION

By far the biggest rival to social science is the legal establishment. Training in the law is the most common preparation for public life in government. Lawyers are commonly regarded as 'all purpose intellectuals'. Any problem that is not clearly scientific, or possibly economic, is likely to be handed to lawyers. This means that lawyers tend to play a larger role in the issues which social science addresses than do social scientists themselves. The lawyers with whom I have discussed this matter say that the prominent position of lawyers is as it should be and can easily be defended. Part of that defence runs along the lines that if expert opinion is needed, they will draw on it. There is a great deal wrong with this answer, and there is a great deal wrong with the current lawyer dominated state of affairs.

For one thing, lawyers can be shockingly ignorant of the possibility of expert opinion when it comes to matters outside of medicine, engineering, economics, and a few other areas. I am not talking about what goes on in litigation, though one could make a few observations there. For example, the courts routinely ignore the potential contributions of social psychology. The use of hypnotically induced evidence by the courts is an example. But courts are very much beside the point. It is influence outside the courts that is the problem.

Lawyers have an enormous influence on public policy. No doubt this has something to do with the fact that much policy implementation requires changing or introducing some laws. Lawyers must play a part at that stage, but it should only be a small part. The dominant part should come from informed specialists. And of course a good deal of policy formulation and implementation does not require law making. Among the many examples are the policy views of political parties, White Papers, and similar investigations leading to policy. These are routinely headed and managed by lawyers. In many instances this has unfortunate consequences.

Government decision-making on public health is an interesting example. The relationship between the political process and decisions on what to say to the public about food dangers, for example, and when to forbid marketing of possibly dangerous food has been investigated on a number occasions. The bias of the legal profession is apparent. The legal mind is inclined to attempt to determine if a responsible figure acted illegally, or improperly. If not, no one is to blame for regrettable consequences. But this is hardly the point. A political scientist, or possibly a sociologist, or even an anthropologist, would be more inclined, and more able, to uncover and analyse the institutions and arrangements that operate in public health, including interactions between natural scientists and politicians, and make useful suggestions for improvement.

A number of safety issues depend on monitoring and enforcing standards undertaken by what we could call communities of agents. There is nothing in the training of a lawyer that particularly equips this profession for the study of peer pressure and other relevant influences on the practices of such agents. Some social scientists are experts on communities, in the sense of knowing much of what is to be known. Admittedly, very often the scientific answer is 'we just do not know', or we have only a very uncertain idea. If that is the case, policy should be formulated in that light, and not on the basis of lawyers coming to firm conclusions by questioning a range of equally uninformed people.

I am not interested in lawyer bashing. They are essential to the operation of the rule of law. However, their influence has extended way beyond what is needed for law making and applying the law. Routinely lawyers can be found doing jobs that would be better done by social scientists. The time has come to acknowledge that.

SCIENCE AND IDEOLOGY

The very idea of approaching social issues in a scientific manner takes some getting used to. Recently a prominent public figure told me he was trying to determine the socialist attitude toward human cloning. Presumably the reasoning goes something like this. 'I am a socialist, hence I believe the socialist position on matters. If I knew the socialist position on cloning, I would know my position on human cloning.' An impolite friend suggested that the socialist position on cloning is that it should be available to everyone. People on the right are equally convinced that their broad ideological position provides compelling answers to all social questions.

Part of the ideological divide comes about because of differences in values, which may have their origins in early experience. Being tall or short, loved or tolerated, attractive or less so, may play a part, and possibly genetic influences on behaviour and perceptions exert an influence as well. None of these factors are likely to operate in a simple, if the first characteristic then the second outcome, kind of way. Being in some sense disadvantaged may induce sympathy for others, or tend towards hostile denial and an attempt to line up with the advantaged. Be that as it may, and no doubt research on these relations is progressing, differences in values, whatever causes them, are part of the story. We will never be rid of ideological positions, nor should we in my view, but they can usefully be tempered by scientific investigation.

One factor which relates to and helps to account for ideological convictions, or leanings, is divergent views about how the world works. Will a big army make me more secure, or am I pretty secure when it comes to foreign invasion in any case? Will a minimum wage mainly reduce female and youth employment, or will it mainly help the poorest workers and have little side effects? Everyone is entitled to a view, as they say, but what about more serious understanding? A more accurate view of how the world works can influence ideological positions.

One could ask how much society has benefited from social science so far. This is the hardest question. Just suppose, for example, that better social knowledge has made more complex, larger and more integrated and mutually dependent societies possible, but these are also more vulnerable to social and natural upheaval. Add in the possibility that the critical race is between new knowledge needed to stave off catastrophe and the complexity generated by existing knowledge. A popular view is that maybe we can stay ahead for awhile, but sooner or later the race will be lost. This is the social equivalent of the Frankenstein monster analogy in natural science. Knowing certain things opens doors best left closed. I very much doubt the validity of this kind of thinking, precisely because it exaggerates the role of social science knowledge.

Another possibility is that when it comes to application, social science is just so much window dressing, so much hand waving, like a frustrated musician who conducts the symphony coming over the radio in his bedroom. The growth of technology through advances in engineering and natural science, combined with accumulation of physical, human and social capital, along with world population growth, are the great engines driving our fate, who knows where, and social science has nothing to do with it. I very much doubt this view as well.

A third view would hold that social science serves a tiny minority of mankind consisting mainly of those with the most wealth and power. It is just another tool in the hands of the dominant club, which it can use to secure and increase its hold over the rest. Better management, more effective marketing, more knowledge of political processes — who is benefiting and will continue to benefit from these advances in understanding? There must be some truth in this effect of knowledge on the ability of powerful manipulators to manipulate.

Think tanks, consulting, and all forms of private information rather suggest something along 'top conspirator' lines. On the other hand, it is impressive how much of the work supported by special interests is made completely public. Is there really a tight club at the top, or more of a mad scramble for wealth and power, often gained and lost in a lifetime, and rarely passed beyond the third generation. And if social science had this capacity to help dominant interests, would not those interests support it more actively?

The fourth view holds that social science did not create society any more than astronomy created the stars. It does have a bit more effect on how society evolves than our knowledge has on the heavens, but only a bit more. Television may have done more to reduce the propensity to make war on distant people than political science. Growth in income per person may owe more to engineering than to economics. That hardly is the point. Knowing more about how society functions can occasionally contribute to a better taxation policy or a better treaty between nations, along with contributing to better use of the resources we put to education, for example. The right question is not who contributes more, but what is the contribution of social science.

If you really want to know how much, and in what way, social science has contributed to the human saga, some progress in addressing that question could be made by undertaking an extensive research project. A lot of social science resources would have to go into shedding light on that question. My guess is that we could come up with an answer of a kind. There would still be a wide margin of uncertainty. In quantitative terms, the truth could easily be half of our best guess answer, or twice as much. Apart from an estimate, there could be other benefits from that research. New and interesting ideas might well come out of such an investigation, even if the answer to the initial question remained almost as much in the dark.

CURIOSITY AND APPLICABILITY

For me, and for many social scientists, the drive to investigate society in a scientific manner is fuelled by a combination of curiosity about what is going on, and faith in rationality. At the level of the individual, it often hurts for a time to know the truth, and maybe for a long time. It certainly is not the case that an improvement in knowledge automatically leads to better actions. Sometimes more knowledge leads to very unfortunate behaviour and has unexpected and unintended consequence. This is true of individuals and of society at large. Moving from the level of the individual to the social level sometimes compounds the uncertainty, and sometimes reduces it.

In spite of the unintended consequences argument, there is a reasonable presumption that improving knowledge has the potential to help with solving problems. Asking for proof is asking for too much. It might be a small thing to know a little more about the effects on battered wives of various measures, such as the provision of shelters. If our investigations add only a little to our understanding, in spite of our best efforts, we need that bit more understanding. It might be a small thing in one sense to know a little more about famines. But in questions of this kind, even knowing a little more is worth a very great deal. I would rather try to find out more than leave it to guesses, emotions, prejudice and ideology. It is a mistake to claim to have made more progress than has actually been achieved. Equally misleading is to sell short the modest advances that have been made.

This book provides a picture of the practice of scientific investigation of social matters. Even in such relatively new subjects such as sociology and social psychology, the construction of knowledge has gone so far that researchers aiming for significant advances must restrict their work to a little corner, a few aspects, a little patch of the whole. To have more than a glimpse one has to specialise. There is no reason to be coy or shy about calling this work scientific. It meets all the tests of being scientific. It is easy to dismiss what one does not understand. On the other hand, making an improvement on existing knowledge in the social sciences is no mean feat, and this is a telling indication of what has already been achieved. As subjects mature, it is very hard to have a big impact. One of the motives for 'pretend social science' is precisely the desire to at least appear to be making a big contribution to knowledge.

When it comes to investigating unexplored territory, there are no guarantees. Social science answers to social questions are not always immediately forthcoming, and when answers are found, they are far from being infallible. Our understanding is continually changing, and over time it is improving. This cumulative aspect of science is its most important feature. Few challenges can match taking part in that process. There is no alternative approach to social questions which comes remotely close to the contribution of social science. Social scientists formulate the best questions, and provide the best answers to the social problems of society. We will all benefit when people in responsible positions pay more heed to a scientific approach to society.

BIBLIOGRAPHY

Abrams, M.; Gerard, D.; Timms, N., (Eds.) *Values and Social Change in Britain*, MacMillan, 1985.

Achenbach, Thomas S. and Edelbrock, Craig, *Behavioral Problems and Competencies Reported by Parents of Normal and Disturbed Children Aged Four through Sixteen*, Monographs of the Society for Research in Child Development, serial no. 188, University of Chicago Press, 1981.

Ahern, M. and Davie, G., Inner City God. *The Nature of Belief in the Inner City*, Hodder and Stroughton, London, 1987.

Aldridge, Alan, "Women priests from exclusion to accommodation", *British Journal of Sociology*, vol. 45, no. 3, September 1994, pp. 501 - 510.

Allen, Douglas W., "Order in the church: A property rights approach", *Journal of Economic Behavior and Organization*, vol. 27, no. 1, June 1995, pp. 97 - 117.

Al-Rasheed, Madawi, "Iraqi Assyrians in London: Beyond the 'Immigrant/Refugee' Divide", *Journal of the Anthropological Society of Oxford*, vol. XXVI, no. 3, Michaelmas, 1995, pp. 241 - 255.

Altemeyer, B., *Right-wing Authoritarianism*, University of Manitoba Press, 1981.

Andrews, Marcellus, "Schools and Jails and the dynamics of an educated underclass", *Journal of Economic Behavior and Organization*, vol. 22, no. 2, October, 1993, pp. 121 - 132.

Ardener, Shirley, "The Comparative Study of Rotating Credit Associations", *Journal of the Royal Anthropological Institute*, vol. 94, 1964, pp. 201 - 209.

Austin, Timothy, "Filipino Self-Help and Peacemaking Strategies: A View from the Mindanao Hinterland", *Human Organization*, vol. 54, no. 1, Spring 1995, pp. 10 - 19.

Barrett, David B., Editor, *World Christian Encyclopedia*, Oxford University Press, 1982.

Barry, H. and Paxon, L., "Infancy and Early Childhood", *Ethnology*, vol. 10, 1971, pp. 466 - 505.

Bateson, C.D.; Fink, C.H.; Schoenrade, P.A.; Fultz, J.; Pych, V., "Religious orientation and overt versus covert racial prejudice", *Journal of Personality and Social Psychology*, vol. 50, 1978, pp. 175 - 181.

Baun, Michael J., "The Maastricht Treaty As High Politics: Germany, France, ands European Integration", *Political Science Quarterly*, vol. 110, no. 4, 1995/1996, pp. 605 - 624.

Beck, A.J. and Shipley, B.E., *Recidivism of young parolees*, Bureau of Justice Statistics Special Report, NCJ-104961, U.S. Department of Justice, 1987.

Beckly, Gloria T. and Burstein, Paul, "Religious Pluralism, Equal Opportunity, and the State", *Western Political Quarterly*, vol. 44, no. 1, March 1991, pp. 185 - 208.

Bell, Brian D., "The Performance of Immigrants in the United Kingdom: Evidence from the GHS", *Economic Journal*, vol. 107, no. 411, March 1997, pp. 333 - 344

Benson, Janet E., "Good Neighbors: Ethnic Relations in Garden City Trailor Courts", *Urban Anthropology*, vol. 19, no. 4, Winter 1990, pp. 361 - 386.

Bernheim, B.D.; Shleifer, A.; Summers, L., "The Strategic Bequest Motive", *Journal of Political Economy*, vol. 93, no. 6, December 1985, pp. 1045 - 1076.

Besley, Timothy and McLaren, John, "Taxes and Bribery: The Role of Wage Incentives", *Economic Journal*, vol. 103, no. 416, January 1993, pp. 119 - 141.

Bird, Rebeca L. Blege and Bird, Douglas W., "Delayed Reciprocity and Tolerated Theft", *Current Anthropology*, vol. 38, no. 1, February 1997, pp. 49 - 78.

Black, Jane; de Meza, David; Jeffreys, David, "Home Prices, the Supply of Collateral and the Enterprise Economy", *Economic Journal*, vol. 106, no. 434, January 1996, pp. 60 - 75.

Bliss, Christopher and Di Tella, Rafael, "Does Competition Kill Corruption?", *Journal of Political Economy*, vol. 105, no. 5, October 1997, pp. 1001 - 1023.

Bohner, Gerd; Weisbrod, Christina; Raymond, Paula; Barvzi, Alexandra; Schwarz, Norbert, "Salience of rape effects self-esteem; The moderating role of gender and rape myth acceptance", *European Journal of Personality*, vol. 23, no. 6, November/December 1995, pp. 561 - 579.

Borjas, George J. and Bronars, Stephen G., "Immigration and the Family", *Journal of Labour Economics*, vol. 9, no. 2, April 1991, pp. 123 - 148.

Boustead, Emma; Cottee, Katherine; Farquhar, Rhona; Jonas, Rebecca; Walter, Joseph; Webley, Paul, "The Perceived Value of a New Coin", *Journal of Social Psychology*, vol. 132, no. 1, February 1992, pp. 143 - 144.

Branscombe, Nyla R.; Owen, Susan; Garstka, Teri A.; Coleman, Jason, "Rape and Accident Counterfactuals: Who Might Have Done Othertwise and Would It Have Changed the Outcome?", *Journal of Applied Social Psychology*, vol. 26, no. 12, June 1996, pp. 1042 - 1067.

Brehm, John and Hamilton, James T., "Noncompliance in Environmental Reporting: Are Violators Ignorant, or Evasive, of the Law?", *American Journal of Political Science*, vol. 40, no. 2, May 1996, pp. 444 - 477.

Brems, Christine and Wagner, Patricia, "Blame of Victim and Perpetrator in Rape Versus Theft", *The Journal of Social Psychology*, vol. 134, no. 3, June 1994.

Brierly, P., UK *ChristianHandbook 1989/90*, Marc Europe, 1988.

Brook, Lindsay; Hedges, Susan; Jowell, Roger; Lewis, Jude; Prior, Gillian; Sebastian, Gary; Taylor, Bridget; Witherspoon, Sharon, *British Social Attitudes Cumulative Sourcebook*, Gower, Aldershot, 1992.

Brumm, Harold J. and Cloninger, Dale O., "Perceived risk of punishment and the commission of homicide: A covariance structure analysis", *Journal of Economic Organization and Behavior*, vol. 31, no. 1, October 1996, pp. 1 - 11.

Buiter, Willem; Corsetti, Giancarlo; Roubini, Nouriel, (with discussion by Repullo, Rafael and Frankel, Jeffrey), "Excessive deficits: sense and nonsense in the Treaty of Maastricht", *Economic Policy,* vol. 16, April 1993, pp. 58 - 100.

Burdett, Ken and Coles, Melvyn G., "Marriage and Class", Quarterly Journal of Economics, vol. CXII, issue 1, February 1997, pp. 141 - 168.

Cannell, Fenella, "The Imitation of Christ in Bicol, Philippines", *Journal of the Royal Anthropological Institute*, vol. 1, no. 2, June 1995, pp. 377 - 394.

Cantu, Lionel, "The Peripheralization of Rural America: A Case Study of Latino Migrants in America's Heartland", *Sociological Perspectives*, vol. 38, no. 3, Fall, 1995, pp. 399 - 414.

Carruthers, Bruce G. and Babb, Sarah, "The Color of Money and the Nature of Value: Greenbacks and Gold in Posbellum America", *American Journal of Sociology*, vol. 101, no. 6, May 1996, pp. 1556 - 1591.

Carsten, Janet, "The Politics of Forgetting: Migration, Kinship and Memory on the Periphery of the Southeast Asian State", *Journal of the Royal Anthropology Institute*, vol. 1, no. 2, June 1995, pp. 317 - 335.

Chhetri, Ram B., "Rotating Credit Associations", *Human Organization*, vol. 54, no. 4, Winter 1995, pp. 449 - 454.

Coleman, William D., "Banking interest intermediation and political power: a framework for comparative analysis", *European Journal of Political Research*, vol. 26, no. 1, July 1994, pp. 31 - 58.

Coltrane, Scott, "Father-Child Relationships and the status of Women: A Cross-Cultural Study", *American Journal of Sociology*, vol. 93,no. 5, March 1988, pp. 1060 - 95.

Coopersmith, S., *Self-esteem inventories*, Consulting Psychologists Press, 1981.

Costin, F. and Kasptanoglu, C., "Beliefs about rape and women's social roles: A Turkish replication", *European Journal of Social Psychology*, vol. 23, no. 3, May/June 1993, pp. 327 - 330.

Davidson, Audrey B., "The medieval monastery as franchise monopolist", *Journal of Economic Behavior and Organization*, vol. 19, no. 1, September 1992, pp. 1 - 15.

Davidson, Aubrey B. and Ekelund, Robert B. Jr., "The medieval church and the rent from marriage market regulations", *Journal of Economic Behavior and Organization*, vol. 32, no. 2, February 1997, pp. 215 - 245.

Davie, Grace, "'An ordinary God': the paradox of religion in contemporary Britain", *British Journal of Sociology*, vol. 41, no. 3, September 1990, pp. 395 - 421.

Davis, Nancy J. and Robinson, Robert V., "Are the Rumors of War Exaggerated? Religious Orthodoxy and Moral Progressivism in America", *American Journal of Sociology*, vol. 100, no. 3, November 1996, pp. 756 - 787.

Daly, Martin and Wilson, Margo, *Homicide*, Aldyne de Gruyter, 1988.

Devons, Ely, *Planning in Practice: Essays in Aircraft Planning in War-time*, Cambridge University Press, 1950.

Dewey, Alice, "Capital, Credit and Saving in Javanese Marketing", in *Capital, Saving and Credit in Peasant Societies*, Firth, Raymond and Yamey, Basil, (Eds.), George Allen and Unwin, 1964, pp. 230 - 255.

Dezhbakhsh, Hashem and Rubin, Paul H., "Lives Saved or Lives Lost? The Effects of Concealed-Handgun Laws on Crime", *American Economic Review*, vol. 88, no. 2, May 1998, pp. 468 - 474.

Dixon, Jo, "The Organizational Context of Criminal Sentencing", *American Journal of Sociology*, vol. 100, no. 5, March 1995, pp. 1157 -1198.

Dodd, Nigel, "Money and the Nation-State: Contested Boundaries of Monetary Sovereignty in Geopolitics", *International Sociology*, vol. 10, no. 2, June 1995, pp. 139 - 154.

Donohue, John J. III and Levitt, Steven D., "Guns, Violence, and the Efficiency of Illegal Markets", *American Economic Review*, vol. 88, no. 2, May 1998, pp. 463 - 467.

Dornbusch, R., *Priorities of Economic Reform in Eastern Europe and the Soviet Union*, Occasional Paper no. 5, Centre for Economic Policy Research, London, 1991.

Echabe, Augustin Echebarria and Castro, Jose L. Gonzales, "Images of immigrants: a study of the xenophobia and permeability of intergroup boundaries", *European Journal of Social Psychology*, vol. 26, issue 3, May/June 1996, pp. 341 - 352.

Ekelund, Robert B. Jr.; Hebert, Robert F.; Tollison, Robert D., "The economics of sin and redemption: Purgatory as a market-pull innovation?", *Journal of Economic Behavior and Organization*, vol 19, no. 1, September 1992, pp. 1 - 15.

Elander, Ingemar, "Good Dwellings for All: The Case of Social Rented Housing in Sweden", *Housing Studies*, vol. 6, no. 1, January 1991, pp. 29 - 43.

Eliade, Mircea, *The Sacred and the Profane*, Harcourt Brace, 1959.

Elliot, Delbert S.; Ageton, Susan S.; Huizinga, David; Knowles, Brian A.; Canter, Raquelle J., *The Prevalence and Incidence of Delinquent Behavior: 1876 - 1980*, National Youth Survey Report No. 26, Behavior Research Institute, 1983.

Erman, Tahire, "Women and the Housing Environment: The Experiences of Turkish Migrant Women in Squatter (Gecekondu) and Apartment Housing", *Environment and Behavior*, vol. 28, no. 6, November 1996, pp. 764 - 798.

Eysneck, S.B.J.; Eysenck, H.L.; Barrett, P., "A revised version of the Psychoticism Scale", *Personality and Individual Differences*, vol. 6, 1985, pp. 21 - 29.

Farmer, Amy and Tiefenthaler, Jill, "Domestic Violence: The Value of Services as Signals", *American Economic Review*, vol. 86, no. 2, May 1996, pp. 274 - 279.

Feather, N.T., "Variables relating to the allocation of pocket money to children: Parental reasons and values", *British Journal of Social Psychology*, vol. 30, part 3, September 1991, pp. 221 - 234.

Felson, Richard B.; Liska, Allen E.; South, Scott J.; McNulty, Thomas L., "The Subculture of Violence and Delinquency: Individual vs. School Context Effects", *Social Forces*, vol. 73, no. 1, September 1994, pp. 155 - 173.

Finch, Janet and Hayes, Lynn, "Inheritance, Death and the Concept of the Home", *Sociology*, vol. 28, no. 2, May 1994, pp. 417 - 433.

Fisher, Randy D.; Derison, Donna; Polly III, Chester F.; Cadman, Jenifer; Johnston, Dana, "Religiousness, Religious Orientation, and Attitudes Towards Gays and Lesbians", *Journal of Applied Social Psychology*, vol. 24, no. 7, April 1994, pp. 614 - 630.

Formoso, Bernard, "Hsiu-Kou-Ku: The Ritual Refining of Restless Ghosts Among the Chinese of Thailand", *Journal of the Royal Anthropological Institute*, vol. 2, no. 2, June 1996, pp. 217 - 234.

Fox, R.A., *Parent Behavior Checklist*, Clinical Psychology Publishing, 1994.

Francis, L.C.;Brown, L.B.;Philipchalk, R., "The development in an abbreviated form of the Revised Eysenck Personality Questionnaire (EPQR-A): Its use among students in England, Canada, the USA and Australia", *Personality and Individual Differences*, vol. 13, 1992, pp. 243 -246.

Francis, L.C. and Wilcox, C., "Personality, prayer, and church attendance among 16- to 18-year old girls in England", *The Journal of Social Psychology*, vol. 134, no. 2, April 1994, pp. 243 -246.

Francis, Leslie J. and Gibbs, Darryl, "Prayer and Self-Esteem Among 8 –11 Year-Olds in the United Kingdom", *The Journal of Social Psychology*, vol. 136, no. 6, December 1996, pp. 791 -793.

Franselow, Frank, "The Bazaar Economy: Or How Bizzare is the Bazaar Really?", *Man*, vol. 25, no. 2, June 1990, pp. 250 - 285.

Fraser, Nancy, "After the Family Wage; Gender Equity and the Welfare State", *Political Theory*, vol. 22, no. 4, November 1994, pp. 591 - 618.

Fuchs, Lawrence H., *The American Kaleidoscope: Race, Ethnicity and the Civic Culture*, University Press of New England, 1990.

Furnham, A.F., "Many sides of the coin: The psychology of money usage", *Personality and Individual Differences*, vol. 5, 1984, pp. 501 - 509.

Furnham, A.F., "The perceived value of small coins", *Journal of Social Psychology*, vol. 125, no. 5, October 1985, pp. 571 - 575.

Garza, Rodolfo O. de la; Falcon, Angelo; Garcia, F. Chris, "Will the Real Americans Please Stand Up: Anglo and Mexican-American Support of core American Political Values", *American Journal of Political Science*, vol. 40, no. 2, May 1996, pp. 335 - 351.

Gastill, Raymond, *Freedom at Issue*, Freedom House, various years.

Geertz, Clifford, "The Rotating Credit Association: A 'middle rung' in development", *Economic Development and Cultural Change*, vol. 10, no. 3, April 1962, pp. 241 - 263.

Georges, Eugenia, *The Making of a Transnational Community: Migration, Development, and Cultural Change in the Dominican Republic*, Columbia University Press, 1990.

Georgiana, S.L., *The Moral Majority and fundamentalism: Plausibility and dissonance*, Edwin Mellon, 1989.

Gilderbloom, John, I. And Markham, John F., "Housing Modification Needs of the Disabled Elderly: What Really Matters?", *Environment and Behavior*, vol. 28, no. 4, July 1996, pp. 512 - 535.

Gill, Anthony J., "Rendering unto Caesar? Religious Competition and Catholic Political Strategy in Latin America, 1962 - 1979", *American Journal of Political Science*, vol. 38, no. 2, May 1994, pp 403 - 425.

Gillespie, Kate and Okruhlik, Gwenn, "The Political Dimensions of Corruption Cleanups: A Framework for Analysis", *Comparative Politics*, vol. 24, no. 1, October 1991, pp. 77 - 96.

Gillis, A.R., "So long as They Both Shall Live: Marital Dissolution and the Decline of Domestic Homicide in France, 1852 - 1909", *American Journal of Sociology*, vol 101, no. 5, March 1996, pp. 1273 - 1305.

Giorgi, Liana, "Religious involvement in a secularized society: an empirical confirmation of Martin's general theory of secularization", *British Journal of Sociology*, vol. 43, no. 4, December 1992, pp. 639 - 656.

Glaeser, Edward L. and Glendon, Spencer, "Who Owns Guns? Criminals, Victims, and the Culture of violence", *American Economic Review*, vol 88, no. 2, May 1998, pp. 458 - 462.

Glick-Schiller, Nina; Basch, L.; Blanc-Szanton, C., (Eds.), *Towards a Transnational Perspective on migration: Race, Class, Ethnicity, and Nationalism Reconsidered*, New York Academy of Sciences, 1992.

Glenmary Research Centre, *Churches and church membership in the United States*, 1980, Glenmary Research Centre, Washington D.C., 1982.

Goldberg, D.P., *Manual of the General Health Questionnaire*, Windsor, UK:NFER, 1978.

Goodhart, Charles, "European Monetary Integration", *European Economic Review*, vol. 40, 1996, pp. 1083 - 1090.

Ghosh, E.S.K. and Huq, M.M., "A study of social identity in two ethnic groups in India and Bangladesh", *Journal of Multilingual and Multicultural Development*, vol. 6, nos. 3 and 4, 1985, pp. 239 - 251.

Grauwe, Paul De, "Monetary union and convergence economies", *European Economic Review*, vol. 40, 1996, pp. 1091 - 1101.

Greer, J.E., "The Persistance of Religion: A Study of Sixth-Form Pupils in Northern Ireland, 1968 - 1988", *The Journal of Social Psychology*, vol. 130, no. 5, October 1990, pp. 573 - 581.

Greer, John E. and Francis, Lelie J., "Religious Experiences and Attitude Toward Christianity Among Secondary School Children in Northern Ireland", *The Journal of Social Psychology*, vol. 132, no. 2, April 1992, pp. 277 - 279.

Grogger, Jeffrey, "The Effects of Arrests on the Employment and Earnings of Young Men", *The Quarterly Journal of Economics*, vol. CX, no. 1, February 1995, pp. 51 - 71.

Gudjonsson, G.H., *The Manual to the Gudjonsson Suggestibility Scales*, Psychological Press, Hove, 1997.

Guth, James L. and Green, John C., "Politics in a New Key: Religiosity and Participation Among Political Activists", *Western Political Quarterly*, vol. 43, no. 1, March 1990, pp. 153 - 179.

Hagen, John and McCarthy, Bill, "Streetlife and delinquency", *British Journal of Sociology*, vol. 43, no. 4, December 1992, pp. 533 - 561.

Hagendorn, Louk and Henke, Roger, "The effect of multiple category membership on intergroup evaluations in a north Indian context: Class, caste and religion", *British Journal of Social Psychology*, vol. 30, part 3, September 1991, pp. 247 – 260.

Hagle, Timothy M., "But Do They Have to See It to Know It? The Supreme Court's Obscenity and Pornography Decisions", *Western Political Quarterly*, vol. 44, no. 4, December 1991, pp. 1039 - 1054.

Hatton, Timothy J. and Williams, Jeffery G., "What Explains Wage Gaps between Farm and City? Exploring the Todaro Model with American Evidence, 1890 – 1941", *Economic Development and Cultural Change*, vol. 40, no. 2, January 1992, pp. 267 - 290.

Hayes, Bernadette, C., "Religious identification and moral attitudes: the British case", *British Journal of Sociology*, vol. 46, no. 3, September 1995, pp. 457 - 474.

Hayes, Bernadette C., "Gender differences in religious mobility in Great Britain", *British Journal of Sociology*, vol. 47, no. 4, December 1996, pp. 643 - 656.

Heath, W.C.; Waters, M.S.; Watson, J.K., "Religionand economic welfare: An empirical analysis of state per capita income", *Journal of Economic Behavior and Organization*, vol. 27, n0. 1, June 1995, pp. 129 - 142.

Herek, G.M., "Religious orientation and prejudice: A comparison of racial and sexual attitudes", *Personality and Social Psychology Bulletin*, vol. 13, 1987, pp. 34 – 44.

Herek, G.M., "Can functions be measured? A new perspecitve on the functional approach to attitudes", *Social Psychology Quarterly*, vol. 50, 1987, pp. 285 - 303.

Heyman, Josiah McC, "Putting Power in the Anthropology of Bureaucracy: The Immigration and Naturalization Service at the Mexico-United States Border", *Current Anthropology*, vol. 36, no. 2, April 1995, pp. 261 - 287.

Hirschi, Travis, *Causes of Delinquency*, University of California, 1969.

Hoddinott, John, "Rotten Kids or Manipulative Parents: Are Children Old Age Security in Western Kenya?", *Economic Development and Cultural Change*, vol. 40, no. 3, April 1992, pp. 545 - 565.

Hoffman, Alexander von, "High Ambitions: Past and Future of American Low-Income Housing Policy", *Housing Policy Debate*, vol. 7, issue 3, 1996, pp. 423 - 446.

Hollifield, James F., "Immigration and the French State: Problems of Policy Implementation", *Comparative Political Studies*, vol. 23, no. 1, April 1990, pp. 56 - 79.

Homant, Robert J.; Kennedy, Daniel B.; Howton, Jimmy D., "Risk Taking and Police Pursuit", *The Journal of Social Psychology*, vol. 139, no. 2, April 1997, pp. 213 - 221.

Hosch, Harmon M.; Chanez, Gloria J.; Bothwell, Robert K.; Munoz, Henry, "A Comparison of Anglo-American and Mexican-american Jurors' Judgements of Mothers Who Fail to Protect Their Children from Abuse", *Journal of Applied Social Psychology*, Vol. 21, no. 20, October 1991, pp. 1687 - 1698.

Houlihan, Barrie, "Policy Implementation and Central-Local Government Relations in England: The Examples of the Sale of Council Houses and Area Improvement", *Housing Studies*, vol. 2, no. 2, April, 1987, pp. 99 - 111.

Howe, Edmund S., "Judged Likelihood of Different Second Crimes: A Function of Judged similarity", *Journal of Applied Social Psychology*, vol. 21, no. 9, May 1991, pp. 697 - 712.

Hull, Brooks B. and Bold, Frederick, "Preaching matters: Replication and extension", *Journal of Economic Behavior and Organization*, vol. 27, no. 1, June 1995, pp. 143 - 149.

Hurwitz, Jon and Peffley, Mark, "Public Perceptions of Race and Crime: The Role of Racial Stereotypes", *American Journal of Political Science*, vol. 41, no. 2, April 1997, pp. 375 - 401.

Hymes, Robert W.; Leinart, Mary; Rowe, Sandra; Rogers, William, "Acquaintance Rape: The Effect of Race of Defendent and Race of Victim on White Juror Decisions", *The Journal of Social Psychology*, vol. 133, no. 5, October 1993, pp. 627 - 634.

Iannaccone, Laurence R., "Risk, Rationality, and Religious Portfolios", *Economic Inquiry*, vol. XXXIII, no. 2, April 1995, pp. 285 - 295.

Jacobs, David and Helsm, Ronald E., "Toward a Political Model of Incarcerations: A Time-series Examination of Multiple Explanations for Prison Admission Rates", *American Journal of Sociology*, vol. 102, no. 2, September 1996, pp. 323 - 357.

Jankowski, Richard and Wlezien, "Substitutability and the Politics of Macroeconomic Policy", *Journal of Politics*, vol. 55, no. 4, November 1993, pp. 1060 -1080.

Jelen, Ted G., "Political Christianity: A Contextual Analysis", *American Journal of Political Science*, vol. 36, no. 3, August 1992, pp. 692 - 714.

Johnston, Les, "The Politics of Private Policing", *Political Quarterly*, vol. 65, no. 3, July/September 1992, pp. 341 - 349.

Jones, Peter, "Respecting Beliefs and Rebunking Rushdie", *British Journal of Political Science*, vol. 20, part 4, October 1990, pp. 415 - 438.

Juergensmeyer, Mark, "The New Religious State", *Comparative Politics*, vol. 27, no. 4 , July 1995, pp. 379 – 392.

Kaljee, Linda M.; Stanton, Bonita; Ricardo, Izabel; Whitehead, Tony L., "Urban African American Adolescents and their Parents' Perceptions of Violence within and against their Communities", *Human Organization*, vol. 54, no. 4, Winter 1995, pp. 373 -382.

Kane, Thomas J. and Staiger, Douglas, "Teen Motherhood and Abortion Access", *Quarterly Journal of Economics*, vol. CXI, issue 2, May 1996, pp. 467 – 506.

Kanekar, Suresh; Shaherwalla, Asma; Franco, Bunny; Kunji, Theresa; Pinto, Anita J., "The Acquaintance Predicament of a Rape Victim", *Journal of Applied Social Psychology*, vol. 21, no. 18, September 1991, pp. 1524 - 1544.

Kassin, Saul M. and Garfield, David A., "Blood and Guts: General and Trial-Specific Effects of Videotaped Crime Scenes on mock Jurors", *Journal of Applied Social Psychology*, vol. 21, no. 18, September 1991, pp. 1459 - 1472.

Kassin, Saul M. and Wrightsman, L.S., "The construction and validation of a juror bias scale", *Journal of Research in Personality*, vol. 17, 1983, pp. 423 - 442.

Kerlinger, F.N., "The structure and content of social attitude referents: A preliminary study", *Educational and Psychological Measurement*, vol. 62, 1972, pp. 379 - 383.

Kerlinger, F.N.; Middendorp, C.; Amon, J., "The structure of social attitudes in three countries: Tests of critical referent theory", *International Journal of Psychology*, vol. 11, 1976, pp. 265 – 279.

Keynes, J.M., "Art and the State", *The Listener*, 26 August 1936.

King, K.;Abernathy, T.J.; Robinson, I.E.; Balswick, J.O., "Religiosity and sexual attitudes and behaviour among college students", *Adolescence*, vol. 11, 1976, pp. 535 - 539.

Kiyotaki, Nobuhiro and Wright, Randall, "On Money as a Medium of Exchange", *Journal of Political Economy*, vol. 97, no. 4, August 1989, pp. 927 - 954.

Kleinke, Chris L.; Wallis, Robert; Stalder, Kevin, "Evaluation of a Rapist as a Function of Expressed Intent and Remorse", *The Journal of Social Psychology*, vol. 132, no. 4, August 1992, pp. 525 - 537.

Knight, John, "Municipal Matchmaking in Rural Japan", *Anthropology Today*, vol. 11, no. 2, August 1995, pp. 9 - 17.

Kposowa, Augustine J.; Breault, Kevin D.; Harrison, Beatrice M., "Reassessing the structural covariates of violent and property crimes in the USA: a county level analysis", *British Journal of Soiciology*, vol. 45, no. 1, March 1995, pp. 79 - 105.

Krause, George A., "Federal Reserve Policy Decision Making: Political and Bureaucratic Influences", American Journal of Political Science, vol. 38, no. 1, February 1994, pp. 124 - 144.

Kuran, Timur, "The Discontents of Islamic Economic Morality", *American Economic Review*, vol. 86, no. 2, May 1986, pp. 438 - 442.

Kurtz, Donald V. and Showman, Margaret, "The Tanda: A rotating credit association in Mexico", *Ethology*, vol. 17, 1977, pp. 65 – 74.

Lalonde, R.N. and Cameron, J.E., "Behavioral responses to discrimination: A focus on action", in Zannna, M.P. and Olsen, J.M. (eds.), *The Psychology of Prejudice: The Ontario Symposium*, vol. 7, Lawerence Erlbaum, 1994, pp. 257 - 288,

Lalonde, Richard N.; Majumder, Shilpi; Parris, Roger D., "Preferred Responses to Situations of Housing and Employment Discrimination", *Journal of Applied Social Psychology*, vol. 25, no. 12, June 1995, pp. 1105 - 1119.

Larsen, Kjersti, "Morality and the rejection of spirits. A Zanzibari case", *Social Anthropology*, vol. 6, no. 1, February 1998, pp. 61 - 75.

Lea, S.E.G., "Decimalisation and the estimated size of coins", *Journal of Economic Psychology*, vol. 1, 1981, pp. 79 - 81.

Lempert, Richard and Monsma, Karl, "Cultural Differences and Discrimination: Samoans Before A Public Housing Eviction Board", *American Socilogical Review*, vol. 59, no. 6, December 1994, pp. 890 - 910.

Levine, Nancy E. and Silk, Joan B., "Why Polyandry Fails", *Current Anthropology*, vol. 38, no. 3, June 1997, pp. 375 – 398.

LeVine, Robert A. and LeVine, Sarah E., "House Design and ther Self in an African Culture", *The Psychoanalytic Study of Society*, edited by Boyer, L. Bruce and Boyer, Ruth M., vol. 16, chapter 6, 1991, pp. 87 - 109.

Levitt, Mairi, "Sexual identity and religious socialization", British Journal of *Sociology*, vol. 46, no. 3, September 1995, p.529 - 536.

Lewis, Jane, "Anxieties about the Family: A New Parenthood Contract", *Political Quarterly*, vol. 67, no. 2, 1996, pp. 92 – 100.

Lienhardt, Peter, "Family Waaf in Zanzibar", *Journal of the Anthropological Society of Oxford*, vol. XXVII, no. 2, Trinity 1996, pp. 95 - 106.

Lipford, Jody; McCormick, Robert E.; Tollison, Robert D., "Preaching matters", *Journal of Economic Behavior and Organization*, vol. 21, no. 3, August 1993, pp. 235 – 250.

Logan, John R. and Spitze, Glenda D., "Family Neighbors", *American Journal of Sociology*, vol. 100, no. 2, September 1994, pp. 453 - 476.

Lott, John and Mustard, David, "Crime, Deterrence, and Right-to-Carry Concealed Handguns", *Journal of Legal Studies*, vol. 26, no. 1, January 1997, pp. 1 - 68.

Luhtanen, R. and Croker, J., "A collective self-esteem scale: Self-evaluation of one's social identity", *Personality and Social Psychology* Bulletin, Vol. 18, 1992, pp. 302 - 318.

Lynn, Richard, ""'Sex Differences in Competitiveness and the Valuation of Money in Twenty Countries", *Journal of Social Psychology*, vol. 133, no. 4, August 1993, pp.507 - 511.

Macrae, C. Neil and Shepherd, John W., "Do criminal stereotypes mediate juridic judgements?", *British Journal of Social Psychology*, vol. 28, part 1, March 1989, pp. 189 - 191.

Madigan, Ruth and Munro, Moira, "House Beautiful: Style and Consumption in the Home", *Sociology*, vol. 30, no. 1, February 1996, pp. 41 - 57.

Maguire, Joseph, "Preliminary observations on globalisation and the migration of sport labour", *Sociological Review*, vol. 42, no. 3, August 1994, pp. 452 - 480.

Maio, Gregory R.; Bell, David W.; Esses, Victoria M., "Ambivalence and Persuasion: The Processing of Messages about Immigrant Groups", *Journal of Experimental Social Psychology*, vol. 32, no. 6, November 1996, pp. 513 - 536.

Maltby, John, "Personality, Prayer, and Church Attendance Among U.S. Female Adults", *The Journal of Social Psychology*, vol. 135, no. 4, August 1995, pp. 529 - 531.

Markowitz, Fran, "Living in Limbo: Bosnian Refugees in Israel", *Human Organization*, vol. 55, no. 2, September 1996, pp. 127 - 132.

Martin, D., *A General Theory of Secularization*, Basil Blackwell, Oxford, 1978.

Massey, Douglas S. and Espinosa, Kristin E., "What's Driving Mexico-U.S. Migration? A Theoretical, Empirical, and Policy Analysis", *American Journal of Sociology*, vol. 102, no. 4, January 1997, pp. 939 - 999.

McCarthy, Bill and Hagan, John, "Mean Streets: The Theoretical Significance of Situational Delinquency among Homeless Youths", *American Journal of Sociology*, vol. 98, no. 3, November 1992, pp. 597 - 627.

McCauliff, C.M.A., "Burdens of proof: Degrees of belief, quanta of evidence, or constitutional guarentees?", *Vanderbilt Law Review*, vol. 35, 1982, pp. 1293 - 1335.

McLeay, E.M., "Defining Policing Policies and the Political Agenda", *Political Studies*, vol. XXXVIII, no. 4, December 1990, pp. 620 - 637.

McMahon, Doreen; Heath, Anthony; Harrop, Martin; Curtice, John, "The Electoral Consequences of North-South Migration", *British Journal of Political Science*, vol. 22, part 14, October 1992, pp. 419 - 443.

Meier, Kenneth J., "The Politics of Drug Abuse: Laws, Implementation, and Consequences", *Western Political Quarterly*, vol. 45, no. 1, March 1992, pp. 41 - 70.

Merton, Robert K., *Social Theory and Social Structure*, Free Press, 1957.

Messerschmidt, Donald A., "Dhikurs: Rotating credit Associations in Nepal", Himalayan Anthropology: *The Indo-Tibet Interface*, edited by Fisher, James F., Mouton, 1978.

Miles, Willaim F.S., "The Rally as Ritual: Dramaturgical Politics in Nigerian Hausaland", *Comparative Politics*, vol. 21, no. 3, April 1989, pp. 323 - 328.

Miller, Beatrice D., "Ganye and Kidu: Two formalized systems of mutual aid among Tibetans", *Southwestern Journal of Anthropology*, vol. 12, 1956, pp. 157 - 170.

Miller, Warren B. and Pasta, David J., "The Relative Influence of Husbands and Wives on the Choice of Oral Contraception, a Diaphram, and Condums", *Journal of Applied Psychology*, vol. 26, no. 19, October 1996, pp. 1749 - 1774.

Moberg, Mark, "Transnational Labour and Refugee Enclaves in a Central American Banana Industry", *Human Organization*, vol. 55, no. 4, Winter 1996, pp. 425 - 435.

Montgomery, James D., "Contemplations on the Economic Approach to Religious Behavior", *American Economic Review*, vol. 86, no. 2, May 1996, pp. 443 - 447.

Moreno-Black, Geraldine and Price, Lisa Leimar, "The Marketing of Gathered Food As an Economic Strategy of Women in Northeastern Thailand", *Human Organization*, vol. 52, no. 4, Winter 1993, pp. 398 - 404.

Mosse, David, "South Indian Christians, Purity/Impurity, and the Caste system: Death Ritual in a Tamil Roman Catholic Community", *Journal of the Royal Anthropological Institute*, vol. 2, no. 3, September 1996, pp. 461 - 483.

Muir, Grant; Lonsway, Kimberly A.; Payne, Diana L., "Rape Myth Acceptance Among Scottis and American Students", The Journal of Social Psychology, vol. 136, no. 2, April 1996, pp. 261 - 262.

Munnell, Alicia H.; Tootell, Geoffrey, M.B.; Browne, Lynn E.; McEneaney, James, "Mortgage Lending in Boston: Interpreting HMDA Data", *American Economic Review*, vol. 86, no. 1, March 1996, pp. 25 - 53.

Murdock, G.P., *Ethnographic Atlas*, University of Pittsburgh Press, 1967.

Murdock, G.P. and White, D., "Standard Cross-Cultural Sample", *Ethnology*, vol. 7, 1969, pp. 329 -369.

Mutlu, Kayham, "Examining religious beliefs among university students in Ankara", *British Journal of Sociology*, vol. 45, no. 2, June 1996, pp. 353 - 359.

Nadeua, Kathy and Sumingutt, Vel. J., "A Response to Austin's 'Filipino Self-Help and Peacemaking Strategies: A view from the Mindanao Hinterland", *Human Organization*, vol. 55, no. 2, Summer 1996, pp. 245 - 247.

Need, Ariana and De Graaf, Nan Dirk, "'Losing my religion': a dynamic analysis of leaving the church in the Netherlands", *European Sociological Review*, vol. 12, no. 1, May 1996, pp. 87 - 99.

Nice, David C., "The States and the Death Penalty", Western Political Quarterly, vol. 45, no. 4, *December* 1992, pp. 1037 - 1048.

Noor, Noraini M., "Work and Family Roles in Relations to Women's Well-being: A Longitudinal Study", *British Journal of Social Psychology*, vol. 34, part III, March 1995, pp. 87 - 106.

Norris, Clive; Fielding, Nigel; Kemp, Charles; Fielding, Jane, "Black and blue: an analysis of the influence of race on being stopped by the police", *British Jouranl of Sociology*, vol. 43, no. 2, June 1992, pp. 207 - 224.

Olshan, Marc A., "The Opening of Amish Society; Cottage Industry as Trojan Horse", *Human Organization*, vol. 50, no. 4, Winter 1991, pp. 378 - 384.

Ong, Aithwa, "Cultural Citizenship as Subject Making", *Current Anthropology*, vol. 37, no. 5, December 1996, pp. 737 - 762.

Osgood, Charles E.; Suci, George C.; Tannenbaum, Perry H, *The Measurement of Meaning*, University of Illinois Press, 1975.

Pagan, Jose A., "Employer sanctions on hiring illegal labor: An experimental analysis of firm compliance", *Journal of Economic Behavior and Organization*, vol. 34, no. 1, February 1998, pp. 87 - 100.

Palmonari, Augusto; Kirchler, Erich; Pombeni, Maria Luisa, "Differential Effects of Identification with Family and Peers on Coping with Developmental Tasks in Adolescence", *European Journal of Social Psychology*, vol. 21, issue 5, September/October 1991, pp. 381 - 402.

Pampel, Fred C. and Gartner, Rosemary, "Age Structure, Soicio-Political Institutions, and National Homicide Rates", *European Sociological Review*, vol. 11, no. 3, December 1995, pp. 243 - 260.

Parcel, Toby L. and Menagham, Elizabeth G., "Early Parental Work, Family Social Capital, and Early Childhood Outcomes", *American Journal of Sociology*, vol. 99,no. 4, January 1994, pp. 972 - 1009.

Parker, Keith D.; McMorris, Barbara J.; Smith, Earl; Murty, Komanduris, "Fear of Crime and the Likelihood of Victimization: A Bi-Ethic Comparison2, *The Journal of Social Psychology*, vol. 133, no. 5, October 1993, pp. 723 - 732.

Parker, R.A., "Child Care: The Roots of a Dilemma", *Political Quarterly*, vol. 57, no. 3, July-September, 1986, pp. 305 - 314.

Paulus, Paul B.; Nagar, Dinesh; Larey, Timothy S.; Camacho, Luz M., "Environment, Lifestyle, and Psychological Factors in the Health and Well-Being of Military Families", *Journal of Applied Social Psychology*, vol. 26, no. 23, December 1996, pp. 2063 - 2075.

Payne, Diana L., *The structure and assessmant of rape myths*, Unpublished doctoral dissertation, University of Illinois, 1993.

Pearse, J.; Gudjonsson, G.H.; Clare, I.C.H.; Rutter, S., "Police Interviewing and Psychological Vulrnerabilities: Predicting the Likelihood of a Confession", *Journal of Community & Applied Social Psychology*, vol. 8, no. 1, January/February 1998, pp. 1 - 21.

Peck, Sheryl Dickerson, "The Orthogonality of Liberalism and Conservatism Among American Evangelical Protestants", *The Journal of Social Psychology*, vol. 136, no. 5, October 1996, pp. 639 - 645.

Pernice, Regina and Brook, Judith, "Refugees' and Immigrants' Mental Health: Association of Demographic and Post-Immigration Factors", *Journal of Social Psychology*, vol. 136, no. 4, August 1996, pp. 511 - 519.

Petee, Thomas A., "Recommended for Release on Recognizance: Factors Affecting Pretrial Release Recommendations", *The Journal of Social Psychology*, vol. 134, no. 3, June 1994, pp. 375 - 382.

Phillips, Daphne, "The Internationalization of labour: The migration of nurses from Trinidad and Tobago", *International Sociology*, vol. 11, no. 1, March 1996, pp. 109 - 127.

Phinney, J.S., "The multigroup ethnic identity measure: A new scale for use with diverse groups", *Journal of Adolescent Research*, vol. 7, 1992, pp. 156 - 173.

Power, Anne, "The Crisis in Council Housing — Is Public Housing Manageable?", *Political Quarterly*, vol. 58, no. 3, July/September 1987, pp. 283 - 295.

Presley, John R. and Sessions, John G., "Islamic Economics: The emergence of a New Paradigm", *Economic Journal*, vol. 104, no. 424, May 1994, pp. 584 - 596.

Purcell, Terry, "Experiencing American and Australian High- and Popular-Style Houses", *Environment and Behavior*, vol. 27, no. 6, November 1995, pp. 771 - 800.

Quinton, Wendy J.; Cowan, Gloria; Watson, Breet D., "Personality and Attitudinal Predictors of Support for Proposition 187 — California's Anti-Illegal Immigrant Initiative", *Journal of Applied Social Psychology*, vol. 26, no. 24, December 1996, pp. 2204 - 2223.

Rabinowitz, Fredric E.; Colmar, Cyndee; Elgie, Damon; Hale, Donna; Niss, Stacey; Sharp, Brian; Sinclitico, Jessica, "Dishonesty, Indifference, or Carelessness in Souvenir Shop Transactions", *The Journal of Social Psychology*, vol. 133, no. 1, February 1993, pp. 73 - 77.

Randall, Vicky, "The Irresponsible State? The Politics of Day Care Provision in Britain", *British Journal of Political Science*, vol. 25, part 3, July1995, pp. 327 – 348.

Rasinski, K.A., "What's fair is fair — or is it? Value differences underlying public views about social justice", *Journal of Personality and Social Psychology*, vol. 53, 1987, pp. 201 – 211.

Rhode, Deborah L., "Adolescent Pregnancy and Public Policy", *Political Science Quarterly*, vol. 108, no. 11, Winter 1993 – 94, pp. 635 - 669.

Robinson, Dawn T.; Smith-Lovin, Lynn; Tsoudis, Olga, "Heinious Crime or Unifortunate Accident? The Effects of Remorse on Responses to Mock Criminal Confessions", *Social Forces*, vol. 73, no. 1, September 1994, pp. 175 - 190.

Rodman, Margaret C., "Contemporary Custom: Redefining Domestic Space in Longana, Vanuatu", *Contemporary Ethnology*, vol. XXIV, no. 4, October 1985, pp. 269 - 279.

Roper, William L., "The Prevention of Minority Youth Violence Must Begin Despite Risks and Imperfect Understanding", *Public Health Reports*, vol. 106, 1991, pp. 229 -231.

Ross, M., "Political Decision Making and Conflict", *Ethnology*, vol. 22, 1983, pp. 169 - 192.

Ruback, R. Barry and Pandey, Janak, "Gender Differences in Perceptions of Household Crowding: Stress, Affiliation, and Role Obligations in Rural India", *Journal of Applied Social Psychology*, vol. 26, no. 5, March 1996, pp. 417 - 436.

Rubin, Z. and Peplau, A., "Belief in a just world and reactions to another's lot: A study of participants in a national draft lottery", *Journal of Social Issues*, vol. 29, 1975, pp. 73 - 93.

Sagie, Abraham, "Measurement of Religiosity and Work Obligations Among Israeli Youth", *The Journal of Social Psychology*, vol. 133, no. 4, August 1993, pp. 529 - 537.

Santos, Michael D.; Leve, Craig; Pratkanis, Anthony R.; "Hey Buddy, Can You Spare Seventeen Cents?: Mindful Persuasion and the Pique Technique", *Journal of Applied Social Psychology*, vol. 24, no. 9, May 1994, pp. 755 - 781.

Schlesinger, Philip; Tumber, Howard; Murdock, Graham, "The media politics of crime and criminal justice", *British Journal of Sociology*, vol. 42, no. 3, September 1991, pp. 397 - 420.

Schmidtchen, G., *Ethic und Protest,* Leske+Budrich, 1992, plus the supplement, 1993.

Schneider, Jane and Schneider, Peter, "Mafia, Antimafia, and the Question of Sicilian Culture", *Politics and Society*, vol. 22, no. 2, June 1994, pp. 237 – 258.

Schnonell, F.J. and Goodacre, E.J., *The Psychology and Teaching of Reading* (5th Edition), Oliver & Boyd/Longman, Harlow, 1974.

Schrader, Heiko, "Professional Moneylenders and the Emergence of Capitalism in India and Indonesia", *International Sociology*, vol. 9, no. 2, June 1994, pp. 185 - 208.

Schuler, Sidney Ruth and Hashemi, Syed M., "Family Planning Outreaxh and Credit Programs in Rural Bangladesh", *Human Organization*, vol. 54, no. 4, Winter 1995, pp. 455 - 461.

Shaffer, David R. and Kerwin, Jeffrey, "On Adhering to Judicial Instructions: Reactions of Dogmatic and non dogmatic Juries to the Judge's Charges in an Entrapment Case", *Journal of Applied Social Psychology*, vol. 22, no. 14, July 1992, pp. 1133 - 1147.

Sheeran, Pascal; Abrams, Dominic; Abraham, Charles; Spears, Russell, "Religiosity and adolescents' premarital sexual attitudes and behaviour: An empirical study of conceptual issues", *European Journal of Social Psychology*, vol. 23, issue 1, Janaury/February 1993, pp. 39 - 52.

Shore, Chris, "Virgin births and Sterile Debates", *Current Anthropology*, vol. 33, no. 3, June 1992, pp. 295 - 314.

Siegrist, Michael, "Church Attendance, Denomination and Suicide Ideology", The *Journal of Social Psychology*, vol. 136, no. 5, October 1996, pp. 559 - 566.

Simpson, Bob, "Bringing the 'Unclear' Family into Focus: Divorce and Re-Marriage in Contemporary Britain", *Man*, New Series, vol. 29, no. 4, December 1994, pp. 831 - 851.

Smith, Adam and David, Nicholas, "The Production of Space and the House of the Xidi Suker", *Current Anthropology*, vol. 36, no. 3, June 1995, pp. 441 - 471.

Solis-Camara, Pedro and Fox, Robert A., "Parenting among Mothers with Young Children in Mexico and the United States", *Journal of Social Psychology*, vol. 135, no. 5, 1995, pp. 591 - 599.

Spence, J.; Helmreich, R.; Stapp, J., "A short version of the Attitudes Towards Women Scale (AWS)", *Bulletin of the Psychonomic Society*, vol. 29, 1973, pp. 219 - 220.

Spielberger, C.D.; Gorsuch, R.; Lushene, R.E., *State-Trait Anxiety Inventory Manual*, Consulting Psychologists Press, Palo Alto, California, 1970.

Stein, Jeremy C., "Prices and Trading Volume in the Housing Market: A Model with Down-Payment Effects", *Quarterly Journal of Economics*, vol. 110, issue 2, May 1995, pp. 379 - 406.

Steuer, Max, "Miracles and Alien Abduction", *Discussion Paper Series*, Centre for the Philosophy of the Natural and the Social Sciences, DP 38/99, March 1999.

Suzuki, Motoshi, "Domestic political determinants of inflation", *European Journal of Political Research*, vol. 28, no. 3, April 1993, pp. 245 - 259.

Tamney, Joseph R., "Conservative Government Support for the Religious Institution: Religious Education in English Schools", *British Journal of Sociology*, vol. 45, no. 2, June 1994, pp. 195 - 210.

Thornton, Arland; Axinn, William G.; Hill, Daniel, H., "Reciprocal Effects of Religiosity: Cohabitation and Marriage", *American Journal of Sociology*, vol. 98, no. 3, November 1992, pp. 628 - 651.

Todaro, M.P., "A Model of Urban Unemployment in Less Developed Countries", *American Economic Review*, vol. 59, no. 1, March 1969, pp. 138 - 148.

U.S. Department of Commerce, *Bureau of the Census, County and City Data Book*, 1983.

Velez-Iba™ez, Carlos G., "Social Diversity, Commercialization, and Organizational Complexity of Urban Mexican/Chicano Rotating Credit Associations: Theoretical and empirical issues of adaptation", *Human Organization*, vol. 4, no. 2, 1982, pp. 107 - 120.

Varese, Federico, "The Transition to the Market and Corruption in Post-socialist Russia", *Political Studies*, vol. XLV, Special Issue, 1997, pp. 579 - 596.

Vigil, James Diego, "Street Baptism: Chicago Gang Initiation", *Human Organization*, vol. 55, no. 2, Summer 1994, pp. 149 - 159

Villalon, Leonardo A., "Sufi Rituals as Rallies: Religious Ceremonies in the Politics of Sengalese State-Society Relations", *Comparative Politics*, vol. 26, no. 4, July 1994, pp. 415 - 438.

Viñals, Josė, "European monetary intergration: A narrow or a wide EMU?", *European Economic Review*, vol. 40, 1996, pp. 1103 - 1109.

Vinding, Michael, "Making a Living in the Nepal Himalayas: The case of the Thakalis of Mustang District", *Contribution to Nepalese Studies*, vol. 12, no. 1, 1984, pp. 51 - 106.

Vrij, Albert, "Credibility Judgements of Detectives: The Impact of Nonverbal Behavior, Social Skills, and Physical Characteristics on Impression Formation", *Journal of Social Psychology*, vol. 133, no. 5, October 1993, pp. 601 - 610.

Vrij, Aldert and Dingemans, Liesbeth, "Physical Effort of Police Officers as a Determinant of Their Behavior Towards Criminals", *The Journal of Social Psychology*, vol. 135, no. 4, August 1996.

Wagstaff, Graham F.; Vella, Marilyn; Perfect, Tim, "The Effect of Hypnotically Elicited Testimony on Jurors' Judgements of Guilt and Innocence", *Journal of Social Psychology*, vol. 132, no. 5, October 192, pp. 591 - 595.

Wald, Kenneth D.; Owen, Dennis E.; Hill, Samuel S., "Churches as Political Communities", *American Political Science Review*, vol. 82, no. 2, June 1988, pp. 531 - 548.

Weber, Linda R.; Mircale, Andrew; Skehan, Tom, "Family bonding and Delinquency: Racial and Ethnic influences among U.S. Youth", *Human Organization*, vol. 54, no. 4, Winter 1995, pp. 363 - 372.

Wechsler, D., *WAIS-R Manual*, Psychological Corporation, New York, 1981.

Whalen, D.H. and Blanchard, F.A., "Effects of photographic evidence on mock juror judgement", *Journal of Applied Social Psychology*, vol. 12, no. 1, January-February 1982, pp. 30 - 41.

Wiegand, Bruce, "Black Money in Belize: The Ethnicity and Social Structure of Blacl-market Crime", *Social Forces*, vol. 73, no. 1, September 1994, pp. 135 - 154.

Wiener, Richard L; Habert, Kristen; Shkodriani, Gina; Staebler, Caryn, "The Social Psychology of Jury Nullification: Predicting When Juries Disobey the Law", *Journal of Applied Social Psychology*, vol 21, no. 17, September 1991, pp. 1379 - 1401.

Wilcox, C., "Evangelicals and fundamentalists in the new Christian right: Religious differences in the Ohio Moral Majority", *Journal for the Scientific Study of Religion*, vol. 25, no. 3, 1986, pp. 355 - 363.

Wilk, Richard and Miller, Stephen, "Some Methodological Issues in Counting Communities and Households", *Human Organization*, vol. 56, no. 1, Spring 1997, pp. 64 - 70.

Winkelman, Michael, "Cultural Factors in Criminal Defence Proceedings", *Human Organization*, vol. 55, no. 2, Summer 1996, pp. 154 - 159.

Winter, Michael and Short, Christopher, "Believing and belonging: religion in rural England", *British Journal of Sociology*, vol. 44, no. 4, December 1993, pp. 635 – 657.

Wober, J.M.; Brosius, H-B.; Weinmann, G., "The European election of 1989: British television viewers' knowledge, attitudes and voting behaviour", *British Journal of Social Psychology*, vol. 35, no. 2, June 1996, pp. 233 - 244.

Wolfgang, M.E. and Ferracuti, F., The Subculture of Violence, Tavistock, 1967.

Wright, Gerald; Erickson, Robert; McIver, John, "Measuring State Partisanship and Ideology with Survey Data", *Journal of Politics*, vol. 47,no. 2, May 1985, pp. 469 - 489.

Wu, David Y.H., "To Kill Three Birds With One Stone: The rotating credit association of the Papua New Guinea Chinese", *American Ethologist*, vol 1, 1974, pp. 565 - 584.

Yinon, Yoel and Levian, Emanual, "Presence of Other Drivers as a Determinant of Traffic Violations", *The Journal of Social Psychology*, vol. 135, no. 3, June 1995, pp. 299 - 304.

Yperen, Nico W. van and Buunk, Bram P., "A longitudinal study of equity and satisfaction in intimate relationships", *European Journal of Social Psychology*, vol. 20, no. 5 May/June 1990, pp. 287 – 309.

Zelizer, Viviana A., "The Social Meaning of Money: 'Special Monies'", American Journal of Sociology, vol. 95, no. 2, September 1989, pp. 342 – 3

NAMES INDEX

SUBJECT INDEX

C

D

H

I

J

N

O

P

R

S

T

U

V

W

X

Z

JOURNALS

Note: There are a number of important journals in each discipline that do not appear on this list. They do not appear on the list because in the period under consideration, they did not publish a scientific paper on any one of the six topics used in this study.

Anthropology
- Anthropology Today
- Contemporary Ethnology
- Current Anthropology
- Ethnology
- Human Organization
- Journal of the Royal Anthropology Institute
- Journal of the Anthropological Society of Oxford
- Man
- Social Anthropology
- Urban Anthropology

Economics
- American Economic Review
- Economic Development and Cultural Change
- Economic Inquiry
- Economic Journal
- Economic Policy
- European Economic Review
- Journal of Economic Organization and Behavior

Journal of Labour Economics
Journal of Political Economy
Quarterly Journal of Economics

Political Science
American Journal of Political Science
British Journal of Political Science
Comparative Political Studies
Comparative Politics
European Journal of Political Research
Housing Studies
Journal of Politics
Political Quarterly
Political Science Quarterly
Political Studies
Political Theory
Western Political Quarterly

Social Psychology
British Journal of Social Psychology
Environment and Behavior
European Journal of Personality
European Journal of Social Psychology
Journal of Applied Social Psychology
Journal of Community and Applied Social Psychology
Journal of Cross-cultural Psychology
Journal of Economic Psychology
Journal of Experimental Social Psychology
Journal of Personality and Social Psychology
Journal of Social Psychology
Personality and Individual Differences
Personality and Social Psychology Bulletin
Social Psychology Quarterly

Sociology
American Journal of Sociology
British Journal of Sociology
European Sociological Review
International Sociology
Social Forces
Sociological Perspectives
Sociological Review
Sociology

Printed in the United Kingdom
by Lightning Source UK Ltd.
100913UKS00001B/42

9 781402 073212